# RUSSIAN
# Vocabulary

**Second Edition**

**Eli Hinkel, Ph.D.**
Seattle University
Seattle, Washington

BARRON'S

*All inquiries should be addressed to:*
Barron's Educational Series, Inc.
250 Wireless Boulevard
Hauppauge, NY 11788
*www.barronseduc.com*

Library of Congress Control Number: 2008932188

ISBN-13: 978-0-7641-3970-3
ISBN-10: 0-7641-3970-3

PRINTED IN CHINA
9 8 7 6 5

# CONTENTS

# HOW TO USE THIS BOOK

*Russian Vocabulary* is a thematically organized English to Russian vocabulary reference book. The text is oriented toward learners of Russian with various levels of proficiency, from beginning to advanced. Because the vocabulary is organized thematically, beginners can consult the book when looking for terms associated with a certain domain of activity or life. On the other hand, because the text includes advanced vocabulary items and deals with various culture-specific notions, it also can serve the needs of proficient students striving to expand their vocabulary range. The thematic organization makes the text ideal for students preparing presentations or papers on a particular topic. It can also prove very helpful for those who are involved in communications with native speakers of Russian, be it in the United States or in the former Soviet Union.

A large number of items include morphological derivations from stems, e.g., **любо́вь—люби́мый—люби́ть** (*love—beloved—to love*). As the lexical structure in Russian relies heavily on morphology in word formation, attention to the included derived items can assist learners in the acquisition of Russian syllabic parsing.

In addition to the thematic organization, the vocabulary and topics are cross-referenced in the *Word finder*, which allows learners quick access to the translation of an English item into Russian and also indicates the sections that cover vocabulary associated with a particular thematic domain.

The thematic domains are further divided into smaller units, each following a similar format. Every alphabetized English word is located in the left column, the Russian word in the middle column, and the pronunciation guide in the right column. All nouns are listed in the singular, except those without a singular form. All verbs are given in the infinitive. Idioms and examples of sentences with some grammatical structures are provided at the end of each chapter.

Correct pronunciation and word stress are essential for intelligibility in Russian. This book provides a detailed pronunciation guide presented in a form that is easy to understand. The pronunciation guide adheres to the sound transcription symbols familiar to most language learners, except when colloquial imperatives dictate otherwise. The division of words into syllables with a consistent parsing at the boundaries of inflections permits learners to familiarize themselves with the syllabic structure of the words. The advantage of syllabic parsing is that learners do not need to work on the pronunciation of inflections each time they appear. Instead, having learned a pronunciation of a particular suffix or inflection, they can use their pronunciation skills with its subsequent occurrences.

Because no two languages are alike in their lexicon and its pragmatic usage, the vocabulary contained in the text reflects aspects of Russian culture, discourse patterns, lexical characteristics, and collocations. The selection of lexis in the text is appropriate for learners of the Russian language and conveys its cultural and literary flavor. In this sense, the text is unique as it provides for a relatively wide vocabulary range accessible to diverse learner populations.

## ORGANIZATION OF THE BOOK

*Russian Vocabulary* includes 5,000 to 6,000 words and associated idiomatic expressions with pronunciation. The book includes nine chapters, further divided into subsections to include the vocabulary associated with certain activities. For example, the chapter *Travel* contains seven units: *Choosing a Destination; Packing and Going Through Customs; Traveling by Air; On the Road; Train, Bus, Trolley, and Subway; Hotels and Motels;* and *On Vacation.* This design allows the reader to refer directly to the vocabulary dealing with a particular activity.

Each page is divided into three columns, which contain the English word, the corresponding Russian word, and the pronunciation of the Russian word. The symbols used in the pronunciation column are found in the *Pronunciation Guide.* The English words are arranged in alphabetical order within each unit. Grammatical peculiarities, morphological derivatives, related items, and specific uses are also presented.

Example #1: Morphological Derivatives

| | | |
|---|---|---|
| **atmosphere** | атмосфера | *at-mas-fyé-ra* |
| • **atmospheric** | атмосферный | *at-mas-fyér-nyj* |

| | | | |
|---|---|---|---|
| Main | Derived | Russian | Pronunciation |
| item | item | equivalent | guide |

Example #2: Related Items

| | | |
|---|---|---|
| **watch, clock** | часы | *chi-sý* |
| • **alarm clock** | будильник | *bu-díl'-nik* |
| • **dial** | циферблат | *tsy-fir-bláht* |
| • **hand** | стрелка | *stryél-ka* |

| | |
|---|---|
| Main | Related |
| item | items |

Example #3: Specific Uses

| **line** | очередь | *ó-chi-rit'* |
| • **stand in line** | стоять в очереди | *sta-yáht' v ó-chi-ri-di* |

| Main | Use in a specific |
| item | expression |

 Most nouns are listed in the singular form, unless marked *(pl)* for plural. The gender of Russian nouns can usually be determined by their endings, for example, стол, which ends in a consonant, is masculine, окнó is neuter, and рýчка is feminine. In the text, the gender of the noun is indicated only in the case of exceptions. For example, коллега can be both masculine and feminine and is marked *(m&f)*. Similarly, лóкоть is masculine and is marked *(m)*.
 Verbs are given in their infinitive forms, which usually end in -ть. All verbs are accompanied by a reference to their aspect, *(p)* for perfective and *(i)* for imperfective. In most cases, both forms are presented. Occasionally, Russian verbs require a prefix or a change in the suffix for different aspects [kiss: поцеловáть *(p)* and целовáть *(i)*]. In this case, both forms are given.
 Most frequently, adjectives are presented in the masculine singular form. Because Russian adverbs are largely derived from adjectives, most adjectives are listed together with the adverbs derived from their stems. In this case, both the adjective and the adverb are marked:

Example #4:

| **weak** | слабый *(adj)* | *sláh-byj* |
| | слабо *(adv)* | *sláh-ba* |

 Focus sections provide additional information and examples of words and their usages in a specific unit. Idiomatic expressions and proverbs are interspersed throughout the book.

## IDENTIFYING PARTS OF SPEECH

 Most Russian nouns and their gender, verbs, adjectives, and adverbs can be identified by their inflectional endings. The following chart provides the listing of common Russian endings for the four parts of speech.

## NOUNS *(in the nominative case)*

### Masculine

— End in consonants: -б, -в, -г, -д, -ж, -з, -к, -л, -м, -н, -п, -р, -с, -т, -ф, -х, -ч, -ш, -щ, and -й, e.g., гриб (mushroom), друг (friend), дом (house), рост (height), воздух (air), трамвай (tram).

— Some nouns end in -ь, e.g., словарь (dictionary), локоть (elbow).

— A few nouns end in -a, -я; most refer to persons of masculine gender, e.g., мужчина (man), юноша (young man), папа (dad);

### Feminine

— End in -a, -я/-ия, e.g., картина (picture), семья (family), фамилия (last name), except those that end in -мя.

— Some nouns end in -ь, e.g., мать (mother), тетрадь (notebook).

### Neuter

— End in -o, -e/-ие/-ье, and -мя, e.g., письмо (letter), платье (dress), здание (building), имя (name).

## VERBS

— End in -ть, -ти, and -чь in the infinitive form, with the addition of -ся/-сь in the reflexive form, e.g., читать (read), рисовать (draw), мыться (bathe), смеяться (laugh), мести (sweep), расти (grow), нестись (rush), печь (bake), помочь (help), беречься (safeguard).

## ADJECTIVES *(in the nominative case)*

### Masculine

— End in -ый/-ий and -ой, e.g., новый (new), старый (old), маленький (small), хороший (good), молодой (young), плохой (bad), большой (big).

### Feminine

— End in -ая/-яя, e.g., новая (new), молодая (young), хорошая (good), синяя (blue).

### Neuter

— End in -oe/-ee, e.g., новое (new), молодое (young), хорошее (good), синее (blue).

## ADVERBS

— Most end in -o, e.g., быстро (quickly), хорошо (well), тепло (warmly), грустно (sadly).

— Some adverbs of place and time have a variety of endings: -ом, -a, -то -нибудь, and -ью, e.g., пешком (on foot), всегда (always), где-то (somewhere), когда-нибудь (sometime), ночью (at night).

## PRONUNCIATION GUIDE

The charts that follow identify the quality of a particular Russian sound. Unstressed Russian vowels are always reduced, and the voicing of a consonant is determined by the sound that follows it, that is, a consonant can be voiced in front of a vowel or another voiced consonant, and voiceless in front of a voiceless consonant or at the end of a word. The stressed vowel is marked with

### *VOWELS*

Vowel pronunciation frequently varies depending on whether a vowel is stressed or unstressed.

---

### *NOT PALATALIZED*

| Russian | English Equivalent | Pronunciation | Symbol |
|---|---|---|---|
| **а** | | | |
| *полка* (unstressed) | s<u>o</u>fa | *pól-k<u>a</u>* | *a* |
| *краска* (stressed) | f<u>a</u>ther | *kr<u>áh</u>s-ka* | *ah* |
| | | | |
| **э** | | | |
| *элита* (unstressed) | No English equivalent | *y-lí-ta* | |
| *этого* (stressed) | No English equivalent | *éh-ta-va* | *eh* |
| | | | |
| **ы** | | | |
| *бутылка* (stressed or unstressed) | p<u>i</u>ll | *bu-t<u>ý</u>l-ka* | *y* |
| | | | |
| **о** | | | |
| *облако* (stressed) | m<u>o</u>ld | *<u>ó</u>b-la-ka* | |
| *Москва* (unstressed) | s<u>o</u>fa | *m<u>a</u>sk-váh* | *a* |
| | | | |
| **у** | | | |
| *мука* (unstressed) | p<u>u</u>sh | *m<u>u</u>-káh* | |
| *булка* (stressed) | n<u>oo</u>dle | *b<u>óo</u>l-ka* | *oo* |

## PALATALIZED

| Russian | English Equivalent | Pronunciation | Symbol |
|---------|--------------------|---------------|--------|
| **я** | | | |
| *вишня* (unstressed; final position) | <u>ya</u>rdstick | *vísh-n<u>ya</u>* | *ya* |
| *завязать* (unstressed; middle position) | b<u>ea</u>t | *za-v<u>i</u>-záht'* | *i* |
| *яблоко* (stressed) | <u>ya</u>cht | *<u>yáh</u>b-la-ka* | *yah* |
| | | | |
| **е** | | | |
| *белый* (stressed) | <u>ye</u>sterday | *b<u>yé</u>-lyj* | *ye* |
| *метла* (unstressed; initial or middle position) | b<u>ea</u>t | *m<u>i</u>t-láh* | *i* |
| *красные* (unstressed; final position) | <u>ye</u>sterday | *kráhs-ny-<u>ye</u>* | *ye* |
| | | | |
| **и** | | | |
| *вилка* (stressed or unstressed) | b<u>ea</u>t | *v<u>í</u>l-ka* | *i* |
| | | | |
| **ю** | | | |
| *юг* (stressed or unstressed) | <u>you</u> | *<u>yu</u>k* | *yu* |
| | | | |
| **ё** (always stressed) *тёмный* | <u>yo</u>lk | *t<u>yó</u>m-nyj* | *yo* |

## CONSONANTS

The following chart lists consonants and their English equivalents.

| Russian | English Equivalent | Pronunciation | Symbol |
|---|---|---|---|
| б<br>*банк* | <u>b</u>ank | *<u>b</u>áhnk* | *b* |
| в<br>*ваза* | <u>v</u>ase | *<u>v</u>áh-za* | *v* |
| г<br>*гусь* | <u>g</u>oose | *<u>g</u>oos'* | *g* |
| д<br>*дама* | <u>d</u>ame | *<u>d</u>áh-ma* | *d* |
| ж<br>*лежать* | lei<u>s</u>ure | *li-<u>zh</u>áht'* | *zh* |
| з<br>*зуб* | <u>z</u>oo | *<u>z</u>oop* | *z* |
| й<br>*бой* | bo<u>y</u> | *bo<u>j</u>* | *j* |
| к<br>*клиент* | <u>c</u>lient | *<u>k</u>li-yént* | *k* |
| л<br>*лампа* | <u>l</u>amp | *<u>l</u>áhm-pa* | *l* |
| м<br>*мост* | <u>m</u>ost | *<u>m</u>ost* | *m* |
| н<br>*нос* | <u>n</u>ose | *<u>n</u>os* | *n* |
| п<br>*пост* | <u>p</u>ost | *<u>p</u>ost* | *p* |
| р<br>*рост* | <u>r</u>oast | *<u>r</u>ost* | *r* |

| | | | |
|---|---|---|---|
| **с** *соль* | <u>s</u>alt | <u>s</u>ol' | s |
| **т** *табак* | <u>t</u>obacco | <u>t</u>a-báhk | t |
| **ф** *фото* | <u>f</u>an | <u>f</u>ó-ta | f |
| **Х** *хоккей* | <u>h</u>ockey | <u>kh</u>a-kyéj | kh |
| **ц** *цапля* | ki<u>ts</u> | <u>ts</u>áhp-lya | ts |
| **ч** *чек* | <u>ch</u>eck | <u>ch</u>yek | ch |
| **ш** *шок* | <u>sh</u>ock | <u>sh</u>ok | sh |
| **щ** *щи* | fre<u>sh</u> <u>ch</u>eese | <u>shch</u>i | shch |
| **ъ** (short pause followed by palatalization) *подъём* | – | pad'-yóm | , |
| **ь** (palatalization of preceding sound) *мать* | – | maht' | , |

The following consonants are VOICED but can be pronounced as VOICELESS in front of other voiceless consonants or at the end of a word.

| Russian | English Equivalent | Pronunciation | Symbol |
|---|---|---|---|
| **б** *куб* | cu<u>p</u> | koo<u>p</u> | p |
| **д** *сад* | sa<u>t</u> | sah<u>t</u> | t |

| | | | |
|---|---|---|---|
| **ж**<br>*паж* | po<u>sh</u> | *pah<u>sh</u>* | *sh* |
| **з**<br>*таз* | pa<u>ss</u> | *tah<u>s</u>* | *s* |

The following consonants are always VOICED.

| Russian | English Equivalent | Pronunciation | Symbol |
|---|---|---|---|
| **л**<br>*лапа* | <u>l</u>eft | <u>*l*</u>*áh-pa* | *l* |
| **м**<br>*моль* | <u>m</u>ouse | <u>*m*</u>*ol'* | *m* |
| **н**<br>*нора* | <u>n</u>arrow | <u>*n*</u>*a-ráh* | *n* |
| **р**<br>*рама* | <u>r</u>oam | <u>*r*</u>*áh-ma* | *r* |

The following consonants are always VOICELESS.

| Russian | English Equivalent | Pronunciation | Symbol |
|---|---|---|---|
| **й**<br>*чай* | ma<u>y</u> | *chah<u>j</u>* | *j* |
| **х**<br>*хор* | <u>h</u>urry | <u>*kh*</u>*or* | *kh* |
| **ц**<br>*цапля* | mi<u>ts</u> | <u>*ts*</u>*áhp-lya* | *ts* |
| **ч**<br>*часы* | <u>ch</u>unk | <u>*ch*</u>*i-sý* | *ch* |
| **щ**<br>*плащ* | <u>sh</u>y | *plah<u>shch</u>* | *shch* |

**COMMON SOUND COMBINATIONS**

*VOWELS AND CONSONANTS*

| Russian | English Equivalent | Pronunciation | Symbol |
|---|---|---|---|
| **ero/oro** (stressed) *моего, одного* | none | *ma i-vó, ad-na-vó* | *i-vo, a-vo* |
| **его/oro** (unstressed) *синего, этого* | none | *sí-ni-va, éh-ta-va* | *i-va, a-va* |
| **же, ше, це** (stressed) *женщина, шея* | none | *zhéhn-shchi-na, shéh-ya* | *eh* |
| **же, ше, це** (unstressed) *жена, шестёрка* | p**i**ll | *zhy-náh, shys-tyór-ka* | *y* |
| **жи, ши, ци** *живот, ширина* | m**i**ss | *zhy-vót, shy-ri-náh* | *y* |
| **жё, шё, цё** (always stressed) *жёлтый, шёпот* | m**o**ld | *zhól-tyj, shó-pat* | |
| **тся/ться** *боятся, учиться* | none | *ba-yáh-tsa, u-chí-tsa* | *tsa* |

# ABBREVIATIONS

| | |
|---|---|
| *adj* | adjective |
| *adv* | adverb |
| *coll* | collective |
| *f* | feminine noun |
| *fam* | familiar *you* (ты) form and verb |
| *i* | imperfective form of verb |
| *indecl* | indeclinable noun |
| *m* | masculine noun |
| *n* | neuter noun/noun |
| *p* | perfective form of verb |
| *pl* | plural noun or form |
| *pol* | polite *you* (вы) form and verb |
| *sg* | singular noun or form |

## BASIC INFORMATION

*1. ARITHMETIC*

## a. CARDINAL NUMBERS

| | | |
|---|---|---|
| **zero** | ноль *(m)* | *nol'* |
| **one** | один | *a-dín* |
| **two** | два | *dvah* |
| **three** | три | *tri* |
| **four** | четыре | *chi-tý-ri* |
| **five** | пять | *pyaht'* |
| **six** | шесть | *shehst'* |
| **seven** | семь | *syem'* |
| **eight** | восемь | *vó-sim'* |
| **nine** | девять | *dyé-vit'* |
| **ten** | десять | *dýe-sit'* |
| **eleven** | одиннадцать | *a-di-na-tsat'* |
| **twelve** | двенадцать | *dvi-náh-tsat'* |
| **thirteen** | тринадцать | *tri-náh-tsat'* |
| **fourteen** | четырнадцать | *chi-týr-na-tsat'* |
| **fifteen** | пятнадцать | *pit-náh-tsat'* |
| **sixteen** | шестнадцать | *shys-náh-tsat'* |
| **seventeen** | семнадцать | *sim-náh-tsat'* |
| **eighteen** | восемнадцать | *va-sim-náh-tsat'* |
| **nineteen** | девятнадцать | *di-vit-náh-tsat'* |
| **twenty** | двадцать | *dváh-tsat'* |
| **twenty-one** | двадцать один | *dváh-tsat' a-dín* |
| **twenty-two** | двадцать два | *dváh-tsat' dvah* |
| **twenty-three** | двадцать три | *dváh-tsat' tri* |
| **twenty-four** | двадцать четыре | *dváh-tsat' chi-tý-ri* |
| **twenty-five** | двадцать пять | *dváh-tsat' pyaht'* |
| **twenty-six** | двадцать шесть | *dváh-tsat' shehst'* |
| **twenty-seven** | двадцать семь | *dváh-tsat' syem'* |
| **twenty-eight** | двадцать восемь | *dváh-tsat' vó-sim'* |
| **twenty-nine** | двадцать девять | *dváh-tsat' dyé-vit'* |
| **thirty** | тридцать | *trí-tsat'* |
| **thirty-one** | тридцать один | *trí-tsat' a-dín* |
| **thirty-two** | тридцать два | *trí-tsat' dváh* |
| **thirty-three** | тридцать три | *trí-tsat' tri* |
| **...** | | |
| **forty** | сорок | *só-rak* |
| **forty-one** | сорок один | *só-rak a-dín* |

| | | |
|---|---|---|
| **forty-two** | сорок два | *só-rak dvah* |
| **forty-three** | сорок три | *só-rak tri* |
| ... | | |
| **fifty** | пятьдесят | *pi-di-syáht* |
| **fifty-one** | пятьдесят один | *pi-di-syáht a-dín* |
| **fifty-two** | пятьдесят два | *pi-di-syáht dvah* |
| **fifty-three** | пятьдесят три | *pi-di-syáht tri* |
| ... | | |
| **sixty** | шестьдесят | *shys-di-syáht* |
| ... | | |
| **seventy** | семьдесят | *syém'-di-sit* |
| ... | | |
| **eighty** | восемьдесят | *vó-sim-di-sit* |
| ... | | |
| **ninety** | девяносто | *di-vi-nó-sta* |
| ... | | |
| **one hundred** | сто/сотня | *sto/sót-nya* |
| **one hundred and one** | сто один | *sto a-dín* |
| **one hundred and two** | сто два | *sto dvah* |
| ... | | |
| **two hundred** | двести | *dvyés-ti* |
| **two hundred and one** | двести один | *dvyés-ti a-dín* |
| ... | | |
| **three hundred** | триста | *trís-ta`* |
| ... | | |
| **one thousand** | тысяча | *tý-si-cha* |
| **one thousand and one** | тысяча один | *tý-si-cha a-dín* |
| ... | | |
| **two thousand** | две тысячи | *dvye tý-si-chi* |
| **two thousand and one** | две тысячи один | *dvye tý-si-chi a-dín* |
| ... | | |
| **three thousand** | три тысячи | *tri tý-si-chi* |
| ... | | |
| **four thousand** | четыре тысячи | *chi-tý-ri tý-si-chi* |
| ... | | |
| **one hundred thousand** | сто тысяч | *sto tý-sich* |
| ... | | |
| **two hundred thousand** | двести тысяч | *dvyés-ti tý-sich* |
| ... | | |
| **one million** | миллион | *mi-li-ón* |
| **one million and one** | миллион один | *mi-li-ón a-dín* |
| **one million and two** | миллион два | *mi-li-ón dvah* |
| ... | | |
| **two million** | два миллиона | *dvah mi-li-ó-na* |

...

| three million | три миллиона | *tri mi-li-ó-na* |

...

| one hundred million | сто миллионов | *sto mi-li-ó-naf* |

...

| one billion | миллиард | *mi-li-áhrt* |

...

| two billion | два миллиарда | *dvah mi-li-áhr-da* |

## b. ORDINAL NUMBERS (msg form)

| **first** | первый | *pyér-vyj* |
| **second** | второй | *fta-rój* |
| **third** | третий | *trýe-tij* |
| **fourth** | четвёртый | *chit-vyór-tyj* |
| **fifth** | пятый | *pyáh-tyj* |
| **sixth** | шестой | *shys-tój* |
| **seventh** | седьмой | *sid'-mój* |
| **eighth** | восьмой | *vas'-mój* |
| **ninth** | девятый | *di-vyáh-tyj* |
| **tenth** | десятый | *di-syáh-tyj* |
| **eleventh** | одиннадцатый | *a-dí-na-tsa-tyj* |
| **twelfth** | двенадцатый | *dvi-náh-tsa-tyj* |
| ... | | |
| **twenty-third** | двадцать третий | *dváh-tsat' trýé-tij* |
| ... | | |
| **thirty-third** | тридцать третий | *trí-tsat' trýé-tij* |
| ... | | |
| **forty-third** | сорок третий | *só-rak trýé-tij* |
| ... | | |
| **hundredth** | сотый | *só-tyj* |
| ... | | |
| **thousandth** | тысячный | *tý-sich-nyj* |
| ... | | |
| **millionth** | миллионный | *mi-li-ó-nyj* |
| ... | | |
| **billionth** | миллиардный | *mi-li-áhrd-nyj* |

## c. FRACTIONS

| **one-half** | пол-/половина | *pol-/pa-la-ví-na* |
| **one-third** | треть *(f)*/одна треть *(f)* | *tryet'/ad-náh tryet'* |

| **one-quarter** | четверть *(f)*/одна | *chyét-virt'/ad-náh* |
| | четверть *(f)* | *chyét-virt'* |
| ... | | |
| **two-thirds** | две трети *(f, pl)* | *dvye tryé-ti* |
| ... | | |
| **three-elevenths** | три одиннадцатых | *tri a-dí-na-tsa-tykh* |
| | *(f, pl)* | |

## d. TYPES OF NUMBERS

| **number** | число *(n)* | *chis-ló* |
| • **numeral** | цифра | *tsýf-ra* |
| • **numerical** | числовой/цифровой | *chis-la-vój/tsyf-ra-vój* |
| **Arabic number** | арабская цифра | *a-ráhp-ska-ya tsýf-ra* |
| **cardinal** | количественный | *ka-lí-chis-tvi-nyj* |
| **complex** | сложный | *slózh-nyj* |
| **digit** | знак | *znahk* |
| **even** | чётный | *chyót-nyj* |
| **fraction** | дробь *(f)* | *drop'* |
| • **fractional** | дробный | *drób-nyj* |
| **imaginary** | воображаемый | *va-ab-ra-zháh-i-myj* |
| **integer** | целое число | *tséh-la-ye chis-ló* |
| **irrational** | нерациональный | *ni-ra-tsy-a-náhl'-nyj* |
| **natural** | натуральный | *na-tu-ráhl'-nyj* |
| **negative** | отрицательный | *at-ri-tsáh-til'-nyj* |
| **odd** | нечётный | *ni-chyót-nyj* |
| **ordinal** | порядковый | *pa-ryáht-ka-vyj* |
| **positive** | положительный | *pa-la-zhý-til'-nyj* |
| **prime** | простое (число) *(n)* | *pras-tó-ye (chis-ló)* |
| **rational** | рациональный | *ra-tsy-a-náhl'-nyj* |
| **real** | действительное | *dist-ví-til'-na-ye (chis-ló)* |
| | (число) *(n)* | |
| **reciprocal** | обратная (величина) | *ab-ráht-na-ya* |
| | *(f)* | *(vi-li-chi-náh)* |
| **Roman** | римский | *ríms-kij* |

## e. BASIC OPERATIONS

| **add** | сложить *(p)* | *sla-zhýt'* |
| | складывать *(i)* | *skláh-dy-vat'* |
| • **addition** | сложение | *sla-zhéh-ni-ye* |
| • **plus** | плюс | *plyus* |
| • **two plus two** | два плюс два | *dvah plyus dvah* |

| | | |
|---|---|---|
| **equals four** | равняется/ | *rav-nyáh-i-tsa/* |
| | получается | *pa-lu-cháh-i-tsa* |
| | четыре | *chi-tý-ri* |
| **subtract** | вычесть *(p)* | *vý-chist'* |
| | вычитать *(i)* | *vý-chi-táht'* |
| • **subtraction** | вычитание | *vy-chi-táh-ni-ye* |
| • **minus** | минус | *mí-nus* |
| • **three minus two** | три минус два | *trí mí-nus dvah* |
| **equals one** | равняется один | *rav-nyáh-i-tsa a-dín* |
| **multiply** | умножить *(p)* | *um-nó-zhyt'* |
| | умножать *(i)* | *um-na-zháht'* |
| • **multiplication** | умножение | *um-na-zhéh-ni-ye* |
| • **multiplication** | таблица умножения | *tab-lí-tsa* |
| **table** | | *um-na-zhéh-ni-ya* |
| • **multiplied by** | умноженный на | *um-nó-zhy-nyj na* |
| • **three times two** | три умножить на | *tri um-nó-zhyt' na dvah* |
| **equals six** | два равняется | *rav-nyáh-i-tsa shehst'* |
| | шесть | |
| **divide** | разделить *(p)* | *raz-di-lít'* |
| | делить *(i)* | *di-lít'* |
| • **divided by** | делённый/ | *di-lyó-nyj / raz-di-lýo-nyj* |
| | разделённый | |
| • **division** | деление | *di-lyé-ni-ye* |
| • **six divided by** | шесть разделить на | *shehst' raz-di-lít' na* |
| **three equals** | три получается | *tri pa-lu-cháh-i-tsa* |
| **two** | два | *dvah* |
| **raise to power** | возвести *(p)* в | *vaz-vis-tí f styé-pin'* |
| | степень *(f)* | |
| | возводить *(i)* | *vaz-va-dít'* |
| • **to the power of** | в степень *(f)* | *f styé-pin'* |
| • **squared** | в квадрате | *f kvad-ráh-ti* |
| • **cubed** | в кубе | *f kóo-bi* |
| • **to the fourth** | в четвёртой | *f chit-vyór-taj* |
| **power** | степени | *styé-pi-ni* |
| • **to the *n*th power** | в энную степень *(f)* | *v éh-nu-yu styé-pin'* |
| • **two squared** | два в квадрате | *dvah f kvad-ráh-ti* |
| **equals four** | равняется четыре | *rav-nyáh-i-tsa chi-tý-ri* |
| **extract a root** | найти *(p)* корень *(m)* | *naj-tí kó-rin'* |
| | находить *(i)* | *na-kha-dít'* |
| • **square root** | квадратный корень | *kvad-ráht-nyj kó-rin'* |
| | *(m)* | |
| • **cube root** | кубический корень | *ku-bí-chis-kij kó-rin'* |
| | *(m)* | |
| • ***n*th root** | энный корень *(m)* | *éhn-yj kó-rin'* |
| • **(the) square root** | квадратный корень | *kvad-ráht-nyj kó-rin' iz* |
| **of nine is three** | из девяти три | *di-vi-tí tri* |

| | | |
|---|---|---|
| **ratio** | отношение | *at-na-shéh-ni-ye* |
| • **twelve is to four** | двенадцать | *dvi-náh-tsat' at-nó-si-tsa k* |
| **as nine is to three** | относится к | *chi-ty-ryóm kahk dyé-* |
| | четырём как | *vit' k tryom* |
| | девять к трём | |

## f. ADDITIONAL MATHEMATICAL CONCEPTS

| | | |
|---|---|---|
| **algebra** | алгебра | *áhl-gi-bra* |
| • **algebraic** | алгебраический | *al-gi-bra-í-chis-kij* |
| **arithmetic** | арифметика | *arif-myé-ti-ka* |
| • **arithmetical** | арифметический | *a-rif-mi-tí-chis-kij* |
| • **arithmetical** | арифметические | *a-rif-mi-tí-chis-ki-ye* |
| **operations** | функции *(pl)* | *fóonk-tsy-i* |
| **average** | среднее *(n)* | *sryéd-ni-ye* |
| • **calculate** | вычислить *(p)* | *vý-chis-lit'* |
| | вычислять *(i)* | *vy-chis-lyáht'* |
| • **calculation** | вычисление | *vy-chis-lyé-ni-ye* |
| **constant** | постоянное *(n)* | *pa-sta-yáh-na-ye* |
| **count** | считать *(i)* | *shchi-táht'* |
| **decimal** | десятичный | *di-si-tích-nyj* |
| **difference** | разница | *ráhz-ni-tsa* |
| **equality** | равенство | *ráh-vin-stva* |
| **equals** | равняется *(i)* | *rav-nyáh-i-tsa* |
| • **does not equal** | не равняется *(i)* | *ni rav-nyáh-i-tsa* |
| • **is equivalent to** | равен | *ráh-vin* |
| • **is greater than** | больше | *ból'-she* |
| • **is less than** | меньше | *myén'-sheh* |
| • **is similar to** | подобно *(adv)* | *pa-dób-na* |
| **equation** | уравнение | *u-rav-nyé-ni-ye* |
| **factor** | множитель *(m)* | *mnózhy-til'* |
| | коэффициент | *ka-y-fí-tsy-éhnt* |
| • **factor** | разложить *(p)* на | *raz-la-zhýt' na* |
| | множители *(pl)* | *mnózhy-ti-li* |
| | разлагать *(i)* | *raz-la-gáht'* |
| • **factorization** | найти *(p)* общий | *naj-tí óp-schchij mnó-zhy-* |
| | множитель *(m)* | *til'* |
| | находить *(i)* | *na-kha-dít'* |
| **function** | функция | *fóonk-tsy-ya* |
| **logarithm** | логарифм | *la-ga-rífm* |
| • **logarithmic** | логарифмический | *la-ga-rif-mí-chis-kij* |
| **multiple** | кратное *(n)* | *kráht-na-ye* |
| **percent** | процент | *pra-tséhnt* |
| • **percentage** | часть *(f)* | *chahst'* |
| | доля | *dó-lya* |

*FOCUS: Arithmetical Operations*

Addition — Сложение
$2 + 3 = 5$    two plus three equals five    два плюс три равняется пять

Subtraction — Вычитание
$9 - 3 = 6$    nine minus three equals six    девять минус три равняется шесть

Division — Деление
$10 : 2 = 5$    ten divided by two equals five    десять поделить на два получается пять

Raising to a power — Возведение в степень
$3^2 = 9$    three squared (to the second power) equals nine    три в квадрате (во второй степени) равняется девять

$2^3 = 8$    two cubed (to the third power) equals eight    два в кубе (в третьей степени) равняется восемь

$2^4 = 16$    two to the fourth power equals sixteen    два в четвёртой степени равняется шестнадцать

$x^n$    x to the nth power    x в энной степени

Extraction of root — Найти корень
$\sqrt[2]{4} = 2$    the square root of four is two    квадратный корень из четырёх равняется два

$\sqrt[3]{27} = 3$    the cube root of twenty-seven is three    кубический корень из двадцати семи равняется три

$\sqrt[n]{x}$    the nth root of x    энный корень из x

Ratio — Отношение
$12:4 = 9:3$    twelve is to four as nine is to three    двенадцать относится к четырём, как девять к трём

| problem | задача | za-dáh-cha |
| • problem solved | разрешённая задача | raz-ri-shó-na-ya |
| | | za-dáh-cha |
| product | произведение | pra-iz-vi-dýe-ni-ye |
| quotient | частное *(n)* | chást-na-ye |
| set | множество *(n)* | mnó-zhyst-va |
| solution | решение *(n)* | ri-shéh-ni-ye |
| • solve | решить *(p)* | ri-shýt' |
| | решать *(i)* | ri-sháht' |
| statistics | статистика | sta-tís-tika |
| • statistical | статистический | sta-tis-tíchis-kij |
| sum | сумма | sóom-a |
| • sum up | суммировать *(i)* | su-mí-ra-vat' |
| symbol | знак | znahk |
| variable | переменная | pi-ri-mýé-na-ya |
| | величина | vi-li-chi-náh |

## 2. GEOMETRY

### a. FIGURES

| **Plane figures** | плоскостные | plós-kas-ny-ye fi-góo-ry |
| | фигуры | |
| circle | круг | krook |
| • center | центр | tsehntr |
| • circumference | окружность *(f)* | ak-róozh-nast' |
| • diameter | диаметр | di-áh-mitr |
| • radius | радиус | ráh-di-us |
| • tangent | тангенс | táhn-gins |
| four-sided figures | четырёхугольники | chi-ty-ryokh-u-gól'-ni-ki |
| • parallelogram | параллелограмм | pa-ra-li-la-gráhm |
| • rectangle | прямоугольник | pri-ma-u-gól'-nik |
| • rhombus | ромб | romp |
| • square | квадрат | kvad-ráht |
| • trapezoid | трапеция | tra-pýe-tsy-ya |
| *n*-sided figures | многосторонние | mna-ga-sta-ró-ni-ye |
| | фигуры *(pl)* | fi-góo-ry |
| • pentagon | пятиугольник | pi-ti-u-gól'-nik |
| • hexagon | шестиугольник | shys-ti-u-gól'-nik |
| • heptagon | семиугольник | si-mi-u-gól'-ník |
| • octagon | восьмиугольник | vas'-mi-u-gól'-nik |
| • decagon | десятиугольник | di-si-ti-u-gól'-nik |
| triangle | треугольник | tri-u-gól'-nik |
| • acute angle | острый угол | óst-ryj óo-gal |
| • equilateral | равносторонний | rav-na-sta-ró-nij |
| • obtuse angle | широкий угол | shy-ró-kij óo-gal |

*FOCUS: Geometrical Figures*

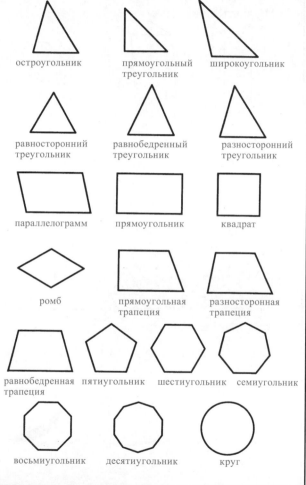

*FOCUS: Geometrical Solids*

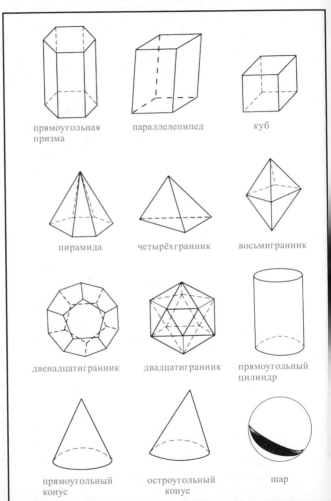

прямоугольная призма

параллелепипед

куб

пирамида

четырёхгранник

восьмигранник

двенадцатигранник

двадцатигранник

прямоугольный цилиндр

прямоугольный конус

остроугольный конус

шар

*FOCUS: Angles*

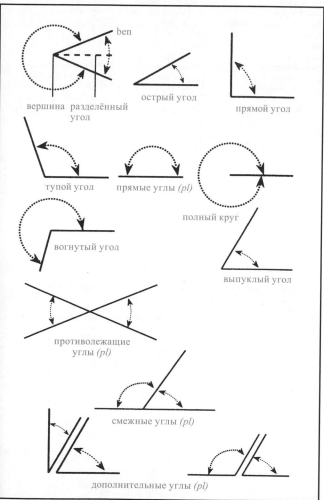

| | | |
|---|---|---|
| • **right-angled** | прямоугольный | *pri-ma-u-ngól'-nyj* |
| • **scalene** | разносторонний | *raz-na-sta-ró-nij* |
| **Solid figures** | объёмные фигуры *(pl)* | *ab'-yóm-ny-ye fi-góo-ry* |
| **cone** | конус | *kó-nus* |
| **cube** | куб | *koop* |
| **cylinder** | цилиндр | *tsy-líndr* |
| **parallelepiped** | параллелепипед | *pa-ra-li-li-pí-pit* |
| **polyhedron** | многогранник | *mna-ga-gráh-nik* |
| • **tetrahedron** | четырёхгранник | *chi-ty-ryókh-gráh-nik* |
| • **octahedron** | восьмигранник | *vas'-mi-gráh-nik* |
| • **dodecahedron** | десятигранник | *di-si-ti-gráh-nik* |
| **prism** | призма | *príz-ma* |
| **pyramid** | пирамида | *pi-ra-mí-da* |
| **sphere** | шар | *shahr* |

**b. CONCEPTS**

| | | |
|---|---|---|
| **angle** | угол | *óo-gal* |
| • **acute** | острый | *ós-tryj* |
| • **adjacent** | смежный | *smyézh-nyj* |
| • **bisector** | биссектриса | *bi-sik-trí-sa* |
| • **complementary** | дополнительный | *da-pal-ní-til'-nyj* |
| • **concave** | вогнутый | *vóg-nu-tyj* |
| • **consecutive** | последовательный | *pas-lyé-da-va-til'-nyj* |
| • **convex** | выпуклый | *vý-puk-lyj* |
| • **obtuse** | широкий | *shy-ró-kij* |
| • **one turn (360°)** | полный круг | *pól-nyj krook* |
| • **opposite** | противолежащий | *pra-ti-va-li-zháh-shchij* |
| • **right** | прямой | *pri-mój* |
| • **side** | сторона | *sta-ra-náh* |
| • **straight** | прямой | *pri-mój* |
| • **supplementary** | дополнительный | *da-pal-ní-til'-nyj* |
| • **vertex** | вершина | *vir-shý-na* |
| **axis** | ось *(f)* | *os'* |
| **coordinate** | координат | *ka-ar-di-náht* |
| **degree** | градус | *gráh-dus* |
| **draw** | чертить/рисовать *(i)* | *chir-tít' /ri-sa-váht'* |
| **drawing instruments** | чертёжные инструменты *(pl)* | *chir-tyózh-ny-ye in-stru-myén-ty* |
| • **compass** | циркуль *(m)* | *tsýr-kul'* |
| • **eraser** | ластик | *láhs-tik* |
| • **pen** | ручка | *róoch-ka* |
| • **pencil** | карандаш | *ka-ran-dáhsh* |
| • **protractor** | транспортир | *trans-par-tír* |

| | | |
|---|---|---|
| • ruler | линейка | *li-nyéj-ka* |
| • template | шаблон | *shab-lón* |
| geometry | геометрия | *gi-a-myét-ri-ya* |
| • geometrical | геометрический | *gi-a-mit-rí-chis-kij* |
| line | линия/черта | *lí-ni-ya/chir-táh* |
| • broken | раздробленная *(adj, f)* | *raz-dróp-li-na-ya* |
| • curved | округлая *(adj, f)* | *ak-róog-la-ya* |
| • parallel | параллельная *(adj, f)* | *pa-ra-lyél'-na-ya* |
| • perpendicular | перпендикулярная *(adj, f)* | *pir-pin-di-ku-lyáhr-na-ya* |
| • segment | сегмент | *sig-myént* |
| • straight | прямая *(adj, f)* | *pri-máh-ya* |
| point | точка | *tóch-ka* |
| space | пространство | *prast-ráhn-stva* |
| trigonometry | тригонометрия | *tri-ga-na-myét-ri-ya* |
| • trigonometric | тригонометрический | *tri-ga-na-mit-rí-chis-kij* |
| • cosecant | косеканс | *ka-si-káhns* |
| • cosine | косинус | *kó-si-nus* |

*FOCUS: Lines*

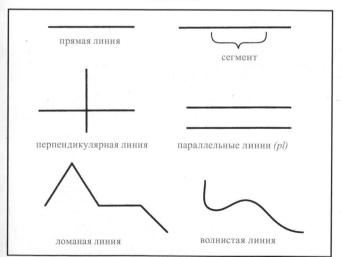

прямая линия

сегмент

перпендикулярная линия

параллельные линии *(pl)*

ломаная линия

волнистая линия

| | | |
|---|---|---|
| • **cotangent** | котангенс | *ka-táhn-gins* |
| • **secant** | секанс | *si-káhns* |
| • **sine** | синус | *sí-nus* |
| • **tangent** | тангенс | *táhn-gins* |
| **vector** | вектор | *vyék-tar* |

## 3. QUANTITY AND SPACE

### a. WEIGHTS AND MEASURES

| | | |
|---|---|---|
| **area** | площадь *(f)* | *pló-shchit'* |
| • **hectare** | гектар | *gik-táhr* |
| • **square centimeter** | квадратный сантиметр | *kvad-ráht-nyj san-ti-myétr* |
| • **square kilometer** | квадратный километр | *kvad-ráht-nyj ki-la-myétr* |
| • **square meter** | квадратный метр | *kvad-ráht-nyj myétr* |
| • **square millimeter** | квадратный миллиметр | *kvad-ráht-nyj mi-li-myétr* |
| **length** | длина | *dli-náh* |
| • **centimeter** | сантиметр | *san-ti-myétr* |
| • **kilometer** | километр | *ki-la-myétr* |
| • **meter** | метр | *myetr* |
| • **millimeter** | миллиметр | *mi-li-myétr* |
| **volume** | объём | *ab'-yóm* |
| • **cubic centimeter** | кубический сантиметр | *ku-bí-chis-kij san-ti-myétr* |
| • **cubic kilometer** | кубический километр | *ku-bí-chis-kij ki-la-myétr* |
| • **cubic millimeter** | кубический миллиметр | *ku-bí-chis-kij mi-li-myétr* |
| • **liter** | литр | *litr* |
| **weight** | вес | *vyes* |
| • **gram** | грамм | *grahm* |
| • **kilogram** | килограмм | *ki-la-gráhm* |

### b. WEIGHING AND MEASURING

| | | |
|---|---|---|
| **dense** | плотный | *plót-nyj* |
| • **density** | плотность *(f)* | *plót-nast'* |
| **dimension** | измерение | *iz-mi-ryé-ni-ye* |
| **extension** | продолжение | *pra-dal-zhéh-ni-ye* |
| **heavy** | тяжёлый | *ti-zhó-lyj* |
| **light** | лёгкий | *lyókh-kij* |

| long | длинный | *dlí-nyj* |
| mass | масса | *máh-sa* |
| maximum | максимум | *máhk-si-mum* |
| measure | мера | *myé-ra* |
| • measuring tape | измерительная лента | *iz-mi-rí-til'-na-ya léhn-ta* |
| medium | середина | *si-ri-dí-na* |
| minimum | минимум | *mí-ni-mum* |
| narrow | узкий | *óos-kij* |
| short (thing) | короткий | *ka-rót-kij* |
| speed | скорость *(f)* | *skó-rast'* |
| • per hour | в час | *f chahs* |
| • per minute | в минуту | *v mi-nóo-ty* |
| • per second | в секунду | *f si-kóon-du* |
| size | размер | *raz-myér* |
| tall | высокий | *vy-só-kij* |
| thick | толстый | *tóls-tyj* |
| thin | тонкий | *tón-kij* |
| weigh | весить *(i)* | *vyé-sit'* |
| wide | широкий | *shy-ró-kij* |
| • width | ширина | *shy-ri-náh* |

## c. CONCEPTS OF QUANTITY

| add (quantity) | добавить *(p)* | *da-báh-vit'* |
| | добавлять *(i)* | *da-bav-lyáht'* |
| a lot, much | много | *mnó-ga* |
| all, everyone | все | *fsye* |
| almost, nearly | почти | *pach-tí* |
| approximately | приблизительно *(adv)* | *pri-bli-zí-til'-na* |
| as much as | столько, сколько | *stól'-ka, skól'-ka* |
| big, large | большой | *bal'-shój* |
| • become big | увеличиться *(p)* | *u-vi-lí-chi-tsa* |
| | увеличиваться *(i)* | *u-vi-lí-chi-va-tsa* |
| both | оба, обе | *ó-ba, ó-bi* |
| capacity | ёмкость *(f)* | *yóm-kast'* |
| decrease *(n)* | уменьшение *(n)* | *u-min-shéh-ni-ye* |
| • decrease | уменьшиться *(p)* | *u-myén'-shy-tsa* |
| | уменьшаться *(i)* | *u-min'-sháh-tsa* |
| double | двойной | *dvaj-nój* |
| empty | пустой/порожний | *pus-tój/pa-rózh-nij* |
| • empty | опорожнить *(p)* | *a-pa-razh-nít'* |
| | опоражнивать *(i)* | *a-pa-ráhzh-ni-vat'* |
| enough | достаточно *(adv)* | *das-táh-tach-na* |

| entire | целый *(adj)*, | *tséh-lyj, tsy-li-kóm* |
|---|---|---|
| | целиком *(adv)* | |
| every, each | каждый | *káhzh-dyj* |
| everything | всё | *fsyo* |
| fill | наполнить *(p)* | *na-pól-nit'* |
| | наполнять *(i)* | *na-pal-nyáht'* |
| • full | полный | *pól-nyj* |
| grow | вырасти *(p)* | *vý-ras-ti* |
| | расти *(i)* | *ras-tí* |
| • growth | рост | *rost* |
| half | пол, половина | *pol, pa-la-ví-na* |
| how much | сколько | *skól'-ka* |
| increase | увеличиться *(p)* | *u-vi-lí-chi-tsa* |
| | увеличиваться *(i)* | *u-vi-lí-chi-va-tsa* |
| • increase | увеличение | *u-vi-li-chyé-ni-ye* |
| less | меньше | *myén'-she* |
| little | мало *(adv)* | *máh-la* |
| • a little | немного/немножко | *ni-mnó-ga/ni-mnó-zhka* |
| many | много | *mnó-ga* |
| more | больше, ещё | *ból'-she, i-shchyó* |
| no one | никто | *nik-tó* |
| nothing | ничего | *ni-chi-vó* |
| pair | пара | *páh-ra* |
| part | часть *(f)* | *chahst'* |
| piece | кусок | *ku-sók* |
| portion | порция | *pór-tsy-ya* |
| quantity | количество | *ka-lí-chist-va* |
| several | несколько | *nyés-kal'-ka* |
| small | маленький, малый | *máh-lin'-kij, máh-lyj* |
| • become small | уменьшиться *(p)* | *u-myén'-shy-tsa* |
| | уменьшаться *(i)* | *u-min'-sháh-tsa* |
| some | некоторое | *nyé-ka-ta-ra-ye* |
| suffice | быть *(i)* | *byt' das-táh-tach-nym* |
| | достаточным | |
| • sufficiently | достаточно | *das-táh-tach-na* |
| too much (more than | больше чем | *ból'-shy chyem das-táh-* |
| enough) | достаточно *(adv)* | *tach-na* |
| triple | в три раза | *f tri ráh-za* |

*Expressions*

| | | |
|---|---|---|
| **No more/enough** | = Больше не надо/хватит | |
| **Double quantity/dose** | = Двойное количество | |
| **How much do you want?** | = Сколько ты хочешь? *(fam)*/ | |
| | вы хотите? *(pol)* | |

## d. CONCEPTS OF LOCATION

| above | вверху | *vvir-khóo* |
|---|---|---|
| across | напротив | *na-pró-tif* |
| ahead, forward | вперёд | *fpi-ryót* |
| among, between | между | *myézh-du* |
| away | от | *at* |
| back, backward | назад | *na-záht* |
| beside, next to | рядом | *ryáh-dam* |
| beyond | за | *za* |
| bottom | дно, низ | *dno, nis* |
| • at the bottom | на дне, внизу | *na dnye, vni-zóo* |
| compass | компас | *kóm-pas* |
| direction | направление | *nap-rav-lyé-ni-ye* |
| distance | расстояние | *ras-ta-yáh-ni-ye* |
| down | вниз | *vnis* |
| east | восток | *vas-tók* |
| • eastern | восточный | *vas-tóch-nyj* |
| • to the east | на востоке | *na vas-tó-ki* |
| edge | край | *krahj* |
| far | далеко | *da-li-kó* |
| fast | быстро *(adv)* | *býst-ra* |
| from | от | *at* |
| here | здесь | *zdyes'* |
| horizontal | горизонтальный | *ga-ri-zan-táhl'-nyj* |
| in | в | *v/f* |
| • inside | внутри | *vnut-rí* |
| in front of | перед | *pyé-rit* |
| in the middle | в середине | *f si-ri-dí-ni* |
| left | левый *(adj)* | *lyé-vyj* |
| • to the left | налево *(adv)* | *na-lyé-va* |
| level | уровень *(m)* | *óo-ra-vin'* |
| near | вблизи, близко *(adv)* | *vbli-zí, blís-ka* |
| north | север | *syé-vir* |
| • northern | северный | *syé-vir-nyj* |
| • to the north | на север | *na syé-vir* |
| nowhere | никуда | *ni-ku-dáh* |
| outside | снаружи, извне *(adv)* | *sna-róo-zhy, iz-vnyé* |
| position | позиция/положение | *pa-zí-tsy-ya/ pa-la-zhéh-ni-ye* |
| place | место | *myés-ta* |
| right | правый *(adj)* | *práh-vyj* |
| • to the right | направо *(adv)* | *nap-ráh-va* |
| somewhere | куда-либо, куда-нибудь | *ku-dáh-li-ba, ku-dáh-ni-but'* |
| south | юг | *yuk* |

*FOCUS: Compass Points*

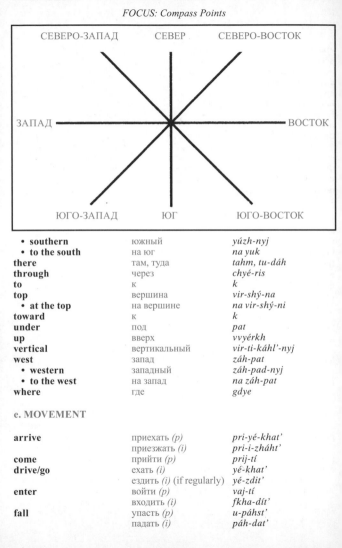

| | | |
|---|---|---|
| • **southern** | южный | *yúzh-nyj* |
| • **to the south** | на юг | *na yuk* |
| **there** | там, туда | *tahm, tu-dáh* |
| **through** | через | *chyé-ris* |
| **to** | к | *k* |
| **top** | вершина | *vir-shý-na* |
| • **at the top** | на вершине | *na vir-shý-ni* |
| **toward** | к | *k* |
| **under** | под | *pat* |
| **up** | вверх | *vvyérkh* |
| **vertical** | вертикальный | *vir-ti-káhl'-nyj* |
| **west** | запад | *záh-pat* |
| • **western** | западный | *záh-pad-nyj* |
| • **to the west** | на запад | *na záh-pat* |
| **where** | где | *gdye* |

**e. MOVEMENT**

| | | |
|---|---|---|
| **arrive** | приехать *(p)* | *pri-yé-khat'* |
| | приезжать *(i)* | *pri-i-zháht'* |
| **come** | прийти *(p)* | *prij-tí* |
| **drive/go** | ехать *(i)* | *yé-khat'* |
| | ездить *(i)* (if regularly) | *yé-zdit'* |
| **enter** | войти *(p)* | *vaj-tí* |
| | входить *(i)* | *fkha-dít'* |
| **fall** | упасть *(p)* | *u-páhst'* |
| | падать *(i)* | *páh-dat'* |

| follow | следовать *(i)* | *slyé-da-vat'* |
|---|---|---|
| get up, rise | подняться *(p)* | *pad-nyáht'-tsa* |
| | подниматься *(i)* | *pad-ni-máh-tsa* |
| go | идти *(i)* | *it-tí* |
| | ходить *(i)* | *kha-dít'* |
| • go away | уйти *(p)* | *uj-tí* |
| | уходить *(i)* | *u-kha-dít'* |
| • go down | спуститься *(p)* | *spus-tí-tsa* |
| | спускаться *(i)* | *spus-káh-tsa* |
| • go on foot | идти *(i)* пешком | *it-tí pish-kóm* |
| • go out, exit | выйти *(p)* | *vэj-ti* |
| | выходить *(i)* | *vy-kha-dít'* |
| • go up, climb | взойти *(p)* | *vzaj-tí* |
| | всходить *(i)* | *fskha-dít'* |
| leave, depart | уйти *(p)* | *uj-tí* |
| | уходить *(i)* | *u-kha-dít'* |
| | уехать *(p)* | *u-yé-khat'* |
| | уезжать *(i)* | *u-i-zháht'* |
| lie down | лечь *(p)* | *lyech* |
| | ложиться *(i)* | *la-zhý-tsa* |
| lift | поднять *(p)* | *pad-nyáht'* |
| | поднимать *(i)* | *pad-ni-máht'* |
| motion | движение | *dvi-zhéh-ni-ye* |
| move | двинуть *(p)* | *dví-nut'* |
| | двигать *(i)* | *dví-gat'* |
| • move oneself | двинуться *(p)* | *dví-nu-tsa* |
| | двигаться *(i)* | *dví-ga-tsa* |
| • movement | движение | *dvi-zhéh-ni-ye* |
| pass by | пройти *(p)* | *praj-tí* |
| | проходить *(i)* | *pra-kha-dít'* |
| pull | потянуть *(p)* | *pa-ti-nóot'* |
| | тянуть *(i)* | *ti-nóot'* |
| push | толкать *(i)* | *tal-káht'* |
| | толкнуть *(p)* | *talk-noot'* |
| put | поставить *(p)* | *pas-táh-vit'* |
| | ставить *(i)* | *stáh-vit'* |
| • put down | положить *(p)* | *pa-la-zhýt'* |
| | класть *(i)* | *klahst'* |
| quickly | быстро *(adv)* | *být-ra* |
| return | вернуть *(p)* | *vir-nóot'* |
| | возвращать *(i)* | *vaz-vra-shcháht'* |
| • come back | вернуться *(p)* | *vir-nóo-tsa* |
| | возвратиться *(p)* | *vaz-vra-tí-tsa* |
| | возвращаться *(i)* | *vaz-vra-shcháh-tsa* |
| run | бегать *(i)* | *byé-gat'* |
| | бежать *(i)* | *bi-zháht'* |
| send | послать *(p)* | *pas-láht'* |
| | посылать *(i)* | *pa-sy-láht'* |

| | | |
|---|---|---|
| **sit down** | сесть *(p)* | *syest'* |
| | сидеть *(i)* | *si-dyét'* |
| **slow** | медленный *(adj)* | *myéd-li-nyj* |
| • **slowly** | медленно *(adv)* | *myéd-li-na* |
| **stop** | остановиться *(p)* | *as-ta-na-ví-tsa* |
| | останавливаться *(i)* | *as-ta-náhv-li-va-tsa* |
| **turn** | повернуть *(p)* | *pa-vir-nóot'* |
| | поворачивать *(i)* | *pa-va-ráh-chi-vat'* |
| | повернуться *(p)* | *pa-vir-nóo-tsa* |
| | поворачиваться *(i)* | *pa-va-ráh-chi-va-tsa* |
| **walk** | идти *(i)* | *it-tí* |
| | ходить *(i)* | *kha-dít'* |
| • **walk** *(n)* | прогулка | *pra-góol-ka* |

*4. TIME*

## a. GENERAL EXPRESSIONS OF TIME

| | | |
|---|---|---|
| **afternoon** | вторая половина дня | *fta-ráh-ya pa-la-ví-na dnyah* |
| • **in the afternoon** | во второй половине дня | *va fta-rój pa-la-ví-ni dnyah* |
| • **this afternoon** | сегодня во второй половине дня | *si-vód-nya va fta-rój pa-la-ví-ni dnyah* |
| • **tomorrow afternoon** | завтра во второй половине дня | *záhft-ra va fta-rój pa-la-ví-ni dnyah* |
| **dawn** | рассвет | *ras-vyét* |
| **day** | день *(m)* | *dyen'* |
| • **all day** | весь день *(m)* | *vyes' dyen'* |
| **evening** | вечер | *vyé-chir* |
| • **in the evening** | вечером *(adv)* | *vyé-chi-ram* |
| • **this evening** | сегодня вечером | *si-vód-nya vyé-chi-ram* |
| • **tomorrow evening** | завтра вечером | *záhft-ra vyé-chi-ram* |
| **long ago** | давно | *dav-nó* |
| **midnight** | полночь *(f)* | *pól-nach* |
| • **at midnight** | в полночь *(f)* | *f pól-nach* |
| **morning** | утро | *óot-ra* |
| • **in the morning** | утром *(adv)* | *óot-ram* |
| • **this morning** | сегодня утром | *si-vód-nya óot-ram* |
| • **tomorrow morning** | завтра утром | *záhft-ra óot-ram* |
| **night** | ночь *(f)* | *noch* |
| • **at night** | ночью | *nóch'-yu* |
| • **last night** | вчера вечером | *fchi-ráh vyé-chi-ram* |
| | вчера ночью | *fchi-ráh nóch'-yu* |

| | | |
|---|---|---|
| • tomorrow night | завтра вечером | *záhft-ra vyé-chi-ram* |
| | следующая ночь *(f)* | *slyé-du-yu-shcha-ya noch* |
| • this night | сегодня ночью | *si-vód-nya nóch-yu* |
| **noon** | полдень *(m)* | *pól-din'* |
| • at noon | в полдень | *f pól-din'* |
| **occasionally** | иногда | *i-nag-dáh* |
| **recently** | недавно | *ni-dáhv-na* |
| **sunset** | закат | *za-káht* |
| **temporary** | временный | *vryé-min-nyj* |
| **time (in general)** | время | *vryé-mya* |
| • time (as in every time) | раз | *rahs* |
| **today** | сегодня | *si-vód-nya* |
| **tomorrow** | завтра | *záhft-ra* |
| • day after tomorrow | послезавтра | *pas-li-záhft-ra* |
| **tonight** | вечером | *vyé-chi-ram* |
| **yesterday** | вчера | *fchi-ráh* |
| • day before yesterday | позавчера | *pa-zaf-chi-ráh* |
| • yesterday morning | вчера утром | *fchi-ráh óot-ram* |
| • yesterday afternoon | вчера днём | *fchi-ráh dnyom* |

*Expressions*

| | | |
|---|---|---|
| **Time is money** | = | Время — деньги |
| **Time flies** | = | Время летит |
| **Many years ago** | = | Много лет назад, много лет тому назад |

## b. TELLING TIME

| | | |
|---|---|---|
| **What time is it?** | Который сейчас час? | *ka-tó-ryj si-cháhs chahs* |
| | Сколько сейчас времени? | *skól'-ka si-cháhs vryé-mi-ni* |
| • It's 1:00 | Час | *chahs* |
| | Сейчас час | *si-cháhs chahs* |
| • It's 2:00 P.M. | Два часа | *dvah chi-sáh* |
| | Сейчас два часа | *si-cháhs dvah chi-sáh* |
| • It's 3:00 A.M. | Три часа | *tri chi-sáh* |
| | Сейчас три часа | *si-cháhs tri chi-sáh* |
| **It's midnight.** | Полночь | *pól-nach* |
| | Сейчас полночь | *si-cháhs pól-nach* |

| | | |
|---|---|---|
| • It's exactly 3:00 | Ровно три часа | *róv-na tri chi-sáh* |
| | Сейчас ровно три часа | *si-cháhs róv-na tri chi-sáh* |
| • It's almost 3:00 | Почти три (часа) | *pach-tí tri (chi-sáh)* |
| • It's 1:10 | Десять минут второго | *dyé-sit' mi-nóot fta-ró-va* |
| | Сейчас час десять | *si-cháhs chahs dyé-sit'* |
| • It's 4:25 | Двадцать пять (минут) пятого | *dváh-tsat' pyáh' (mi-nóot) pyáh-ta-va* |
| | Сейчас четыре двадцать пять | *si-cháhs chi-tý-ri dváh-tsat' pyáht'* |
| • It's 3:15 | Четверть четвёртого | *chyét-virt' chit-vyór-ta-va* |
| | Сейчас три (часа) пятнадцать (минут) | *si-cháhs tri (chi-sáh) pit-náh-tsat' mi-nóot* |
| • It's 3:30 | Пол(овина) четвёртого | *pól/pa-la-ví-na chit-vyór-ta-va* |
| | Три тридцать | *tri trí-tsat'* |
| • It's 2:45 | Без четверти три | *bis chyét-vir-ti tri* |
| | Два сорок пять | *dváh só-rak pyáht'* |
| • It's 5:50 | Без десяти шесть | *bis di-si-tí shehst'* |
| | Пять пятьдесят | *pyaht' pi-di-syáht* |

---

**Note: Russian official time is similar to U.S. military time, e.g., 9:00, 18:00, or 22:00 hours. The A.M. and P.M. distinctions are not used.**

---

| | | |
|---|---|---|
| • It's 1:00 A.M. | Час ночи | *chahs nó-chi* |
| | Сейчас час ночи | *si-cháhs chahs nó-chi* |
| • It's 1:00 P.M. | Час дня | *chahs dnyah* |
| | Сейчас час дня | *si-cháhs chahs dnyah* |
| • It's 5:00 A.M. | Пять часов утра | *pyaht' chi-sóf ut-ráh* |
| | Сейчас пять часов утра | *si-cháhs pyaht' chi-sóf ut-ráh* |
| • It's 5:00 P.M. | Пять часов дня | *pyaht' chi-sóf dnyah* |
| | Сейчас пять часов дня | *si-cháhs pyaht' chi-sóf dnyah* |
| • It's 10:00 A.M. | Десять часов утра | *dyé-sit' chi-sóf ut-ráh* |
| • It's 10:00 P.M. | Десять часов вечера | *dyé-sit' chi-sóf vyé-chi-ra* |
| At what time? | В которое время? | *f ka-tó-ra-ye vryé-mya* |
| | В какое время? | *f ka-kó-ye vryé-mya* |
| | В который час? | *f ka-tó-ryj chahs* |
| • At 1:00 | В час (дня/ночи) | *f chahs (dnyah/nó-chi)* |

| | | |
|---|---|---|
| • **At 2:00** | В два (часа) | *v dvah (chi-sáh)* |
| • **At 3:00** | В три (часа) | *f tri (chi-sáh)* |

## c. UNITS OF TIME

| | | |
|---|---|---|
| century | век (века *pl*) | *vyek (vi-káh)* |
| day | день *(m)* (дни *pl*) | *dyen' (dni)* |
| • daily | ежедневно *(adv)* | *i-zhy-dnyév-na* |
| decade | декада | *dy-káh-da* |
| | десятилетка | *di-si-ti-lyét-ka* |
| hour | час | *chahs* |
| • hourly | ежечасный | *y-zhy-cháhs-nyj* |
| instant | мгновение | *mgna-vyé-ni-ye* |
| minute | минута | *mi-nóo-ta* |
| moment | момент | *ma-myént* |
| month | месяц | *myé-sits* |
| • monthly | ежемесячный | *y-zhy-myé-sich-nyj* |
| second | секунда | *si-kóon-da* |
| week | неделя | *ni-dyé-lya* |
| • weekly | еженедельный | *i-zhy-ni-dyél'-nyj* |
| year | год (года *pl*) | *got (ga-dáh)* |
| • yearly, annually | годовой | *ga-da-vój* |
| | ежегодный | *i-zhy-gód-nyj* |

## d. TIMEPIECES

| | | |
|---|---|---|
| alarm clock | будильник | *bu-díl'-nik* |
| clock | часы *(pl)* | *chi-sý* |
| dial | циферблат | *tsy-fír-bláht* |
| grandfather clock | часы с боем | *chi-sý s bó-yem* |
| hand (of a clock) | стрелка | *stryél-ka* |
| watch | часы *(pl)* | *chi-sý* |
| • watchband | ремешок для часов | *ri-mi-shók dlya chi-sóf* |
| • watch battery | батарейка для часов | *ba-ta-ryéj-ka dlya chi-sóf* |
| wristwatch | ручные часы | *ruch-ný-ye chi-sý* |

*Expressions*

| | | |
|---|---|---|
| **Day to day** | = | Изо дня в день |
| **This watch is fast** | = | Эти часы спешат |
| **This watch is slow** | = | Эти часы отстают |

## e. CONCEPTS OF TIME

| | | |
|---|---|---|
| **after** | после | *pós-li* |
| **again** | опять, снова | *a-pyáht', snó-va* |
| **almost never** | почти никогда | *pach-tí ni-kag-dáh* |
| **already** | уже | *u-zhéh* |
| **always** | всегда | *fsig-dáh* |
| | постоянно | *pas-ta-yáh-na* |
| **as soon as** | как только | *kahk tól'-ka* |
| **at the same time** | в то же время | *f to zhy vryé-mya* |
| | в одно и то же время | *vad-nó i to zhy vryé-mya* |
| **be about to** | почти | *pach-tí* |
| **become** | стать *(p)* | *staht'* |
| | становиться *(i)* | *sta-na-ví-tsa* |
| **before** | до, перед | *da, pyé-rid* |
| **before long** | в ближайшем будущем | *v bli-zháhj-shym bóo-du-shchim* |
| | в скором будущем | *v skó-ram bóo-du-shchim* |
| **begin** | начать *(p)* | *na-cháht'* |
| | начинать *(i)* | *na-chi-náht'* |
| • **beginning** | начало | *na-cháh-la* |
| **brief** | короткий | *ka-rót-kij* |
| | краткий | *kráht-kij* |
| **by now** | к настоящему времени | *k nas-ta-yáh-shchi-mu vryé-mi-ni* |
| **change** | переменить (-ся) *(p)* | *pi-ri-mi-nít' (-tsa)* |
| | переменять (-ся) *(i)* | *pi-ri-mi-nyáht' (-tsa)* |
| **continue** | продолжить (-ся) *(p)* | *pra-dól-zhyt'* |
| | продолжать (-ся) *(i)* | *pra-dal-zháh-tsa* |
| • **continually** | в течение продолжительного времени | *f ti-chyé-ni-ye pra-dal-zhý-til'-na-va vryé-mi-ni* |
| **during** | во время | *va vryé-mya* |
| **early** | рано | *ráh-na* |
| • **arrive early** | прийти *(p)* рано | *pri-tí ráh-na* |
| | приходить *(i)* | *pri-kha-dít'* |
| **end, finish** | кончить *(p)* | *kón-chit'* |
| | кончать *(i)* | *kan-cháht'* |
| • **end** | конец | *ka-nyéts* |
| **for** | на | *na* |
| **frequent** | частый *(adj)* | *cháhs-tyj* |
| • **frequently** | часто *(adv)* | *cháhs-ta* |
| **future** | будущее | *bóo-du-shchi-ye* |
| **happen, occur** | случиться *(p)* | *slu-chí-tsa* |
| | случаться *(i)* | *slu-cháh-tsa* |

| | | |
|---|---|---|
| **in an hour** | через час | *chí-ris chahs* |
| • **in two minutes** | через две минуты | *chí-ris dve mi-nóo-ty* |
| **in the meantime** | пока что | *pa-káh shto* |
| **in time** | во время | *vó vrye-mya* |
| **irregular** | неравномерный | *ni-rav-na-myér-nyj* |
| **just now** | только сейчас | *tól'-ka si-cháhs* |
| | только что | *tól'-ka shto* |
| **last** | продолжиться *(p)* | *pra-dól-zhyt'-tsa* |
| | продолжаться *(i)* | *pra-dal-zháht'-tsa* |
| • **last a long time** | продолжаться | *pra-dal-zháht'-tsa* |
| | длинное время | *dlí-na-ye vryé-mya* |
| • **last a short time** | продолжаться | *pra-dal-zháht'-tsa* |
| | короткое время | *ka-rót-ka-ye vryé-mya* |
| **last** | последний | *pas-lyéd-nij* |
| • **last month** | прошлый месяц | *prósh-lyj myé-sits* |
| • **last year** | прошлый год | *prósh-lyj got* |
| **late** | поздно *(adv)* | *póz-na* |
| • **to be late** | опоздать *(p)* | *a-paz-dáht'* |
| | опаздывать *(i)* | *a-páhz-dy-vat'* |
| **long-term** | продолжительный | *pra-dal-zhý-til'-nyj* |
| **never** | никогда | *ni-kag-dáh* |
| • **almost never** | почти никогда | *pach-tí ni-kag-dáh* |
| **now** | сейчас/теперь | *si-cháhs/ti-pyér'* |
| • **for now** | пока (что) | *pa-káh (shto)* |
| • **from now on** | начиная с | *na-chi-náh-ya s si-vód-* |
| | сегодняшнего дня | *nish-ni-va dnyah* |
| **nowadays** | теперь/сейчас/ | *ti-pyér'/si-cháhs/* |
| | нынче/нонче | *nýn-chi/nón-chi* |
| **occasionally** | иногда | *i-nag-dáh* |
| **often** | часто *(adv)* | *cháhs-ta* |
| | частенько *(adv)* | *chas-tyén'-ka* |
| **once** | однажды | *ad-náhzh-dy* |
| | один раз | *a-dín rahs* |
| • **once in a while** | периодически | *pi-ri-a-dí-chis-ki* |
| • **once more** | ещё раз | *i-shchyó rahs* |
| • **once upon a time** | давным давно | *dav-ným dav-nó* |
| **only** | только | *tól'-ka* |
| **on time** | во время | *vó vrye-mya* |
| **past** | прошлое | *prósh-la-ye* |
| • **in the past** | в прошлом | *f prósh-lam* |
| **present** | настоящее | *nas-ta-yáh-shchi-ye* |
| • **presently** | в настоящее время | *v nas-ta-yáh-shchi-ye* |
| | | *vryé-mya* |
| **previous** | предыдущий | *pri-dy-dóo-shchij* |
| • **previously** | в предыдущем | *f pri-dy-dóo-shchim* |
| **rare** | редкий *(adj)* | *ryét-kij* |
| • **rarely** | редко *(adv)* | *ryét-ka* |

| | | |
|---|---|---|
| recent | недавний *(adj)* | *ni-dáhv-nij* |
| • recently | недавно *(adv)* | *ni-dáhv-na* |
| regular | обычный | *a-bých-nyj* |
| | регулярный | *ri-gu-lyáhr-nyj* |
| right away | сейчас, сейчас же | *si-cháhs, si-cháhs zhy* |
| short-term | краткосрочный | *krat-ka-sróch-nyj* |
| simultaneous | одновременный | *ad-na-vri-myé-nyj* |
| since | с, в течение | *s, f ti-chyé-ni-ye* |
| • since Monday | с понедельника | *s pa-ni-dyél'-ni-ka* |
| • since yesterday | со вчерашнего дня | *sa fchi-ráhsh-ni-va dnyah* |
| • for three days | в течение трёх дней | *f ti-chyé-ni-i tryokh dnyej* |
| slow | медленный *(adj)* | *myéd-li-nyj* |
| • slowly | медленно *(adv)* | *myéd-li-na* |
| soon | скоро | *skó-ra* |
| • as soon as | как только | *kahk tól'-ka* |
| • sooner or later | рано или поздно | *ráh-na i-li póz-na* |
| spend time | провести время | *pra-vis-tí vryé-mya* |
| sporadic | спорадический | *spo-rah-dí-chis-skij* |
| still | ещё пока | *i-shchyó pa-káh* |
| take place | иметь *(i)* место | *i-myét' myés-ta* |
| temporary | временный | *vryé-mi-nyj* |
| • temporarily | временно | *vryé-mi-na* |
| then | тогда | *tag-dáh* |
| timetable, schedule | расписание | *ras-pi-sáh-ni-ye* |
| to this day | до сего дня | *da si-vó dnyah* |
| | до сегодняшнего дня | *da si-vód-nish-ni-va dnyah* |
| until | до тех пор | *da tyekh por* |
| usually | обычно | *a-bých-na* |
| • as usual | как обычно | *kahk a-bých-na* |
| wait | подождать *(p)* | *pa-dazh-dáht'* |
| | ждать *(i)* | *zhdaht'* |
| while | пока | *pa-káh* |
| within | в течение | *f ti-chyé-ni-ye* |
| yet | ещё | *i-shchyó* |

*Expressions*

---

**Better late than never** = Лучше поздно, чем никогда

---

## 5. DAYS, MONTHS, AND SEASONS

### a. DAYS OF THE WEEK

| | | |
|---|---|---|
| days of the week | дни недели | *dni ni-dyé-li* |
| • Monday | понедельник | *pa-ni-dyél'-nik* |

- **Tuesday**  вторник  *ftór-nik*
- **Wednesday**  среда  *sri-dáh*
- **Thursday**  четверг  *chit-vyérk*
- **Friday**  пятница  *pyáht-ni-tsa*
- **Saturday**  суббота  *su-bó-ta*
- **Sunday**  воскресенье (-ние)  *vas-kri-syé-n'ye*

**holiday**  праздник  *práhz-nik*
**weekend**  конец недели  *ka-nyéts ni-dyé-li*
**What day is it?**  Какой сегодня день?  *ka-kój si-vód-nya dyen'*
**workday**  рабочий день *(m)*  *ra-bó-chij dyen'*

## b. MONTHS OF THE YEAR

**month of the year**  месяц года  *myé-sits gó-da*
- **January**  январь *(m)*  *yn-váhr'*
- **February**  февраль *(m)*  *fiv-ráhl'*
- **March**  март  *mahrt*
- **April**  апрель *(m)*  *ap-ryél'*
- **May**  май  *mahj*
- **June**  июнь *(m)*  *i-yún'*
- **July**  июль *(m)*  *i-yúl'*
- **August**  август  *áhv-gust*
- **September**  сентябрь *(m)*  *sin-tyáh-bar'*
- **October**  октябрь *(m)*  *ak-tyáh-bar'*
- **November**  ноябрь *(m)*  *na-yáh-bar'*
- **December**  декабрь *(m)*  *di-káh-bar'*

**academic year**  учебный год  *u-chyéb-nyj got*
**calendar**  календарь *(m)*  *ka-lin-dáhr'*
- **calendar year**  календарный год  *ka-lin-dáhr-nyj got*

**leap year**  високосный год  *vi-sa-kós-nyj got*
**monthly**  месячный  *myé-sich-nyj*
  ежемесячный  *y-zhy-myé-sich-nyj*
**school year**  школьный год  *shkól'-nyj got*

## c. SEASONS

**season**  время года  *vryé-mya gó-da*
- **spring**  весна  *vis-náh*
- **summer**  лето  *lyé-ta*
- **fall**  осень *(f)*  *ó-sin'*
- **winter**  зима  *zi-máh*

**equinox**  равноденствие  *rav-na-dyéns-tvi-ye*
**moon**  луна  *lu-náh*

FOCUS: The Seasons

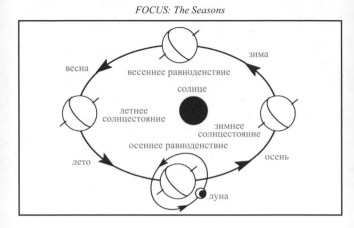

| solstice | солнцестояние | *son-tse-sta-yáh-ni-ye* |
| sun | солнце | *són-tse* |

## d. EXPRESSING THE DATE

| What's today's date? | Какое сегодня число? | *ka-kó-ye si-vód-nya chis-ló* |
| • **October first** | первое октября | *pyér-va-ye ak-tib-ryáh* |
| • **January second** | второе января | *fta-ró-ye in-va-ryáh* |
| • **May third** | третье мая | *tryét'-ye máh-ya* |
| What year is it? | Какой сейчас год? | *ka-kój si-cháhs got* |
| • **It's 1993** | тысяча девятьсот девяносто третий | *tý-si-cha di-vi-tsót di-vi-nós-ta tryé-tij* |
| When were you born? | Когда вы родились? *(pol)* | *kag-dáh vy ra-di-lís'* |
| | Когда ты родился? *(fam, m)* | *kag-dáh ty ra-díl-sya* |
| | Когда ты родилась? *(fam, f)* | *kag-dáh ty ra-di-láhs'* |

| • **I was born in 1973** | Я родился *(m)* [родилась *(f)*] в семьдесят третьем году | *yah ra-díl-sya (ra-di-láhs') f syém-di-syat tryét'-yem ga-doó* |

## e. IMPORTANT DATES

| **Christmas** | Рождество (Христово) | *razh-dist-vó (khris-tó-va)* |
| **Easter** | Пасха | *páhs-kha* |
| **First of May** | Первое мая | *pyér-va-ye máh-ya* |
| **New Year** | Новый год | *nó-vyj god* |
| **New Year's Day** | Новогодний день *(m)* | *na-va-gód-nij dyen'* |
| **New Year's Eve** | канун Нового года | *ka-nóon nó-va-va gó-da* |
| **Women's Day** | Женский день | *zhéhn-skij dyen'* |

## 6. TALKING ABOUT THE WEATHER

## a. GENERAL WEATHER VOCABULARY

| **air** | воздух | *vóz-dukh* |
| **atmosphere** | атмосфера | *at-mas-fyé-ra* |
| • **atmospheric conditions** | атмосферные условия | *at-mas-fyér-ny-ye us-ló-vi-ya* |
| **awful** | ужасный | *u-zháhs-nyj* |
| • **awful weather** | ужасная погода | *u-zháhs-na-ya pa-gó-da* |
| **beautiful weather** | прекрасная погода | *prik-ráhs-na-ya pa-gó-da* |
| | замечательная погода | *za-mi-cháh-til'-na-ya pa-gó-da* |
| **clear** | ясно | *yáhs-na* |
| • **The sky is clear** | Небо ясное | *nyé-ba yáhs-na-ye* |
| **climate** | климат | *klí-mat* |
| • **cold** | холодный | *kha-lód-nyj* |
| • **continental** | континентальный | *kan-ti-nin-táhl'-nyj* |
| • **dry** | сухой | *su-khój* |
| • **hot** | жаркий | *zháhr-kij* |
| • **humid** | влажный | *vláhzh-nyj* |
| • **maritime** | морской | *mars-kój* |
| • **Mediterranean** | средиземный | *sri-di-zyém-nyj* |
| • **subtropical** | субтропический | *sup-tra-pí-chis-kij* |
| **cloud** | облако | *ób-la-ka* |
| • **cloudy** | облачный | *ób-lach-nyj* |

| | | |
|---|---|---|
| **cold** | холод *(n)* | *khó-lad* |
| • **cold** | холодно *(adv)* | *khó-lad-na* |
| • **I am cold** | Мне холодно | *mnye khó-lad-na* |
| **cool** | прохладный | *prakh-láhd-nyj* |
| • **become cooler** | стать *(p)* прохладнее | *staht' prakh-láhd-ni-ye* |
| | становиться *(i)* прохладнее | *sta-na-ví-tsa prakh-láhd-ni-ye* |
| **dark** | тёмный *(adj)* | *tyóm-nyj* |
| | темно *(adv)* | *tim-nó* |
| • **It's dark already** | Уже темно | *u-zhéh tim-nó* |
| **drizzle** | моросить *(i)* | *ma-ra-sít'* |
| | мелкий дождь *(n, m)* | *myél-kij dozht'* |
| **drop (of rain)** | капля (дождя) | *káhp-lya (dazh-dyáh)* |
| **dry** | сухой | *su-khój* |
| **fog** | туман | *tu-máhn* |
| • **foggy** | туманный | *tu-máhn-yj* |
| **freeze** | замёрзнуть *(p)* | *za-myórz-nut'* |
| | замерзать *(i)* | *za-mir-záht'* |
| • **frozen** | замёрзший | *za-myór-shyj* |
| **hail** | град | *graht* |
| • **It's hailing** | Град идёт | *graht i-dyót* |
| **How's the weather?** | Как погода? | *kak pa-gó-da* |
| • **It's a bit hot (cold, etc.)** | Немножко жарко (холодно) | *nim-nósh-ka zháhr-ka (khó-lad-na)* |
| • **It's awful** | Ужасно (-ная погода) | *u-zháhs-na (-na-ya pa-gó-da)* |
| • **It's beautiful** | Прекрасно (-ная погода) | *prik-ráhs-na (-na-ya pa-gó-da)* |
| | Замечательно | *za-mi-cháh-til'-na* |
| • **It's cloudy** | Облачно | *ób-lach-na* |
| • **It's cold** | Холодно | *khó-lad-na* |
| • **It's cool** | Прохладно | *prakh-láhd-na* |
| • **It's foul** | Отвратительно | *at-vra-tí-til'-na* |
| | Противно | *pra-tív-na* |
| • **It's hot** | Жарко | *zháhr-ka* |
| • **It's humid** | Влажная погода | *vláhzh-na-ya pa-gó-da* |
| • **It's mild** | Мягкая погода | *myáhkh-ka-ya pa-gó-da* |
| • **It's pleasant** | Приятная погода | *pri-yáht-na-ya pa-gó-da* |
| • **It's raining** | Дождливо | *dazhd-lí-va* |
| | Дождь *(m)* идёт | *dosht' i-dyót* |
| • **It's snowing** | Снег идёт | *snyek i-dyót* |
| • **It's sunny** | Солнечно | *sól-nich-na* |
| • **The sun is shining** | Солнце светит | *són-tsy svyé-tit* |
| • **It's thundering** | Гром гремит | *grom gri-mít* |
| • **It's very cold** | Очень холодно | *ó-chin' khó-lad-na* |

| | | |
|---|---|---|
| • It's very hot | Очень жарко | *ó-chin' zháhr-ka* |
| • It's windy | Ветренно | *vyét-ri-na* |
| • There is lightning | Молния сверкает | *mól-ni-ya svir-káh-it* |
| humid, damp | влажно *(adv)* | *vláhzh-na* |
| • humidity | влажность *(f)* | *vláhzh-nast'* |
| hurricane | ураган | *u-ra-gáhn* |
| ice | лёд | *lyot* |
| • ice over | покрыться *(p)* льдом | *pak-rý-tsa l'dom* |
| | покрываться *(i)* | *pak-ry-váh-tsa* |
| light | свет | *svyet* |
| • become lighter | посветлеть *(p)* | *pas-vit-lyét'* |
| | светлеть *(i)* | *svit-lyét'* |
| lightning | молния | *mól-ni-ya* |
| moon | луна | *lu-náh* |
| • moonlight | лунный свет | *lóon-yj svyet* |
| mugginess | сырость *(f)* | *sý-rast'* |
| • muggy weather | сырая погода | *sy-ráh-ya pa-gó-da* |
| overcast | обложенное (небо) | *ab-ló-zhy-na-ye (nyé-ba)* |
| precipitation | осадки *(pl)* | *a-sáhd-ki* |
| rain | дождь *(m)* | *dosht'* |
| • rainy | дождливый | *dazhd-lí-vyj* |
| sea | море | *mó-rye* |
| shadow, shade | тень *(f)* | *tyen'* |
| sky | небо | *nyé-ba* |
| snow | снег | *snyek* |
| • blizzard | буран | *bu-ráhn* |
| • flakes | хлопья *(pl)* | *khlóp'-ya* |
| • snowy | снежный | *snyézh-nyj* |
| • snow cover | снежный покров | *snyézh-nyj pak-róf* |
| • snowfall | снегопад | *sni-ga-páht* |
| • snow in | занести *(p)* снегом | *za-nis-tí snyé-gam* |
| | заносить *(i)* | *za-na-sít'* |
| star | звезда | *zviz-dáh* |

*Expressions*

| | |
|---|---|
| It's raining cats and dogs (Rain pours as if from a bucket) | = Дождь идёт, как из ведра |
| The sun is shining | = Солнце светит |
| The weather is beautiful | = Прекрасная (замечательная, восхитительная) погода |
| Weather permitting (depending on the weather) | = В зависимости от погоды |

| | | |
|---|---|---|
| **storm** | буря | *bóo-rya* |
| • **stormy** | бурный | *bóor-nyj* |
| **sun** | солнце | *són-tse* |
| • **sunny** | солнечный | *sól-nich-nyj* |
| **thunder** | гром | *grom* |
| • **thunderclap** | удар грома | *u-dáhr gró-ma* |
| **tornado** | смерч | *smyérch* |
| **weather** | погода | *pa-gó-da* |

## b. REACTING TO THE WEATHER

| | | |
|---|---|---|
| **catch a chill (cold)** | простудиться *(p)* | *pras-tu-dí-tsa* |
| | простужаться *(i)* | *pras-tu-zháh-tsa* |
| **I am cold** | Мне холодно | *mnye khó-lad-na* |
| **I am hot** | Мне жарко | *mnye zháhr-ka* |
| **(I) can't stand the cold** | Невыносимо холодно | *ni-vy-na-sí-ma khó-lad-na* |
| **(I) can't stand the heat** | Невыносимо жарко | *ni-vy-na-sí-ma zháhr-ka* |
| **I like cold weather** | Мне нравится холодная погода | *mnye nráh-vi-tsa kha-lód-na-ya pa-gó-da* |
| **I like warm weather** | Мне нравится тёплая погода | *mnye nráh-vi-tsa tyóp-la-ya pa-gó-da* |
| **perspire** | потеть *(i)* | *pa-tyét'* |
| **warm up** | согреться *(p)* | *sag-ryé-tsa* |
| | греться *(i)* | *gryé-tsa* |

*Expressions*

| | | |
|---|---|---|
| **A lot of snow has fallen** | = | Много снега навалило |
| **Changeable/variable weather** | = | Переменная (переменчивая) погода |
| **Chilled to the bone** | = | Промёрзнуть до кости |
| **Cold as ice** | = | Холодный, как лёд |
| **(His) teeth were chattering** | = | (У него) зуб на зуб не попадал |
| **Perspire profusely** | = | Обливаться потом |
| **Snowman** | = | Снежная баба, снеговик |
| **The snow has melted** | = | Снег растаял |
| **Usual (seasonal) weather** | = | Обычная погода |
| **White (pale) as snow** | = | Белый, как снег |

## c. WEATHER-MEASURING INSTRUMENTS AND ACTIVITIES

| | | |
|---|---|---|
| **barometer** | барометр | *ba-ró-mitr* |
| • **barometric pressure** | баромерное давление | *ba-ró-mir-na-ye dav-lyé-ni-ye* |
| **Celsius** | Цельсий | *tséhl'-sij* |
| **degree** | градус | *gráh-dus* |
| **Fahrenheit** | Фаренгейт | *fa-rin-gyéjt* |
| **mercury** | ртуть *(f)* | *rtoot'* |
| **minus** | минус | *mí-nus* |
| **plus** | плюс | *plyus* |
| **temperature** | температура | *tim-pi-ra-tóo-ra* |
| • **average** | средняя | *sryéd-ni-ya* |
| • **high** | высокая | *vy-só-ka-ya* |
| • **low** | низкая | *nís-ka-ya* |
| • **maximum** | максимальная | *mak-si-máhl'-na-ya* |
| **thermometer** | термометр | *tir-mó-mitr* |
| • **boiling point** | температура кипения | *tim-pi-ra-tóo-ra ki-pyé-ni-ya* |
| • **melting point** | температура таяния | *tim-pi-ra-tóo-ra táh-i-ni-ya* |
| **thermostat** | термостат | *tir-ma-stáht* |
| **weather forecast** | прогноз/сводка погоды | *prag-nós/svót-ka pa-gó-dy* |
| • **forecast** | предсказывать *(i)* предсказать *(p)* погоду | *prit-skáh-zy-vat' prit-ska-záht' pa-gó-du* |
| **zero** | ноль | *nol'* |
| • **above zero** | выше ноля/тепла | *vý-shy na-lyáh/tip-láh* |
| • **below zero** | ниже ноля/мороза | *ní-zhy na-lyáh/ma-ró-za* |

## 7. COLORS

### a. BASIC COLORS

| | | |
|---|---|---|
| **What color is it?** | Какого это цвета? | *ka-kó-va éh-ta tsvyé-ta* |
| • **beige** | бежевый | *byé-zhy-vyj* |
| • **black** | чёрный | *chyór-nyj* |
| • **blue** | синий | *sí-nij* |
| • **dark blue** | тёмно-синий | *tyóm-na-sí-nij* |
| • **light blue** | голубой | *ga-lu-bój* |
| • **bluish** | синеватый | *si-ni-váh-tyj* |
| • **brown** | коричневый | *ka-rích-ni-vyj* |
| • **gold** | золотой | *za-la-tój* |
| • **gray** | серый | *syé-ryj* |

- **green** — зелёный — *zi-lyó-nyj*
- **maroon** — вишнёвый — *vish-nyó-vyj*
- **off white** — кремовый — *kréh-ma-vyj*
- **orange** — оранжевый — *a-ráhn-zhy-vyj*
- **pink** — розовый — *ró-za-vyj*
- **purple** — лиловый — *li-ló-vyj*
- **red** — красный — *kráhs-nyj*
- **silver** — серебряный — *si-ryéb-ri-nyj*
- **white** — белый — *byé-lyj*
- **yellow** — жёлтый — *zhól-tyj*
- **yellow-green** — жёлто-зелёный — *zhol-to-zi-lyó-nyj*

## Expressions

| | | |
|---|---|---|
| **Gray day** | = | Пасмурный день |
| **Green (young, inexperienced)** | = | Зелёный |
| **Red as a tomato** | = | Красный, как помидор |
| **Red Square** | = | Красная Площадь |
| **To become blue (from the cold)** | = | Посинеть (от холода) |
| **To become green (with envy, anger)** | = | Позеленеть |
| | | (от зависти, злости) |

## b. DESCRIBING COLORS

| | | |
|---|---|---|
| **bichromatic, two-color** | двухцветный | *dvukh-tsvyét-nyj* |
| **bright** | яркий | *yáhr-kij* |
| **dark** | тёмный | *tyóm-nyj* |
| **dull** | тусклый/мутный | *tóosk-lyj/móot-nyj* |
| **light** | светлый | *svyét-lyj* |
| **monochromatic** | одноцветный | *ad-na-tsvyét-nyj* |
| **multicolored** | многоцветный | *mna-ga-tsvyét-nyj* |
| **opaque** | непрозрачный | *ni-praz-ráhch-nyj* |
| **pure** | чистый | *chís-tyj* |
| **shiny** | светящийся | *svi-tyáh-shchij-sya* |
| **sparkling** | сверкающий | *svir-káh-yu-shchij* |
| **transparent** | прозрачный | *praz-ráhch-nyj* |

## c. ADDITIONAL VOCABULARY FOR COLORS

| color | цвет | *tsvyet* |
|---|---|---|
| • color | окрасить *(p)* | *ak-ráh-sit'* |
| | покрасить *(p)* | *pa-kráh-sit* |
| | красить *(i)* | *kráh-sit'* |
| • colored | окрашенный | *ak-ráh-shy-nyj* |
| • coloring | окраска | *ak-ráhs-ka* |
| • food coloring | съедобная окраска | *s'ye-dób-na-ya ak-ráhs-ka* |
| colored pencil | цветной карандаш | *tsvit-nój ka-ran-dáhsh* |
| paint | краска | *kráhs-ka* |
| painter (workman) | маляр | *ma-lyáhr* |
| painter (artist) | художник (-ница) | *khu-dózh-nik (-ni-tsa)* |
| pen | ручка | *róoch-ka* |
| tint | оттенок | *at-tyé-nak* |
| • tint | подкрашивать *(i)* | *pat-kráh-shy-vat'* |

*8. BASIC GRAMMAR*

## a. GRAMMATICAL TERMS

| adjective | прилагательное | *pri-la-gáh-til'-na-ye* |
|---|---|---|
| • comparative | сравнительное | *srav-ní-til'-na-ye* |
| • demonstrative | указательное | *u-ka-záh-til'-na-ye* |
| • descriptive | описательное | *a-pi-sáh-til'-na-ye* |
| • indefinite | неопределённое | *ni-ap-ri-di-lyó-na-ye* |
| • possessive | притяжательное | *pri-ti-zháh-til'-na-ye* |
| • short (form) | краткое | *kráht-ka-ye* |
| • superlative | превосходная | *pri-vas-khód-na-ya* |
| | степень *(f)* | *styé-pin'* |
| adverb | наречие | *na-ryé-chi-ye* |
| alphabet | алфавит | *al-fa-vít* |
| • alphabetical | алфавитный | *al-fa-vít-nyj* |
| order | порядок | *pa-ryáh-dak* |
| • consonant | согласная | *sag-láhs-na-ya* |
| • letter | буква | *bóok-va* |
| • capital letter | большая буква | *bal'-sháh-ya bóok-va* |
| • small letter | маленькая буква | *máh-lin'-ka-ya bóok-va* |
| • phonetics | звуковая система | *zvu-ka-váh-ya sis-tyé-ma* |
| • pronunciation | произношение | *pra-iz-na-shéh-ni-ye* |
| • vowel | гласная | *gláhs-na-ya* |
| • stressed | ударная | *u-dáhr-na-ya* |
| • unstressed | безударная | *bi-zu-dáhr-na-ya* |
| article | there are no articles in Russian grammar | |
| aspect | вид | *vit* |

| | | |
|---|---|---|
| • **imperfective** | несовершенный | *ni-sa-vir-shéh-nyj* |
| • **perfective** | совершенный | *sa-vir-shéh-nyj* |
| **clause** | предложение | *prid-la-zhéh-ni-ye* |
| • **main** | главное | *gláhv-na-ye* |
| • **relative** | относительное | *at-na-sí-til'-na-ye* |
| • **subordinate** | подчинённое | *pat-chi-nýo-na-ye* |
| **comparison** | сравнение | *srav-nyé-ni-ye* |
| **conjunction** | союз | *sa-yús* |
| **discourse** | обороты речи | *a-ba-ró-ty ryé-chi* |
| • **direct** | прямая речь *(f)* | *pri-máh-ya ryech* |
| • **indirect** | косвенная речь *(f)* | *kós-vi-na-ya ryech* |
| **gender** | род | *rot* |
| • **feminine** | женский | *zhéhn-skij* |
| • **masculine** | мужской | *mush-skój* |
| • **neuter** | средний | *sryéd-nij* |
| **grammar** | грамматика | *gra-máh-ti-ka* |
| **idiomatic expression** | идиоматическое выражение/ поговорка | *i-di-a-ma-tí-chis-ka-ye vy-ra-zhéh-ni-ye/ pa-ga-vór-ka* |
| **interrogative** | вопросительный | *vap-ra-sí-til'-nyj* |
| **intonation** | интонация | *in-ta-náh-tsy-ya* |
| **mood** | наклонение | *nak-la-nyé-ni-ye* |
| • **conditional** | условное | *us-lóv-na-ye* |
| • **imperative** | повелительное | *pa-vi-lí-til'-na-ye* |
| • **indicative** | указательное | *u-ka-záh-til'-na-ye* |
| **noun** | существительное | *su-shchis-tví-til'-na-ye* |
| • **declension** | склонение | *skla-nyé-ni-ye* |
| • **case** | падеж | *pa-dyésh* |
| • **nominative** | именительный | *i-mi-ní-til'-nyj* |
| • **genitive** | родительный | *ra-dí-til'-nyj* |
| • **dative** | дательный | *dáh-til'-nyj* |
| • **accusative** | винительный | *vi-ní-til'-nyj* |
| • **instrumental** | творительный | *tva-rí-til'-nyj* |
| • **prepositional** | предложный | *prid-lózh-nyj* |
| **number** | число | *chis-ló* |
| • **plural** | множественное | *mnó-zhys-tvi-na-ve* |
| • **singular** | единственное | *i-díns-tvi-na-ye* |
| **numeral** | числительное | *chis-lí-til'-na-ye* |
| • **cardinal** | количественное | *ka-lí-chis-tvi-na-ye* |
| • **collective** | собирательное | *sa-bi-ráh-til'-na-ye* |
| • **ordinal** | порядковое | *pa-ryáht-ka-va-ye* |
| **object** | дополнение | *da-pal-nyé-ni-ye* |
| • **direct** | прямое | *pri-mó-ye* |
| • **indirect** | косвенное | *kós-vi-na-ye* |
| **participles** (verbal adjectives) | причастие | *pri-cháhs-ti-ye* |

| | | |
|---|---|---|
| • participial phrase | причастный оборот | *pri-cháhs-nyj a-ba-rót* |
| person | лицо | *li-tsó* |
| • first | первое | *pyér-va-ye* |
| • second | второе | *fta-ró-ye* |
| • third | третье | *tryét'-ye* |
| predicate | сказуемое | *ska-zóo-i-ma-ye* |
| preposition | предлог | *prid-lók* |
| pronoun | местоимение | *mis-ta-i-myé-ni-ye* |
| • demonstrative | указательное | *u-ka-záh-til'-na-ye* |
| • interrogative | вопросительное | *vap-ra-sí-til'-na-ye* |
| • indirect | косвенное | *kós-vi-na-ye* |
| • possessive | притяжательное | *pri-ti-zháh-til'-na-ye* |
| • reflexive | возвратное | *vaz-vráht-na-ye* |
| • relative | относительное | *at-na-sí-til'-na-ye* |
| proverb | пословица | *pas-ló-vi-tsa* |
| sentence | предложение | *prid-la-zhéh-ni-ye* |
| • complex | сложное | *slózh-na-ye* |
| • compound | составное | *sas-tav-nó-ye* |
| • declarative | повествовательное | *pa-vist-va-váh-til'-na-ye* |
| • indefinite | неопределённое | *ni-ap-ri-di-lyó-na-ye* |
| • interrogative | вопросительное | *vap-ra-sí-til'-na-ye* |
| • main | главное | *gláhv-na-ye* |
| • simple | простое | *pras-tó-ye* |
| stress (accent) | ударение | *u-da-ryé-ni-ye* |
| subject | подлежащее | *pad-li-zháh-shchi-ye* |
| syllable | слог | *slok* |
| tense | время | *vryé-mya* |
| • future | будущее | *bóo-du-shchi-ye* |
| • past | прошедшее | *pra-shéht-shy-ye* |
| • present | настоящее | *nas-ta-yáh-shchi-ye* |
| verb | глагол | *gla-gól* |
| • conjugation | спряжение | *spri-zhéh-ni-ye* |
| • first | первое | *pyér-va-ye* |
| • second | второе | *fta-ró-ye* |
| • mixed | смешанное | *smyé-sha-na-ye* |
| • impersonal | безличный | *biz-lích-nyj* |
| • intransitive | непереходный | *ni-pi-ri-khód-nyj* |
| • irregular | неправильный | *ni-práh-vil'-nyj* |
| • reflexive | возвратный | *vaz-vráht-nyj* |
| • regular | правильный | *práh-vil'-nyj* |
| • transitive | переходный | *pi-ri-khód-nyj* |
| verbal adverbs | деепричастие | *di-i-pri-cháhs-ti-ye* |
| voice | залог | *za-lók* |
| • active | действительный | *dist-ví-til'-nyj* |
| • passive | страдательный | *stra-dáh-til'-nyj* |

| **word** | слово | *sló-va* |
|---|---|---|
| • **complex** | сложное | *slózh-na-ye* |
| • **compound** | составное | *sas-tav-nó-ye* |
| • **prefix** | приставка | *pris-táhf-ka* |
| • **root** | корень *(m)* | *kó-rin'* |
| • **simple** | простое | *pras-tó-ye* |
| • **suffix** | суффикс | *soó-fiks* |

## b. DEMONSTRATIVE ADJECTIVES

**this**

| | | |
|---|---|---|
| Nom. | этот *(m)*, это *(n)*, эта *(f)* | *éh-tat, éh-ta, éh-ta* |
| Genitive | этого *(m&n)*, этой *(f)* | *éh-ta-va, éh-taj* |
| Dative | этому *(m&n)*, этой *(f)* | *éh-ta-mu, éh-taj* |
| Acc. | этот/этого *(m)*, это *(n)*, эту *(f)* | *éh-tat/éh-ta-va, éh-ta, éh-tu* |
| Instr. | этим *(m&n)*, этой *(f)* | *éh-tim, éh-taj* |
| Prep. | этом *(m&n)*, этой *(f)* | *éh-tam, éh-taj* |

**that**

| | | |
|---|---|---|
| Nom. | тот *(m)*, то *(n)*, та *(f)* | *tot, to, tah* |
| Genitive | того *(m&n)*, той *(f)* | *ta-vó, toj* |
| Dative | тому *(m&n)*, той *(f)* | *ta-móo, toj* |
| Acc. | тот/того *(m)*, то *(n)*, ту *(f)* | *tot/ta-vó, to, too* |
| Instr. | тем *(m&n)*, той *(f)* | *tyem, toj* |
| Prep. | том *(m&n)*, той *(f)* | *tom, toj* |

**those**

| | | |
|---|---|---|
| Nom. | те *(pl)* | *tye* |
| Genitive | тех | *tyekh* |
| Dative | тем | *tyem* |
| Acc. | те/тех | *tye/tyekh* |
| Instr. | теми | *tyé-mi* |
| Prep. | тех | *tyekh* |

**all, every**

| | | |
|---|---|---|
| Nom. | весь *(m)*, всё *(n)*, вся *(f)* | *vyes', fsyo, fsyah* |
| Genitive | всего *(m&n)*, всей *(f)* | *fsi-vó, fsyej* |
| Dative | всему *(m&n)*, всей *(f)* | *fsi-móo, fsyej* |
| Acc. | весь/всего *(m)*, всё *(n)*, всю *(f)* | *vyes'/fsi-vó, fsyo, fsyu* |
| Instr. | всем *(m&n)*, всей *(f)* | *fsyem, fsyej* |
| Prep. | всём *(m&n)*, всей *(f)* | *fsyom, fsyej* |

## c. PERSONAL AND POSSESSIVE PRONOUNS

**I/we**
| | | |
|---|---|---|
| Nom. | я, мы | *yah, my* |
| Genitive | меня, нас | *mi-nyáh, nahs* |
| Dative | мне, нам | *mnye, nahm* |
| Acc. | меня, нас | *mi-nyáh, nahs* |
| Instr. | мной, нами | *mnoj, náh-mi* |
| Prep. | мне, нас | *mnye, nahs* |

**you** *(fam, pol)*
| | | |
|---|---|---|
| Nom. | ты, вы | *ty, vy* |
| Genitive | тебя, вас | *ti-byáh, vahs* |
| Dative | тебе, вам | *ti-byé, vahm* |
| Acc. | тебя, вас | *ti-byáh, vahs* |
| Instr. | тобой, вами | *ta-bój, váh-mi* |
| Prep. | тебе, вас | *ti-byé, vahs* |

**he, it, she**
| | | |
|---|---|---|
| Nom. | он *(m)*, оно *(n)*, она *(f)* | *on, a-nó, a-náh* |
| Genitive | его *(m&n)*, её *(f)* | *ye-vó, ye-yó* |
| Dative | ему *(m&n)*, ей *(f)* | *i-móo, yej* |
| Acc. | его *(m&n)*, её *(f)* | *ye-vó, ye-yó* |
| Instr. | им *(m&n)*, ей/ею *(f)* | *im, yej/yé-yu* |
| Prep. | нём *(m&n)*, ней *(f)* | *nyom, nej* |

**they**
| | | |
|---|---|---|
| Nom. | они | *a-ní* |
| Genitive | их | *ikh* |
| Dative | им | *im* |
| Acc. | их | *ikh* |
| Instr. | ими | *í-mi* |
| Prep. | них | *nikh* |

**my**
| | | |
|---|---|---|
| Nom. | мой *(m)*, моё *(n)*, моя *(f)*, мои *(pl)* | *moj, ma-yó, ma-yáh, ma-í* |
| Genitive | моего *(m&n)*, моей *(f)* моих | *ma-i-vó, ma-yéj, ma-íkh* |
| Dative | моему *(m&n)*, моей *(f)*, моим | *ma-i-móo, ma-yéj, ma-ím* |
| Acc. | мой/моего *(m)*, моё *(n)*, мою *(f)*, мои/моих | *moj/ma-i-vó, ma-yó, ma-yú, ma-í/ma-íkh* |
| Instr. | моим *(m&n)*, моей *(f)*, моими | *ma-ím, ma-yéj, ma-í-mi* |
| Prep. | моём *(m&n)*, моей *(f)*, моих | *ma-yóm, ma-yéj, ma-íkh* |

**your** *(fam)*

| | | |
|---|---|---|
| Nom. | твой *(m)*, твоё *(n)*, твоя *(f)*, твои *(pl)* | tvoj, tva-yó, tva-yáh, tva-í |
| Genitive | твоего *(m&n)*, твоей *(f)*, твоих | tva-i-vó, tva-yéj, tva-íkh |
| Dative | твоему *(m&n)*, твоей *(f)*, твоим | tva-i-móo, tva-yéj, tva-ím |
| Acc. | твой/твоего *(m)*, твоё *(n)*, твою *(f)*, твои/твоих *(pl)* | tvoj/tva-i-vó, tva-yó, tva-yú, tva-í/tva-íkh |
| Instr. | твоим *(m&n)*, твоей *(f)*, твоими | tva-ím, tva-yéj, tva-í-mi |
| Prep. | твоём *(m&n)*, твоей *(f)*, твоих | tva-yóm, tva-yéj, tva-íkh |

**your** *(pl/pol)*

| | | |
|---|---|---|
| Nom. | ваш *(m)*, ваше *(n)*, ваша *(f)*, ваши *(pl)* | vahsh, váh-shy, ván-sha, váh-shy |
| Genitive | вашего *(m&n)*, вашей *(f)*, ваших *(pl)* | váh-shy-va, váh-shyj, váh-shykh |
| Dative | вашему *(m&n)*, вашей *(f)*, вашим *(pl)* | váh-shy-moo, váh-shyj, váh-shym |
| Acc. | ваш/вашего *(m)*, ваше *(n)*, вашу *(f)*, ваши/ваших *(pl)* | vahsh/váh-shy-va, váh-shy, váh-shu, váh-shy/váh-shykh |
| Instr. | вашим *(m&n)*, вашей *(f)*, вашими *(pl)* | váh-shym, váh-shyj, váh-shy-mi |
| Prep. | вашем *(m&n)*, вашей *(f)*, ваших *(pl)* | váh-shym, váh-shyj, váh-shykh |

**our**

| | | |
|---|---|---|
| Nom. | наш *(m)*, наше *(n)*, наша *(f)*, наши *(pl)* | nahsh, náh-shy, náh-sha, náh-shy |
| Genitive | нашего *(m&n)*, нашей *(f)*, наших *(pl)* | náh-shy-va, náh-shyj, náh-shykh |
| Dative | нашему *(m&n)*, нашей *(f)*, нашим *(pl)* | náh-shy-moo, náh-shyj, náh-shym |
| Acc. | наш/нашего *(m)*, наше *(n)*, нашу *(f)*, наши/наших *(pl)* | nahsh/náh-shy-va, náh-shy, náh-shu, náh-shy/náh-shykh |
| Instr. | нашим *(m&n)*, нашей *(f)*, нашими *(pl)* | náh-shym, náh-shyj, náh-shy-mi |

| Prep. | нашем *(m&n)*, нашей | *náh-shym, náh-shyj,* |
|-------|----------------------|------------------------|
|       | *(f)*, наших *(pl)*  | *náh-shykh*            |
| **their** | их *(for all cases)* | *ikh* |

## d. PREPOSITIONS

| | | |
|-----------------------|--------------------|-------------------------|
| **about**             | о, около           | *o, ó-ka-la*            |
| **above, over**       | над                | *naht*                  |
| **along**             | по                 | *pa*                    |
| **at**                | на, в              | *nah, v*                |
| **before, in front**  | перед              | *pyé-rid*               |
| **behind**            | за                 | *za*                    |
| **between, among**    | между              | *myézh-du*              |
| **during**            | в, во, в течение   | *v, va, f ti-chyé-ni-ye* |
| **for**               | для                | *dlyah*                 |
| **from**              | из, от             | *is, ot*                |
| **in**                | в, внутри          | *v, vnut-rí*            |
| **near**              | при, около         | *pri, ó-ka-la*          |
| **of**                | genitive case      |                         |
| **on**                | на                 | *nah*                   |
| **out**               | из                 | *is*                    |
| **through**           | через              | *chyé-ris*              |
| **to**                | к                  | *k*                     |
| **under**             | под                | *pat*                   |
| **with**              | с, со              | *s, so*                 |

## e. REFLEXIVE PRONOUNS

| | | |
|----------------------------------|----------|----------------|
| **myself**                       | себе/-я  | *si-byé/-yáh*  |
| **yourself** *(fam and pol)*     | себе/-я  | *si-byé/-yáh*  |
| **himself/ herself/ itself**     | себе/-я  | *si-byé/-yáh*  |
| **ourselves**                    | себе/-я  | *si-byé/-yáh*  |
| **yourselves**                   | себе/-я  | *si-byé/-yáh*  |
| **(fam and pol)**                |          |                |
| **themselves**                   | себе/-я  | *si-byé/-yáh*  |

## f. RELATIVE PRONOUNS

| | | |
|---------------------------|----------|----------------|
| **that, which**           | что      | *shto*         |
| **who**                   | кто      | *kto*          |
| **whose, of which**       | чей *(m)* | *chyej*       |
|                           | чья *(f)* | *ch'yah*      |
|                           | чьё *(n)* | *ch'yo*       |
| **to whom, to which**     | которому | *ka-tó-ra-mu*  |

## g. INTERROGATIVE PRONOUNS

| who | кто | *kto* |
|---|---|---|
| what | что | *shto* |
| • for what | зачем | *za-chyém* |
| whom | кого | *ka-vó* |
| • to whom | кому | *ka-móo* |
| whose | чей | *chyej* |
| when | когда | *kag-dáh* |
| where | где | *gdye* |
| which | который | *ka-tó-ryj* |
| why | почему | *pa-chi-móo* |

## h. CONJUNCTIONS

| although | хотя | *kha-tyáh* |
|---|---|---|
| and | и | |
| as if | как будто | *kahk bóo-ta* |
| as soon as | как только | *kahk tól'-ka* |
| because | потому что | *pa-ta-móo shta* |
| but | но, а | *no, ah* |
| due to (thanks to) | благодаря (тому) | *bla-ga-da-ryáh (ta-móo)* |
| if | если | *yés-li* |
| or | или | *í-li* |
| provided that | при условии, что | *pri us-ló-vi-i shto* |
| since (causal) | поскольку | *pas-kól'-ku* |
| so, therefore | так что | *tahk shto* |
| until, till | до, пока | *do, pa-káh* |
| when, as | когда | *kag-dáh* |
| whether | ли | *li* |
| while | пока | *pa-káh* |

## 9. REQUESTING INFORMATION

| answer | ответить *(p)* | *at-vyé-tit'* |
|---|---|---|
| | отвечать *(i)* | *at-vi-cháht'* |
| | ответ | *at-vyét* |
| ask someone | спросить (у) кого-нибудь | *spra-sít' ka-vó-ni-but'* |
| • ask for something | попросить что-нибудь (что-то) | *pap-ra-sít' shtó-ni-but'(shtó-ta)* |

| | | |
|---|---|---|
| **Can you tell me...?** | Скажите, пожалуйста... ? *(pol)* | *ska-zhý-ti pa-zháh-lus-ta* |
| | Скажи, пожалуйста... ? *(fam)* | *ska-zhý pa-zháh-lus-ta* |
| | Не могли бы вы мне сказать... ? *(pol)* | *ni mag-lí by vy mnye ska-záht'* |
| | Не можешь ли ты мне сказать... ? *(fam)* | *ni mó-zhysh li ty mnye ska-záht'* |
| **how** | как | *kahk* |
| **How come?** | Как это получается? | *kahk éh-ta pa-lu-cháh-i-tsa* |
| **How do you say that in Russian?** | Как это по-русски сказать? | *kahk éh-ta pa-róo-ski ska-záht'* |
| **How much?** | Сколько? | *skól'-ka* |
| **I don't understand** | Я не понимаю | *yah ni pa-ni-máh-yu* |
| | Я понять не могу | *yah pa-nyáht' ni ma-góo* |
| **So?** | Ну и что? | *nu i shto* |
| | Ну и что из этого? | *nu i shto iz éh-ta-va* |
| **What?** | Что? | *shto* |
| **What does it mean?** | Что это значит (обозначает)? | *shto éh-ta znáh-chit (a-baz-na-cháh-it)* |
| **What is it for?** | Для чего это? | *dlya chi-vó éh-ta* |
| • **What is its purpose?** | Зачем это? | *za-chyém éh-ta* |
| **When?** | Когда? | *kag-dáh* |
| **Where?** | Где? | *gdye* |
| **Where to?** | Куда? | *ku-dáh* |
| **Which (one)?** | Который (из них)? | *ka-tó-ryj iz nikh* |
| **Who?** | Кто? | *kto* |
| **Why?** | Почему? | *pa-chi-móo* |

# PEOPLE

## 10. FAMILY AND FRIENDS

### a. FAMILY MEMBERS

| | | |
|---|---|---|
| **aunt** | тётя | *tyó-tya* |
| **brother** | брат | *braht* |
| • **brother-in-law** | зять *(m)* | *zyaht'* |
| **cousin** | двоюродный брат *(m)* | *dva-yú-rad-nyj braht* |
| | двоюродная сестра *(f)* | *dva-yú-rad-na-ya sist-ráh* |
| **dad** | папа *(m)* | *páh-pa* |
| **daughter** | дочь *(f)*/дочка | *doch/dóch-ka* |
| • **daughter-in-law** | невестка | *ni-vyést-ka* |
| **family** | семья | *si-m'yáh* |
| **father** | отец | *a-tyéts* |
| • **father-in-law** | свёкор | *svyó-kar* |
| **granddaughter** | внучка | *vnóoch-ka* |
| **grandfather** | дед/дедушка *(m)* | *dyet/dyé-dush-ka* |
| **grandmother** | бабка/бабушка | *báhp-ka/báh-bush-ka* |
| **grandson** | внук | *vnook* |
| **husband** | муж | *moosh* |
| **mom** | мама | *máh-ma* |
| **mother** | мать *(f)* | *maht'* |
| • **mother-in-law** | свекровь *(f)* | *svi-króf'* |
| **nephew** | племянник | *pli-myáh-nik* |
| **niece** | племянница | *pli-myáh-ni-tsa* |
| **relative** | родственник | *rót-stvin-ik* |
| **sister** | сестра | *sist-ráh* |
| • **sister-in-law** | невестка | *ni-vyést-ka* |
| **stepbrother** | сводный брат | *svód-nyi braht* |
| **stepfather** | отчим | *ót-chim* |
| **stepmother** | мачеха | *máh-chi-kha* |
| **stepsister** | сводная сестра | *svód-na-ya sist-ráh* |
| **son** | сын | *syn* |
| • **son-in-law** | зять *(m)* | *zyaht'* |
| **twin** | близнец | *bliz-nyéts* |
| **uncle** | дядя/дядька *(m)* | *dyáh-dya/dyáht'-ka* |
| **wife** | жена | *zhy-náh* |

## b. FRIENDS

| | | |
|---|---|---|
| acquaintance | знакомый | *zna-kó-myj* |
| • be acquainted | быть знакомым *(i)* | *byt' zna-kó-mym* |
| • become acquainted | познакомиться *(p)* | *pa-zna-kó-mi-tsa* |
| | знакомиться *(i)* | *zna-kó-mi-tsa* |
| chum | приятель *(m)* | *pri-yáh-til'* |
| | приятельница *(f)* | *pri-yáh-til'-ni-tsa* |
| colleague | коллега *(m&f)* | *ka-lyé-ga* |
| enemy | враг | *vrahk* |
| • be enemies | враждовать *(i)* | *vrazh-da-váht'* |
| fiancé, groom | жених | *zhy-níkh* |
| fiancée, bride | невеста | *ni-vyés-ta* |
| friend | друг/товарищ *(m&f)* | *drook/ta-váh-rishch* |
| • (boy)friend | друг/дружок | *drook/dru-zhók* |
| • (girl)friend | подруга | *pa-dróo-ga* |
| • in a friendly way | по-дружески | *pa-dróo-zhy-ski* |
| • make friends | подружиться *(p)* | *pa-dru-zhý-tsa* |
| • best friend | лучший друг | *lóot-shyj drook* |
| • break off friendship | раздружиться *(p)* | *raz-dru-zhý-tsa* |
| • close friend | близкий друг | *blís-kij drook* |
| • family friend | семейный друг | *si-myéj-nyj drook* |
| | друг семьи | *drook si-m'í* |

*Expressions*

> A friend in need is a friend indeed = Друзья в нужде познаются
>   (In need are friends known)
>
> Love/friendship to the death = До гробовой доски
>   (Till the coffin's plank)
>
> They are such close friends that = Они такие друзья,
> nothing can come between them   их водой не разольёшь
>   (Such friends that water will
>   not unbind them)

| | | |
|---|---|---|
| • friendship | дружба | *dróozh-ba* |
| lover | любовник *(m)* | *lyu-bóv-nik* |
| | любовница *(f)* | *lyu-bóv-ni-tsa* |
| • date | свидание | *svi-dáh-ni-ye* |
| • to date | встречаться *(i)* | *fstri-cháh-tsa* |
| • fall in love | влюбиться *(p)* | *vlyu-bí-tsa* |
| • in love | влюблённый | *vlyub-lyó-nyj* |

## 11. DESCRIBING PEOPLE

### a. GENDER AND APPEARANCE

| | | |
|---|---|---|
| **attractive** | привлекательный | *pri-vli-káh-til'-nyj* |
| **beautiful** | красивый *(adj)* | *kra-sí-vyj* |
| • **beautifully** | красиво *(adv)* | *kra-sí-va* |
| • **good-looking** | интересный | *in-ti-ryés-nyj* |
| • **nice (person)** | симпатичный | *sim-pa-tích-nyj* |
| **beauty** | красота | *kra-sa-táh* |
| **blond** | блондин *(m)* | *blan-dín* |
| | блондинка *(f)* | *blan-dín-ka* |
| **body** | тело | *tyé-la* |
| • **physique** | конституция | *kan-sti-tóo-tsy-ya* |
| • **torso** | туловище | *tóo-la-vi-shche* |
| **boy** | мальчик | *máhl'-chik* |
| **brunet** | брюнет *(m)* | *bryu-nyét* |
| | брюнетка *(f)* | *bryu-nyét-ka* |
| **clean** | чистый *(adj)* | *chís-tyj* |
| | чисто *(adv)* | *chís-ta* |
| **coarse (person)** | грубый *(adj)* | *gróo-byj* |
| • **coarsely** | грубо *(adv)* | *gróo-ba* |
| **curly-haired** | кудрявый | *kud-ryáh-vyj* |
| **dark-haired** | темноволосый | *tim-na-va-ló-syj* |
| **dirty** | грязный *(adj)* | *gryáz-nyj* |
| | грязно *(adv)* | *gryáz-na* |
| **elegance** | элегантность *(f)* | *y-li-gáhnt-nast'* |
| • **elegant** | элегантный *(adj)* | *y-li-gáhnt-nyj* |
| | элегантно *(adv)* | *y-li-gáhnt-na* |
| • **inelegant** | неэлегантный | *ni-y-li-gáhnt-nyj* |
| **facial features** | черты *(pl)* лица | *chir-tý li-tsáh* |
| **fair-haired** | светловолосый | *svit-la-va-ló-syj* |
| **fat** | жирный | *zhýr-nyj* |
| **female** | женский | *zhéhn-skij* |
| • **lady** | дама | *dáh-ma* |
| **feminine** | женственный | *zhéhn-stvi-nyj* |
| **gender** | пол | *pol* |
| **gentleman** | джентельмен | *dzhyn-til'-myén* |
| **girl** | девочка | *dyé-vach-ka* |
| **health** | здоровье | *zda-róv'-ye* |
| • **healthy** | здоровый | *zda-ró-vyj* |
| **height** | рост | *rost* |
| • **How tall are you?** | Какого вы роста? *(pol)* | *ka-kó-va vy rós-ta* |
| | Какого ты роста? *(fam)* | *ka-kó-va ty rós-ta* |

| | | |
|---|---|---|
| • I am tall | Я высокий *(m)* | *yah vy-só-kij* |
| | Я высокая *(f)* | *yah vy-só-ka-ya* |
| • I am... | Мой рост... | *moj rost* |
| centimeters tall | сантиметров | *san-ti-myét-raf* |
| • medium (average) height | средний рост | *sryéd-nij rost* |
| • short | низкий рост | *nís-kij rost* |
| • tall | высокий | *vy-só-kij* |
| male | мужской | *mush-skój* |
| man | мужчина *(m)* | *muzh-chí-na* |
| • old man | старик | *sta-rík* |
| • young man | молодой человек | *ma-la-dój chi-la-vyék* |
| | юноша | *yú-na-sha* |
| | парень *(m)* | *páh-rin'* |
| masculine | мужественный | *móo-zhyst-vin-yj* |
| physical features | физические черты *(pl)* | *fi-zí-chis-ki-i chir-tý* |
| plain-looking, simple | простой *(adj)* | *pra-stój* |
| • plainly, simply | просто *(adv)* | *prós-ta* |
| • plain face | простое лицо | *pra-stó-ye li-tsó* |
| plump | упитанный | *u-pí-ta-nyj* |
| portly | полный | *pól-nyj* |
| red-haired | рыжий | *rý-zhyj* |
| | рыжеволосый | *ry-zhy-va-ló-syj* |
| round | круглый | *króog-lyj* |
| sick | больной | *bal'-nój* |
| • become sick | заболеть *(p)* | *za-ba-lyét'* |
| • disease | болезнь *(f)* | *ba-lyézn'* |
| • sickly | болезненный | *ba-lyéz-ni-nyj* |
| small, little | маленький | *máh-lin'-kij* |
| • little boy | маленький мальчик | *máh-lin'-kij máhl'-chik* |
| • little girl | маленькая девочка | *máh-lin'-ka-ya dyé-vach-ka* |
| stout, full-figured | толстый | *tól-styj* |
| strength | сила | *sí-la* |
| • strong | сильный *(adj)* | *síl'-nyj* |
| • strongly | сильно *(adv)* | *síl'-na* |
| ugly | уродливый | *u-ród-li-vyj* |
| • ugliness | уродство | *u-rót-stva* |
| weak | слабый *(adj)* | *sláh-byj* |
| • weakly | слабо *(adv)* | *sláh-ba* |
| • become weak | ослабеть *(p)* | *a-sla-byét'* |
| | слабеть *(i)* | *sla-byét'* |
| • weak-looking | слабосильный | *sla-ba-síl'-nyj* |
| weakness | слабость *(f)* | *sláh-bast'* |
| weight | вес | *vyes* |

| | | |
|---|---|---|
| • **heavy** | тяжёлый *(adj)* | *ti-zhó-lyj* |
| • **heavily** | тяжело *(adv)* | *ti-zhy-ló* |
| • **How much do you weigh?** | Сколько вы весите? *(pol)* | *skól'-ka vy vyé-si-tye* |
| | Сколько ты весишь? *(fam)* | *skól'-ka ty vyé-sish* |
| • **I weigh...** | Я вешу... | *yah vyé-shu* |
| • **light** | лёгкий *(adj)* | *lyókh-kij* |
| • **lightly** | легко *(adv)* | *likh-kó* |
| • **lose weight** | похудеть *(p)* | *pa-khu-dyét'* |
| | худеть *(i)* | *khu-dyét'* |
| • **skinny** | худой | *khu-dój* |
| • **thin** | тонкий *(adj)* | *tón-kij* |
| • **thinly** | тонко *(adv)* | *tón-ka* |
| • **slim, slender** | худощавый | *khu-da-shcháh-vyj* |
| • **weigh oneself** | взвеситься *(p)* | *vzvyé-si-tsa* |
| | взвешиваться *(i)* | *vzvyé-shy-va-tsa* |
| **woman** | женщина | *zhéhn-shchi-na* |
| • **young woman** | девушка | *dyé-vush-ka* |
| | молодая женщина | *ma-la-dáh-ya zhéhn-shchi-na* |

## b. CONCEPTS OF AGE

| | | |
|---|---|---|
| **adolescence** | переходный возраст | *pi-ri-khód-nyj vóz-rast* |
| • **of the adolescent age** | переходного возраста | *pi-ri-khód-na-va vóz-ras-ta* |
| **adult** | взрослый | *vzrós-lyj* |
| **age** | возраст | *vóz-rast* |
| **baby** | ребёнок | *ri-byó-nak* |
| | младенец | *mla-dyé-nits* |
| **elderly person** | пожилой человек | *pa-zhy-lój chi-la-vyék* |
| **gray-haired** | седоволосый | *si-da-va-ló-syj* |
| **grow up** | вырасти *(p)* | *vý-ras-ti* |
| | расти *(i)* | *ras-tí* |
| **middle-aged** | средних лет | *sryéd-nikh lyet* |
| **old** | старый | *sláh-ryj* |
| • **become old** | постареть *(p)* | *pa-sta-ryét'* |
| | стареть *(i)* | *sta-ryét'* |
| • **become older** | становиться *(i)* старше | *sta-na-ví-tsa stáhr-she* |
| • **How old are you?** | Сколько вам лет? *(pol)* | *skól'-ka vahm lyet* |
| | Сколько тебе лет? *(fam)* | *skól'-ka ti-byé lyet* |

| | | |
|---|---|---|
| • I am ... years old | Мне ... лет | *mnye lyet* |
| • old age | пожилой возраст | *pa-zhy-lój vóz-rast* |
| • older | старше | *stáhr-she* |
| • older brother | старший брат | *stáhr-shyj braht* |
| • older sister | старшая сестра | *stáhr-sha-ya sist-ráh* |
| white-haired | беловолосый | *bí-la-va-ló-syj* |
| young | молодой *(adj)* | *ma-la-dój* |
| • look young | выглядеть *(i)* молодо | *vý-glya-dyet' mó-la-da* |
| • younger | моложе | *ma-ló-zhe* |
| | младше | *mláht-she* |
| • youngest | самый молодой | *sáh-myj ma-la-dój* |
| | самый младший | *sáh-myj mláht-shyj* |
| • younger brother | младший брат | *mláht-shyj braht* |
| • younger sister | младшая сестра | *mláht-sha-ya sist-ráh* |
| youth | юность *(f)* | *yú-nast'* |
| | молодость *(f)* | *mó-la-dast'* |
| • youthful | моложавый | *ma-la-zháh-vyj* |
| • youthfully | молодо *(adv)* | *mó-la-da* |

## c. MARRIAGE AND THE HUMAN LIFE CYCLE

| | | |
|---|---|---|
| anniversary | годовщина | *ga-dav-shchí-na* |
| • golden wedding anniversary | золотая свадьба | *za-la-táh-ya sváhd'-ba* |
| • silver wedding anniversary | серебряная свадьба | *si-ryéb-ti-na-ya sváhd'-ba* |
| bachelor | холостяк | *kha-la-styáhk* |
| birth | рождение | *razh-dyé-ni-ye* |
| • be born | родиться *(p)* | *ra-dí-tsa* |
| | рождаться *(i)* | *razh-dáh-tsa* |
| birthday | день рождения *(m)* | *dyen' razh-dyé-ni-ya* |
| • celebrate one's birthday | праздновать *(i)* день рождения | *práhz-na-vat' dyen' razh-dyé-ni-ya* |
| • Happy birthday! | С днём рождения! | *s dnyom razh-dyé-ni-ya* |
| death | смерть *(f)* | *smyert'* |
| • die | умереть *(p)* | *u-mi-ryét'* |
| | умирать *(i)* | *u-mi-ráht'* |
| divorce | развод | *raz-vód* |
| • divorce | развестись *(p)* | *raz-vis-tís'* |
| | разводиться *(i)* | *raz-va-dí-tsa* |
| • divorced | разведённый | *raz-vi-dyón-yj* |
| engagement | обручение | *a-bru-chyé-ni-ye* |

| | | |
|---|---|---|
| • **become engaged** | обручиться *(p)* | *a-bru-chí-tsa* |
| | обручаться *(i)* | *a-bru-cháh-tsa* |
| • **engaged** | обручённый | *a-bru-chyó-nyj* |
| **fiancé, groom** | жених | *zhy-níkh* |
| **fiancée, bride** | невеста | *ni-vyés-ta* |
| **gift** | подарок | *pa-dáh-rak* |
| • **give (a gift)** | подарить *(p)* | *pa-da-rít'* |
| | дарить *(i)* | *da-rít'* |
| • **give ... as a gift** | подарить... | *pa-da-rít'* |
| | в подарок | *v pa-dáh-rak* |
| **honeymoon** | медовый месяц | *mi-dó-vyj myé-sits* |
| **husband** | муж | *moozh* |
| **kiss** | поцелуй *(m)* | *pa-tsy-lóoj* |
| • **kiss** | поцеловать *(p)* | *pa-tsy-la-váht'* |
| | целовать *(i)* | *tsy-la-váht'* |
| | целоваться *(i)* | *tsy-la-váh-tsa* |
| **life** | жизнь *(f)* | *zhyzn'* |
| • **live** | жить *(i)* | *zhyt'* |
| **love** | любовь *(f)* | *lyu-bóf'* |
| • **love** | любить *(i)* | *lyu-bít'* |
| • **fall in love** | влюбиться *(p)* | *vlyu-bí-tsa* |
| • **in love** | влюблённый | *vlyub-lyó-nyj* |
| **marriage, matrimony** | женитьба | *zhy-nít'-ba* |
| • **get married** (for men) | пожениться *(p)* | *pa-zhy-ní-tsa* |
| | жениться *(i)* | *zhy-ní-tsa* |
| • **get married** (for women) | выйти замуж *(p)* | *výj-ti záh-muzh* |
| | выходить замуж *(i)* | *vy-kha-dít' záh-muzh* |
| • **married** | женатый *(m)* | *zhy-náh-tyj* |
| | замужняя *(f)* | *za-móozh-nya-ya* |
| • **marry (someone)** | жениться *(i)* на *(m)* | *zhy-ní-tsa nah* |
| | выходить *(i)* замуж за *(f)* | *vy-kha-dít' záh-muzh zah* |
| • **unmarried** | неженатый *(m)* | *ni-zhy-náh-tyj* |
| | незамужняя *(f)* | *ni-za-móozh-nya-ya* |
| **newlyweds** | молодожёны *(pl)* | *ma-la-da-zhó-ny* |
| **pregnancy** | беременность *(f)* | *bi-ryé-mi-nast'* |
| • **be pregnant** | беременная | *bi-ryé-mi-na-ya* |
| • **give birth** | родить *(p)* | *ra-dít'* |
| • **have a baby** | иметь *(i)* ребёнка | *i-myét' ri-byón-ka* |
| • **They have a baby** | У них есть ребёнок | *u nikh yest' ri-byó-nak* |
| **separation** | расход | *ras-khód* |
| • **move out** | уйти из дома *(p)* | *uj-tí iz dó-ma* |
| | уходить *(i)* | *u-kha-dít'* |

| | | |
|---|---|---|
| • separate | разойтись *(p)* | *ra-zaj-tís'* |
| | расходиться *(i)* | *ras-kha-dít-tsa* |
| spouse | супруг *(m)* | *sup-róog* |
| | супруга *(f)* | *sup-róo-ga* |
| wedding | свадьба | *sváhd'-ba* |
| • wedding invitation | приглашение на свадьбу | *pri-gla-shéh-ni-ye na sváhd'-bu* |
| • wedding ring | обручальное кольцо | *ab-ru-chyáhl'-na-ye kal'-tsó* |
| widow | вдова *(f)* | *vda-váh* |
| widower | вдовец *(m)* | *vda-vyéts* |
| wife | жена | *zhy-náh* |

## d. RELIGION

| | | |
|---|---|---|
| agnostic | агностик | *ag-nós-tik* |
| atheism | атеизм | *a-ty-ízm* |
| • atheist | атеист | *a-ty-íst* |
| baptism | крестины *(pl)* | *kris-tí-ny* |
| belief | вера | *vyé-ra* |
| • believe | веровать *(i)* | *vyé-ra-vat'* |
| | верить *(i)* | *vyé-rit'* |
| • believer | верующий | *vyé-ru-yu-shchij* |
| Buddhism | буддизм | *bud-ízm* |
| • Buddhist | буддист | *bud-íst* |
| candle | свеча | *svi-cháh* |
| • light a candle | зажечь свечу *(p)* | *za-zhéhch svi-chóo* |
| | зажигать *(i)* | *za-zhy-gáht'* |
| cathedral | собор | *sa-bór* |
| Catholicism | католичество | *ka-ta-lí-chist-vo* |
| • Catholic | католик | *ka-tó-lik* |
| Christian | христианин | *khris-ti-áh-nin* |
| Christianity | христианство | *khris-ti-áhn-stvo* |
| church | церковь *(f)* | *tséhr-kaf'* |
| • church bell | церковный колокол | *tsyr-kóv-nyj kó-la-kal* |
| • church dome | церковный купол | *tsyr-kóv-nyj kóo-pal* |
| deacon | дьякон | *d'yáh-kan* |
| Easter | Пасха | *páhs-kha* |
| Eastern Orthodox | православный | *pra-va-sláhv-nyj* |
| faith | вера | *vyé-ra* |
| God | Бог | *bok (or bokh)* |
| Hindu | индус | *in-dóos* |
| human | человек | *chi-la-vyék* |
| • human being | человеческое существо | *chi-la-vyé-chis-ko-ye su-shchi-stvó* |
| imam | имам | *i-máhm* |

| | | |
|---|---|---|
| • **humanity** | человечество | *chi-la-vyé-chi-stva* |
| **icon** | икона | *i-kó-na* |
| **Islam** | ислам | *is-láhm* |
| • **Islamic** | исламский | *is-láhm-skij* |
| • **Muslim** | мусульманский | *mu-sul'-máhn-skij* |
| **Judaism** | иудейская религия | *iu-dyéj-ska-ya ri-lí-gi-ya* |
| • **Jew** | еврей *(m)* | *yev-ryéj* |
| • **Jewish** | еврейский | *yev-ryéj-skij* |
| **monastery** | монастырь *(m)* | *ma-nas-týr'* |
| **monk** | монах *(m)* | *ma-náhkh* |
| **nun** | монахиня *(f)* | *ma-náh-khi-nya* |
| **pagan** | язычник | *i-zých-nik* |
| **pray** | молиться *(i)* | *ma-lít-tsa* |
| • **prayer** | молитва | *ma-lít-va* |
| **priest** | священник | *svi-shchyé-nik* |
| **rabbi** | раввин | *ra-vín* |
| **religion** | религия | *ri-lí-gi-ya* |
| • **religious** | религиозный | *ri-li-gi-óz-nyj* |
| **ritual** | ритуал | *ri-tu-áhl* |
| **saint** | святой | *svi-tój* |
| **service (prayer)** | служба | *slóozh-ba* |
| **soul** | душа | *du-sháh* |
| **spirit** | дух | *dookh* |
| • **spiritual** | духовный | *du-khóv-nyj* |
| • **spiritually** | духовно | *du-khóv-na* |
| **synagogue** | синагога | *si-na-gó-ga* |
| **temple** | храм | *khrahm* |

## e. CHARACTERISTICS AND SOCIAL TRAITS

| | | |
|---|---|---|
| **activity** | активность *(f)* | *ak-tív-nast'* |
| • **active** | активный *(adj)* | *ak-tív-nyj* |
| • **actively** | активно *(adv)* | *ak-tív-na* |
| **adaptable** | гибкий | *gíp-kij* |
| **aggressiveness** | агрессивность *(f)* | *ag-ri-sív-nast'* |
| • **aggressive** | агрессивный *(adj)* | *ag-ri-sív-nyj* |
| • **aggressively** | агрессивно *(adv)* | *ag-ri-sív-na* |
| **altruism** | альтруизм | *al'-tru-ízm* |
| • **altruist** | альтруист | *al'-tru-íst* |
| • **altruistic** | альтруистичный | *al'-tru-is-tích-nyj* |
| **anger** | гнев | *gnyef* |
| • **angry** | сердитый *(adj)* | *sir-dí-tyj* |
| | гневный *(adj)* | *gnyév-nyj* |
| • **angrily** | сердито *(adv)* | *sir-dí-ta* |
| | гневно *(adv)* | *gnyév-na* |

| | | |
|---|---|---|
| arrogance | нахальство | *na-kháhl'-stva* |
| • arrogant | нахальный *(adj)* | *na-kháhl'-nyj* |
| • arrogantly | нахально *(adv)* | *na-kháhl'-na* |
| avarice, greed | жадность | *zháhd-nast'* |
| • avaricious | жадный | *zháhd-nyj* |
| benevolent | доброжелательный | *da-bra-zhe-láh-til'-nyj* |
| brash | резкий | *ryéz-kij* |
| calmness | покой *(m)* | *pa-kój* |
| • calm | спокойный *(adj)* | *spa-kój-nyj* |
| • calmly | спокойно *(adv)* | *spa-kój-na* |
| character | характер | *kha-ráhk-tir* |
| • characteristic | характеристика | *kha-rak-ti-rís-ti-ka* |
| • characterize | охарактеризовать *(p)* | *a-kha-rak-ti-ri-za-váht'* |
| | характеризовать *(i)* | *kha-rak-ti-ri-za-váht'* |
| conservative | консервативный | *kan-sir-va-tív-nyj* |
| contrary | противоречивый | *pra-ti-va-ri-chí-vyj* |
| courage | отвага | *at-váh-ga* |
| • courageous | отважный *(adj)* | *at-váhzh-nyj* |
| | смелый *(adj)* | *smyé-lyj* |
| • courageously | отважно *(adv)* | *at-váhzh-na* |
| | смело *(adv)* | *smyé-la* |
| courtesy | вежливость *(f)* | *vyézh-li-vast'* |
| • courteous | вежливый | *vyézh-li-vyj* |
| • discourteous | грубый | *gróo-byj* |
| critical | критический | *kri-tí-chis-kij* |
| cry | плакать *(i)* | *pláh-kat'* |
| cultured | культурный | *kul'-tóor-nyj* |
| cunning, crafty | хитрый *(adj)* | *khít-ryj* |
| • cunningly | хитро *(adv)* | *khít-ra* |
| curiosity | любопытство | *lyu-ba-pýt-stva* |
| • curious | любопытный *(adj)* | *lyu-ba-pýt-nyj* |
| • curiously | любопытно *(adv)* | *lyu-ba-pýt-na* |
| delicate | деликатный *(adj)* | *di-li-káht-nyj* |
| • delicately | деликатно *(adv)* | *di-li-káht-na* |
| difficult | тяжёлый *(adj)* | *ti-zhó-lyj* |
| | трудный *(adj)* | *tróod-nyj* |
| diligence | трудолюбие | *tru-da-lyú-bi-ye* |
| • diligent | трудолюбивый | *tru-da-lyú-bi-vyj* |
| • hard-working | работящий | *ra-ba-tyáh-shchij* |
| diplomatic | дипломатичный | *dip-la-ma-tích-nyj* |
| discontent | недовольный | *ni-da-vól'-nyj* |
| disorganized | неорганизованный | *ni-ar-ga-ni-zó-va-nyj* |
| eccentric | эксцентричный | *yk-tsyn-trích-nyj* |
| education | образование | *ab-ra-za-váh-ni-ye* |
| • educated | образованный *(m)* | *ab-ra-zó-va-nyj* |

| | | |
|---|---|---|
| • **uneducated** | необразованный | *ni-ab-ra-zó-van-yj* |
| **egoism** | эгоизм | *y-ga-ízm* |
| • **egotist** | эгоист | *y-ga-íst* |
| • **egotistic** | эгоистичный | *y-ga-is-tích-nyj* |
| **eloquence** | образная речь *(f)* | *ób-raz-na-ya ryech* |
| • **eloquent** | образный *(adj)* | *ób-raz-nyj* |
| • **eloquently** | образно *(adv)* | *ób-raz-na* |
| **energy** | энергия | *y-néhr-gi-ya* |
| • **energetic** | энергичный | *y-nyr-gích-nyj* |
| **envy** | зависть *(f)* | *záh-vist'* |
| • **envious** | завистливый | *za-vís-li-vyj* |
| **erudite** | эрудированный | *y-ru-dí-ra-va-nyj* |
| **faithful** | верный | *vyér-nyj* |
| | преданный | *pryé-da-nyj* |
| **fascination** | интерес | *in-ti-ryés* |
| • **fascinate** | интересовать *(i)* | *in-ti-ri-sa-váht'* |
| • **fascinating** | интересный | *in-ti-ryés-nyj* |
| **fool** | дурак | *du-ráhk* |
| • **foolish** | дурацкий | *du-ráhts-kij* |
| • **silly** | дурашливый | *du-ráhsh-li-vyj* |
| **fretful** | беспокойный *(adj)* | *bis-pa-kój-nyj* |
| • **fretfully** | беспокойно *(adv)* | *bis-pa-kój-na* |
| **friendly** | дружелюбный | *dru-zhy-lyúb-nyj* |
| | приветливый | *pri-vyét-li-vyj* |
| **funny** | смешной | *smish-nój* |
| **fussy** | суетливый | *su-it-lí-vyj* |
| **generosity** | щедрость | *shchyéd-rast'* |
| • **generous** | щедрый *(adj)* | *shchyéd-ryj* |
| • **generously** | щедро *(adv)* | *shchyéd-ra* |
| **gentle** | мягкий *(adj)* | *myáhkh-kij* |
| • **gently** | мягко *(adv)* | *myáhkh-ka* |
| **good** | хороший *(adj)* | *kha-ró-shij* |
| • **well** | хорошо *(adv)* | *kha-ra-shó* |
| **graceful** | грациозный | *gra-tsy-óz-nyj* |
| **grumpy, grumbling** | ворчливый | *varch-lí-vyj* |
| **habit** | привычка | *pri-vých-ka* |
| • **(a person) of habit** | (он) с привычками | *(on) s pri-vých-ka-mi* |
| **happiness** | счастье | *shcháhs-ti-ye* |
| • **happy** | счастливый *(adj)* | *shchis-lí-vyj* |
| • **happily** | счастливо *(adv)* | *shchis-lí-va* |
| • **unhappy** | несчастливый | *ni-shchis-lí-vyj* |
| **hate** | ненависть *(f)* | *nyé-na-vist'* |
| • **hate** | ненавидеть *(i)* | *ni-na-ví-dit'* |
| • **hateful** | ненавистный | *ni-na-vís-nyj* |
| **honesty** | честность *(f)* | *chyés-nast'* |

| | | |
|---|---|---|
| • **honest** | честный *(adj)* | *chyés-nyj* |
| | порядочный *(adj)* | *pa-ryáh-dach-nyj* |
| • **honestly** | честно *(adv)* | *chyés-na* |
| | порядочно *(adv)* | *pa-ryáh-dach-na* |
| • **dishonest** | нечестный | *ni-chyés-nyj* |
| | непорядочный | *ni-pa-ryáh-dach-nyj* |
| **humor** | юмор | *yú-mar* |
| • **(with) a sense of humor** | с чувством юмора | *s chóost-vam yú-ma-ra* |
| **idealism** | идеализм | *i-di-a-lízm* |
| • **idealist** | идеалист | *i-di-a-líst* |
| • **idealistic** | идеалистичный | *i-di-a-lis-tích-nyj* |
| **idiot** | идиот | *i-di-ót* |
| **imagination** | воображение | *va-ab-ra-zhéh-ni-ye* |
| • **imaginative** | с воображением | *s va-ab-ra-zhéh-ni-yem* |
| **impudence** | наглость *(f)* | *náhg-last'* |
| • **impudent** | наглый *(adj)* | *náhg-lyj* |
| • **impudently** | нагло *(adv)* | *náhg-la* |
| **impulse** | импульс | *ím-pul's* |
| • **impulsive** | импульсивный | *im-pul'-sív-nyj* |
| **indecisive** | нерешительный *(adj)* | *ni-ri-shý-til'-nyj* |
| • **indecisively** | нерешительно *(adv)* | *ni-ri-shý-til'-na* |
| **independent** | независимый *(adj)* | *ni-za-ví-si-myj* |
| • **independently** | независимо *(adv)* | *ni-za-ví-si-ma* |
| **indifferent** | безразличный *(adj)* | *biz-raz-lích-nyj* |
| • **indifferently** | безразлично *(adv)* | *biz-raz-lích-na* |
| **individualist** | индивидуалист | *in-di-vi-du-a-líst* |
| **innocence** | невинность *(f)* | *ni-ví-nast'* |
| • **innocent** | невинный *(adj)* | *ni-ví-nyj* |
| • **innocently** | невинно *(adv)* | *ni-ví-na* |
| **intelligent** | умный *(adj)* | *óom-nyj* |
| **intelligentsia** | интеллигенция | *in-ti-li-gyén-tsy-ya* |
| • **member of intelligentsia** | интеллигент | *in-ti-li-gyént* |
| | интеллигентный | *in-ti-li-gyént-nyj* |
| **irony** | ирония | *i-ró-ni-ya* |
| • **ironic** | ироничный | *i-ra-ních-nyj* |
| **irresponsible** | безответственный | *bi-zat-vyét-stvi-nyj* |
| **irritable** | раздражительный | *raz-dra-zhý-til`-nyj* |
| **jealous** | ревнивый *(adj)* | *riv-ní-vyj* |
| • **jealously** | ревниво *(adv)* | *riv-ni-va* |
| **kindness** | доброта | *dab-ra-táh* |
| • **kind** | добрый *(adj)* | *dób-ryj* |
| • **kindly** | добро *(adv)* | *dób-ra* |
| • **kindhearted** | добросердечный | *dab-ra-sir-dyéch-nyj* |
| **laugh** | смеяться *(i)* | *smi-yáh-tsa* |

| | | |
|---|---|---|
| • laughter | смех | *smyekh* |
| laziness | ленивость *(f)* | *li-ní-vast'* |
| • lazy | ленивый *(adj)* | *li-ní-vyj* |
| • lazily | лениво *(adv)* | *li-ní-va* |
| liberal | либеральный | *li-bi-ráhl'-nyj* |
| lively | оживлённый | *a-zhyv-lyó-nyj* |
| love | любовь *(f)* | *lyu-bóf'* |
| • beloved | любимый | *lyu-bí-myj* |
| • love | любить *(i)* | *lyu-bít'* |
| loyal | преданный | *pryé-da-nyj* |
| | постоянный | *pa-sta-yáh-nyj* |
| • disloyal | нелояльный | *niloh-yál-nyj* |
| madness | сумасшествие | *su-ma-shéhst-vi-ye* |
| • crazy, mad | сумасшедший | *su-ma-shéht-shyj* |
| | ненормальный | *ni-nar-máhl'-nyj* |
| malicious | зловредный *(adj)* | *zla-vryéd-nyj* |
| • maliciously | зловредно *(adv)* | *zla-vryéd-na* |
| mean, bad | противный *(adj)* | *pra-tív-nyj* |
| • meanly | противно *(adv)* | *pra-tív-na* |
| modesty | скромность *(f)* | *skróm-nast'* |
| • modest | скромный *(adj)* | *skróm-nyj* |
| • modestly | скромно *(adv)* | *skróm-na* |
| mood | настроение | *na-stra-yé-ni-ye* |
| • bad mood | плохое настроение | *pla-khó-ye na-stra-yé-ni-ye* |
| • good mood | хорошее настроение | *kha-ró-shy-ye na-stra-yé-ni-ye* |
| • moody | с настроением | *s na-stra-yé-ni-yem* |
| naive | наивный *(adj)* | *na-ív-nyj* |
| | наивно *(adv)* | *na-ív-na* |
| neat | аккуратный *(adj)* | *a-ku-ráht-nyj* |
| • neatly | аккуратно *(adv)* | *a-ku-ráht-na* |
| nice, pleasant | приятный *(adj)* | *pri-yáht-nyj* |
| • pleasantly | приятно *(adv)* | *pri-yáht-na* |
| • unpleasant | неприятный *(adj)* | *ni-pri-yáht-nyj* |
| obstinate | неуклонный *(adj)* | *ni-uk-ló-nyj* |
| • obstinately | неуклонно *(adv)* | *ni-uk-ló-na* |
| odd, strange | странный *(adj)* | *stráh-nyj* |
| • oddly, strangely | странно *(adv)* | *stráh-na* |
| optimism | оптимизм | *ap-ti-mízm* |
| • optimist | оптимист | *ap-ti-míst* |
| • optimistic | оптимистичный *(adj)* | *ap-ti-mis-tích-nyj* |
| • optimistically | оптимистично *(adv)* | *ap-ti-mis-tích-na* |
| original | оригинальный | *a-ri-gi-náhl'-nyj* |
| patience | терпение | *tir-pyé-ni-ye* |
| • patient | терпеливый *(adj)* | *tir-pi-lí-vyj* |

| | | |
|---|---|---|
| • **patiently** | терпеливо *(adv)* | *tir-pi-lí-va* |
| • **impatient** | нетерпеливый | *ni-tir-pi-lí-vyj* |
| **perfection** | совершенство | *sa-vir-shéhn-stva* |
| **pessimism** | пессимизм | *pi-si-mízm* |
| • **pessimist** | пессимист | *pi-si-míst* |
| • **pessimistic** | пессимистичный *(adj)* | *pi-si-mis-tích-nyj* |
| • **pessimistically** | пессимистично *(adv)* | *pi-si-mis-tích-na* |
| **picky** | привередливый | *pri-vi-ryéd-li-vyj* |
| | разборчивый | *raz-bór-chi-vyj* |
| **playful** | шутливый *(adj)* | *shut-lí-vyj* |
| • **joker** | шутник | *shut-ník* |
| • **playfully** | шутливо *(adv)* | *shut-lí-va* |
| **poor** | бедный *(adj)* | *byéd-nyj* |
| • **poorly** | бедно *(adv)* | *byéd-na* |
| **practicality** | практичность *(f)* | *prak-tích-nast'* |
| • **practical** | практичный | *prak-tích-nyj* |
| • **impractical** | непрактичный | *ni-prak-tích-nyj* |
| **pretentious** | претенциозный *(adj)* | *pri-tyn-tsy-óz-nyj* |
| • **pretentiously** | претенциозно *(adv)* | *pri-tyn-tsy-óz-na* |
| **proud** | гордый *(adj)* | *gór-dyj* |
| • **proudly** | гордо *(adv)* | *gór-da* |
| **prude** | ханжа *(m&f)* | *khan-zháh* |
| **reckless** | бесшабашный | *bis-sha-báhsh-nyj* |
| **reserved** | сдержанный | *sdyér-zhy-nyj* |
| • **unreserved** | несдержанный | *ni-sdyér-zhy-nyj* |
| **responsibility** | ответственность *(f)* | *at-vyét-stvi-nast'* |
| • **responsible** | ответственный | *at-vyét-stvi-nyj* |
| **restless** | беспокойный *(adj)* | *bis-pa-kój-nyj* |
| • **restlessly** | беспокойно *(adv)* | *bis-pa-kój-na* |
| **rich** | богатый *(adj)* | *ba-gáh-tyj* |
| • **richly** | богато *(adv)* | *ba-gáh-ta* |
| **romantic** | романтичный | *ra-man-tích-nyj* |
| **rude, rough** | грубый *(adj)* | *gróo-byj* |
| • **rudely, roughly** | грубо *(adv)* | *gróo-ba* |
| **sadness** | грусть *(f)* | *groost'* |
| | тоска | *tas-káh* |
| | печаль *(f)* | *pi-cháhl'* |
| • **sad** | грустный | *gróos-nyj* |
| | тоскливый | *task-lí-vyj* |
| | печальный | *pi-cháhl'-nyj* |
| **sarcasm** | сарказм | *sar-káhzm* |
| • **sarcastic** | саркастичный | *sar-kas-tích-nyj* |
| **sensitive** | чувствительный | *chu-ství-til'-nyj* |
| **sentimental** | сентиментальный | *sin-ti-min-táhl'-nyj* |
| **serious** | серьёзный *(adj)* | *sir'-yóz-nyj* |

| | | |
|---|---|---|
| • seriously | серьёзно *(adv)* | *sir'-yóz-na* |
| **shyness** | застенчивость *(f)* | *za-styén-chi-vast'* |
| • shy | застенчивый *(adj)* | *za-styén-chi-vyj* |
| • shyly | застенчиво *(adv)* | *za-styén-chi-va* |
| **simple** | простой *(adj)* | *pras-tój* |
| • simply | просто *(adv)* | *prós-ta* |
| **sincerity** | искренность *(f)* | *ísk-ri-nast'* |
| • sincere | искренний | *ísk-ri-nij* |
| • sincerely | искренно | *ísk-ri-na* |
| **sloppy** | неопрятный | *ni-ap-ryáht-nyj* |
| **smart, clever** | умный *(adj)* | *óom-nyj* |
| | умница *(f)* | *óom-ni-tsa* |
| | сообразительный *(adj)* | *sa-ab-ra-zí-til'-nyj* |
| | смышлёный *(adj)* | *smysh-lyó-nyj* |
| • cleverly | умно *(adv)* | *óom-na* |
| **smile** | улыбка | *u-lýp-ka* |
| • smile | улыбаться *(i)* | *u-ly-báh-tsa* |
| **snobbery** | снобизм | *sna-bízm* |
| • snob | сноб | *snob* |
| **stingy** | жадный | *zháhd-nyj* |
| **straight, blunt** | прямой *(adj)* | *pri-mój* |
| • bluntly | прямо *(adv)* | *pryáh-ma* |
| **strong** | сильный *(adj)* | *síl'-nyj* |
| • strongly | сильно *(adv)* | *síl'-na* |
| **stubborn** | упрямый *(adj)* | *u-pryáh-myj* |
| • stubbornly | упрямо *(adv)* | *u-pryáh-ma* |
| **stupid** | глупый *(adj)* | *glóo-pyj* |
| • stupidly | глупо *(adv)* | *glóo-pa* |
| **superstitious** | суеверный | *su-ye-vér-nyj* |
| **sweet** | милый *(adj)* | *mí-lyj* |
| • sweetly | мило *(adv)* | *mí-la* |
| **talk** | разговор | *raz-ga-vór* |
| • talkative | разговорчивый | *raz-ga-vór-chi-vyj* |
| | болтливый | *balt-lí-vyj* |
| **unyielding** | непреклонный | *ni-pri-kló-nyj* |
| **use, help** | польза | *pól'-za* |
| • useful | полезный | *pa-lyéz-nyj* |
| • useless | бесполезный | *bis-pa-lyéz-nyj* |
| **vain** | тщеславный | *tshchi-sláhv-nyj* |
| **warm** | тёплый *(adj)* | *tyóp-lyj* |
| • warmly | тепло *(adv)* | *tip-ló* |
| • warm-hearted | теплосердечный | *tip-la-sir-dyéch-nyj* |
| **weak** | слабый *(adj)* | *sláh-byj* |
| • weakly | слабо *(adv)* | *sláh-ba* |

| well-bred | хорошо | *kha-ra-shó vas-pí-ta-nyj* |
| | воспитанный | |
| well-mannered | с хорошими | *s kha-ró-shy-mi* |
| | манерами *(pl)* | *ma-nyé-ra-mi* |
| willing | готовый | *ga-tó-vyj* |
| • willing to help | готов помочь | *ga-tóf pa-móch* |
| wisdom | мудрость *(f)* | *móod-rast'* |
| • wise | мудрый *(adj)* | *móod-ryj* |
| • wisely | мудро *(adv)* | *móod-ra* |
| witty | остроумный | *ast-ra-óom-nyj* |
| | остряк *(m)* | *ast-ryáhk* |

*Expressions*

| As a fifth wheel for a carriage | = Как телеге пятое колесо |
| He is bright | = У него голова золотая |
| (He has a golden head) | |
| Jack of all trades | = Мастер на все руки |
| Patience and work will | = Терпение и труд всё перетрут |
| overcome anything | |
| She lost her spirit (faith) | = У неё руки опустились |
| (Her hands fell) | |
| To look/act like a fool | = (С-)валять дурака |
| What a fool! | = Вот дурак какой! |

## f. BASIC PERSONAL INFORMATION

| address | адрес | *áhd-res* |
| • boulevard | бульвар | *bul'-váhr* |
| • highway | шоссе | *shy-séh* |
| • street | улица | *óo-li-tsa* |
| | переулок | *pi-ri-óo-lak* |
| • to live on | жить *(i)* на | *zhyt' nah* |
| • Where do you live? | Где вы живёте? *(pol)* | *gdye vy zhy-vyó-ti* |
| | Где ты живёшь? *(fam)* | *gdye ty zhy-vyósh* |
| • I live on ... street | Я живу на ... улице | *yah zhy-vóo nah óo-li-tsy* |

| | | |
|---|---|---|
| • **house number** | номер дома *(m)* | *nó-mir dó-ma* |
| **career** | карьера | *kar'-yé-ra* |
| **come from** | приехать *(p)* из | *pri-yé-khat' iz* |
| • **move** | переехать *(p)* | *pi-ri-yé-khat'* |
| • **city, town** | город | *gó-rad* |
| • **country** | страна | *stra-náh* |
| • **state** | государство | *ga-su-dáhr-stva* |
| | штат | *shtaht* |
| **date and year of birth** | день и год рождения | *dyen' i god razh-dyé-ni-ya* |
| **education** | образование | *ab-ra-za-váh-ni-ye* |
| • **go to school** | посещать школу *(i)* | *pa-si-shchyáht' shkó-lu* |
| | посетить *(p)* | *pa-si-tít'* |
| • **finish school,** | кончить школу *(p)* | *kón-chit' shkó-lu* |
| **graduate** | кончать *(i)* | *kan-cháht'* |
| • **graduate** | кончить *(p)* | *kón-chit'* |
| **(from institute,** | (институт, | *(in-sti-tóot,* |
| **university)** | университет) | *u-ni-vir-si-tyét)* |
| • **higher education** | высшее образование | *výsh-shy-ye* |
| | | *ab-ra-za-váh-ni-ye* |
| • **high school** | среднее образование | *sryéd-ni-ye* |
| **education** | | *ab-ra-za-váh-ni-ye* |
| • **diploma** | диплом | *dip-lóm* |
| **identification** | удостоверение | *u-das-ta-vi-ryé-ni-ye* |
| | личности | *lích-nas-ti* |
| • **passport** | паспорт | *páhs-part* |
| **job, work** | работа | *ra-bó-ta* |
| • **line (sphere) of** | область *(f)* работы | *ób-last' ra-bó-ty* |
| **work** | | |
| **marital status** | семейное | *si-myéj-na-ye* |
| | положение | *pa-la-zhéh-ni-ye* |
| **married** | женатый *(m)* | *zhi-náh-tyj* |
| | замужняя *(f)* | *zá-moozh-nya-ya* |
| **single, unmarried** | неженатый *(m)* | *ni-zhi-náh-tyj* |
| | незамужняя *(f)* | *ni-zá-moozh-nya-ya* |
| **name** | имя *(n)* | *í-mya* |
| • **be called** | называть *(i)* | *na-zy-váht'* |
| • **first name** | имя *(n)* | *í-mya* |
| • **family name** | фамилия | *fa-mí-li-ya* |
| • **patronymic** | отчество | *ót-chist-va* |
| • **How do you spell** | Как ваше имя | *kahk váh-shy í-mya* |
| **your name?** | пишется? *(pol)* | *pí-shyt-tsa* |
| | Как твоё имя | *kahk tva-yó í-mya* |
| | пишется? *(fam)* | *pí-shyt-tsa* |
| • **Print your name** | Напишите ваше имя | *na-pi-shý-tye váh-shy* |
| | *(pol)* | *í-mya* |
| | Напиши твоё имя *(fam)* | *na-pi-shý tva-yó í-mya* |
| • **What's your** | Как вас зовут? *(pol)* | *kahk vahs za-vóot* |
| **name?** | Как тебя зовут? *(fam)* | *kahk ti-byáh za-vóot* |

| • My name is... | Меня зовут... | *mi-nyáh za-vóot* |
| • sign | подписаться *(p)* | *pat-pi-sáh-tsa* |
| | подписываться *(i)* | *pat-pí-sy-vat-tsa* |
| • signature | подпись *(f)* | *pót-pis'* |
| nationality | национальность *(f)* | *na-tsy-a-náhl'-nast'* |
| place of birth | место рождения | *myés-ta razh-dyé-ni-ya* |
| place of employment | место работы | *myés-ta ra-bó-ty* |
| place of residence | место жительства | *myés-ta zhý-til'-stva* |
| profession | специальность *(f)* | *spi-tsáhl'-nast'* |
| | профессия | *pra-fyé-si-ya* |
| • professional | профессиональный работник | *pra-fi-si-a-náhl'-nyj ra-bót-nik* |
| telephone number | номер телефона | *nó-myer ti-li-fó-na* |

## 12. THE BODY

### a. PARTS OF THE BODY

| abdomen | живот | *zhy-vót* |
| ankle | щиколотка | *shchí-ka-lat-ka* |
| arm | рука | *ru-káh* |
| back | спина | *spi-náh* |
| beard | борода | *ba-ra-dáh* |
| blood | кровь *(f)* | *krof'* |
| bone | кость *(f)* | *kost'* |
| brain | мозг | *mosk* |
| breast, chest | грудь *(f)* | *grood'* |
| buttock | ягодица | *yáh-ga-di-tsa* |
| cheek | щека | *shchi-káh* |
| chin | подбородок | *pad-ba-ró-dak* |
| ear | ухо | *óo-kha* |
| elbow | локоть *(m)* | *ló-kat'* |
| eye | глаз | *glahs* |
| eyebrow | бровь *(f)* | *brof'* |
| eyelash | ресница | *ris-ní-tsa* |
| eyelid | веко | *vyé-ka* |
| face | лицо | *li-tsó* |
| finger | палец | *páh-lits* |
| fingernail | ноготь *(m)* | *no-gat'* |
| foot, leg | нога | *na-gáh* |
| forehead | лоб | *lop* |
| genitals | половые органы *(pl)* | *pa-la-vý-ye ór-ga-ny* |
| gland | железа | *zhy-li-záh* |
| hair | волос(ы) *(m)* | *vó-las(-y)* |
| head | голова | *ga-la-váh* |

| heart | сердце | *syér-tse* |
|---|---|---|
| hip | бедро | *bid-ró* |
| index finger | указательный палец | *u-ka-záh-til'-nyj páh-lyets* |
| intestines | кишечник | *ki-shéhch-nik* |
| | кишки *(pl)* | *kish-kí* |
| jaw | челюсть *(f)* | *chýe-lyust'* |
| joint | сустав | *sus-táhv* |
| kidney | почка | *póch-ka* |
| knee | колено | *ka-lyé-na* |
| lip | губа | *gu-báh* |
| liver | печень *(f)* | *pyé-chin'* |
| lung | лёгкое *(n)* | *lyókh-ka-ye* |

*FOCUS: Parts of the Body*

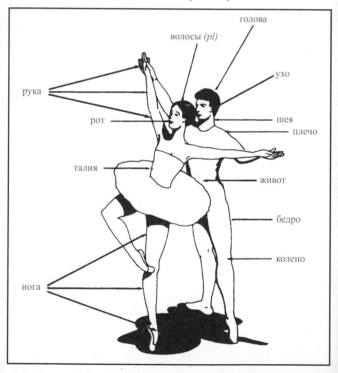

голова
волосы *(pl)*
ухо
рука
рот
шея
плечо
талия
живот
бедро
колено
нога

| middle finger | средний палец | sryéd-nij páh-lits |
| moustache | ус(ы) *(m)* | óos(ý) |
| mouth | рот | rot |
| muscle | мышца | mýsh-tsa |
| neck | шея | shéh-ya |
| nose | нос | nos |
| nostril | ноздря | nazd-ryáh |
| organ | орган | ór-gan |
| pancreas | поджелудочная железа | pad-zhy-lóo-dach-na-ya zhy-li-záh |
| shoulder | плечо | pli-chó |
| skin | кожа | kó-zha |
| spine, backbone | позвоночник | paz-va-nóch-nik |
| stomach | желудок | zhy-lóo-dak |
| thigh | ляжка | lyáhsh-ka |
| thumb | большой палец | bal'-shój páh-lits |
| toe | палец ноги | páh-lits na-gí |
| tongue | язык | i-zýk |
| tooth | зуб | zoop |
| waist | талия | táh-li-ya |
| wrist | кисть *(f)* | kist' |

## b. PHYSICAL STATES AND ACTIVITIES

| be hungry | быть *(i)* голодным | byt' ga-lód-nym |
| • hungry | голодный | ga-lód-nyj |
| • hunger | голод | gó-lad |
| thirst | жажда | zháhzh-da |
| • I need something to drink | Мне нужно/надо что-нибудь попить | mnye nóozh-na/náh-da shtó-ni-bud' pa-pít' |
| tired | усталый | u-stáh-lyj |
| breathe | дышать *(i)* | dy-sháht' |
| drink | пить *(i)* | pit' |
| eat | есть *(i)* | yest' |
| | кушать *(i)* | kóo-shat' |
| fall asleep | заснуть *(p)* | za-snóot' |
| | засыпать *(i)* | za-sy-páht' |
| feel bad | плохо себя чувствовать *(i)* | pló-kha si-byáh chóost-va-vat' |
| feel well | хорошо себя чувствовать *(i)* | kha-ra-shó si-byáh chóost-va-vat' |
| get up | встать *(p)* | fstaht' |
| | вставать *(i)* | fsta-váht' |
| go to sleep/go to bed | идти спать *(i)* | it-tí spaht' |

| | | |
|---|---|---|
| **I am cold** | Мне холодно | *mnye khó-la-dna* |
| **I am hot** | Мне жарко | *mnye zháhr-ka* |
| **rest** | отдыхать *(i)* | *ad-dy-kháht'* |
| **run** | бегать *(i)* | *byé-gat'* |
| **sleep** | спать *(i)* | *spaht'* |
| **wake up** | проснуться *(p)* | *pra-snóot-tsa* |
| | просыпаться *(i)* | *pra-sy-páh-tsa* |
| **walk** | ходить *(i)* | *kha-dít'* |

*Expressions*

| | | |
|---|---|---|
| **A glass of water** | = | Стакан воды |
| **Could you give me a glass of water?** | = | Не могли бы вы мне дать стакан воды? |
| **Hungry as a wolf** | = | Голодный как волк |
| **To get up early in the morning** | = | Проснуться с утра пораньше, проснуться утром рано |
| **To sleep like a log (To sleep like a corpse)** | = | Спать как убитый |

## c. SENSORY PERCEPTION

| | | |
|---|---|---|
| **blind** | слепой *(adj)* | *sli-pój* |
| | слепо *(adv)* | *slyéh-pa* |
| • **blindness** | слепота | *sli-pa-táh* |
| **deaf** | глухой *(adj)* | *glu-khój* |
| | глухо *(adv)* | *glóo-kha* |
| • **deafness** | глухота | *glu-kha-táh* |
| **hear** | слышать *(i)* | *slýsh-at'* |
| • **hearing** | слух | *slookh* |
| **listen to** | слушать *(i)* | *slóo-shat'* |
| **look** | смотреть *(i)* | *smat-ryét'* |
| | глядеть *(i)* | *gli-dyét'* |
| **mute** | немой | *ni-mój* |
| **noise** | шум | *shoom* |
| **noisy** | шумный *(adj)* | *shóom-nyj* |
| | шумно *(adv)* | *shóom-na* |
| **perceive** | воспринять *(p)* | *vas-pri-nyáht'* |
| | воспринимать *(i)* | *vas-pri-ni-máht'* |
| • **perception** | восприятие | *vas-pri-yáh-ti-ye* |
| **see** | видеть *(i)* | *ví-dit'* |

| • vision | видение | *ví-di-ni-ye* |
| sense, feel | чувствовать *(i)* | *chóost-va-vat'* |
| • sense | чувство | *chóo-stva* |
| smell | нюхать *(i)* | *nyú-khat'* |
| • smell | запах | *záh-pakh* |
| sound | звучать *(i)* | *zvu-cháht'* |
| | звук | *zvook* |
| taste | вкус | *fkoos* |
| touch | коснуться *(p)* | *kas-nóo-tsa* |
| | касаться *(i)* | *ka-sáh-tsa* |
| • touch | прикосновение | *pri-kas-na-vyé-ni-ye* |

## d. PERSONAL CARE

| bald | лысый | *lý-syj* |
| barber | мужской | *muzh-skój pa-rik-máh-khir* |
| | парикмахер | |
| • barber shop | парикмахерская | *pa-rik-máh-khir-ska-ya* |
| beautician | косметичка *(f)* | *kas-mi-tích-ka* |
| brush | щётка | *shchyót-ka* |
| • brush, comb | расчесать *(p)* | *ras-chi-sáht' vó-la-sy* |
| one's hair | волосы *(pl)* | |
| | расчёсывать *(i)* | *ras-chyó-sy-vat'* |
| clean | чистить *(i)* | *chís-tit'* |
| | очищать *(i)* | *a-chi-shcháht'* |
| • clean oneself | очиститься *(p)* | *a-chís-tit-tsa* |
| comb | гребень *(m)* | *gryé-bin'* |
| | гребёнка *(f)* | *gri-byón-ka* |
| curls | кудри *(pl)* | *kóod-ri* |
| cut one's hair | остричь волосы *(p)* | *a-strích vó-la-sy* |
| | постричься *(p)* | *pa-strích-sya* |
| deodorant | деодорант | *di-ó-da-rant* |
| dirty | грязный | *gryáz-nyj* |
| dry oneself | вытереться *(p)* | *vý-ti-rit-tsa* |
| | вытираться *(i)* | *vy-ti-ráh-tsa* |
| grooming | привести *(p)* себя в | *pri-vis-tí si-byáh v* |
| | порядок | *pa-ryáh-dak* |
| | приводить *(i)* | *pti-va-dít'* |
| hairdresser | женский | *zhéhn-skij pa-rik-máh-khir* |
| | парикмахер | |
| hair dryer | сушилка для волос | *su-shýl-ka dlya va-lós* |
| | фен | *fyen* |
| hair spray | лак для волос | *lahk dlya va-lós* |
| hygiene | гигиена | *gi-gi-yé-na* |
| • hygienic | гигиеничный | *gi-gi-i-ních-nyj* |

| | | |
|---|---|---|
| **makeup** | мэйк-ап | *méhjk-ap* |
| | краска для лица | *kráhs-ka dlya li-tsáh* |
| • put on makeup | покраситься *(p)* | *pa-kráh-si-tsa* |
| | краситься *(i)* | *kráh-si-tsa* |
| **manicure** | маникюр | *ma-ni-kyur* |
| **mascara** | тушь *(f)* для ресниц | *toosh dlya ris-níts* |
| **massage** | массаж | *ma-sáhzh* |
| **nail polish** | лак для ногтей | *lahk dlya nag-tyéj* |
| **perfume** | духи *(pl)* | *du-khí* |
| • put on perfume | подушиться *(p)* | *pa-du-shý-tsa* |
| | душиться *(i)* | *du-shý-tsa* |
| **permanent wave** | постоянная завивка | *pas-ta-yáh-na-ya za-víf-ka* |
| **razor** | бритва | *brít-va* |
| • electric razor | электрическая бритва | *y-lyek-trí-chyes-ka-ya brít-va* |
| **scissors** | ножницы *(pl)* | *nózh-ni-tsy* |
| **shampoo** | шампунь *(m)* | *sham-póon'* |
| **shave** | побриться *(p)* | *pa-brí-tsa* |
| | бриться *(i)* | *brí-tsa* |
| **shower** | душ | *doosh* |
| • take a shower | принять душ *(p)* | *pri-nyáht' doosh* |
| | принимать *(i)* | *pri-ni-máht'* |
| **soap** | мыло | *mý-la* |
| **toothbrush** | зубная щётка | *zub-náh-ya shchyót-ka* |
| **toothpaste** | зубная паста | *zub-náh-ya páhs-ta* |
| **towel** | полотенце | *pa-la-tyén-tsy* |
| **wash** | мыть *(i)* | *myt'* |
| • wash oneself | помыться *(p)* | *pa-mýt-tsa* |
| | мыться *(i)* | *mýt-tsa* |
| • wash one's hair | вымыть/помыть *(p)* голову | *vý-myt'/pa-mýt' gó-la-vu* |

## THE PHYSICAL, PLANT, AND ANIMAL WORLDS

### 13. THE PHYSICAL WORLD

#### a. THE UNIVERSE

| | | |
|---|---|---|
| **astronomy** | астрономия | *ast-ra-nó-mi-ya* |
| **comet** | комета | *ka-myé-ta* |
| **cosmos** | космос | *kós-mas* |
| **eclipse** | затмение | *zat-myé-ni-ye* |
| • **lunar eclipse** | затмение луны | *zat-myé-ni-ye lu-ný* |
| • **solar eclipse** | затмение солнца | *zat-myé-ni-ye són-tsa* |
| **galaxy** | галактика | *ga-láhk-ti-ka* |
| **gravitation** | притяжение | *pri-ti-zhéh-ni-ye* |
| **light** | свет | *svyét* |
| • **infrared light** | инфракрасный свет | *in-fra-kráhs-nyj svyet* |
| • **light year** | световой год | *svi-ta-vój got* |
| • **ultraviolet light** | ультрафиолетовый свет | *ul't-ra-fi-a-lyé-ta-vyj svyet* |
| **meteor** | метеор | *mi-ti-ór* |
| **moon** | луна | *lu-náh* |
| • **half moon** | полумесяц | *pa-lu-myé-sits* |
| • **full moon** | полная луна | *pól-na-ya lu-náh* |
| • **moonlight** | лунный свет | *lóon-yj svyet* |
| • **new moon** | новая луна | *nó-va-ya lu-náh* |
| | молодая луна | *ma-la-dáh-ya lu-náh* |
| **orbit** | орбита | *ar-bí-ta* |
| • **orbit** | вращаться *(i)* по/на орбите | *vra-shcháh-tsa pa/na ar-bí-ti* |
| **planet** | планета | *pla-nyé-ta* |
| • **Earth** | Земля | *zim-lyáh* |
| • **Jupiter** | Юпитер | *yu-pí-tir* |
| • **Mars** | Марс | *mahrs* |
| • **Mercury** | Меркурий | *mir-kóo-rij* |
| • **Neptune** | Нептун | *nip-tóon* |
| • **Saturn** | Сатурн | *sa-tóorn* |
| • **Uranus** | Уран | *u-ráhn* |
| • **Venus** | Венера | *vi-nyé-ra* |
| **dwarf planet** | карликовая планета | *kár-li-ka-va-ya pla-nyé-ta* |
| • **Pluto** | Плутон | *plu-tón* |
| **satellite** | спутник | *spóot-nik* |
| **space** | космос/пространство | *kós-mas/prast-ráhnst-va* |

| | | |
|---|---|---|
| • **two-dimensional space** | двухмерное пространство | *dvukh-myér-na-ye prast-ráhnst-va* |
| • **three-dimensional space** | трёхмерное пространство | *tryokh-myér-na-ye prast-ráhnst-va* |
| • **narrow space** | узкое пространство | *óos-ka-ye prast-ráhnst-va* |
| • **wide space** | широкое пространство | *shy-ró-ka-ye prast-ráhnst-va* |
| **star** | звезда *(sg)* | *zviz-dáh* |
| | звёзды *(pl)* | *zvyóz-dy* |
| **sun** | солнце | *són-tse* |
| • **sunlight** | солнечный свет | *sól-nich-nyj svyet* |
| • **sun ray** | луч солнца | *looch són-tsa* |
| | солнечный луч | *sól-nich-nyj looch* |
| • **solar system** | солнечная система | *sól-nich-na-ya sis-tyé-ma* |
| **universe** | вселенная | *fsi-lyé-na-ya* |
| **world** | мир | *mir* |

*Expressions*

| | |
|---|---|
| **Gravitational force** | = Сила притяжения |
| **To become (act) stupid** (He has an eclipse of the brain.) | = У него затмение мозга |
| **To shed light on the subject** | = Осветить предмет |
| **To shine brightly** | = Ярко светить |
| **With the speed of lightning** (To fly by like a meteor) | = Промчаться как метеор |

# b. THE ENVIRONMENT

| | | |
|---|---|---|
| **air** | воздух | *vóz-dukh* |
| **archipelago** | архипелаг | *ar-khi-pi-láhk* |
| **atmosphere** | атмосфера | *at-mas-fyé-ra* |
| • **atmospheric** | атмосферный | *at-mas-fyér-nyj* |
| **basin, pool** | бассейн | *ba-syéjn* |
| **bay** | бухта | *bóokh-ta* |
| **beach** | берег/пляж | *byé-rik/plyahzh* |
| **channel (canal)** | канал | *ka-náhl* |
| **cloud** | облако *(sg)* | *ób-la-ka* |
| | облака *(pl)* | *ab-la-káh* |
| **coast** | побережье | *pa-bi-ryézh'-ye* |
| **desert** | пустыня | *pus-tý-nya* |

| | | |
|---|---|---|
| earthquake | землетрясение | *zim-li-tri-syé-ni-ye* |
| environment | окружающая среда | *ak-ru-zháh-yu-shcha-ya sri-dáh* |
| farmland | пахотная земля | *páh-khat-na-ya zim-lyáh* |
| field | поле | *pó-li* |
| forest, woods | лес *(sg)* | *lyes* |
| | леса *(pl)* | *li-sáh* |
| grass | трава | *tra-váh* |
| gulf | залив | *za-líf* |
| hill | холм | *kholm* |
| horizon | горизонт | *ga-ri-zónt* |
| ice | лёд | *lyot* |
| • iceberg | айсберг | *áhjs-birk* |
| island | остров | *óst-raf* |
| lake | озеро *(sg)* | *ó-zi-ra* |
| | озёра *(pl)* | *a-zyó-ra* |
| land | земля | *zim-lyáh* |
| landscape | пейзаж | *pij-záhsh* |
| | ландшафт | *lant-sháhft* |
| layer | слой/прослойка | *sloj/pras-lój-ka* |
| mountain | гора | *ga-ráh* |
| • mountain chain | горная цепь *(f)* | *gór-na-ya tsehp'* |
| • mountainous | гористый | *ga-rís-tyj* |
| • peak | вершина | *vir-shý-na* |
| nature | природа | *pri-ró-da* |
| • natural | естественный | *is-tyést-vi-nyj* |
| ocean | океан | *a-ki-áhn* |
| • Antarctic Ocean | Антарктический океан | *an-tark-tí-chis-kij a-ki-áhn* |
| • Arctic | Арктика | *áhrk-ti-ka* |
| • Atlantic | Атлантический | *at-lan-tí-chis-kij* |
| • Indian | Индийский | *in-díjs-kij* |
| • Pacific | Тихий | *tí-khij* |
| pebbles | галька | *gáhl'-ka* |
| peninsula | полуостров | *pa-lu-óst-raf* |
| plain | равнина | *rav-ní-na* |
| river | река | *ri-káh* |
| • bed | русло | *róos-la* |
| • bottom | дно | *dno* |
| • flow, current | течение | *ti-chyé-ni-ye* |
| rock, stone | камень *(m, sg)* | *káh-min'* |
| | камни *(pl)* | *káhm-ni* |
| sand | песок | *pi-sók* |
| sea | море | *mó-rye* |
| sky | небо *(sg)* | *nyé-ba* |
| | небеса *(pl)* | *ni-bi-sáh* |

| storm cloud | туча | *tóo-cha* |
|---|---|---|
| tide | прилив | *pri-líf* |
| valley | долина | *da-lí-na* |
| vegetation | растительность *(f)* | *ras-tí-til'-nast'* |
| volcano | вулкан | *vul-káhn* |
| • eruption | извержение | *iz-vir-zhéh-ni-ye* |
| • lava | лава | *láh-va* |
| water | вода | *va-dáh* |
| wave | волна | *val-náh* |

## c. MATTER AND THE ENVIRONMENT

| acid | кислота | *kis-la-táh* |
|---|---|---|
| air | воздух | *vóz-dukh* |
| ammonia | аммиак | *a-mi-áhk* |
| atom | атом | *áh-tam* |
| • charge | заряд | *za-ryáht* |
| • electron | электрон | *y-likt-rón* |
| • neutron | нейтрон | *nijt-rón* |
| • nucleus | ядро | *id-ró* |
| • proton | протон | *pra-tón* |
| bronze | бронза | *brón-za* |
| carbon | углерод | *ug-li-rót* |
| chemical | химический | *khi-mí-chis-kij* |
| • chemistry | химия | *khí-mi-ya* |
| chlorine | хлор | *khlor* |
| coat | покрыть *(p)* | *pak-rýt'* |
| | покрывать *(i)* | *pak-ry-váht'* |
| compound | состав | *sas-táhf* |
| copper | медь *(f)* | *myet'* |
| cotton | хлопок | *khló-pak* |
| electrical | электрический | *y-likt-rí-chis-kij* |
| • electricity | электричество | *y-likt-rí-chist-va* |
| element | элемент | *y-li-myént* |
| energy | энергия | *y-néhr-gi-ya* |
| • fossil fuel | ископаемое топливо | *is-ka-páh-ye-ma-ye tóp-li-va* |
| • nuclear energy | ядерная энергия | *yáh-dir-na-ya y-néhr-gi-ya* |
| • radioactive wastes | радиоактивные отходы | *ra-di-a-ak-tív-ny-ye at-khó-dy* |
| • solar energy | солнечная энергия | *sól-nich-na-ya y-néhr-gi-ya* |
| fiber | волокно | *va-lak-nó* |
| fuel | топливо | *tóp-li-va* |
| gas | газ | *gahs* |

| | | |
|---|---|---|
| • gasoline | бензин | *bin-zín* |
| • natural gas | натуральный газ | *na-tu-ráhl'-nyj gahs* |
| gold | золото | *zó-la-ta* |
| heat | теплота | *tip-la-táh* |
| hydrogen | водород | *va-da-rót* |
| industry | промышленность *(f)* | *pra-mýsh-li-nast'* |
| • industrial | промышленный | *pra-mýsh-li-nyj* |
| iodine | йод | *jot* |
| iron | железо | *zhy-lyé-za* |
| laboratory | лаборатория | *la-ba-ra-tó-ri-ya* |
| lead | свинец *(n)* | *svi-nyéts* |
| • lead *(adj)* | свинцовый *(adj)* | *svin-tsó-vyj* |
| leather | кожа *(n)* | *kó-zha* |
| • leather *(adj)* | кожаный *(adj)* | *kó-zha-nyj* |
| liquid | жидкость *(f)* | *zhýt-kast'* |
| material | материал | *ma-ti-ri-áhl* |
| matter | вещество | *vi-shchist-vó* |
| mercury | ртуть *(f)* | *rtoot'* |
| metal | металл | *mi-táhl* |
| • metal *(adj)* | металлический | *mi-tah-lí-chis-kij* |
| methane | метан | *mi-táhn* |
| microscope | микроскоп | *mik-ras-kóp* |
| mineral | минерал | *mi-ni-ráhl* |
| molecule | молекула | *ma-lyé-ku-la* |
| • molecular | молекулярная | *ma-li-ku-lyáhr-na-ya* |
| formula, | формула, | *fór-mu-la,* |
| structure | структура | *struk-tóo-ra* |
| nitrogen | азот | *a-zót* |
| oil | масло | *máhs-la* |
| organic | органический | *ar-ga-ní-chis-kij* |
| • inorganic | неорганический | *ni-ar-ga-ní-chis-kij* |
| oxygen | кислород | *kis-la-rót* |
| particle | частица | *chis-tí-tsa* |
| petroleum | нефть *(f)* | *nyeft'* |
| physics | физика | *fí-zi-ka* |
| • physical | физический | *fi-zí-chis-kij* |
| plastic | пластик | *pláhs-tik* |
| platinum | платина | *pláh-ti-na* |
| pollution | загрязнение | *zag-riz-nyé-ni-ye* |
| salt | соль *(f)* | *sol'* |
| silk | шёлк | *sholk* |
| silver | серебро | *si-rib-ró* |
| smoke | дым | *dym* |
| sodium | натрий | *náht-rij* |
| solid | твёрдый | *tvyór-dyj* |
| steel | сталь *(f)* | *stahl'* |

| | | |
|---|---|---|
| • **stainless steel** | нержавеющая сталь *(f)* | *nir-zha-vyé-yu-shchi-ya stahl'* |
| **substance** | вещество | *vi-shchist-vó* |
| **sulfur** | сера | *syé-ra* |
| • **sulfuric acid** | серная кислота | *syér-na-ya kis-la-táh* |
| **textile** | текстиль *(m)* | *tiks-tíl'* |
| **vapor** | пар | *pahr* |
| **water** | вода | *va-dáh* |
| **wool** | шерсть *(f)* | *shehrst'* |

## d. CHARACTERISTICS OF MATTER

| | | |
|---|---|---|
| **artificial** | искусственный *(adj)* | *is-kóost-vi-nyj* |
| • **artificially** | искусственно *(adv)* | *is-kóost-vi-na* |
| **authentic** | настоящий | *nas-ta-yáh-shchij* |
| | подлинный | *pód-li-nyj* |
| **ductile** | ковкий | *kóf-kij* |
| | тягучий | *ti-góo-chij* |
| **elastic** | эластичный | *y-las-tích-nyj* |
| **hard, firm** | твёрдый *(adj)* | *tvyór-dyj* |
| • **firmly** | твёрдо *(adv)* | *tvyór-da* |
| **heavy** | тяжёлый *(adj)* | *ti-zhó-lyj* |
| • **heavily** | тяжело *(adv)* | *ti-zhy-ló* |
| **light** | лёгкий *(adj)* | *lyókh-kij* |
| • **lightly** | легко *(adv)* | *likh-kó* |
| **malleable** | ковкий | *kóf-kij* |
| **opaque** | непрозрачный | *nip-raz-ráhch-nyj* |
| | светонепро- ницаемый | *svye-ta-nip-ra-ni- tsáh-i-myj* |
| **pure** | чистый *(adj)* | *chís-tyj* |
| • **purely** | чисто *(adv)* | *chís-ta* |
| **resistant** | стойкий | *stój-kij* |
| **robust** | крепкий | *kryép-kij* |
| **rough** | грубый *(adj)* | *gróo-byj* |
| • **roughly** | грубо *(adv)* | *gróo-ba* |
| **smooth** | гладкий *(surface) (adj)* | *gláht-kij* |
| | плавный *(motion) (adj)* | *pláhv-nyj* |
| • **smoothly** | гладко *(adv)* | *gláht-ka* |
| | плавно *(adv)* | *pláhv-na* |
| **soft** | мягкий *(adj)* | *myáhkk-kij* |
| • **softly** | мягко *(adv)* | *myáhkk-ka* |
| **soluble** | растворимый | *rast-va-rí-myj* |
| **stable** | устойчивый | *us-tój-chi-vyj* |

| **strong** | крепкий *(adj)* | *kryép-kij* |
| | сильный *(adj)* | *síl'-nyj* |
| • **strongly** | крепко *(adv)* | *kryép-ka* |
| | сильно *(adv)* | *síl'-na* |
| **synthetic** | синтетический | *syn-ty-tí-chis-kij* |
| **transparent** | прозрачный | *praz-ráhch-nyj* |
| **weak** | слабый *(adj)* | *sláh-byj* |
| • **weakly** | слабо *(adv)* | *sláh-ba* |

## e. GEOGRAPHY

| **Antarctic Circle** | Южный полярный круг | *yúzh-nyj pa-lyáhr-nyj krook* |
| **Arctic Circle** | Северный полярный круг | *syé-vir-nyj pa-lyáhr-nyj krook* |
| **area** | местность *(f)* | *myés-nast'* |
| | область *(f)* | *ób-last'* |
| | площадь *(math) (f)* | *pló-shchat'* |
| **border** | граница | *gra-ní-tsa* |
| • **border on** | граничить с *(i)* | *gra-ní-chit' s* |
| **city** | город | *gó-rat* |
| • **capital** | столица | *sta-lí-tsa* |
| **continent** | континент | *kan-ti-nyént* |
| • **continental** | континентальный | *kan-ti-nin-táhl'-nyj* |
| **country** | страна | *stra-náh* |
| **equator** | экватор | *yk-váh-tar* |
| **geography** | география | *gi-ag-ráh-fi-ya* |
| • **geographical** | географический | *gi-ag-ra-fí-chis-kij* |
| **globe** | земной шар | *zim-nój shahr* |
| • **globe (model)** | глобус | *gló-bus* |
| **hemisphere** | полушарие | *pa-lu-sháh-ri-ye* |
| • **hemispheric** | полусферический | *pa-lu-sfi-rí-chis-kij* |
| **latitude** | широта | *shy-ra-táh* |
| **location** | местонахождение | *myes-ta-na-khazh-dyé-ni-ye* |
| | месторасположение | *myes-ta-ras-pa-la-zhéh-ni-ye* |
| • **located** | расположенный | *ras-pa-ló-zhy-nyj* |
| | размещённый | *raz-mi-shchyó-nyj* |
| • **be located** | находиться *(i)* | *na-kha-dí-tsa* |
| | быть расположенным *(i)* | *byt' ras-pa-ló-zhyn-ym* |
| **longitude** | долгота | *dal-ga-táh* |
| **map** | карта | *káhr-ta* |

МОЛДОВА
(Moldova)

БЕЛАРУС
(Belarus)

САНКТ ПЕТЕРБУРГ
(St. Petersburg)

СМОЛЕНСК
(Smolensk)

МОСКВА (Moscow)

КУРСК
(Kursk)

ВЛАДИМИР
(Vladimir)

УКРАИНА
(Ukraine)

АЛЕКСАНДРОВСК
(Aleksandrovsk)

РОСТОВ-НА-ДОНУ
(Rostov-on-Don)

КРАСНОДАР
(Krasnodar)

ВОЛГОГРАД
(Volgograd)

ОРЕНБУРГ
(Orenburg)

ОМСК
(Omsk)

АРМЕНИЯ
(Armenia)

КАЗАХСТАН
(Kazakhstan)

НОВОСИБИРСК
(Novosibirsk)

ТУРКМЕНИСТАН
(Turkmenistan)

АЗЕРБАЙДЖАН
(Azerbaijan)

УЗБЕКИСТАН
(Uzbekistan)

КЫРГЫЗСТАН
(Kyrgyzstan)

ТАДЖИКИСТАН
(Tajikistan)

| | | |
|---|---|---|
| **meridian** | меридиан | *mi-ri-di-áhn* |
| • **prime meridian** | первый меридиан | *pyér-vyj mi-ri-di-áhn* |
| **nation** | страна | *stra-náh* |
| • **state (country)** | государство | *ga-su-dáhr-stva* |
| • **national** | национальный | *na-tsy-a-náhl'-nyj* |
| | государственный | *ga-su-dáhrst-vi-nyj* |
| **pole** | полюс | *pó-lyus* |
| • **North Pole** | Северный полюс | *syé-vir-nyj pó-lyus* |
| • **South Pole** | Южный полюс | *yúzh-nyj pó-lyus* |
| **province** | провинция | *pra-vín-tsy-ya* |
| **region** | район | *raj-ón* |
| | область *(f)* | *ób-last'* |
| • **regional center** | центр района, области | *tséhntr raj-ó-na, ób-las-ti* |
| **state (U.S.)** | штат | *shtaht* |
| **territory** | территория | *ti-ri-tó-ri-ya* |
| **tropic** | тропик | *tró-pik* |
| • **tropical zone** | тропическая зона | *tra-pí-chis-ka-ya zó-na* |
| **village** | деревня | *di-ryév-nya* |
| • **large village** | село | *si-ló* |

## 14. PLANTS

### a. GENERAL VOCABULARY

| | | |
|---|---|---|
| **agriculture** | сельское хозяйство | *syél'-ska-ye kha-zyáhjst-va* |
| **bloom** | цветок *(sg)* | *tsvi-tók* |
| | цветы/цветки *(pl)* | *tsvi-tý/tsvit-kí* |
| • **bloom** | расцвести *(p)* (за-) | *ras-tsvis-tí* |
| | расцветать *(i)* (за-) | *ras-tsvi-táht'* |
| **botanical** | ботанический | *ba-ta-ní-chis-kij* |
| • **botany** | ботаника | *ba-táh-ni-ka* |
| **branch** | ветка | *vyét-ka* |
| **bud** | бутон | *bu-tón* |
| **bulb** | луковица | *lóo-ka-vi-tsa* |
| **cell** | клетка | *klyét-ka* |
| • **membrane** | мембрана | *mimb-ráh-na* |
| • **nucleus** | ядро | *id-ró* |
| **chlorophyll** | хлорофил | *khla-ra-fíl* |
| **cultivate** | обрабатывать *(i)* | *ab-ra-báh-ty-vat'* |
| | обработать *(p)* | *ab-ra-bó-tat'* |
| | растить *(i)* | *ras-tít'* |
| | выращивать *(i)* | *vy-ráh-shchi-vat'* |

| | | |
|---|---|---|
| • cultivation | обработка | *ab-ra-bót-ka* |
| dig | вырыть *(p)/* выкопать *(p)* | *vý-ryt'/vý-ka-pat'* |
| | рыть *(i)/* копать *(i)* | *ryt'/ ka-páht'* |
| flower | цветок *(sg)* | *tsvi-tók* |
| | цветы *(pl)* | *tsvi-tý* |
| foliage | листва *(coll)* | *list-váh* |
| gather, reap | пожать *(p)/* собрать *(p)* | *pa-zháht'/sab-ráht'* |
| | жать *(i)/*собирать *(i)* | *zhaht'/sa-bi-ráht'* |
| grain | зерно | *zir-nó* |
| greenhouse | теплица | *tip-lí-tsa* |
| hedge | живая изгородь *(f)* | *zhy-váh-ya íz-ga-rat'* |
| horticulture | садоводство | *sa-da-vót-stva* |
| irrigation | ирригация | *i-ri-gáh-tsy-yu* |
| • irrigation network | ирригационная сеть *(f)* | *i-ri-ga-tsy-ón-na-ya syet'* |
| leaf | лист *(sg)* | *list* |
| | листья *(pl)* | *líst'-ya* |
| petal | лепесток | *li-pis-tók* |
| photosynthesis | фотосинтез | *fo-ta-sín-tis* |
| plant | растение (-ье) | *ras-tyé-ni-ye* |
| • raise | вырастить *(p)* | *vý-ras-tit'* |
| | растить *(i)* | *ras-tít'* |
| | выращивать *(i)* | *vy-ráh-shchi-vat'* |
| plough | вспахать *(p)* | *fspa-kháht'* |
| | пахать *(i)* | *pa-kháht'* |
| pollen | пыльца | *pyl'-tsáh* |
| reproduce | размножать (-ся) | *raz-mna-zháht' (-tsa)* |
| • reproduction | размножение | *raz-mna-zhéh-ni-ye* |
| ripe | зрелый | *zryé-lyj* |
| • ripen | созреть *(p)* | *saz-ryét'* |
| | зреть *(i)* | *zryet'* |
| root | корень *(m, sg)* | *kó-rin'* |
| | корни *(pl)* | *kór-ni* |
| rotten | гнилой | *gni-lój* |
| seed | семя *(sg)* | *syé-mya* |
| | семена *(pl)* | *si-mi-náh* |
| sow | сеять *(i)* | *syé-it'* |
| species | вид | *vit* |
| stem | стебель *(m)* | *styé-bil'* |
| transplant | пересадить *(p)* | *pi-ri-sa-dít'* |
| | пересаживать *(i)* | *pi-ri-sáh-zhy-vat'* |
| trunk | ствол | *stvohl* |
| water | вода | *va-dáh* |

|  |  |  |
|---|---|---|
| • water | полить *(p)* | *pa-lít'* |
|  | поливать *(i)* | *pa-li-váht'* |
| **winter crop** | озимые | *a-zí-my-ye* |

## b. FLOWERS

|  |  |  |
|---|---|---|
| **aster** | астра | *áhst-ra* |
| **bird cherry blossom** | черёмуха *(coll)* | *chi-ryó-mu-kha* |
| **bluebell** | колокольчик | *ka-la-kól'-chik* |
| **carnation** | гвоздика | *gvaz-dí-ka* |
| **chamomile** | ромашка | *ra-máhsh-ka* |
| **daffodil** | нарцисс | *nar-tsýs* |
| **daisy** | маргаритка | *mar-ga-rít-ka* |
| **flower** | цветок *(sg)* | *tsvi-tók* |
|  | цветы *(pl)* | *tsvi-tý* |
| • bouquet | букет | *bu-kyét* |
| • bunch | охапка (цветов) | *a-kháhp-ka tsvi-tóf* |
| • flower bed | клумба | *klóom-ba* |
| • flower scent | запах цветов | *záh-pakh tsvi-tóf* |
| • flower wreath | венок из цветов | *vi-nók is tsvi-tóf* |
| • fresh flowers | свежие цветы | *svyé-zhy-ye tsvi-tý* |
| • wilted flowers | увядшие (цветы) | *u-vyáht-shy-ye (tsvi-tý)* |
| **forget-me-not** | незабудка | *ni-za-bóot-ka* |
| **gladiolus** | гладиолус | *gla-di-ó-lus* |
| **lilac** | сирень *(f)* | *si-ryén'* |
| **lily-of-the-valley** | ландыш | *láhn-dysh* |
| **nasturtium** | настурция | *nas-tóor-tsy-ya* |
| **pansies** | анютины глазки *(pl)* | *a-nyú-ti-ny gláhs-ki* |
| **petal** | лепесток *(sg)* | *li-pis-tók* |
|  | лепестки *(pl)* | *li-pist-kí* |
| **petunia** | петунья | *pi-tóon'-ya* |
| **pick flowers** | собрать цветы *(p)* | *sab-ráht' tsvi-tý* |
|  | собирать цветы *(i)* | *sa-bi-ráht' tsvi-tý* |
| **poppy** | мак | *mahk* |
| **rose** | роза | *ró-za* |
| **thorn** | шип | *shyp* |
| **tulip** | тюльпан | *tyul'-páhn* |
| **violet** | фиалка | *fi-áhl-ka* |

## c. TREES

|  |  |  |
|---|---|---|
| **alder** | ольха | *al'-kháh* |
| **ash** | ясень *(m)* | *yáh-sin'* |
| **bark** | кора | *ka-ráh* |

| birch | берёза | *bi-ryó-za* |
|---|---|---|
| cedar | кедр | *kyedr* |
| cottonwood | тополь *(m)* | *tó-pal'* |
| cypress | кипарис | *ki-pa-rís* |
| fruit tree | фруктовое дерево *(sg)* | *fruk-tó-va-ye dyé-ri-va* |
| | фруктовые деревья *(pl)* | *fruk-tó-vy-ye di-ryév'-ya* |
| • apple tree | яблоня | *yáhb-la-nya* |
| • cherry tree | вишня | *vísh-nya* |
| • pear tree | груша | *gróo-sha* |
| • plum tree | слива | *slí-va* |
| larch | лиственница | *líst-vi-ni-tsa* |
| maple | клён | *klyon* |
| mountain ash | рябина | *ri-bí-na* |
| oak | дуб | *doop* |
| palm | пальма | *páhl'-ma* |
| pine | сосна | *sas-náh* |
| silver fir tree | пихта | *píkh-ta* |
| snowball tree | калина | *ka-lí-na* |
| tree | дерево *(sg)* | *dyé-ri-va* |
| | деревья *(pl)* | *di-ryév'-ya* |
| willow | ива | *í-va* |

## d. FRUITS

| apple | яблоко | *yáhb-la-ka* |
|---|---|---|
| apricot | абрикос | *ab-ri-kós* |
| banana | банан | *ba-náhn* |
| blueberry | черника | *chir-ní-ka* |
| cherry | вишня *(coll)* | *vísh-nya* |
| • sour cherry | черешня *(coll)* | *chi-ryésh-nya* |
| chestnut | каштан | *kash-táhn* |
| citrus | цитрус | *tsýt-rus* |
| date | финик | *fí-nik* |
| fruit | фрукт | *frookt* |
| grapefruit | грейпфрут | *gryéjp-fróot* |
| grapes | виноград *(coll)* | *vi-nag-ráht* |
| | виноградина *(sg)* | *vi-nag-ráh-di-na* |
| lemon | лимон | *li-món* |
| mandarin | мандарин | *man-da-rín* |
| melon | дыня | *dý-nya* |
| orange | апельсин | *a-pil'-sín* |
| peach | персик | *pyér-sik* |
| pear | груша | *gróo-sha* |

| | | |
|---|---|---|
| pineapple | ананас | *a-na-náhs* |
| plum | слива | *slí-va* |
| prune | чернослив *(coll)* | *chir-na-slíf* |
| raspberry | малина *(coll)* | *ma-lí-na* |
| strawberry | клубника *(coll)* | *klub-ní-ka* |
| walnut | грецкий орех | *gryéts-kij a-ryékh* |
| watermelon | арбуз | *ar-bóos* |

## e. VEGETABLES AND HERBS

| | | |
|---|---|---|
| artichoke | артишок | *ar-ti-shók* |
| asparagus | спаржа | *spáhr-zha* |
| bean | боб | *bop* |
| • green beans | стручковые бобы *(pl)* | *struych-kó-vy-ye ba-bý* |
| • kidney bean | фасоль *(f)* | *fa-sól'* |
| beet | свёкла | *svyók-la* |
| • sugar beet | сахарная свёкла | *sáh-khar-na-ya svyók-la* |
| cabbage | капуста | *ka-póos-ta* |
| carrot | морковь *(f)* | *mar-kóf'* |
| cauliflower | цветная капуста | *tsvit-náh-ya ka-póos-ta* |
| celery | сельдерей | *sil'-di-ryéj* |
| corn | кукуруза | *ku-ku-róo-za* |
| • corn ear | початок | *pa-cháh-tak* |
| cucumber | огурец | *a-gu-ryéts* |
| dill | укроп *(coll)* | *uk-róp* |
| eggplant | баклажан | *bak-la-zháhn* |
| garden | сад | *saht* |
| • vegetable garden | огород | *a-ga-rót* |
| garlic | чеснок *(coll)* | *chis-nók* |
| grass | трава | *tra-váh* |
| lettuce | салат | *sa-láht* |
| mint | мята | *myáh-ta* |
| mushroom | гриб | *grip* |
| onion | лук | *look* |
| parsley | петрушка | *pit-róosh-ka* |
| pea | горох *(coll)* | *ga-rókh* |
| | горошина *(sg)* | *ga-ró-shy-na* |
| potato | картофель *(coll, m)* | *kar-tó-fil'* |
| | картошка *(coll)* | *kar-tósh-ka* |
| • new potato | молодая картошка | *ma-la-dáh-ya kar-tósh-ka* |
| pumpkin | тыква | *týk-va* |
| scallions | зелёный лук | *zi-lyó-nyj look* |
| spinach | шпинат | *shpi-náht* |
| squash | кабачок | *ka-ba-chók* |

| | | |
|---|---|---|
| **tomato** | помидор | *pa-mi-dór* |
| **turnip** | репа | *ryé-pa* |
| **vegetable** | овощ *(m)* | *ó-vashch* |

## 15. THE ANIMAL WORLD

### a. ANIMALS

| | | |
|---|---|---|
| **animal** | животное | *zhy-vót-na-ye* |
|   • domesticated | домашнее | *da-máhsh-ni-ye* |
|   • wild | дикое | *dí-ka-ye* |
| **bat** | летающая мышь *(f)* | *li-táh-yu-shchi-ya mysh* |
| **bear** | медведь *(m)* | *mid-vyét'* |
| **beast** | зверь *(m)* | *zvyer'* |
| **buffalo** | бизон | *bi-zón* |
| **bull** | бык | *byk* |
| **camel** | верблюд | *virb-lyút* |
| **cat** | кот *(m)* | *kot* |
| | кошка *(f)* | *kósh-ka* |
|   • meow | мяукать *(i)* | *mi-óo-kat'* |
| **cow** | корова | *ka-ró-va* |
| **crane** | журавль *(m)* | *zhu-ráhvl'* |
| **deer** | олень *(m)* | *a-lyén'* |
| | олениха *(f)* | *a-li-ní-kha* |
| **dog** | собака | *sa-báh-ka* |
|   • bark | лаять *(i)* | *láh-it'* |
| **donkey** | осёл | *a-syól* |
| **elephant** | слон | *slohn* |
| **farm** | ферма | *fyér-ma* |
|   • barn | сарай | *sa-ráhj* |
|   • farmer | фермер | *fyér-mir* |
| **fence** | забор/ограда | *za-bór/ag-ráh-da* |
| **fox** | лиса | *li-sáh* |
| **giraffe** | жираф | *zhy-ráhf* |
| **goat** | козёл *(m)* | *ka-zyól* |
| | козлиха *(f)* | *kaz-lí-kha* |
| **hare** | заяц | *záh-its* |
| **hippopotamus** | бегемот/ гиппопотам | *bi-gi-mót/gi-pa-pa-táhm* |
| **horse** | лошадь *(f)* | *ló-shat'* |
|   • colt | жеребёнок | *zhy-ri-byó-nak* |
| **human being** | человек | *chi-la-vyék* |
| **hunter** | охотник | *a-khót-nik* |
|   • hunt | охотиться *(i)* | *a-khó-ti-tsa* |
| **hyena** | гиена | *gi-yé-na* |

*FOCUS: Some Common Animals*

| | | | |
|---|---|---|---|
| кошка | корова | лисица | собака |
| тигр | лев | олень | лошадь |
| волк | свинья | слон | медведь |

| | | |
|---|---|---|
| **lamb** | ягнёнок | *ig-nyó-nak* |
| **leopard** | леопард | *li-a-páhrt* |
| **lion** | лев *(sg)* | *lyef* |
| | львы *(pl)* | *l'vy* |
| • **roar** | рычать *(i)* | *ry-cháht'* |
| **mammal** | млекопитающееся животное | *mli-ka-pi-táh-yu-shchij-sya zhy-vót-na-ye* |
| **mole** | крот | *krot* |
| **monkey** | обезьяна | *a-biz'-yáh-na* |
| **mouse** | мышь *(f)* | *mysh* |
| **mule** | мул | *mool* |
| **ox** | вол | *vol* |
| **paw** | лапа | *láh-pa* |

| | | |
|---|---|---|
| **pet** | домашнее животное | *da-máhsh-ni-ye zhy-vót-na-ye* |
| **pig** | свинья | *svin'-yáh* |
| **primate** | примат | *pri-máht* |
| **rabbit** | кролик | *kró-lik* |
| **rat** | крыса | *krý-sa* |
| **rhinoceros** | носорог | *na-sa-rók* |
| **sheep** | баран *(m)* | *ba-ráhn* |
| | овца *(f)* | *af-tsáh* |
| • **bleat** | блеять *(i)* | *blyé-it'* |
| **squirrel** | белка | *byél-ka* |
| **tail** | хвост | *khvost* |
| **tiger** | тигр | *tigr* |
| **vertebrate** | позвоночное | *paz-va-nóch-na-ye* |
| • **invertebrate** | непозвоночное | *ni-paz-va-nóch-na-ye* |
| **wolf** | волк *(m)* | *volk* |
| | волчица *(f)* | *val-chí-tsa* |
| • **howl** | выть *(i)* | *vyt'* |
| **zebra** | зебра | *zyéb-ra* |
| **zoo** | зоопарк | *za-a-páhrk* |
| • **zoological** | зоологический | *za-a-la-gí-chis-kij* |
| • **zoology** | зоология | *za-a-ló-gi-ya* |

*Expressions*

| | | |
|---|---|---|
| **Curiosity killed the cat** | = | Любопытство кошку сгубило |
| **Goatee (beard)** | = | Козлиная борода |
| **...knows which side the bread is buttered on (The cat knows whose sour cream it ate)** | = | Кошка знает, чью сметану съела |
| **Stubborn as a mule** | = | Упрямый, как осёл |
| **The lion's share** | = | Львиная доля |

**b. BIRDS AND FOWL**

| | | |
|---|---|---|
| **albatross** | альбатрос | *al'-bat-rós* |
| **beak** | клюв | *klyuf* |
| **chicken** | цыплёнок | *tsyp-lyó-nak* |
| **dove, pigeon** | голубь *(m)* | *gó-lup'* |
| **duck** | утка *(f)* | *óot-ka* |
| | селезень *(m)* | *syé-li-zin'* |
| **eagle** | орёл | *a-ryól* |

| feather | перо | *pi-ró* |
|---|---|---|
| **flight** | полёт | *pa-lyót* |
| • glide | парить *(i)* | *pa-rít'* |
| • fly | летать *(i)* | *li-táht'* |
| | лететь *(i)* | *li-tyét'* |
| **goose** | гусь *(m)* | *goos'* |
| | гусыня *(f)* | *gu-sý-nya* |
| **hawk** | ястреб | *yáhst-rip* |
| **nightingale** | соловей | *sa-la-vyéj* |
| **ostrich** | страус | *stráh-us* |
| **owl** | сова | *sa-váh* |
| **parrot** | попугай | *pa-pu-gáhj* |
| **pelican** | пеликан | *pi-li-káhn* |
| **penguin** | пингвин | *pin-gvín* |
| **rooster** | петух | *pi-tóokh* |
| **seagull** | чайка | *cháhj-ka* |
| **sparrow** | воробей | *va-ra-byéj* |
| **stork** | аист | *áh-ist* |
| **swallow** | ласточка | *láhs-tach-ka* |
| **turkey** | индейка/индюшка | *in-dyéj-ka/in-dyúsh-ka* |
| **wing** | крыло | *kry-ló* |

*Expressions*

| | |
|---|---|
| **A word is not a bird—once it flies out, you cannot catch it** | = Слово не воробей, вылетит—не поймаешь |
| **Black as a crow** | = Чёрный, как ворона |
| **Crafty, cunning (Web-footed goose)** | = Гусь лапчатый |
| **Repeat incessantly (To repeat like a parrot)** | = Повторять, как попугай |
| **To crow like a rooster** | = Петь петухом |
| **To get up with the sun (To get up with the roosters)** | = Встать с петухами |
| **To walk, march in a single file (To walk goose-style)** | = Идти гуськом |

## c. FISH, REPTILES, AMPHIBIANS, AND MARINE MAMMALS

| **carp** | карп | *kahrp* |
|---|---|---|
| • silver carp | серебряный карп | *si-ryéb-ri-nyj kahrp* |

| catfish | сом | *som* |
|---|---|---|
| codfish | треска | *tris-káh* |
| crocodile | крокодил | *kra-ka-díl* |
| • alligator | аллигатор | *a-li-gáh-tar* |
| dolphin | дельфин | *dil'-fín* |
| eel | угорь *(m)* | *óo-gar'* |
| fish | рыба | *rý-ba* |
| • fin | плавник | *plav-ník* |
| • fish | ловить *(i)* рыбу | *la-vít' rý-bu* |
| • fish bone | рыбная кость *(f)* | *rýb-na-ya kost'* |
| • fisherman | рыбак *(m)* | *ry-báhk* |
| | рыбачка *(f)* | *ry-bách-ka* |
| • fishing rod | удочка/удка | *óo-dach-ka/óot-ka* |
| • hook | крючок | *kryu-chók* |
| flounder | камбала | *kám-ba-lah* |
| frog | лягушка | *li-góosh-ka* |
| goldfish | золотая рыбка | *za-la-táh-ya rýp-ka* |
| herring | сельдь *(f)* | *syel't'* |
| reptile | пресмыкающееся | *pris-my-káh-yu-shchi-i-sya* |
| salmon | сёмга | *syóm-ga* |
| sardine | сардина | *sar-dí-na* |
| seal | тюлень *(m)* | *tyu-lyén'* |
| snake | змея | *zmi-yáh* |
| toad | жаба | *zháh-ba* |
| tuna | тунец | *tu-nyéts* |
| turtle | черепаха | *chi-ri-páh-kha* |
| whale | кит | *kit* |

## d. INSECTS AND OTHER INVERTEBRATES

| ant | муравей | *mu-ra-vyéj* |
|---|---|---|
| bedbug | клоп | *klop* |
| bee | пчела | *pchi-láh* |
| bug | букашка/насекомое | *bu-káhsh-ka/ na-si-kó-ma-ye* |
| butterfly | бабочка | *báh-bach-ka* |
| caterpillar | гусеница | *gu-si-ní-tsa* |
| clam | моллюск | *ma-lyúsk* |
| cockroach | таракан | *ta-ra-káhn* |
| crab | краб | *krahp* |
| flea | блоха | *bla-kháh* |
| fly | муха | *móo-kha* |
| insect | насекомое | *na-si-kó-ma-ye* |
| lobster | омар | *a-máhr* |

| louse | вошь *(sg, f)* | *vosh* |
| | вши *(pl)* | *fshy* |
| microbe | микроб | *mik-róp* |
| mosquito | комар | *ka-máhr* |
| moth | моль *(f)* | *mol'* |
| octopus | осьминог | *as'-mi-nók* |
| oyster | устрица | *óost-ri-tsa* |
| scorpion | скорпион | *skar-pi-ón* |
| shrimp | креветка | *kri-vyét-ka* |
| silkworm | шёлковый червь *(m)* | *shól-ka-vyj chyerf'* |
| spider | паук | *pa-óok* |
| tick | клещ | *klyeshch* |
| wasp | оса | *a-sáh* |
| worm | червь *(m)* | *chyerf'* |
| | червяк | *chir-vyáhk* |

## COMMUNICATING, FEELING, AND THINKING

*16. BASIC SOCIAL EXPRESSIONS*

### a. GREETINGS AND FAREWELLS

| | | |
|---|---|---|
| **Good afternoon!** | Добрый день! | *dób-ryj dyen'* |
| **Good evening!** | Добрый вечер! | *dób-ryj vyé-chir* |
| **Good morning!** | Доброе утро! | *dób-ra-ye óot-ra* |
| **Good night** | Спокойной ночи! | *spa-kój-naj nó-chi* |
| **Good-bye!** | До свидания! | *da svi-dáh-ni-ya* |
| **greet** | приветствовать *(i)* | *pri-vyét-stva-vat'* |
| • **greeting** | приветствие | *pri-vyét-stvyj-ye* |
| **Hello** | Здравствуйте | *zdráhf-stvyj-ti* |
| **How are you?** | Как дела? | *kahk di-láh* |
| **How are you getting along?** | Как ты поживаешь? *(fam)* | *kahk ty pa-zhy-váh-ish* |
| | Как вы поживаете? *(pol)* | *kahk vy pa-zhy-váh-i-ti* |
| • **Bad(ly)** | Плохо | *pló-kha* |
| • **Excellent** | Отлично | *at-lích-na* |
| • **Fine** | Хорошо | *kha-ra-shó* |
| • **Not bad** | Неплохо | *ni-pló-kha* |
| • **Not very well** | Не очень хорошо | *ni ó-chin' kha-ra-shó* |
| • **Quite well** | Довольно хорошо | *da-vól'-na kha-ra-shó* |
| • **So-so** | Так себе | *tahk si-byé* |
| • **Wonderful(ly)** | Прекрасно | *prik-ráhs-na* |
| • **Very well** | Очень хорошо | *ó-chin' kha-ra-shó* |
| **Please give my regards/greetings to...** | Пожалуйста, передай(те) привет... | *pa-zháh-lus-ta pi-ri-dáhj(-ti) pri-vyét* |
| **See you** | Пока | *pa-káh* |
| • **See you soon** | До скорого (свидания) | *da skó-ra-va (svi-dáh-ni-ya)* |
| **shake hands** | пожать *(p)* руки | *pa-zháht' róo-ki* |
| | пожимать *(i)* руки | *pa-zhy-máht' róo-ki* |
| • **handshake** | рукопожатие | *ru-ka-pa-zháh-ti-ye* |

### b. FORMS OF ADDRESS AND INTRODUCTIONS

| | | |
|---|---|---|
| **acquaintance** | знакомый (-ая) | *zna-kó-myj (-a-ya)* |
| **Allow me to introduce myself** | Позвольте представиться | *paz-vól'-ti prit-stáh-vi-tsa* |

| calling card | визитная карточка | vi-zít-na-ya káhr-tach-ka |
|---|---|---|
| **Come in** | Войдите | vaj-dí-ti |
| • enter | войти *(p)* | vaj-tí |
| | входить *(i)* | fkha-dít' |
| • introduction | представление | prit-stav-lyé-ni-ye |
| **meet, run into** | встретить *(p)* | fstryé-tit' |
| **someone** | встречать *(i)* | fstri-cháht' |
| **Delighted** | Очень приятно | ó-chin' pri-yáht-na |
| **Happy to make your** | Очень приятно/рад с | ó-chin' pri-yáht-na/ raht s |
| **acquaintance** | вами | váh-mi |
| | познакомиться | paz-na-kó-mi-tsa |
| **introduce someone** | представить *(p)* | prit-stáh-vit' |
| | представлять *(i)* | prit-stahv-lyáht' |
| **sit** | сесть *(p)* | syest' |
| | сидеть *(i)* | si-dyét' |
| • seat | посадить *(p)* | pa-sa-dít' |
| | сажать *(i)* | sa-zháht' |
| • Be seated | Садитесь | sa-dí-tis' |
| | Присядьте | pri-syáh-ti |
| **title** | форма обращения | fór-ma ab-ra-shchyé-ni-ya |
| • Dr. | доктор | dók-tar |
| • Miss, Ms., Mrs. | госпожа | gas-pa-zháh |
| • Mr. | господин | gas-pá-dín |
| • Prof. | профессор | pra-fyé-sar |
| **What's new?** | Что нового? | shto nó-va-va |
| **What's your name?** | Как тебя зовут? *(fam)* | kahk ti-byáh za-vóot |
| | Как вас зовут? *(pol)* | kahk vahs za-vóot |
| • My name is... | Меня зовут... | mi-nyáh za-vóot |
| • I'm... | Я— ... | yah |

## c. COURTESY

| **All the best!** | Всего хорошего! | fsi-vó kha-ró-shy-va |
|---|---|---|
| | Всего наилучшего! | fsi-vó na-i-lóoch-shy-va |
| **Best wishes!** | Наилучшие | na-i-lóoch-shy-ye |
| | пожелания! | pa-zhy-láh-ni-ya |
| **Bless you!** | Будь здоров! | boot' zda-róf |
| **(after a sneeze)** | *(fam. m)* | |
| | Будьте здоровы! | bóot-i zda-ró-vy |
| | *(pol. pl)* | |
| **Cheers!** | На здоровье! | na zda-róv'-ye |
| | Будем здоровы! | bóo-dim zda-ró-vy |

| | | |
|---|---|---|
| **Congratulations!** | Поздравляю тебя! *(fam)* | *paz-drav-lyáh-yu ti-byáh* |
| | Поздравляю вас! *(pol)* | *paz-drav-lyáh-yu vahs* |
| **Don't mention it!** | Не за что! | *nye za shta* |
| **Excuse me** | Извини (меня) *(fam)* | *iz-vi-ní (mi-nyáh)* |
| | Извините (меня) *(pol)* | *iz-vi-ní-ti (mi-nyáh)* |
| **Good luck!** | Желаю удачи! | *zhy-láh-yu u-dáh-chi* |
| **Happy New Year!** | С Новым годом! | *s nó-vym gó-dam* |
| **Have a good vacation** | Желаю хорошего отпуска | *zhy-láh-yu kha-ró-shy-va ót-pus-ka* |
| **Have a good break** | Желаю хороших каникул | *zhy-láh-yu kha-ró-shykh ka-ní-kul* |
| **Have a good trip** | Счастливого пути | *shchis-lí-va-va pu-tí* |
| **Have a happy birthday!** | С днём рождения! | *s dnyóm razh-dyé-ni-ya* |
| **Many thanks** | Спасибо большое | *spa-sí-ba bal'-shó-ye* |
| **May I (come in)?** | Можно? | *mózh-na* |
| | Можно войти? | *mózh-na vaj-tí* |
| **May I help you?** | Как я вам могу помочь? | *kahk yah vahm ma-góo pa-móch* |
| **Merry Christmas!** | Счастливого Рождества! | *shchis-lí-va-va razh-dist-váh* |
| **No** | Нет | *nyet* |
| **OK, good** | Хорошо | *kha-ra-shó* |
| **Please** | Пожалуйста | *pa-zháh-lus-ta* |
| **Thank you** | Спасибо | *spa-sí-ba* |
| • **Thanks, no** | Нет, спасибо | *net, spa-sí-ba* |
| • **Thanks, but it's not necessary** | Нет, спасибо, не надо | *net, spa-sí-ba, ni náh-da* |
| **Yes** | Да | *dah* |
| **You're welcome** | Пожалуйста | *pa-zháh-lus-ta* |

## 17. SPEAKING AND TALKING

### a. SPEECH ACTIVITIES AND TYPES

| | | |
|---|---|---|
| **advice** | совет | *sa-vyét* |
| • **advise** | посоветовать *(p)* | *pa-sa-vyé-ta-vat'* |
| | советовать *(i)* | *sa-vyé-ta-vat'* |
| **allude to** | сослаться на *(p)* | *sas-láh-tsa nah* |
| | ссылаться на *(i)* | *sy-láh-tsa nah* |
| | упомянуть *(p)* | *u-pa-mi-nóot'* |

| | | |
|---|---|---|
| analogy | аналогия | *a-na-ló-gi-ya* |
| announce | объявить *(p)* | *ab'-i-vit'* |
| | объявлять *(i)* | *ab'-iv-lyáht'* |
| • **announcement** | объявление | *ab'-iv-lyé-ni-ye* |
| answer, response | ответ | *at-vyét* |
| • **answer** | ответить *(p)* | *at-vyé-tit'* |
| | отвечать *(i)* | *at-vi-cháht'* |
| argue | спорить *(i)* | *spó-rit'* |
| | утвердить *(p)* | *ut-vir-dít'* |
| | утверждать *(i)* | *ut-vir-zhdáht'* |
| • **argument** | спор | *spor* |
| articulate (enunciate) | выговаривать *(i)* | *vy-ga-váh-ri-vat'* |
| articulate (express) | выразить *(p)* | *vý-ra-zit'* |
| | выражать *(i)* | *vy-ra-zháht'* |
| ask | спросить *(p)* | *spra-sít'* |
| | спрашивать *(i)* | *spráh-shy-vat'* |
| • **ask a question** | задать *(p)* вопрос | *za-dáht' vap-rós* |
| | задавать *(i)* | *za-da-váht'* |
| call (someone) | позвать *(p)* | *paz-váht'* |
| | звать *(i)* | *zvaht'* |
| call (on the phone) | позвонить *(p)* | *paz-va-nít'* |
| | звонить *(i)* | *zva-nít'* |
| change the subject | изменить *(p)* тему | *iz-mi-nít' tyé-mu* |
| | разговора | *raz-ga-vó-ra* |
| | изменять *(i)* | *iz-mi-nyáht'* |
| chat | болтать *(i)* | *bal-táht'* |
| | трепаться | *tri-páh-tsa* |
| | *(i, colloquial)* | |
| communicate | объясниться *(p)* | *ab'-is-ní-tsa* |
| | объясняться *(i)* | *ab'-is-nyáh-tsa* |
| • **communication** | связь *(f)* | *svyahs'* |
| | сообщение | *sa-ap-shchyé-ni-ye* |
| compare | сравнить *(p)* | *srav-nít'* |
| | сравнивать *(i)* | *sráhv-ni-vat'* |
| • **comparison** | сравнение | *srav-nyé-ni-ye* |
| conclude | заключить *(p)* | *zak-lyu-chít'* |
| | заключать *(i)* | *zak-lyu-cháht'* |
| • **conclusion** | заключение | *zak-lyu-chyé-ni-ye* |
| congratulate | поздравить *(p)* | *pazd-ráh-vit'* |
| | поздравлять *(i)* | *pazd-rav-lyáht'* |
| conversation | разговор | *raz-ga-vór* |
| debate, discuss | обсудить *(p)* | *ap-su-dít'* |
| | обсуждать *(i)* | *ap-suzh-dáht'* |
| | дискутировать *(i)* | *dis-ku-tí-ra-vat'* |
| declare | объявить *(p)* | *ab'-i-vít'* |
| | объявлять *(i)* | *ab'-iv-lyáht'* |

| | | |
|---|---|---|
| **deny** | отрицать *(i)* | *at-ri-tsáht'* |
| **describe** | описать *(p)* | *a-pi-sáht'* |
| | описывать *(i)* | *a-pí-sy-vat'* |
| • **description** | описание | *a-pi-sáh-ni-ye* |
| **dictate** | диктовать *(i)* | *dik-ta-váht'* |
| **digress** | отклониться *(p)* от темы | *at-kla-nít'-sy aht tyé-my* |
| | отклоняться *(i)* | *at-kla-nyáh-tsa* |
| **discussion** | обсуждение | *ap-suzh-dyé-ni-ye* |
| **emphasis** | ударение | *u-da-ryé-ni-ye* |
| • **emphasize** | подчеркнуть *(p)* | *pat-chirk-nóot'* |
| | подчёркивать *(i)* | *pat-chyór-ki-vat'* |
| **excuse (yourself)** | извиниться *(p)* | *iz-vi-ní-tsa* |
| | извиняться *(i)* | *iz-vi-nyáh-tsa* |
| • **excuse** | извинение | *iz-vi-nyé-ni-ye* |
| **explain** | объяснить *(p)* | *ab'-is-nít'* |
| | объяснять *(i)* | *ab'-is-nyáht'* |
| • **explanation** | объяснение | *ab'-is-nyé-ni-ye* |
| **express** | выразить *(p)* | *vý-ra-zit'* |
| | выражать *(i)* | *vy-ra-zháht'* |
| • **expression** | выражение | *vy-ra-zhéh-ni-ye* |
| **figurative speech** | фигуральная речь *(f)* | *fi-gu-ráhl'-na-ya ryech* |
| • **allegory** | аллегория | *a-li-gó-ri-ya* |
| • **literal** | буквальный *(adj)* | *buk-váhl'-nyj* |
| • **literally** | буквально *(adv)* | *buk-váhl'-na* |
| • **metaphor** | метафора | *mi-ta-fó-ra* |
| • **symbol** | символ | *sím-val* |
| **gossip** | сплетня *(sg)* | *splyét-nya* |
| | сплетни *(pl, coll)* | *splyét-ni* |
| • **gossip** | посплетничать *(p)* | *pasp-lyét-ni-chat'* |
| | сплетничать *(i)* | *splyét-ni-chat'* |
| **hesitation** | сомнение | *sam-nyé-ni-ye* |
| • **hesitate** | усомниться *(p)* | *u-sam-ní-tsa* |
| | сомневаться *(i)* | *sam-ni-váh-tsa* |
| **hint** | намёк | *na-myók* |
| • **hint** | намекнуть *(p)* | *na-mik-nóot'* |
| | намекать *(i)* | *na-mi-káht'* |
| **identify** | удостоверить *(p)* | *u-das-ta-vyé-rit'* |
| | удостоверять *(i)* | *u-das-ta-vi-ryáht'* |
| **indicate, point out** | указать *(p)* | *u-ka-záht'* |
| | указывать *(i)* | *u-káh-zy-vat'* |
| • **indication** | указание | *u-ka-záh-ni-ye* |
| | признак | *príz-nak* |
| **inform** | проинформировать *(p)* | *pra-in-far-mí-ra-vat'* |
| | информировать *(i)* | *in-far-mí-ra-vat'* |

| | | |
|---|---|---|
| **interrupt** | прервать *(p)* | *prir-váht'* |
| | прерывать *(i)* | *pri-ry-váht'* |
| • **interruption** | помеха | *pa-myé-kha* |
| | прерывание | *pri-ry-váh-ni-ye* |
| **invite** | пригласить *(p)* | *prig-la-sít'* |
| | приглашать *(i)* | *prig-la-sháht'* |
| **jest, joke** | шутка | *shóot-ka* |
| • **joke** | пошутить *(p)* | *pa-shu-tít'* |
| | шутить *(i)* | *shu-tít'* |
| **lecture** | лекция | *lyék-tsy-ya* |
| • **lecture** | читать *(i)* лекции *(pl)* | *chi-táht' lyék-tsy-i* |
| **me** | ложь *(f)* | *losh* |
| | враньё *(coll)* | *vran'-yó* |
| • **lie** | лгать *(i)* | *lgaht'* |
| | соврать *(p)* | *sa-vráht'* |
| | врать *(i)* | *vraht'* |
| **listen to** | слушать *(i)* | *slóo-shat'* |
| **mean** | значить *(i)* | *znáh-chit'* |
| • **meaning** | значение | *zna-chyé-ni-ye* |
| **mention** | упомянуть *(p)* | *u-pa-mi-nóot'* |
| | упоминать *(i)* | *u-pa-mi-náht'* |
| | заметить *(p)* | *za-myé-tit'* |
| | замечать *(i)* | *za-mi-cháht'* |
| **mumble, murmur** | бормотать *(i)* | *bar-ma-táht'* |
| **nag** | пилить *(i)* | *pi-lít'* |
| **offend** | обидеть *(p)* | *a-bí-dit'* |
| | обижать *(i)* | *a-bi-zháht'* |
| **oral** | устный | *óos-nyj* |
| **order** | приказ | *pri-káhs* |
| • **order** | приказать *(p)* | *pri-ka-záht'* |
| | приказывать *(i)* | *pri-káh-zy-vat'* |
| **outspoken** | прямой/ | *pri-mój/at-kra-vyé-nyj* |
| | откровенный | |
| **praise** | похвалить *(p)* | *pakh-va-lít'* |
| | хвалить *(i)* | *khva-lít'* |
| **pray** | молиться *(i)* | *ma-lí-tsa* |
| • **prayer** | молитва | *ma-lít-va* |
| **preach** | проповедовать *(i)* | *pra-pa-vyé-da-vat'* |
| • **sermon** | проповедь *(f)* | *pró-pa-vit'* |
| **promise** | обещание | *a-bi-shcháh-ni-ye* |
| • **promise** | обещать *(i)* | *a-bi-shcháht'* |
| **pronounce** | произнести *(p)* | *pra-iz-nis-tí* |
| | произносить *(i)* | *pra-iz-na-sít'* |
| • **pronunciation** | произношение | *pra-iz-na-shéh-ni-ye* |

| | | |
|---|---|---|
| **propose** | предложить *(p)* | *prid-la-zhýt'* |
| | предлагать *(i)* | *prid-la-gáht'* |
| **quiet** | тишина | *ti-shy-náh* |
| • **quiet** | тихий *(adj)* | *tí-khij* |
| • **quietly** | тихо *(adv)* | *tí-kha* |
| **recommend** | рекомендовать *(i)* | *ri-ka-min-da-váht'* |
| **relate (narrate)** | рассказать *(p)* | *ras-ka-záht'* |
| | рассказывать *(i)* | *ras-káh-zy-vat'* |
| **relate (connect)** | связать *(p)* | *svi-záht'* |
| | связывать *(i)* | *svyáh-zy-vat'* |
| **repeat** | повторить *(p)* | *paf-ta-rít'* |
| | повторять *(i)* | *paf-ta-ryáht'* |
| • **repetition** | повторение | *paf-ta-ryé-ni-ye* |
| **report** | доклад | *dak-láht* |
| • **report** | доложить *(p)* | *da-la-zhýt'* |
| | докладывать *(i)* | *dak-láh-dy-vat'* |
| **reproach** | упрёк | *up-ryók* |
| • **reproach** | упрекнуть *(p)* | *up-rik-nóot'* |
| | упрекать *(i)* | *up-ri-káht'* |
| **request** | просьба | *prós'-ba* |
| • **request** | попросить *(p)* | *pap-ra-sít'* |
| | просить *(i)* | *pra-sít'* |
| **rhetoric** | риторика | *ri-tó-ri-ka* |
| • **rhetorical** | риторический | *ri-ta-rí-chis-kij* |
| • **rhetorical question** | риторический вопрос | *ri-ta-rí-chis-kij vap-rós* |
| **rumor** | слух | *slookh* |
| **say, tell** | сказать *(p)* | *ska-záht'* |
| | говорить *(i)* | *ga-va-rít'* |
| **shout (ing)** | крик | *krik* |
| • **shout** | крикнуть *(p)* | *krík-nut'* |
| | кричать *(i)* | *kri-cháht'* |
| **shut up** | заткнуться *(p)* | *zatk-nóo-tsa* |
| | затыкаться *(i)* | *za-ty-káh-tsa* |
| **silence** | молчание | *mal-cháh-ni-ye* |
| • **silent** | молчаливый *(adj)* | *mal-cha-lí-vyj* |
| • **silently** | молчаливо *(adv)* | *mal-cha-lí-va* |
| **speak, talk** | говорить *(i)* | *ga-va-rít'* |
| | разговаривать *(i)* | *raz-ga-váh-ri-vat'* |
| • **speech, talk** | речь *(f)* | *ryech* |
| **state** | изложить *(p)* | *iz-la-zhýt'* |
| | излагать *(i)* | *iz-la-gáht'* |
| | заявить *(p)* | *za-i-vít'* |
| | заявлять *(i)* | *za-iv-lyáht'* |

| | | |
|---|---|---|
| • **statement** | изложение | *iz-la-zhéh-ni-ye* |
| | заявление | *za-iv-lyé-ni-ye* |
| **story** | рассказ | *ras-káhs* |
| • **tell a story** | рассказать *(p)* рассказ | *ras-ka-záht' ras-káhs* |
| **suggest** | предложить *(p)* | *prid-la-zhýt'* |
| | предлагать *(i)* | *prid-la-gáht'* |
| **summarize** | суммировать *(i)* | *su-mí-ra-vat'* |
| | резюмировать *(i)* | *ri-zyu-mí-ra-vat'* |
| • **summary** | сводка | *svót-ka* |
| | резюме | *ri-zyu-méh* |
| **swear (in court)** | клясться *(i)* | *klyáhs-tsa* |
| • **swear (profanity)** | ругнуться *(p)* | *rug-nóo-tsa* |
| | ругаться *(i)* | *ru-gáh-tsa* |
| **thank** | поблагодарить *(p)* | *pa-bla-ga-da-rít'* |
| | благодарить *(i)* | *bla-ga-da-rít'* |
| **threat** | угроза | *ug-ró-za* |
| • **threaten** | пригрозить *(p)* | *prig-ra-zít'* |
| | угрожать *(i)* | *ug-ra-zháht'* |
| **toast** | тост | *tost* |
| **translate** | перевести *(p)* | *pi-ri-vis-tí* |
| | переводить *(i)* | *pi-ri-va-dít'* |
| • **translation** | перевод | *pi-ri-vót* |
| **utter (a sound)** | издавать *(i)* (звук) | *iz-da-váht' (zvook)* |
| | произносить *(i)* | *pra-iz-na-sít'* |
| **vocabulary** | словарный запас | *sla-váhr-nyj za-páhs* |
| **warn** | предупредить *(p)* | *pri-dup-ri-dít'* |
| | предупреждать *(i)* | *pri-dup-rizh-dáht'* |
| • **warning** | предупреждение | *pri-dup-rizh-dyé-ni-ye* |
| **whisper** | шепнуть *(p)* | *shyp-nóot'* |
| | шептать *(i)* | *shyp-táht'* |
| **word** | слово | *sló-va* |
| **yawn** | зевок | *zi-vók* |
| • **yawn** | зевнуть *(p)* | *ziv-nóot'* |
| | зевать *(i)* | *zi-váht'* |
| **yell** | орать *(i)* | *a-ráht'* |

## b. USEFUL EXPRESSIONS

| | | |
|---|---|---|
| **Actually,** | Действительно, | *dist-ví-til'-na* |
| | На самом деле | *na sáh-mam dyé-li* |
| **As a matter of fact...** | На самом деле... | *na sáh-mam dyé-li* |
| | Фактически... | *fak-tí-chis-ki* |
| | Представьте себе... | *prit-stáhf'-ti si-byé* |
| **Briefly speaking...** | Короче говоря... | *ka-ró-chi ga-va-ryáh* |
| | Короче... | *ka-ró-chi* |
| **By the way...** | Кстати... | *kstáh-ti* |
| | Между прочим... | *myézh-du pró-chim* |

| | | |
|---|---|---|
| Clearly, | Очевидно, | a-chi-víd-na |
| | Ясное дело, | yáhs-na-ye dyé-la |
| ...correct? | ... правильно? | práh-vil'-na |
| ..., yes? | ..., да? | dah |
| Go ahead! | Давай! *(fam)* | da-váhj |
| I didn't understand | Я не понял(а) | ya ni pó-nil (pa-ni-láh) |
| How do you say ... in Russian? | Как сказать ... по-русски? | kahk ska-záht' pa-róos-ki |
| I'm sure that... | Я уверен(а), что... | yah u-vyé-rin(a) shto |
| | Я не сомневаюсь, что... | yah ni sam-ni-váh-yus' shto |
| Isn't it so? | Не так ли (это)? | ni tahk li (éh-ta) |
| It seems to me that... | Мне кажется, что... | mnye káh-zhy-tsa shto |
| It's not true! | Не правда (это)! | ni práhv-da (éh-ta) |
| It's obvious that... | Очевидно, что ... | a-chi-víd-na shto |
| It's true! | Это правда! | éh-ta práhv-da |
| Listen... | Слушай (те)... | slóo-shaj-ti |
| Now... | А теперь... | a ti-pyér' |
| | А сейчас... | a si-cháhs |
| ..., right? | ..., правда? | práhv-da |
| To sum up... | Подвести итог(и)... | pad-vis-tí i-tók(gi) |
| Uh-huh... | Ага... | a-káh |
| What was I talking about? | Что я начал(а) говорить? | shto yah náh-chal (na-chi-láh) ga-va-rít' |
| | О чём речь шла? | a chyom ryech shlah |
| Who knows...? | Кто знает... ? | kto znáh-yet |
| ...who knows | ... кто его знает | kto i-vó znáh-yet |

## 18. THE TELEPHONE

### a. TELEPHONES AND ACCESSORIES

| | | |
|---|---|---|
| answering machine | телефонная машина | ti-li-fó-na-ya ma-shý-na |
| battery | аккумуляторная батарея | a-ku-mu-lyáh-tar-na-ya ba-ta-ryé-ya |
| | батарейка | ba-ta-ryéj-ka |
| button (key) | кнопка | knóp-ka |
| cable | кабель *(m)* | káh-bil' |
| | трос | tros |
| cell phone | сотовый телефон | so-tó-vyj ti-li-fón |
| | сотовик | sa-tó-vik |
| | мобильный телефон | ma-bíl'-nyj ti-li-fón |
| | мобильник | ma-bíl'-nik |
| charge | зарядить *(p)* | za-rí-dit' |
| | заряжать *(i)* | zari-zháht' |
| contacts (list) | список контактов | spi-sak kan-táhk-tov |
| display | дисплей | dis-plyéj |

| | | |
|---|---|---|
| fax machine | телефакс | *ti-li-fáhks* |
| handset | телефонная трубка | *ti-li-fó-na-ya tróop-ka* |
| intercom | интерком | *in-tir-kóm* |
| memory | память | *pah-mit'* |
| memory card | карта памяти | *káhr-ta páh-mi-ti* |
| (phone) outlet | (телефонная) розетка | *(ti-li-fó-na-ya) ra-zyét-ka* |
| phone book | телефонная книга | *ti-li-fó-na-ya kní-ga* |
| phone camera | телефонная камера | *ti-li-fó-na-ya káh-mi-ra* |
| phone card | телефонная карточка | *ti-li-fó-na-ya káhr-tach-ka* |
| plug | штепсель *(m)* | *shtéhp-sil'* |
| | вилка | *víl-ka* |
| portable phone | переносной телефон | *pi-ri-nas-nój ti-li-fón* |
| receiver (microphone) | микрофон | *mik-ra-fón* |
| • earphone | телефон | *ti-li-fón* |
| ring tone(s) | рингтон | *ríng-tón* |
| | мелодии для сотового телефона | *mi-ló-di-ii dlyah só-ta-va-va ti-li-fó-na* |
| roaming | роуминг | *ró-u-mink* |
| | гостевая сеть | *gas-ti-váh-ya syet'* |
| telecommunication | телесвязь *(f)* | *ti-li-svyáhs'* |
| • telecommunica- tions satellite | спутник связи | *spóot-nik svyáh-zi* |
| telephone (set) | телефон | *ti-li-fón* |
| text messaging | обмен сообщениями | *ab-myén sa-ab-shchyé-ni-ya-mi* |
| voice mail | голосовая почта | *ga-la-sa-váh-ya póch-ta* |
| voice message | голосовое сообщение | *ga-la-sa-vó-ye sa-ab-shchyé-ni-ye* |

## b. USING THE TELEPHONE

| | | |
|---|---|---|
| area code | код города | *kot gó-ra-da* |
| collect call | звонить *(i)* за счёт вызываемого | *zva-nít' za shchyot vy-zy-váh-i-ma-va* |
| dial | набрать (номер) *(p)* | *nab-ráht' (nó-mir)* |
| | набирать (номер) *(i)* | *na-bi-ráht' (nó-mir)* |
| • direct dialing (self-dialing) | набирать самому | *na-bi-ráht' sa-ma-móo* |
| hang up | повесить трубку *(p)* | *pa-vyé-sit' tróop-ku* |
| | вешать трубку *(i)* | *vyé-shat' tróop-ku* |
| information | справочное (бюро) | *spráh-vach-na-ye (byu-ró)* |
| local call | местный разговор | *myés-nyj raz-ga-vór* |
| long-distance call | междугородный телефонный разговор | *mizh-du-ga-ród-nyj ti-li-fó-nyj raz-ga-vór* |
| • international | международный | *mizh-du-na-ród-nyj* |

| make a call | позвонить *(p)* | *paz-va-nít'* |
| | звонить *(i)* | *zva-nít'* |
| • Could you ask<br>... to the phone? | Позовите...,<br>пожалуйста | *pa-za-ví-ti pa-zháh-lus-ta* |
| • Hello! | Алло, Аллё | *a-ló, a-lyó* |
| | Да! | *dah* |
| • May I speak to... | Попросите... | *pap-ra-sí-ti* |
| | Можно (мне)<br>поговорить с... | *mózh-na (mnye) pa-ga-va-<br>rít' s* |
| | Нельзя ли<br>поговорить с... | *nil'-zyáh li pa-ga-va-rít' s* |
| • This is... | Говорит... | *ga-va-rít* |
| • With whom am I<br>speaking? | С кем я<br>разговариваю? | *s kyem yah raz-ga-váh-ri-<br>va-yu* |
| • Wrong number! | (Вы набрали)<br>неправильный<br>номер! | *(vy nab-ráh-li) ni-práh-<br>vil'-nyj nó-mir* |
| message | сообщение, записка | *sa-ap-shchyé-ni-ye,<br>za-pís-ka* |
| • Did he (she)<br>leave a message? | Он(а) просил(а)<br>что-нибудь<br>передать? | *on/a-náh pra-sí-l(a) shtó-<br>ni-but' pí-ri-dáht'* |
| • Is there any<br>message? | Что ему (ей)<br>передать? | *shto i-móo (yej)<br>pi-ri-dáht'* |
| operator | телефонист(ка) | *ti-li-fa-níst(ka)* |
| pick up the phone | взять *(p)* трубку | *vzyáht' tróop-ku* |
| | взять *(p)* телефон | *vzyákt' ti-li-fón* |
| • Pick up the<br>phone! | Возьми(те)<br>телефон! | *vaz'-mí(-ti) tt-lt-fón* |
| switchboard | коммутатор | *ka-mu-táh-tar* |
| telephone | телефон | *ti-li-fón* |
| telephone bill | телефонный счёт | *ti-li-fó-nyj shchyót* |
| telephone call | телефонный звонок | *ti-li-fó-nyj zva-nók* |
| | вызов к телефону | *vý-zaf k ti-li-fó-nu* |
| telephone line | телефонная линия | *ti-li-fó-na-ya lí-ni-ya* |
| • Hold the line<br>(wait a minute) | Подождите минуту | *pa-dazh-dí-ti mi-nóo-tu* |
| • The line is busy | Линия занята | *lí-ni-ya záh-ni-ta* |
| telephone number | телефонный номер | *ti-li-fó-nyj nó-mir* |
| telephone (ring)<br>someone | позвонить *(p)* | *paz-va-nít'* |
| | звонить *(i)* кому-либо | *zva-nít' ka-móo-li-ba* |

*19. E-MAILS AND LETTER WRITING*

## a. ELECTRONIC CORRESPONDENCE

| | | |
|---|---|---|
| **activate** | активировать *(i)* | *ak-ti-ví-ra-vat'* |
| **address (e-mail)** | адрес | *áhd-ris* |
| **address book** | адресная книжка | *áhd-ris-na-ya kнísh-ka* |
| **attachment** | приложение | *pri-la-zhé-ni-ye* |
| **cc** | скопировать *(p)* | *ska-pí-ra-vat'* |
| | копировать *(i)* | *ka-pí-ra-vat'* |
| **character** | символ | *sím-val* |
| **delete** | удалить *(p)* | *u-da-lít'* |
| | удалять *(i)* | *u-da-lyáht'* |
| **distribution list** | список рассылки | *spí-sak ras-sýl-ki* |
| **e-mail** | электронная почта | *i-lik-trón-a-ya póch-ta* |
| **e-mail message** | сообщение | *sa-ap-shchyé-ni-ye* |
| | письмо | *pis'-mó* |
| • **body** | тело сообщения | *tyé-la sa-ap-shchyé-ni-ya* |
| • **sender's name** | имя отправителя | *í-mya at-pra-ví-ti-lya* |
| • **sender's address** | адрес отправителя | *áhd-ris at-pra-ví-ti-lya* |
| **format** | формат | *far-máht* |
| **forward** | форвард | *fór-vard* |
| | переслать *(p)* | *pi-ris-láht'* |
| | пересылать *(i)* | *pi-ri-sy-láht'* |
| **mailbox (inbox)** | почтовый ящик | *pach-tó-vyj yáh-shchik* |
| **password** | пароль | *pa-ról'* |
| **receive** | получить *(p)* | *pa-lu-chít'* |
| | получать *(i)* | *pa-lu-cháht'* |
| **sender** | отправитель | *at-pra-ví-til'* |
| **server** | сервер | *syér-vir* |
| **service provider** | провайдер | *pra-váhj-dir* |
| **signature** | подпись | *pót-pis'* |
| **spam (e-mail)** | почтовый спам | *pach-tó-vyj spahm* |
| **subject (line)** | предмет письма | *prid-myét pis'-máh* |
| | тема | *tyé-ma* |

## b. FORMAL SALUTATIONS AND CLOSINGS

| | | |
|---|---|---|
| **Dear Sir** | Дорогой товарищ/ | *da-ra-gój ta-váh-rishch/* |
| | гражданин | *grazh-da-nín* |
| | Дорогой господин | *da-ra-gój gas-pa-dín* |
| | Уважаемый | *u-va-zháh-i-myj* |

| | | |
|---|---|---|
| **Dear Madam** | Дорогая гражданка | *da-ra-gáh-ya grazh-dáhn-ka* |
| | Дорогая госпожа | *da-ra-gáh-ya gas-pa-zháh* |
| **Gentlemen** | Товарищи | *ta-váh-ri-shchi* |
| | Граждане | *gráhzh-da-ni* |
| **Yours sincerely** | Искренне твой *(fam)* | *ísk-ri-nye tvoj* |
| | (Ваш) *(pol)* | *(vahsh)* |
| **Yours truly** | Преданный тебе *(fam)* | *pryé-da-nyj ti-byé* |
| | (Вам) *(pol)* | *(vahm)* |

## c. CASUAL SALUTATIONS AND CLOSINGS

| | | |
|---|---|---|
| **Dear** | Дорогой *(m)* | *da-ra-gój* |
| | Дорогая *(f)* | *da-ra-gáh-ya* |
| • **My dear** | Мой дорогой | *moj da-ra-gój* |
| | Моя дорогая | *ma-yáh da-ra-gáh-ya* |
| | Мои дорогие | *ma-í da-ra-gí-ye* |
| **Dearest** | Дражайший *(m)* | *dra-zháhj-shyj* |
| | Дражайшая *(f)* | *dra-zháhj-sha-ya* |
| **Yours** | Твой (-я) *(fam)* | *tvoj, tva-yáh* |
| | Ваш (-а) *(pol)* | *vahsh, váh-sha* |
| **Kisses** | Целую | *tsy-lóo-yu* |
| • **Kisses to all** | Целую всех | *tsy-lóo-yu fsyekh* |
| **Hugs** | Обнимаю | *ab-ni-máh-yu* |
| • **Hugs to all** | Обнимаю всех | *ab-ni-máh-yu fsyekh* |
| **With best wishes,** | С наилучшими пожеланиями | *s na-i-lóot-shy-mi pa-zhy-láh-ni-yah-mi* |
| **With love,** | С любовью | *s lyu-bóv'-yu* |

## d. PARTS OF A LETTER AND PUNCTUATION

| | | |
|---|---|---|
| **body (text)** | текст | *tyekst* |
| **closing** | заключение | *zak-lyu-chyé-ni-ye* |
| **date** | дата | *dáh-ta* |
| **heading (address)** | обращение | *ab-ra-shchyé-ni-ye* |
| **punctuation** | знаки препинания | *znáh-ki pri-pi-náh-ni-ya* |
| • **asterisk** | звёздочка | *zvyóz-dach-ka* |
| • **bracket** | скобка | *skóp-ka* |
| • **capital letter** | большая буква | *bal'-sháh-ya bóok-va* |
| • **colon** | двоеточие | *dva-i-tó-chi-ye* |
| • **comma** | запятая | *za-pi-táh-ya* |
| • **exclamation mark** | восклицательный знак | *vask-li-tsáh-til'-nyj znahk* |

| | | |
|---|---|---|
| • **hyphen** | чёрточка | *chyór-tach-ka* |
| • **italics** | курсив | *kur-síf* |
| | курсивный шрифт | *kur-sív-nyj shrift* |
| • **parenthesis** | круглая скобка | *króog-la-ya skóp-ka* |
| • **question mark** | вопросительный знак | *vap-ra-sí-til'-nyj znahk* |
| • **quotation mark** | кавычка | *ka-vých-ka* |
| • **semicolon** | точка с запятой | *tóch-ka s za-pi-tój* |
| • **small letter** | маленькая буква | *máh-lin'-ka-ya bóok-va* |
| • **square bracket** | квадратная скобка | *kvad-ráht-na-ya skóp-ka* |
| • **underline** | подчеркнуть *(p)* | *pat-chirk-nóot'* |
| | подчёркивать *(i)* | *pat-chyór-ki-vat'* |
| **salutation** | приветствие | *pri-vyét-stvi-ye* |
| **signature** | подпись *(f)* | *pót-pis'* |
| • **sign** | подписать *(p)* | *pat-pi-sáht'* |
| | подписывать *(i)* | *pat-pí-sy-vat'* |
| **text** | текст | *tyekst* |
| • **abbreviation** | сокращение | *sak-ra-shchyé-ni-ye* |
| • **begin a new paragraph** | начать *(p)* с красной строки | *na-cháht' s kráhs-naj stra-kí* |
| | начинать *(i)* | *na-chi-náht'* |
| • **letter (of the alphabet)** | буква алфавита | *bóok-va al-fa-ví-ta* |
| • **line** | черта/линия | *chir-táh/lí-ni-ya* |
| **margin(s)** | поле(-я) | *pó-lye (pa-lyáh)* |
| **P.S.** | пост-скриптум | *past-skríp-tum* |
| **paragraph** | абзац | *ab-záhts* |
| **phrase** | фраза/оборот | *fráh-za/a-ba-rót* |
| **sentence** | предложение | *prid-la-zhéh-ni-ye* |
| **spelling** | орфография | *ar-fa-gráh-fi-ya* |
| | правописание | *pra-va-pi-sáh-ni-ye* |
| **word** | слово | *sló-va* |

*FOCUS: Letter*

20-ое апреля 2008
г. Москва
**Дорогая Катя!**
    Мы доехали благополучно и устроились в гостинице.
Москва — огромный город с множеством разных
достопримечательностей.
    Передай привет Пете и Коле.
    Целую всех.
    Оля,

## e. WRITING MATERIALS AND ACCESSORIES

| | | |
|---|---|---|
| adhesive tape | клейкая лента | *klyéj-ka-ya lyén-ta* |
| clip | скрепка | *skryép-ka* |
| envelope | конверт | *kan-vyért* |
| eraser | ластик | *láhs-rik* |
| | резинка | *ri-zín-ka* |
| glue | клей | *klyej* |
| ink | чернила *(pl)* | *chir-ní-la* |
| letter | письмо | *pis'-mó* |
| marker | фломастер | *fla-máhs-ter* |
| pad | блокнот | *blak-nót* |
| page | страница | *stra-ní-tsa* |
| paper | бумага | *bu-máh-ga* |
| pea | ручка | *róoch-ka* |
| • ballpoint pen | шариковая ручка | *sháh-ri-ka-va-ya róoch-ka* |
| pencil | карандаш | *ka-ran-dáhsh* |
| ruler | линейка | *li-nyéj-ka* |
| scissors | ножницы *(pl)* | *nózh-ni-tsy* |
| staple | скобка | *skóp-ka* |
| • stapler | стейплер | *stéhjp-lir* |
| string | верёвка | *vi-ryóf-ka* |
| | бечёвка | *bi-chyóf'-ka* |
| typewriter | пишущая | *pí-shu-shchi-ya* |
| | машинка | *ma-shýn-ka* |
| • carriage | каретка | *ka-ryét-ka* |
| • key | клавиша | *kláh-vi-sha* |
| • keyboard | клавиатура | *kla-vi-a-tóo-ra* |
| • ribbon | лента для машинки | *lyén-ta dlya ma-shýn-ki* |
| • space bar | промежуточная | *pra-mi-zhóo-tach-na-ya* |
| | клавиша | *kláh-vi-sha* |
| • tab | табулятор | *ta-bu-lyáh-tar* |
| word processor | текстовой редактор | *tiks-ta-vój ri-dáhk-tar* |

## f. AT THE POST OFFICE

| | | |
|---|---|---|
| abroad | заграницу | *zag-ra-ní-tsu* |
| address | адрес | *áhd-ris* |
| • return address | возвратный адрес | *vaz-vráht-nyj áhd-ris* |
| addressee | адресат | *ad-ri-sáht* |
| airmail | авиапочта | *a-vi-a-póch-ta* |
| business letter | деловое письмо | *di-la-vó-ve pis'-mó* |
| clerk | служащий (-ая) | *slóo-zha-shchij (-a-ya)* |
| correspondence | переписка | *pi-ri-pís-ka* |
| | письма *(pl)* | *pís'-ma* |

| courier | курьер | *kur'-yér* |
|---|---|---|
| envelope | конверт | *kan-vyért* |
| letter carrier, mailman | почтальон | *pach-tal'-yón* |
| mail | почта | *póch-ta* |
| • mail a letter | послать письмо *(p)* | *pas-láht' pis'-mó* |
| | посылать письмо *(i)* | *pa-sy-táht' pis'-mó* |
| • mail delivery | доставка почты | *das-táhf-ka póch-ty* |
| mailbox | почтовый ящик | *pach-tó-vyj yáh-shchik* |
| note | записка | *za-pís-ka* |
| package | посылка | *pa-sýl-ka* |
| post office | почта, почтовое отделение | *póch-ta, pach-tó-va-ye at-di-lyé-ni-ye* |
| postage | стоимость *(f)* пересылки | *stó-i-mast' pi-ri-sýl-ki* |
| | почтовые расходы | *pach-tó-vy-ye ras-khó-dy* |
| postal rate | почтовый тариф | *pach-tó-vyj ta-ríf* |
| postcard | открытка | *at-krýt-ka* |
| printed matter | бандероль *(f)* | *ban-dy-ról'* |
| registered letter | заказное письмо | *za-kaz-nó-ye pis'-mó* |
| receive | получить *(p)* | *pa-lu-chít'* |
| | получать *(i)* | *pa-lu-cháht'* |
| reply | ответ(-ное письмо) | *at-vyét (-na-ye pis'-mó)* |
| • reply | ответить *(p)* | *at-vyé-tit'* |
| | отвечать *(i)* | *at-vi-cháht'* |
| send | отправить *(p)* | *at-práh-vit'* |
| | отправлять *(i)* | *at-prav-lyáht'* |
| | послать *(p)* | *pas-láht'* |
| | посылать *(i)* | *pa-sy-láht'* |
| sender | отправитель *(m&f)* | *at-pra-ví-til'* |
| special delivery | спешная почта | *spyésh-na-ya póch-ta* |
| stamp | марка | *máhr-ka* |

*FOCUS: Form of an Envelope Address*

> **Россия**
> **г. Москва**
> **ул. Шевченко, дом 5, кв. 52**
> **Николаеву Павлу Михайловичу**

*Remarks:* The address begins with the name of the country/region, followed by the city, street, house number, apartment number, and, finally, the name of the addressee.

| | | |
|---|---|---|
| **wait for, expect** | ждать *(i)* | *zhdaht'* |
| | ожидать | *a-zhy-dáht'* |
| | (поджидать) *(i)* | *(pad-zhy-dáht')* |
| **write** | писать *(i)* | *pi-sáht'* |
| **zip code** | почтовый индекс | *pach-tó-vyj ín-dyks* |

## 20. THE MEDIA

### a. PRINT MEDIA

| | | |
|---|---|---|
| **appendix (supplement)** | приложение | *pri-la-zhéh-ni-ye* |
| **atlas** | атлас | *áht-las* |
| **author** | автор *(m&f)* | *áhf-tar* |
| **book** | книга | *kní-ga* |
| **comics** | комиксы | *kó-mik-sy* |
| **cover** | обложка | *ab-lósh-ka* |
| **fiction** | беллетристика | *bi-lit-rís-ti-ka* |
| | художественная литература | *khu-dó-zhyst-vi-na-ya li-ti-ra-tóo-ra* |
| • **nonfiction** | документальная литература | *da-ku-min-táhl'-na-ya li-ti-ra-tóo-ra* |
| **index** | указатель *(m)* | *u-ka-záh-til'* |
| **library** | библиотека | *bib-li-a-tyé-ka* |
| • **reading hall** | читальня | *chi-táhl'-nya* |
| **magazine** | журнал | *zhur-náhl* |
| **newspaper** | газета | *ga-zyé-ta* |
| • **advertisement** | объявление | *ab'-iv-lyé-ni-ye* |
| • **article** | статья | *stat'-yáh* |
| • **criticism** | критика | *krí-ti-ka* |
| • **editor** | редактор *(m&f)* | *ri-dáhk-tar* |
| • **editorial** | редакционная статья | *ri-dak-tsy-ó-na-ya stat'-yáh* |
| • **front page** | первая страница | *pyér-va-ya stra-ní-tsa* |
| • **headline** | заголовок *(sg)* | *za-ga-ló-vak* |
| | заголовки *(pl)* | *za-ga-lóf-ki* |
| • **illustration** | иллюстрация | *i-lyust-ráh-tsy-ya* |
| | картинка | *kar-tín-ka* |
| • **interview** | интервью | *in-tyr-v'yú* |
| • **journalist** | журналист (-ка) | *zhur-na-líst (-ka)* |
| • **news** | новость *(sg, f)* | *nó-vast'* |
| • **photo** | фотография | *fa-ta-gráh-fi-ya* |
| • **reader** | читатель *(m)* (-ница) | *chi-táh-til' (-ni-tsa)* |
| • **reporter** | корреспондент (-ка) | *ka-ris-pan-dyént (-ka)* |
| • **review** | обозрение | *a-baz-ryé-ni-ye* |
| **note** | заметка | *za-myét-ka* |

| | | |
|---|---|---|
| • **footnote** | сноска | *snós-ka* |
| **novel** | роман | *ra-máhn* |
| • **adventure** | приключение | *prik-lyu-chyé-ni-ye* |
| • **best-seller** | бест-селлер | *byest-syé-lyer* |
| • **mystery** | детективный роман | *dy-tyk-tív-nyj ra-máhn* |
| • **plot** | сюжет | *syu-zhéht* |
| • **romance** | роман | *ra-máhn* |
| • **science fiction** | научная фантастика | *na-óoch-na-ya fan-táhs-ti-ka* |
| **page** | страница | *stra-ní-tsa* |
| **pamphlet, brochure** | брошюра | *bra-shóo-ra* |
| **play** | пьеса | *p'yé-sa* |
| • **comedy** | комедия | *ka-myé-di-ya* |
| • **drama** | драма | *dráh-ma* |
| • **tragedy** | трагедия | *tra-gyé-di-ya* |
| **poem (short)** | стихотворение | *sti-khat-va-ryé-ni-ye* |
| **poem (long)** | поэма | *pa-éh-ma* |
| **poetry** | поэзия | *pa-éh-zi-ya* |
| **print media (printed word)** | печатное слово | *pi-cháht-na-ye sló-va* |
| • **print** | шрифт | *shrift* |
| • **printing** | печатание | *pi-cháh-ta-ni-ye* |
| **publish** | опубликовать *(p)* | *a-pub-li-ka-váht'* |
| | публиковать *(i)* | *pub-li-ka-váht'* |
| • **publisher** | издатель *(m)* (-ница) | *iz-dáh-til' (-ni-tsa)* |
| **read** | читать *(i)* | *chi-táht'* |
| **reference book** | справочник | *spráh-vach-nik* |
| • **definition** | определение | *ap-ri-di-lyé-ni-ye* |
| • **dictionary** | словарь *(m)* | *sla-váhr'* |
| • **encyclopedia** | энциклопедия | *yn-tsy-kla-pyé-di-ya* |
| **short story** | короткий рассказ | *ka-rót-kij ras-káhs* |
| **title** | заглавие | *zag-láh-vi-ye* |
| | заголовок | *za-ga-ló-vak* |
| **turn pages** | переворачивать *(i)* страницы | *pi-ri-va-ráh-chi-vat' stra-ní-tsy* |

## b. ELECTRONIC MEDIA (COMPUTERS)

| | | |
|---|---|---|
| **battery** | аккумуляторная батарея | *a-ku-mu-lyáh-tar-na-ya ba-ta-ryé-ya* |
| | батарейка | *ba-ta-ryéj-ka* |
| **byte** | байт | *bahjt* |
| **browser** | браузер | *bráh-u-zir* |
| **browsing** *(n)* | обзор | *ab-zór* |
| **buffer** | буфер | *bóo-fir* |
| **button (key)** | кнопка | *knóp-ka* |
| **charge** | зарядить *(p)* | *za-ri-dít'* |
| | заряжать *(i)* | *za-ri-zháht'* |

| | | |
|---|---|---|
| click *(n)* | щелчок | shchil-chók |
| click *(v)* | щёлкнуть *(p)* | shchyólk-nut' |
| | щёлкать *(i)* | shchyól-kat' |
| • double-click *(n)* | двойной щелчок | dvaj-nój shchil-chók |
| • double-click *(v)* | кликнуть/щёлкнуть | klík-nut' / shchyólk-nut' |
| | два раза | dvah ráh-za |
| compatible | совместимый | sav-mis-tí-myj |
| computer | компьютер | kamp'-yú-tar |
| | вычислительная | vy-chis-lí-til'-na-ya |
| | машина | ma-shý-na |
| • computer language | компьютерный язык | kamp'-yú-tar-nyj y-zýk |
| • computer science | кибернетика | ki-bir-néh-ti-ka |
| contacts | список контактов | spí-sak kan-táhk-taf |
| cookie | куки | koó-ki |
| copy | скопировать *(p)* | ska-pí-ra-vat' |
| | копировать *(i)* | ka-pí-ra-vat' |
| • copy a file | скопировать *(p)* файл | ska-pí-ra-vat' fahjl |
| cursor | курсор | kóor-sar |
| database | база данных | báh-za dáh-nykh |
| data | данные | dáhn-y-ye |
| • database | база данных | báh-za dáh-nykh |
| • data processing | обработка данных | ab-ra-bót-ka dáh-nykh |
| dialogue | диалог | di-a-lók |
| directory | директория | di-rik-tó-ri-ya |
| disk | диск | disk |
| drive *(n)* | дисковод | dis-ka-vót |
| drive (disk) | драйв | drahjf |
| document | документ | da-ku-myént |
| edit *(v)* | отредактировать *(p)* | at-ri-dak-tí-ra-vat' |
| | редактировать *(i)* | ri-dak-tí-ra-vat' |
| error | ошибка | a-shýp-ka |
| file *(n)* | файл | fahjl |
| | папка | páhp-ka |
| • copy *(v)* | скопировать *(p)* | ska-pí-ra-vat' |
| | копировать *(i)* | ka-pí-ra-vat' |
| • create *(v)* a file | создать *(p)* файл | saz-dáht' fahjl |
| | создавать *(i)* | saz-da-váht' |
| • creating files *(pl)* | создание файлов *(pl)* | saz-dáh-ni-ye fáhjl-of |
| • delete | удалить *(p)* | u-da-lít' |
| | удалять *(i)* | u-da-lyáht' |
| • empty *(adj)* file | пустая папка | pus-táh-ya páhp-ka |
| • move *(v)* | переместить *(p)* | pi-ri-mis-tít' |
| | перемещать *(i)* | pi-ri-mi-shchyáht' |
| • open *(v)* | открыть *(p)* | at-krýt' |
| | открывать *(i)* | at-kry-váht' |
| • rename | переименовать *(p)* | pi-ri-mi-na-váht' |
| | переименовывать *(i)* | pi-ri-mi-nó-vy-vat' |
| flash drive | флэш-брелок | fléhsh-bri-lók |
| flowchart | диаграмма, схема | di-a-gráh-ma, skhyé-ma |

| | | |
|---|---|---|
| **font** | шрифт | *shrift* |
| • **bold face** | жирный шрифт | *zhýr-nyj shrift* |
| • **italics** | курсив | *kur-síf* |
| **function** | функция | *fóonk-tsy-ya* |
| **hard drive** | жесткий диск | *zhóst-kij disk* |
| **hardware** | техническое | *tich-ní-chis-ka-ye* |
| | обеспечение | *a-bis-pi-chyé-ni-ye* |
| **icon** | картинка | *kar-tín-ka* |
| **insert** | вставить *(p)* | *fstáh-vit'* |
| | вставлять *(i)* | *fstav-lyáht'* |
| • **insert a disk** | вставлять дискету | *fstav-lyáht' dis-kyé-tu* |
| **integrated circuit** | микросхема | *mik-ra-skhyé-ma* |
| **interface** | интерфейс | *in-tyr-féhjs* |
| **key** | клавиша | *kláh-vi-sha* |
| **keyboard** | клавиатура | *kla-vi-a-tóo-ra* |
| **laptop** | лаптоп | *léhp-tóp* |
| **mainframe** | мейнфрейм | *myéjn-fryéjm* |
| **memory** | запоминающее | *za-pa-mi-náh-yu-shchi-ye* |
| | устройство | *ust-rójst-va* |
| | память *(f)* | *páh-mit'* |
| • **random access** | оперативное | *a-pi-ra-tív-na-ye* |
| **memory** | запоминающее | *za-pa-mi-náh-yu-* |
| | устройство | *shchi-ye ust-rójst-va* |
| | (ОЗУ) | *(AZOO)* |
| | память *(f)* | *páh-mit'* |
| **menu** | меню | *mi-nyóo* |
| **microcomputer** | микрокомпьютер | *mik-ra-kamp'-yú-tar* |
| **modem** | модем | *mó-dym* |
| **monitor** | монитор | *ma-ni-tór* |
| | экран | *ik-rán* |
| **mouse** | мышь *(f)* | *mysh* |
| **multimedia** | мультимедия | *móol'-ti-mí-di-ya* |
| • **multimedia file** | мультимедийный файл | *mul'-ti-mi-díj-nyj fahjl* |
| **network** | сеть | *syet'* |
| • **local network** | местная сеть | *myést-na-ya syet'* |
| | локальная | *la-káhl'-na-ya* |
| • **network** | сетевое соединение | *si-ti-vó-ye sa-i-di-* |
| **connection** | | *nyé-ni-ye* |
| **next** | следующее *(adj) (n)* | *slyé-du-yu-shchi-ye* |
| **notebook** | ноутбук | *nó-ut-buk* |
| | книжка-раскладушка | *knísh-ka-ras-kla-dóosh-ka* |
| **open a browser** | открыть *(p)* браузер | *at-krýt' bráh-u-zir* |
| | открывать *(i)* | *at-kry-váht'* |
| **open a file** | открыть *(p)* файл | *at-krýt' fahjl* |
| | открывать *(i)* | *at-kry-váht'* |
| **open a program** | открыть *(p)* программу | *at-krýt' prag-ráh-mu* |
| | открывать *(i)* | *at-kry-váht'* |
| | войти *(p)* в программу | *vaj-tí f prag-ráh-mu* |
| | идти *(i)* | *it-tí* |

| | | |
|---|---|---|
| **opening** *(n)* | открытие | *at-krý-ti-ye* |
| **operating system** | оперативная система | *a-pi-ra-tív-na-ya* |
| | | *sis-tyé-ma* |
| **option** | опция | *óp-tsy-ya* |
| **output** | аутпут | *áh-ut-put* |
| **parallel port** | параллельный порт | *pa-ra-lyél'-nyj port* |
| **peripherals** | периферические | *pi-ri-fi-rí-chis-ki-ye* |
| | устройства | *ust-rójst-va* |
| **permissions** *(pl)* | права *(pl)* доступа | *pra-váh dós-tu-pa* |
| **personal computer** | персональный | *pir-sa-náhl'-nyj* |
| | компьютер | *kamp'-yú-tar* |
| **print** *(n)* | распечатка *(n)* | *ras-pi-cháht-ka* |
| **print** *(v)* | напечатать *(p)* | *na-pi-cháh-tat'* |
| | печатать *(i)* | *pi-cháh-tat'* |
| | вывести *(p)* на печать | *vý-vis-ti na pi-cháht'* |
| | выводить *(i)* | *vy-va-dít'* |
| **printer** | принтер | *prín-tyr* |
| | печатник | *pi-cháht-nik* |
| • **black-and-white** | черный-белый *(adj) (m)* | *chór-nyj-byé-lyj* |
| • **color** | цветной *(adj) (m)* | *tsvit-nój* |
| • **inkjet** | струйный *(adj) (m)* | *stróoj-nyj* |
| | чернильный *(adj) (m)* | *chir-níl'-nyj* |
| • **laser** | лазерный *(adj) (m)* | *láh-zir-nyj* |
| **printer cartridge** | картридж | *káhrt-ridzh* |
| **printing** *(n)* | вывод на печать | *vý-vat na pi-cháht'* |
| **processor** | процессор | *pra-tséh-sar* |
| **program (software)** | программа | *prag-ráh-ma* |
| | прога *(slang)* | *pró-ga* |
| • **programmer** | программист | *prag-ra-míst* |
| • **programming** | программирование | *prag-ra-mí-ra-va-ni-ye* |
| • **programming language** | машинный язык | *ma-shý-nyj i-zýk* |
| **properties** *(pl)* | свойства *(pl)* | *svójst-va* |
| **save** | сохранить *(p)* | *sakh-ra-nít'* |
| | сохранять *(i)* | *sakh-ra-nyáht'* |
| **save as** | сохранить *(p)* как | *sakh-ra-nít' kahk* |
| | сохранять *(i)* | *sakh-ra-nyáht'* |
| **scanner** | сканнер | *skáh-nir* |
| **screen, monitor** | экран | *yk-ráhn* |
| **scroll down** | сместить *(p)* | *smis-tít' koór-sar vnis* |
| | курсор вниз | |
| | смещать *(i)* | *smi-shchyáht'* |
| **scroll up** | сместить *(p)* | *smis-tít' koór-sar* |
| | курсор вверх | *vvyerkh* |
| | смещать *(i)* | *smi-shchyáht* |
| **screen, monitor** | экран | *yk-ráhn* |
| **software** | математическое | *ma-ti-ma-tí-chis-ka-ye* |
| | обеспечение | *a-bis-pi-chyé-ni-ye* |

| | | |
|---|---|---|
| **speakers** *(pl)* | колонки *(pl)* | *ka-lón-ki* |
| | спикеры *(pl)* | *spí-ki-ry* |
| **terminal** | терминал | *tir-mi-náhl* |
| **turn on (a computer)** | включить *(p)* | *fklyu-chít'* |
| | (компьютер) | *(kamp'-yu-tar)* |
| | включать *(i)* | *fklyu-cháht'* |
| **turn off (a computer)** | выключить *(p)* | *vý-klyu-chit'* |
| | (компьютер) | *(kamp'-yú-tar)* |
| | выключать *(i)* | *vy-klyu-cháht'* |
| **videogame** | видио-игра | *ví-di-a-ig-ráh* |
| **virus** | вирус | *ví-rus* |
| **warning** | предупреждение | *pri-dup-rizh-dyé-ni-ye* |
| **window** | окно | *ak-nó* |
| **word processing** | обработка текста | *ab-ra-bót-ka tyéks-ta* |
| • **word processor** | текстовой редактор | *tiks-ta-vój ri-dáhk-tar* |

*Expressions*

| | | |
|---|---|---|
| **The computer is hanging/ crashed.** | = | Компьютер зависает/завис/полетел. |
| **The computer program is hanging.** | = | Программа зависла/повисла. |
| **The disk is bad (is dead).** | = | Дискета/дискетка сдохла/полетела. |

## c. COLLOQUIAL EXPRESSIONS AND COMPUTER-RELATED TERMS

| | | |
|---|---|---|
| **Runglish and Runglish language** | = | Рунглиш, рунглийский язык |
| **Attachment, to attach** | = | Аттачмент, приаттачить |
| **FAQ (Frequently Asked Questions)** | = | ФЭК (also ФАК) |
| | | ЧаВо (частые вопросы) |
| **Host, hosting (on the Internet)** | = | Хост, хостинг |
| **ICQ (I seek you)** | = | Аська, ася |
| **IMHO** | = | ИМХО |
| **Internet forum** | = | Форум |
| **Mail and e-mail** | = | Мыло, майл, мейл, е-мейл, е-майл |
| **Subj (Subject in e-mail)** | = | Сабж |
| **Patch** | = | Патч, заплатка |
| **Upgrade** *(v)* | = | Апгрейдить *(p)* |
| **Off-topic** | = | Оффтопик |
| **Shareware** | = | Шареварная *(adj)* |
| **Antivirus** | = | Антивирус |
| **Firewall** | = | Файрвол |

## d. THE WORLDWIDE WEB AND THE INTERNET

| | | |
|---|---|---|
| **animation** | анимация | *a-ni-máh-tsy-ya* |
| • **animated gif** | гиф-анимация | *gíf-a-ni-máh-tsy-ya* |
| **blog** | блог | *blok* |
| **browser** | браузер | *bráh-u-zir* |
| **chat** | чат | *chyet* |
| | беседа | *bi-syé-da* |
| **chat room** | комната для бесед | *kóm-na-ta dlyah bi-syét* |
| **domain** | домен | *da-myén* |
| **download** *(v)* | скачать *(p)* | *ska-cháht'* |
| | скачивать *(i)* | *skáh-chi-vat'* |
| **forum** | форум | *fo-rum* |
| • **web forum** | веб-форум | *vyép-fó-rum* |
| **HTML** | язык HTML | *i-zyk kha-ta-am-éhl* |
| | эйч-ти-эм-эл | *éhjch-ti-am-éhl* |
| | хэтээмэл | *kha-ta-am-éhl* |
| **home page** | домашняя страница | *da-máhsh-ni-ya stra-ní-tsa* |
| **Internet** | Интернет | *in-tyr-nyét* |
| • **I-net** | И-Нет | *i-nyét* |
| • **connect to the** | соединиться *(p)* | *sa-i-di-ní-tsa s* |
| **Internet** | с Интернет | *in-tyr-nyét* |
| | соединяться *(i)* | *sa-i-di-nyáh-tsa* |
| • **Internet auction** | Интернет-аукцион | *in-tyr-nyét-a-uk-tsy-ón* |
| • **Internet browser** | Интернет-броузер | *in-tyr-nyét-bráh-u-zir* |
| • **Internet service provider (ISP)** | Интернет-провайдер | *in-tyr-nyét-pra-váhj-dyr* |

| | | |
|---|---|---|
| • **Internet user** | пользователь | *pól'-za-va-til'* |
| | интернета | *in-tyr-nyé-ta* |
| **link** | веб-ссылка | *vyép-ssýl-ka* |
| **messenger** | мессенджер | *myé-sin-dzhyr* |
| **moderator** | модератор | *ma-di-ráh-tar* |
| **online** | он-лайн | *an-láhjn* |
| **portal** | портал | *pór-tal* |
| **properties** *(pl)* | свойства *(pl)* | *svójst-va* |
| **Ru-net** | рунет | *roó-nyet* |
| **(Russian Internet)** | | |
| **search** *(n)* – | поиск | *pó-isk* |
| **search** *(v)* | поискать *(p)* | *pa-is-káht'* |
| | искать *(i)* | *is-káht'* |
| **search engine** | поисковая система | *pa-is-kó-va-ya sis-tyé-ma* |
| **security** | безопасность | *bi-za-páhs-nast'* |
| **upload** | поместить *(p)* на сервер | *pa-mis-tít' na syér-vir* |
| | помещать *(i)* | *pa-mi-shcháht'* |
| | загрузить *(p)* файл | *zag-ru-zít' fahjl* |
| | загружать *(i)* | *zag-ru-zháht'* |
| **URL** | урл (also уэрэл, урла) | *oórl (also u-e-réhl,* |
| | (spelled *url*) | *oór-la)* |
| **virtual reality** | виртуальная | *vir-tu-áhl'-na-ya* |
| | реальность | *ri-áhl'-nast'* |
| **virtual space** | виртуальное | *vir-tu-áhl'-na-ye* |
| | пространство | *prast-ráhn-stva* |
| **visit** *(v)* (go to) | посетить *(p)* веб-сайт | *pa-si-tít' vyép-sáhjt* |
| **(a website)** | посещать *(i)* | *pa-si-shchyáht'* |
| **web designer** | веб-дизайнер | *vyép-di-záhj-nir* |
| **web link** | веб-ссылка | *vyép-ssýl-ka* |
| **web-page** | страница | *stra-ní-tsa* |
| • **interactive** | интерактивная | *in-tyr-ak-tív-na-ya* |
| **web-page** | страница | *stra-ní-tsa* |
| **website** | веб-сайт | *vyép-sáhjt* |
| | сайт | *sahjt* |
| | веб-узел | *vyép-oó-zil* |
| **website visitor** | посетитель узла | *pa-si-ti-tíl' uz-láh* |
| **wikipedia** | википедия | *vi-ki-pí-di-ya* |
| • **wiki** | вики | *ví-ki* |
| **world-wide web** | всемирная паутина | *vsi-mír-na-ya pa-u-tí-na* |
| **www(. -dot)** | вэ-вэ-вэ /три вэ | *véh-véh-véh/tri véh* |
| | (-точка) | *(-tóch-ka)* |
| | три дабл ю | *trí dáhbl yu* |

## e. ELECTRONIC MEDIA (ENTERTAINMENT)

| | | |
|---|---|---|
| **AM (amplitude** | АМ (амплитудная | *am-pli-tóod-na-ya* |
| **modulation)** | модуляция) | *ma-du-lyáh-tsi-ya* |
| **antenna** | антенна | *an-téh-na* |
| **audio equipment** | звуковое | *zvu-ka-vó-ye* |
| | оборудование | *a-ba-róo-da-va-ni-ye* |

| | | |
|---|---|---|
| • cassette tape | кассета | ka-syé-ta |
| • compact disc | компактный-диск | kám-páhkt-nyj disk |
| • disc player | дисковод | dis-ka-vód |
| • DVD | дивиди | di-vi-di |
| • DVD player | дивиди проигрыватель | di-vi-di pra-íg-ry-va-tel' |
| • headphones | наушники | na-óosh-ni-ki |
| • loudspeaker | громкоговоритель (m) | grom-ka-ga-va-rí-til' |
| • microphone | микрофон | mik-ra-fón |
| • play (a disk) | поставить (p) диск | pas-táh-vit' disk |
| • receiver, tuner | приёмник | pri-yóm-nik |
| • record | пластинка | plas-tín-ka |
| • record | записывать (i) (музыку) | za-pí-sy-vat' móo-zy-ku |
| • record player | проигрыватель (m) | pra-íg-ry-va-til' |
| • stereo | стерео | styé-ri-a |
| FM (frequency modulation) | ФМ (частотная модуляция) | chas-tót-na-ya ma-du-lyáh-tsi-ya |
| program | программа | prag-ráh-ma |
| projector | проектор | pra-éhk-tar |
| • slide projector | проектор для диапозитивов | pra-éhk-tar dlya di-a-pa-zi-tí-vaf |
| radio | радио | ráh-di-a |
| • car radio | радио в машине | ráh-di-a v ma-shý-nye |
| • listen to | слушать (i) | slóo-shat' |
| • newscast | новости (pl) | nó-vas-ti |
| • pocket radio | карманное радио | kar-máh-na-ye ráh-di-a |
| • portable radio | транзисторный приёмник | tran-zís-tar-nyj pri-yóm-nik |
| • station | радиостанция | ra-di-a-stáhn-tsy-ya |
| short wave | короткие волны | ka-rót-ki-ye vól-ny |
| show (movies) | сеанс | si-áhns |
| • TV | передача | pi-ri-dáh-cha |
| • exhibition | выставка | výs-taf-ka |
| sound track | звуковая дорожка | zvu-ka-váh-ya da-rósh-ka |
| television | телевидение | ti-li-ví-di-ni-ye |
| • channel | канал | ka-náhl |
| • closed circuit | внутреннее телевидение | vnóot-ri-ni-ye ti-li-ví-di-ni-ye |
| • documentary | документальный фильм | da-ku-min-táhl'-nyj fil'm |
| interview | интервью | in-tyr-v'yú |
| look at, watch | смотреть (i) | smat-ryét' |
| network | сеть (f) | syet' |
| news report | передача новостей | pi-ri-dáh-cha na-vas-tyéj |
| remote control | дистанционное управление | dis-tan-tsy-ó-na-ye up-rav-lyé-ni-ye |
| series (TV) | многосерийная передача | mna-ga-si-ríj-na-ya pi-ri-dáh-cha |
| television set | телевизор | ti-li-ví-zar |

| transmission | передача | *pi-ri-dáh-cha* |
|---|---|---|
| **VCR** | видеомагнитофон | *vi-di-a-mag-ni-ta-fón* |
| **videocassette** | видеокассета | *vi-di-a-ka-syé-ta* |
| **videotape** | видеоплёнка | *vi-di-a-plyón-ka* |
| **turn off** | выключить *(p)* | *výk-lyu-chit'* |
| | выключать *(i)* | *vyk-lyu-cháht'* |
| **turn on** | включить *(p)* | *fklyu-chít'* |
| | включать *(i)* | *fklyu-cháht'* |

## 21. FEELINGS

## a. MOODS, ATTITUDES, AND EMOTIONS

| affection | привязанность | *pri-vyáh-zan-nast'* |
|---|---|---|
| • **affectionate** | ласковый | *láhs-ka-vyj* |
| **agree** | согласиться *(p)* | *sag-la-sí-tsa* |
| | соглашаться *(i)* | *sag-la-sháh-tsa* |
| **angry** | сердитый | *sir-dí-tyj* |
| **anxiety** | беспокойство | *bis-pa-kój-stva* |
| | озабоченность *(f)* | *a-za-bó-chi-nast'* |
| • **anxious** | озабоченный | *a-za-bó-chi-nyj* |
| | неспокойный | *ni-spa-kój-nyj* |
| **assure** | уверить *(p)* | *u-vyé-rit'* |
| | уверять *(i)* | *u-vi-ryáht'* |
| • **You may rest assured** | Можете быть уверены | *mó-zhy-ti byt' u-vyé-ri-ny* |
| **attitude** | отношение | *at-na-shéh-ni-ye* |
| **boring** | скучный | *skóoch-nyj* |
| • **become bored** | заскучать *(p)* | *zas-ku-cháht'* |
| • **I'm bored** | Мне скучно | *mnye skóoch-na* |
| • **boredom** | скука | *skóo-ka* |
| **complain** | жаловаться *(i)* | *zháh-la-va-tsa* |
| • **complaint** | жалоба | *zháh-la-ba* |
| **crying** | плач | *plahch* |
| • **cry** | плакать *(i)* | *pláh-kat'* |
| **depressed** | подавленный | *pa-dáhv-li-nyj* |
| | удручённый | *ud-ru-chyó-nyj* |
| • **depression** | депрессия | *dip-ryé-si-ya* |
| **desperate** | отчаянный | *at-cháh-i-nyj* |
| • **desperation** | отчаяние | *at-cháh-i-ni-ye* |
| **disagree** | не согласиться *(p)* | *ni sag-la-sí-tsa* |
| | не соглашаться *(i)* | *ni sag-la-sháh-tsa* |
| • **disagreement** | разногласие | *raz-na-gláh-si-ye* |
| | расхождение | *ras-khazh-dyé-ni-ye* |
| • **be against** | быть *(i)* против | *byt' pró-tif* |

| | | |
|---|---|---|
| **dissatisfaction** | недовольство | *ni-da-vól'st-va* |
| • **dissatisfied** | недовольный | *ni-da-vól-nyj* |
| **encourage** | подбодрить *(p)* | *pad-bad-rít'* |
| | подбодрять *(i)* | *pad-bad-ryáht'* |
| • **encouragement** | ободрение | *a-bad-ryé-ni-ye* |
| | поощрение | *pa-ashch-ryé-ni-ye* |
| **faith, trust** | доверие | *da-vyé-ri-ye* |
| • **trust** | доверить *(p)* | *da-vyé-rit'* |
| | доверять *(i)* | *da-vi-ryáht'* |
| **fear** | боязнь *(f)* | *ba-yáhzn'* |
| | страх | *strahkh* |
| | опасение | *a-pa-syé-ni-ye* |
| • **be afraid** | бояться *(i)* | *ba-yáh-tsa* |
| | опасаться *(i)* | *a-pa-sáh-tsa* |
| **feel** | чувствовать *(i)* | *chóost-va-vat'* |
| • **feeling** | чувство | *chóost-va* |
| **flatter** | льстить *(i)* | *l'stit'* |
| • **flattery** | лесть *(f)* | *lyest'* |
| **fun, enjoyment** | забава/потеха | *za-báh-va/pa-tyé-kha* |
| • **to have a good time** | хорошо провести *(p)* время | *kha-ra-shó pra-vis-tí vryé-mya* |
| | проводить *(i)* | *pra-va-dít'* |
| • **to have fun** | веселиться *(i)* | *vi-si-lí-tsa* |
| **happiness** | счастье | *shcháhst'-ye* |
| • **happy, lucky** | счастливый | *shchis-lí-vyj* |
| **hope** | надежда | *na-dyézh-da* |
| • **hope** | надеяться *(i)* | *na-dyé-i-tsa* |
| **indifference** | безразличие | *biz-raz-lí-chi-ye* |
| • **indifferent** | безразличный | *biz-raz-lích-nyj* |
| **joy** | радость *(f)* | *ráh-dast'* |
| • **joyous** | радостный | *ráh-das-nyj* |
| **laugh** | смеяться *(i)* | *smi-yáh-tsa* |
| • **laughter** | смех | *smyekh* |
| **mood** | настроение | *nast-ra-yé-ni-ye* |
| • **bad mood** | плохое настроение | *pla-khó-ye nast-ra-yé-ni-ye* |
| • **good mood** | хорошее настроение | *kha-ró-shy-ye nast-ra-yé-ni-ye* |
| **need** | нужда | *nuzh-dáh* |
| | необходимость *(f)* | *ni-ap-kha-dí-mast'* |
| • **need** | нуждаться *(i)* | *nuzh-dáh-tsa* |
| **patience** | терпение | *tir-pyé-ni-ye* |
| • **have patience** | иметь *(i)* терпение | *i-myét' tir-pyé-ni-ye* |
| • **patient** | терпеливый *(adj)* | *tir-pi-lí-vyj* |
| • **patiently** | терпеливо *(adv)* | *tir-pi-lí-va* |
| **relief** | облегчение | *ab-likh-chyé-ni-ye* |

| | | |
|---|---|---|
| **sad** | грустный/ тоскливый | *gróos-nyj/task-lí-vyj* |
| • **sadness** | грусть *(f)* | *groost'* |
| | тоска | *tas-káh* |
| **satisfaction** | удовлетворение | *u-dav-lit-va-ryé-ni-ye* |
| • **satisfied** | удовлетворён(-ный) | *u-dav-lit-va-ryón(-yj)* |
| | довольный | *da-vól'-nyj* |
| **shame** | стыд | *styt* |
| • **be ashamed** | стыдиться *(i)* | *sty-dí-tsa* |
| **smile** | улыбка | *u-lýp-ka* |
| • **smile** | улыбнуться *(p)* | *u-lyb-nóo-tsa* |
| | улыбаться *(i)* | *u-ly-báh-tsa* |
| **sorrow** | печаль *(f)* | *pi-cháhl* |
| | скорбь *(f)* | *skorp'* |
| **surprise** | удивление | *u-div-lyé-ni-ye* |
| • **surprise** | удивиться *(p)* | *u-di-ví-tsa* |
| | удивляться *(i)* | *u-di-vlyáh-tsa* |
| **sympathy** | сочувствие | *sa-chóost-vi-ye* |
| • **sympathetic** | сочувственный | *sa-chóost-vi-nyj* |
| **thankfulness** | благодарность *(f)* | *bla-ga-dáhr-nast'* |
| • **thankful** | благодарный | *bla-ga-dáhr-nyj* |
| • **thank** | благодарить *(i)* | *bla-ga-da-rít'* |
| **tolerance** | терпимость *(f)* | *tir-pí-mast'* |
| • **tolerate** | терпеть *(i)* | *tir-pyét'* |
| | допустить *(p)* | *da-pus-tít'* |
| | допускать *(i)* | *da-pus-káht'* |
| **want to** | хотеть *(i)* | *kha-tyét'* |

## b. LIKES AND DISLIKES

| | | |
|---|---|---|
| **accept** | принять *(p)* | *pri-nyáht'* |
| | принимать *(i)* | *pri-ni-máht'* |
| • **acceptable** | приемлемый | *pri-yém-li-myj* |
| • **unacceptable** | неприемлемый | *ni-pri-yém-li-myj* |
| **approval** | одобрение | *a-dab-ryé-ni-ye* |
| • **approve** | одобрить *(p)* | *a-dób-rit'* |
| | одобрять *(i)* | *a-dab-ryáht'* |
| **detestable** | отвратительный | *at-vra-tí-til'-nyj* |
| **disgust** | отвращение | *at-vra-shchyé-ni-ye* |
| • **disgusting** | отвратительный | *at-vra-tí-til'-nyj* |
| **hate, detest** | ненавидеть *(i)* | *ni-na-ví-dit'* |
| • **hatred** | ненависть *(f)* | *nyé-na-vist'* |
| **kiss** | поцелуй | *pa-tsy-lóoj* |
| **like** | нравиться *(i)* | *nráh-vi-tsa* |
| • **dislike** | не нравиться *(i)* | *ni nráh-vi-tsa* |

| love | любовь *(f)* | *lyu-bóf'* |
| • love | любить *(i)* | *lyu-bít'* |
| pleasant | приятный | *pri-yáht-nyj* |
| • unpleasant | неприятный | *ni-pri-yáht-nyj* |
| prefer | предпочесть *(p)* | *prit-pa-chyést'* |
| | предпочитать *(i)* | *prit-pa-chi-táht'* |
| • preferable | предпочтительный | *prit-pach-tí-til'-nyj* |
| • preference | предпочтение | *prit-pach-tyé-ni-ye* |

## c. EXPRESSING EMOTIONS

| A minute of quiet, please! | Пожалуйста, минуту тишины! | *pa-zháh-lus-ta, mi-nóo-tu ti-shy-ný* |
| Are you joking? | Ты что, шутишь? *(fam)* | *ty shto shóo-tish* |
| | Вы шутите! *(pol)* | *vy shóo-ti-ti* |
| Be careful! | Осторожно! | *as-ta-rózh-na* |
| Beat it! | Отвали (отваливай) отсюда! | *at-va-lí (at-váh-li-vaj) at-tsóo-da* |
| Enough! | Хватит! | *khváh-tit* |
| • Enough already! | Хватит уже! | *khváh-tit u-zhéh* |
| Generally, ... | Вообще, ... | *va-ap-shchyé* |
| • Generally speaking, | Вообще говоря, | *va-ap-shchyé ga- va-ryáh* |
| • On the whole, | В общем, | *v óp-shchim* |
| Go to hell! | Иди к чёрту! | *i-dí k chyór-tu* |
| I can't stand it! | Я не могу этого выносить! | *yah ni ma-góo éh-ta-va vy-na-sít'* |
| I couldn't care less! | Мне без разницы! | *mnye biz ráhz-ni-tsy* |
| | Мне до лампочки! | *mnye da láhm-pach-ki* |
| I don't feel like... | Мне неохота... | *mnye ni-a-khó-ta* |
| I don't understand anything. | Я ничего не понимаю. | *yah ni-chi-vó ni pa-ni-máh-yu* |
| I hate him! | Я его ненавижу! | *yah i-vó ni-na-ví-zhu* |
| • I can't stand him! | Я его терпеть не могу! | *yah i-vó tir-pyét' ni ma-góo* |
| I wish! | Мне бы так... | *mnye by tahk* |
| | Мне бы того... | *mnye by ta-vó* |
| I'm absolutely sure! | Я совершенно уверен(а)! | *yah sa-vir-shéh-na u-vyé-rin(a)* |
| I'm serious! | Я всерьёз говорю! | *yah fsir'-yós ga-va-ryú* |
| I'm sorry! | Прости(-те) меня, пожалуйста! | *pras-tí(-ti) mi-nyáh pa-zháh-lus-ta* |
| I'm tired (of it)! | Мне надоело! | *mnye na-da-yé-la* |
| It can't be! | Не может этого быть! | *ni mó-zhyt éh-ta-va byt'* |
| It doesn't matter | Не имеет значения | *ni i-myé-it zna-chyé-ni-ya* |
| Knock it off! | Прекрати! | *prik-ra-tí* |
| | Перестань! | *pi-ri-stáhn'* |

| | | |
|---|---|---|
| **Look here!** | Ты смотри (мне)! | *ty smat-rí (mnye)* |
| **My God!** | Боже мой! | *bó-zhy moj* |
| **Poor man!** | Бедняга! | *bid-nyáh-ga* |
| **Poor woman!** | Бедняжка! | *bid-nyáhsh-ka* |
| **Quiet!** | Тихо! | *tí-kha* |
| **Really?** | Действительно? | *dist-ví-til'-na* |
| | Правда? | *práhv-da* |
| | На самом деле? | *na sáh-mam dyé-li* |
| **Shut up!** | Заткнись! | *zatk-nís'* |
| **Stop pretending!** | Кончай (перестань) притворяться! | *kan-cháhj (pi-ris-láhn') prit-va-ryáh-tsa* |
| **Thank God!** | Слава Богу! | *sláh-va bó-gu* |
| **That's none of your business!** | Не твоё дело! | *ni tva-yó dýe-la* |
| **This is impossible!** | Это просто невозможно! | *éh-ta prós-ta ni-vaz-mózh-na* |
| **This is intolerable!** | Это невыносимо! | *éh-ta ni-vy-na-sí-ma* |
| **This is terrible/ awful!** | Это ужасно! | *éh-ta u-zháhs-na* |
| | Это кошмар! | *éh-ta kash-máhr* |
| **This is wonderful!** | Это замечательно! | *éh-ta za-mi-cháh-til'-na* |
| **Too bad** | Жаль | *zhahl'* |
| | (Как) жалко! | *(kahk) zháhl-ka* |
| **You don't say!** | Да что ты говоришь! *(fam)* | *dah shto ty ga-va-rísh* |
| | Да что вы говорите! *(pol)* | *dah shto vy ga-va-rí-ti* |
| **Wait a minute!** | Одну минуту! | *ad-nóo mi-nóo-tu* |
| **What a bore!** | Какая скука! | *ka-káh-ya skóo-ka* |
| **What do you think you're doing?** | Ты что же это делаешь? | *ty shto zhy éh-ta dyé-la-ish* |
| **What luck!** | Вот, повезло! | *vot pa-viz-ló* |
| • **What bad luck!** | Вот, не повезло! | *vot ni pa-viz-ló* |
| **What's got into you?** | Что с тобой? | *shto s ta-bój* |

## 22. THINKING

### a. DESCRIBING THOUGHT

| | | |
|---|---|---|
| **complicated** | сложный | *slózh-nyj* |
| **concept** | понятие | *pa-nyáh-ti-ye* |
| **consciousness** | сознание | *saz-náh-ni-ye* |
| • **conscious** | сознательный | *saz-náh-til'-nyj* |
| **difficult** | трудный | *tróod-nyj* |
| **doubt** | сомнение | *sam-nyé-ni-ye* |
| **easy** | лёгкий *(adj)* | *lyókh-kij* |

| | | |
|---|---|---|
| • **easily** | легко *(adv)* | *likh-kó* |
| • **Easy!** | Чепуха! | *chi-pu-kháh* |
| **existence** | существование | *su-shchi-stva-váh-ni-ye* |
| **hypothesis** | гипотеза | *gi-pó-ti-za* |
| **idea** | идея | *i-dyé-ya* |
| **ignorant** | невежественный | *ni-vyé-zhyst-vi-nyj* |
| | неосведомлённый | *ni-as-vi-dam-lyó-nyj* |
| **imagination** | воображение | *va-ab-ra-zhéh-ni-ye* |
| **interesting** | интересный *(adj)* | *in-ti-ryés-nyj* |
| • **interestingly** | интересно *(adv)* | *in-ti-ryés-na* |
| **judgment** | решение | *ri-shéh-ni-ye* |
| | благоразумие | *bla-ga-ra-zóo-mi-ye* |
| **justice** | справедливость *(f)* | *spra-vid-lí-vast'* |
| **knowledge** | знание | *znáh-ni-ye* |
| **knowledgeable** | знающий | *znáh-yu-shchij* |
| **mind** | ум | *oom* |
| **opinion** | мнение | *mnyé-ni-ye* |
| • **in my opinion** | по моему мнению | *pa ma-i-móo mnyé-ni-yu* |
| **problem** | проблема | *prab-lyé-ma* |
| • **No problem!** | Никаких проблем! | *ni-ka-kíkh prab-lyém* |
| **reason** | причина | *pri-chí-na* |
| | основание | *as-na-váh-ni-ye* |
| **simple** | простой *(adj)* | *pras-tój* |
| • **simply** | просто *(adv)* | *prós-ta* |
| **thought** | мысль *(f)* | *mysl'* |
| | мышление | *mysh-lyé-ni-ye* |
| **wisdom** | мудрость *(f)* | *móod-rast'* |

## b. BASIC THOUGHT PROCESSES

| | | |
|---|---|---|
| **agree** | согласиться *(p)* | *sa-gla-sí-tsa* |
| | соглашаться *(i)* | *sa-gla-sháh-tsa* |
| **be interested in** | интересоваться *(i)* | *in-ti-ri-sa-váh-tsa* |
| **be right** | быть *(i)* правым | *byt' práh-vym* |
| **be wrong** | быть *(i)* неправым | *byt' ni-práh-vym* |
| **believe** | поверить *(p)* | *pa-vyé-rit'* |
| | верить *(i)* | *vyé-rit'* |
| **convince** | убедить *(p)* | *u-bi-dít'* |
| | убеждать *(i)* | *u-bizh-dáht'* |
| **demonstrate** | показать *(p)* | *pa-ka-záht'* |
| | показывать *(i)* | *pa-káh-zy-vat'* |
| **doubt** | сомневаться *(i)* | *sam-ni-váh-tsa* |
| **forget** | забыть *(p)* | *za-být'* |
| | забывать *(i)* | *za-by-váht'* |

| | | |
|---|---|---|
| **imagine** | вообразить *(p)* | *va-ab-ra-zít'* |
| | воображать *(i)* | *va-ab-ra-zháht'* |
| **know** | знать *(i)* | *znaht'* |
| **learn** | научиться *(p)* | *na-u-chí-tsa* |
| | учиться *(i)* | *u-chí-tsa* |
| **persuade, convince** | убедить *(p)* | *u-bi-dít'* |
| | убеждать *(i)* | *u-bizh-dáht'* |
| **reason** | причина | *pri-chí-na* |
| | основание | *as-na-váh-ni-ye* |
| **reflect** | отразить *(p)* | *at-ra-zít'* |
| | отражать *(i)* | *at-ra-zháht'* |
| **remember** | вспомнить *(p)* | *fspóm-nit'* |
| | помнить *(i)* | *póm-nit'* |
| **study** | изучить *(p)* | *iz-u-chít'* |
| | изучать *(i)* | *iz-u-cháht'* |
| **think** | подумать *(p)* | *pa-dóo-mat'* |
| | думать *(i)* | *dóo-mat'* |
| **understand** | понять *(p)* | *pa-nyáht'* |
| | понимать *(i)* | *pa-ni-máht'* |

## DAILY LIFE

*23. AT HOME*

### a. PARTS OF THE HOUSE

| | | |
|---|---|---|
| **attic** | чердак | *chir-dáhk* |
| **awning** | навес | *na-vyés* |
| **balcony** | балкон | *bal-kón* |
| **basement** | подвал | *pad-váhl* |
| **bathtub** | ванна | *váhn-a* |
| **ceiling** | потолок | *pa-ta-lók* |
| **chimney** | труба | *tru-báh* |
| **corridor** | коридор | *ka-ri-dór* |
| **door** | дверь *(f)* | *dvyer'* |
| **doorbell** | звонок | *zva-nók* |
| **entrance** | вход | *vkhot* |
| • **entrance hall** | прихожая | *pri-khó-zha-ya* |
| **faucet** | кран | *krahn* |
| **fireplace** | камин | *ka-mín* |
| **floor** | пол | *pol* |
| **floor (level)** | этаж | *y-táhzh* |
| **garage** | гараж | *ga-ráhzh* |
| **garden** | сад | *saht* |
| • **vegetable garden** | огород | *a-ga-rót* |
| **hallway** | коридор | *ka-ri-dór* |
| **house** | дом | *dom* |
| **lawn** | лужайка/газон | *lu-zháhj-ka/ga-zón* |
| **lawn mower** | косилка/газонокосилка | *ka-síl-ka/ga-zó-na-ka-síl-ka* |
| • **lawn mower (motor)** | механическая газонокосилка | *mi-kha-ní-chis-ka-ya ga-zó-na-ka-síl-ka* |
| • **push mower** | ручная газонокосилка | *ruch-náh-ya ga-zó-na-ka-síl-ka* |
| • **riding lawn mower** | райдер | *ráhj-dir* |
| **mailbox** | почтовый ящик | *pach-tó-vyj yáh-shchik* |
| **parking** | парковка | *par-kóf-ka* |
| **porch** | крыльцо | *kryl'-tsó* |
| **roof** | крыша | *krý-sha* |
| **shelf** | полка | *pól-ka* |
| **shower** | душ | *doosh* |
| **sink** | раковина | *ráh-ka-vi-na* |
| **stairs** | лестница | *lyéhs-ni-tsa* |
| • **step** | ступень *(f)* | *stu-pyén'* |
| **switch** | выключатель *(m)* | *vy-klyu-cháh-til'* |
| | переключатель *(m)* | *pi-ri-klyu-cháh-til'* |

| | | |
|---|---|---|
| swimming pool | бассейн | *ba-syén* |
| | плавательный бассейн | *pláh-va-til'-nyj ba-syén* |
| tennis court | теннисный корт | *téh-nis-nyj kórt* |
| terrace | терраса | *ti-ráh-sa* |
| toilet (fixture) | унитаз | *u-ni-táhz* |
| TV station | телестанция | *ti-li-stáhn-tsy-ya* |
| wall | стена | *sti-náh* |
| window | окно | *ak-nó* |
| window frame | оконная рама | *a-kó-na-ya ráh-ma* |
| window sill | подоконник | *pa-da-kón-ik* |

## b. ROOMS

| | | |
|---|---|---|
| bathroom | ванная (комната) | *váh-na-ya (kóm-na-ta)* |
| bedroom | спальня | *spáhl'-nya* |
| cellar | погреб | *pó-grib* |
| closet | чулан | *chu-láhn* |
| cupboard | шкаф | *shkáhf* |
| dining room | столовая | *sta-ló-va-ya* |
| kitchen | кухня | *kóokh-nya* |
| living room | гостиная | *gas-tí-na-ya* |
| room | комната | *kóm-na-ta* |
| toilet (room) | туалет | *tu-a-lyét* |
| | уборная | *u-bór-na-ya* |

## c. FURNITURE AND DECORATION

| | | |
|---|---|---|
| armchair | кресло | *kryés-la* |
| bed | кровать *(f)* | *kra-váht'* |
| bedside table | ночной столик | *nach-nój stól-ik* |
| bookcase | книжный шкаф | *knízh-nyj shkáhf* |
| carpet, rug | ковёр | *kav-yór* |
| chair | стул | *stool* |
| chest of drawers/dresser | комод | *ka-mót* |
| curtain | занавесь *(f)* (-ка) | *záh-na-vis' (za-na-vyés-ka)* |
| decorated | украшенный | *u-kráh-shy-nyj* |
| drawer | ящик | *yáh-shchik* |
| furniture | мебель *(f, coll)* | *myé-bil'* |
| • furnished | обставленный | *ap-stáhv-li-nyj* |
| | меблированный | *mi-bli-ró-va-nyj* |
| lamp | лампа | *láhm-pa* |
| mirror | зеркало | *zyér-ka-la* |
| painting | картина | *kar-tí-na* |
| sofa | диван/софа | *di-váhn/sa-fáh* |
| stool | табурет | *ta-bu-ryét* |
| table | стол | *stol* |
| writing desk | письменный стол | *pís'-mi-nyj stol* |

## d. APPLIANCES AND COMMON HOUSEHOLD ITEMS

| | | |
|---|---|---|
| **bag** | сумка | *sóom-ka* |
| | мешок | *mi-skók* |
| **bar** | бар | *bahr* |
| • bar stool | барный стул | *báhr-nyj stool* |
| **barbeque** | барбекю (also -кью) | *bar-bi-kyú* (also *-k'yu*) |
| • a place for a barbeque | место для барбекю | *myés-ta dlyah bar-bi-kyú* |
| **barrel** | бочка | *bóch-ka* |
| **basket** | корзина (-нка) | *kar-zí-na (-nka)* |
| **blanket** | одеяло | *a-di-yáh-la* |
| • blanket case | пододеяльник | *pa-da-di-yáhl'-nik* |
| **blender** | блендер | *blyén-dir* |
| **bottle** | бутылка | *bu-týl-ka* |
| **box (small)** | коробка | *ka-róp-ka* |
| **box (large), case** | ящик | *yáh-shchik* |
| **broom** | веник, метла | *výe-nik, mit-láh* |
| **cabinet (wall)** | настенный шкаф | *nas-tyén-nyj shkahf* |
| **calculator** | калькулятор | *kal'-ku-lyáh-tyr* |
| **calendar** | календарь | *ka-lin-dáhr'* |
| **clothes hanger** | вешалка | *vyé-shyl-ka* |
| **coffee grinder** | кофемолка | *ka-fi-mól-ka* |
| **coffee-maker** | кофеварка | *ka-fi-váhr-ka* |
| • espresso-machine | кофеварка эспрессо | *ka-fi-váhr-ka yks-pryé-sa* |
| **coffee pot** | кофейник | *ka-fyéj-nik* |
| **cup** | чашка | *cháhsh-ka* |
| **dish drainer** | сушилка для посуды | *su-shýl-ka dlya pa-sóo-dy* |
| **dishes** | посуда *(coll)* | *pa-sóo-da* |
| **dishwasher** | посудомоечная машина | *pa-sóo-da-mó-ich-na-ya ma-shý-na* |
| | посудомойка | *pa-su-da-mój-ka* |
| **dryer (clothes)** | сушильная машина | *su-shýl'-na-ya ma-shý-na* |
| | сушилка (для белья) | *su-shýl-ka (dlyah bil'-yáh)* |
| **dustpan** | совок | *sa-vók* |
| **electric current converter** | конвертер | *kan-vyér-tyr* |
| **fire pit (lit. garden fireplace)** | садовый камин | *sa-dó-vyj ka-mín* |
| **food processor** | кухонный комбайн | *ku-khón-nyj kam-báhjn* |
| **fork** | вилка | *víl-ka* |
| **glass (drinking)** | стакан | *sta-káhn* |
| **grill** | гриль | *gril'* |
| **Jacuzzi** | джакузи | *dzha-kóo-zi* |
| **juicer** | соковыжималка | *só-ka-vy-zhy-máhl-ka* |

| kettle | чайник | *cháhj-nik* |
| key | ключ | *klyuch* |
| **kitchen furniture** | кухонная мебель | *ku-khón-na-ya myé-bil'* |
| knife | нож | *nozh* |
| • **blade** | лезвие | *lyéz-vi-ye* |
| • **handle** | ручка | *róoch-ka* |
| lid | крышка | *krý-sha* |
| **microwave oven** | микроволновая печь | *mík-ra-val-nó-va-ya pyech* |
| | микроволновка | *mík-ra-val-nóf-ka* |
| mixer | миксер | *mík-sir* |
| napkin | салфетка | *sal-fyét-ka* |
| oven | духовка | *du-khóf-ka* |
| pail | ведро | *vid-ró* |
| pan | сковорода | *ska-va-ra-dáh* |
| pillow | подушка | *pa-dóosh-ka* |
| • **pillowcase** | наволочка | *náh-va-lach-ka* |
| plate | тарелка | *ta-ryél-ka* |
| pot | кастрюля | *kast-ryúh-lya* |
| radio | радио | *ráh-di-a* |
| rag | тряпка | *tryáhp-ka* |
| refrigerator | холодильник | *kha-la-díl'-nik* |
| saucer | блюдце | *blyú-tsy* |
| **sewing machine** | швейная машина | *shvyéj-na-ya ma-shý-na* |
| **sheet (bed)** | простыня | *pras-ty-nyáh* |
| spoon | ложка | *lósh-ka* |
| • **soup spoon** | суповая (большая) ложка | *su-pa-váh-ya (bal-sháh-ya) lósh-ka* |
| • **teaspoon** | чайная (маленькая) ложка | *cháhj-na-ya (máh-lin'-ka-ya) lósh-ka* |
| steamer | пароварка | *pa-ra-váhr-ka* |
| stove | плита | *pli-táh* |
| tablecloth | скатерть *(f)* | *skáh-tirt'* |
| tableware | посудный прибор | *pa-sóod-nyj pri-bór* |
| teapot | заварной чайник | *za-var-nój cháhj-nik* |
| toaster | тостер | *tós-ter* |
| tools | инструменты | *in-stru-myén-ty* |
| tray | поднос | *pad-nós* |
| **vacuum cleaner** | пылесос | *py-li-sós* |
| vase | ваза | *váh-za* |
| **washing machine** | стиральная машина | *sti-ráhl'-na-ya ma-shý-na* |

## e. SERVICES

| | | |
|---|---|---|
| **air conditioner** | кондиционер | *kan-di-tsy-a-nyér* |
| **air conditioning** | кондиционирование воздуха | *kan-di-tsy-a-ní-ra-va-ni-ye vóz-du-kha* |
| **electricity** | электричество | *y-lik-trí-chi-stva* |
| **gas** | газ | *gahs* |
| **heating** | отопление | *a-tap-lyé-ni-ye* |
| **light** | свет | *svyet* |
| **telephone** | телефон | *ti-li-fón* |
| **TV** | телевидение | *tye-lye-ví-dye-ni-ye* |
| • **TV set** | телевизор | *tye-lye-ví-zar* |
| **water** | вода | *va-dáh* |
| • **hot water** | горячая вода | *ga-ryáh-chi-ya va-dáh* |

## f. ADDITIONAL HOUSEHOLD VOCABULARY

| | | |
|---|---|---|
| **at home** | дома | *dó-ma* |
| **build** | строить *(i)* | *stró-it'* |
| **buy** | купить *(p)* | *ku-pít'* |
| **clean** | очистить *(p)* | *a-chís-tit'* |
| | чистить *(i)* | *chís-tit'* |
| **clear the table** | убрать *(p)* со стола | *u-bráht' sa sta-láh* |
| | убирать *(i)* | *u-bi-ráht'* |
| **dish towel** | кухонное полотенце | *ku-khó-na-ye pa-la-tyén-tsa* |
| **dry the dishes** | вытереть *(p)* посуду | *vý-ti-rit' pa-sóo-du* |
| | вытирать *(i)* | *vy-ti-ráht'* |
| **live in** | жить *(i)* в/на | *zhyt' v/na* |
| **make the bed** | застлать *(p)* постель | *za-stláht' pas-tyél'* |
| | застелить *(p)* | *za-sti-lit'* |
| | застеливать *(i)* | *zas-tyé-li-vat'* |
| **move** | переехать *(p)* | *pi-ri-yé-khat'* |
| | переезжать *(i)* | *pi-ri-y-zháht'* |
| **paint** | покрасить *(p)* | *pa-kráh-sit'* |
| | красить *(i)* | *kráh-sit'* |

| | | |
|---|---|---|
| **put a room in order** | убрать *(p)* комнату | *u-bráht' kóm-na-tu* |
| | убирать *(i)* | *u-bi-ráht'* |
| **set the table** | накрыть *(p)* на стол | *na-krýt' na stol* |
| **tidy up** | убрать *(p)* | *ub-ráht'* |
| | убирать *(i)* | *u-bi-ráht'* |
| **wash** | помыть *(p)* | *pa-mýt'* |
| | мыть *(i)* | *myt'* |
| • **wash clothes** | постирать *(p)* | *pa-sti-ráht'* |
| | стирать *(i)* | *sti-ráht'* |
| • **wash dishes** | помыть *(p)* посуду | *pa-mýt' pa-sóo-du* |
| | мыть *(i)* посуду | *myt' pa-sóo-du* |

## g. LIVING IN AN APARTMENT

| | | |
|---|---|---|
| **apartment** | квартира | *kvar-tí-ra* |
| **apartment building** | квартирный дом | *kvar-tír-nyj dom* |
| **co-op** | кооператив | *ka-a-pi-ra-tíf* |
| **elevator** | лифт | *lift* |
| **landlord** | хозяин дома | *kha-zyáh-in dó-ma* |
| **rent (m)** | плата за квартиру | *pláh-ta za kvar-tí-ru* |
| • **rent (v)** | снять *(p)* | *snyaht'* |
| | снимать *(i)* | *sni-máht'* |
| **tenant** | арендатор | *a-rin-dáh-tar* |
| | квартирант | *kvar-ti-ráhnt* |

## 24. EATING AND DRINKING

### a. MEALS

| | | |
|---|---|---|
| **breakfast** | завтрак | *záhft-rak* |
| **dinner** | ужин | *óo-zhyn* |
| **food** | еда/пища | *i-dáh/pí-shcha* |
| **lunch** | обед | *a-byét* |
| **business lunch** | бизнис ланч | *bíz-nis lánch* |
| **snack (m)** | закуска | *za-kóos-ka* |
| • **snack (v)** | закусить *(p)* | *za-ku-sít'* |
| | перекусить *(p)* | *pi-ri-ku-sít'* |

### b. PREPARATION OF FOOD

| | | |
|---|---|---|
| **boil (food)** | варить *(i)* | *va-rít'* |
| **boil (water)** | кипятить *(i)* | *ki-pi-tít'* |
| • **boiled** | варёный | *va-ryó-nyj* |
| | кипячёный | *ki-pi-chyó-nyj* |

| cook | приготовить *(p)* | *pri-ga-tó-vit'* |
| | готовить *(i)* | *ga-tó-vit'* |
| cooked | приготовленный | *pri-ga-tóv-li-nyj* |
| fry | жарить *(i)* | *zháh-rit'* |
| rare | кровавое (мясо) | *kra-váh-va-ye (myáh-sa)* |
| stew/simmer | тушить *(i)* | *tu-shýt'* |
| well-done (fried) | прожаренный | *pra-zháh-ri-nyj* |
| well-done (boiled) | проваренный | *pra-váh-ri-nyj* |
| with sauce | с соусом | *s só-u-sam* |

## c. MEAT AND POULTRY

| beef | говядина | *ga-vyáh-di-na* |
| bologna | докторская колбаса | *dók-tar-ska-ya kal-ba-sáh* |
| chicken | курица | *kóo-ri-tsa* |
| | цыплёнок | *tsyp-lyó-nak* |
| duck | утка | *óot-ka* |
| ham | ветчина | *vi-chi-náh* |
| lamb | баранина | *ba-ráh-ni-na* |
| liver | печёнка | *pi-chyón-ka* |
| meat | мясо | *myáh-sa* |
| • ground meat | молотое мясо | *mó-la-ta-ye myáh-sa* |
| pork | свинина | *svi-ní-na* |
| salami | колбаса твёрдого копчения | *kal-ba-sáh tvyór-da-va kap-chyé-ni-ya* |
| sausage | колбаса | *kal-ba-sáh* |
| turkey | индейка | *in-dyéj-ka* |
| veal | телятина | *ti-lyáh-ti-na* |

## d. FISH, SEAFOOD, AND SHELLFISH

| caviar | икра | *ik-ráh* |
| • black | чёрная | *chyór-na-ya* |
| • red | красная | *kráhs-na-ya* |
| clam | моллюск | *ma-lyúhsk* |
| cod | треска | *tris-ká* |
| eel | угорь *(m)* | *óo-gar'* |
| fish | рыба | *rý-ba* |
| flounder | камбала | *kám-ba-lah* |
| herring | сельдь *(f)* (селёдка) | *syel'd' (si-lyót-ka)* |
| lobster | омар | *a-máhr* |
| mussel | мидия | *mí-di-ya* |
| oyster | устрица | *óost-ri-tsa* |
| perch | окунь | *ó-kun'* |
| salmon | сёмга | *syóm-ga* |

| sardine | сардина | *sar-dí-na* |
| shrimp | креветка | *kri-vyét-ka* |
| trout | форель *(f)* | *fa-rýel'* |
| tuna | тунец *(m)* | *tu-nyéts* |

## e. VEGETABLES

| artichoke | артишок | *ar-ti-shók* |
| asparagus | спаржа | *spáhr-zha* |
| bean | боб | *bob* |
| beet | свёкла | *svyók-la* |
| cabbage | капуста | *ka-póos-ta* |
| carrot | морковь *(f)* (-вка) | *mar-kóf'* |
| cauliflower | цветная капуста | *tsvit-náh-ya ka-póos-ta* |
| celery | сельдерей | *sil'-di-ryéj* |
| cucumber | огурец [-рцы *(pl)*] | *a-gu-ryéts (a-gur-tsý)* |
| dill | укроп | *uk-róp* |
| eggplant | баклажан | *bak-la-zháhn* |
| lettuce | салат | *sa-láht* |
| mushroom | гриб | *grip* |
| onion | лук | *look* |
| pea | горох *(coll)* | *ga-rókh* |
| | горошина *(sg)* | *ga-ró-shy-na* |
| potato | картофель *(coll)* | *kar-tó-fil'* |
| | картофелина *(sg)* | *kar-tó-fi-li-na* |
| | картошка *(sg, coll)* | *kar-tósh-ka* |
| potato salad | картофельный салат | *kar-tó-fil'-nyj sa-láht* |
| salad | салат | *sa-láht* |
| scallions | зелёный лук | *zi-lyó-nyj look* |
| spinach | шпинат | *shpi-náht* |
| squash | кабачок [-чки *(pl)*] | *ka-ba-chók* |
| string bean | стручковая фасоль | *struych-kó-va-ya fa-sól'* |
| tomato | помидор | *pa-mi-dór* |
| vegetables | овощи | *ó-va-shchi* |

## f. FRUITS AND NUTS

| apple | яблоко | *yáhb-la-ka* |
| apricot | абрикос | *ab-ri-kós* |
| banana | банан | *ba-náhn* |
| blueberry | черника | *chir-ní-ka* |
| cantaloupe | дыня | *dý-nya* |

| cherry | вишня *(sg, coll)* | *vísh-nya* |
|---|---|---|
| • sour cherry | черешня *(sg, coll)* | *chi-ryésh-nya* |
| date | финик | *fí-nik* |
| fig | инжир | *in-zhýr* |
| fruit | фрукт | *frookt* |
| grapefruit | грейпфрут | *gryéjp-fróot* |
| grapes | виноград *(coll)* | *vi-na-gráht* |
| | виноградина *(sg)* | *vi-na-gráh-di-na* |
| lemon | лимон | *li-món* |
| mandarin | мандарин | *man-da-rín* |
| nut | орех | *a-ryékh* |
| orange | апельсин | *a-pil'-sín* |
| peach | персик | *pyér-sik* |
| peanut | арахис *(coll)* | *a-ráh-khis* |
| pineapple | ананас | *a-na-náhs* |
| plum | слива | *slí-va* |
| prune | чернослив *(coll)* | *chir-na-slíf* |
| raspberry | малина *(coll)* | *ma-lí-na* |
| strawberry | клубника *(coll)* | *klub-ní-ka* |
| walnut | грецкий орех | *gryéts-kij a-ryékh* |
| watermelon | арбуз | *ar-bóos* |

## g. MEAL AND MENU COMPONENTS

| appetizer | закуска | *za-kóos-ka* |
|---|---|---|
| • as an appetizer | на закуску | *na za-kóos-ku* |
| borscht | борщ | *borshch* |
| broth, bouillon | бульон | *bul'-yón* |
| cake | кекс | *kyeks* |
| cookies | печенье *(coll)* | *pi-chyén'-ye* |
| crepe | блин | *blin* |
| • stuffed crepe | блинчик | *blín-chik* |
| cutlet | котлета | *kat-lyé-ta* |
| dessert | десерт, сладкое | *di-syért, sláht-ka-ye* |
| fillet | филе | *fi-lyé* |
| first course | первое блюдо | *pyér-va-ye bl ú-da* |
| fish | рыба | *rý-ba* |
| • fried fish | жареная рыба | *zháh-ri-na-ya rý-ba* |
| fried eggs | яичница | *i-ýsh-ni-tsa* |
| fried potatoes | жареный картофель *(f)* | *zháh-ri-nyj kar-tó-fil'* |
| goulash | гуляш | *gu-lyáhsh* |
| herring | сельдь *(f)* (селёдка) | *syel'd' (si-lyót-ka)* |
| hot cereal | каша | *káh-sha* |
| • oatmeal | овсяная каша | *af-syáh-na-ya káh-sha* |

| • cracked wheat | манная каша | *máh-na-ya káh-sha* |
| hot dog | сосиска | *sa-sís-ka* |
| macaroni | макароны | *ma-ka-ró-ny* |
| mashed potatoes | (картофельное) пюре | *(kar-tó-fil'-na-ye) pyu-réh* |
| menu | меню | *mi-nyú* |
| noodles | лапша *(coll)* | *lap-sháh* |
| omelet | омлет | *am-lyét* |
| pastry | пирожное | *pi-rózh-na-ye* |
| pea soup | гороховый суп | *ga-ró-kha-vyj soop* |
| pie | пирог | *pi-rók* |
| pork chop | свиная отбивная | *svi-náh-ya at-biv-náh-ya* |
| rice | рис | *ris* |
| roast beef | ростбиф | *rast-bíf* |
| roll | булка | *bóol-ka* |
| salad | салат | *sa-láht* |
| sandwich | бутерброт | *bu-ter-brót* |
| sausage | колбаса | *kal-ba-sáh* |
| scrambled eggs | яичница-болтунья | *i-ýsh-ni-tsa-bal-tóon'-ya* |
| soup | суп | *soop* |
| • cabbage soup with meat stock | щи | *shchi* |
| steak | бифштекс | *bif-shtéhks* |
| stew | тушёное мясо | *tu-shó-na-ye myáh-sa* |
| | рагу | *ra-góo* |
| • stewed beef | тушёная говядина | *tu-shó-na-ya ga-vyáh-di-na* |
| sweets | сладкое | *sláht-ka-ye* |
| vermicelli | вермишель *(f)* | *vir-mi-shéhl'* |

## h. DAIRY PRODUCTS, EGGS, AND RELATED FOODS

| butter | масло | *máhs-la* |
| buttermilk | кефир | *ki-fír* |
| cheese | сыр | *syr* |
| cream | сливки *(pl)* | *slíf-ki* |
| dairy products | молочные продукты | *ma-lóch-ny-ye pra-dóok-ty* |
| egg | яйцо | *ij-tsó* |
| ice cream | мороженое | *ma-ró-zhy-na-ye* |
| milk | молоко | *ma-la-kó* |
| smoked cheese | копчёный сыр | *kap-chyó-nyj syr* |
| sour cream | сметана | *smi-táh-na* |
| Swiss cheese | швейцарский сыр | *shvij-tsáhr-skij syr* |
| whipped cream | взбитые сливки *(pl)* | *vzbí-ty-ye slíf-ki* |

## i. GRAINS AND GRAIN PRODUCTS

| barley | ячмень *(m)* | *ich-myén'* |
|---|---|---|
| bread | хлеб *(coll)* | *khlyep* |
|  | хлеба *(pl)* | *kli-báh* |
| • black bread | чёрный хлеб | *chyór-nyj khlyep* |
| • rye bread | ржаной хлеб | *rzha-nój khlyep* |
| • slice (of bread) | ломоть *(m)* | *ló-mat'* |
| • white bread | белый хлеб | *byé-lyj khlyep* |
| corn | кукуруза | *ku-ku-róo-za* |
| flour | мука | *mu-káh* |
| grain | зерно | *zir-nó* |
| oats | овёс | *a-vyós* |
| rice | рис | *ris* |
| rye | рожь *(f)* | *rozh* |
| wheat | пшеница | *pshy-ní-tsa* |

## j. CONDIMENTS AND SPICES

| bay leaf | лавровый лист | *lav-ró-vyj list* |
|---|---|---|
| cinnamon | корица | *ka-rí-tsa* |
| cloves | гвоздика | *gvaz-dí-ka* |
| garlic | чеснок | *chis-nók* |
| honey | мёд | *myot* |
| jam | варенье | *va-ryé-n'ye* |
| mayonnaise | майонез | *ma-i-néhs* |
| mint | мята | *myáh-ta* |
| oil | масло | *máhs-la* |
| parsley | петрушка | *pit-róosh-ka* |
| pepper | перец | *pyé-rits* |
| salt | соль *(f)* | *sol'* |
| sugar | сахар | *sáh-khar* |
| vinegar | уксус | *óok-sus* |

## k. DRINKS

| alcoholic drink | алкогольный напиток | *al-ka-gól'-nyj na-pí-tak* |
|---|---|---|
| beer | пиво | *pí-va* |
| carbonated water | газированная вода | *ga-zi-ró-va-na-ya va-dáh* |
| champagne | шампанское | *sham-páhns-ka-ye* |
| • dry | сухое | *su-khó-ye* |
| • sweet | сладкое | *sláht-ka-ye* |
| coffee | кофе | *kó-fi* |

| | | |
|---|---|---|
| • coffee with milk | кофе с молоком | *kó-fì s ma-la-kóm* |
| cognac | коньяк | *kan'-yáhk* |
| drink | напиток | *na-pí-tak* |
| gin | джин | *dzhyn* |
| hot chocolate | какао | *ka-káh-o* |
| juice | сок | *sok* |
| kissel | кисель *(m)* | *ki-syél'* |
| lemonade (carbonated) | лимонад | *li-ma-nát* |
| liqueur | ликёр | *li-kyór* |
| milk | молоко | *ma-la-kó* |
| mineral water | минеральная вода | *mi-ni-ráhl'-na-ya va-dáh* |
| rum | ром | *rom* |
| soft drink | безалкогольный напиток | *biz-al-ka-gól'-nyj na-pí-tak* |
| stewed fruit drink | компот | *kam-pót* |
| tea | чай | *chahj* |
| vodka | водка | *vót-ka* |
| water | вода | *va-dáh* |
| whiskey | виски | *vís-ki* |
| wine | вино | *vi-nó* |
| • dry wine | сухое вино | *su-khó-ye vi-nó* |
| • dessert wine | сладкое вино | *sláht-ka-ye vi-nó* |

## l. AT THE TABLE

| | | |
|---|---|---|
| bottle | бутылка | *bu-týl-ka* |
| bowl | миска | *mís-ka* |
| cup | чашка | *cháhsh-ka* |
| cutlery, tableware | столовый прибор *(sg)* | *sta-ló-vyj pri-bór* |
| fork | вилка | *víl-ka* |
| glass | стакан | *sta-káhn* |
| knife | нож | *nosh* |
| napkin | салфетка | *sat-fyét-ka* |
| plate | тарелка | *ta-ryél-ka* |
| platter, dish | блюдо | *blyú-da* |
| saucer | блюдце | *blyú-tse* |
| shot glass | стаканчик | *sta-káhn-chik* |
| spoon | ложка | *lósh-ka* |
| table | стол | *stol* |
| tablecloth | скатерть *(f)* | *skáh-tirt'* |
| teaspoon | чайная ложка | *cháhj-na-ya lósh-ka* |
| toothpick | зубочистка | *zu-ba-chíst-ka* |
| tray | поднос | *pad-nós* |
| wine glass | рюмка | *ryúm-ka* |

*Expressions*

| | |
|---|---|
| A man can't live by bread alone | = Не хлебом единым жив человек |
| A sated man cannot understand a starving one | = Сытый голодного не понимает |
| Everything is done for him (Everything for him, as if on a tray) | = Всё ему, как на подносе |
| He does not lack for anything (His house is like a full cup) | = Его дом — полная чаша |
| Like a fish in water | = Как рыба в воде |
| Sick and tired of (Full up to the neck) | = Сыт(-а) по горло |
| To finish a meal | = Встать из-за стола |
| To sit down to a meal | = Сесть за стол |

## m. DINING OUT

| | | |
|---|---|---|
| **bill, check** | счёт | *shchot* |
| **bistro** | забегаловка | *za-bi-gáh-laf-ka* |
| **cafeteria** | кафетерий/столовая | *ka-fi-téh-rij/sta-ló-va-ya* |
| **cover charge** | плата за вход | *pláh-ta za fkhot* |
| **fixed price** | фиксированная цена | *fik-sí-ra-va-na-ya tsy-náh* |
| **pizzeria** | пицерия | *pi-tsy-rí-ya* |
| **price** | цена | *tsy-náh* |
| **reservation** | заказанный стол (-ик) | *za-káh-za-nyj stol (-ik)* |
| • **reserved** | заказано | *za-káh-za-na* |
| **restaurant** | ресторан | *ris-ta-ráhn* |
| **service** | обслуживание | *ap-slóo-zhy-va-n'ye* |
| • **self-service** | самообслуживание | *sá-ma-ap-slóo-zhy-va-n'ye* |
| **snack bar** | закусочная | *za-kóo-sach-na-ya* |
| **tip** | чаевые *(pl)* | *chi-i-vý-i* |
| • **tip (v)** | дать на чай *(p)* | *daht' na cháhj* |
| | давать на чай *(i)* | *da-váht' na cháhj* |
| **waiter** | официант | *a-fi-tsi-áhnt* |
| • **waitress** | официантка | *a-fi-tsi-áhnt-ka* |
| **wine list** | карта (карточка) вин | *káhr-ta (káhr-tach-ka) vin* |

## n. BUYING FOOD AND DRINK

| bakery | булочная | *bóo-lach-na-ya* |
|---|---|---|
| butcher shop | мясной магазин | *mis-nój ma-ga-zín* |
| dairy (products) | молочные продукты | *ma-lóch-ny-i pra-dóok-ty* |
| delicatessen | магазин-кулинария | *ma-ga-zín ku-li-ná-ri-ya* |
| fish store | рыбный магазин | *rýb-nyj ma-ga-zín* |
| grocery store | продуктовый магазин | *pra-duk-tó-vyj ma-ga-zín* |
| | гастроном | *gast-ra-nóm* |
| ice cream parlor | кафе-мороженое | *ka-féh-ma-ró-zhy-na-ye* |
| market | рынок | *rý-nak* |
| produce market | овощной рынок | *a-va-shchnój rý-nak* |
| supermarket | супермаркет | *su-pir-máhr-kit* |
| | супер | *sóo-pir* |
| sweets | кондитерская | *kan-dí-tirs-ka-ya* |
| wine store | винные товары | *vín-y-ye ta-váh-ry* |

## o. FOOD AND DRINK: ACTIVITIES

| add up the bill | подвести *(p)* счёт | *pad-vis-tí shchot* |
|---|---|---|
| | подводить *(i)* | *pad-va-dit'* |
| be hungry | быть *(i)* голодным *(m)* | *byt' ga-lód-nym* |
| | быть *(i)* голодной *(f)* | *byt' ga-lód-naj* |
| be thirsty | хотеть *(i)* пить | *kha-tyét' pit'* |
| clear the table | убрать *(p)* со стола | *ub-ráht' sa sta-láh* |
| | убирать *(i)* | *u-bi-ráht'* |
| cook | готовить *(i)* | *ga-tó-vit'* |
| cost | стоить *(i)* | *stó-it'* |
| cut | разрезать *(p)* (по-, на-) | *raz-ryé-zat' (pa-, na-)* |
| | резать *(i)* | *ryé-zat'* |
| drink | выпить *(p)* | *vý-pit'* |
| | пить *(i)* | *pit'* |
| • to drink occasionally | выпивать *(i)* | *vy-pi-váht'* |
| • drinking party | выпивка | *vý-pif-ka* |
| | пьянка | *p'yáhn-ka* |
| drunk | пьяный | *p'yáh-nyj* |
| | выпивший | *vý-pif-shyj* |
| • habitual drunk | пьяница | *p'yáh-ni-tsa* |
| eat | поесть/покушать *(p)* | *pa-yést'/pa-kóo-shat'* |
| | есть/кушать *(i)* | *yest'/kóo-shat'* |
| have a snack | закусить *(p)* | *za-ku-sít'* |
| | закусывать *(i)* | *za-kóo-sy-vat'* |

|                   | перекусить *(p)*          | *pi-ri-ku-sít'*            |
|                   | перекусывать *(i)*        | *pi-ri-kóo-sy-vat'*        |
| have lunch        | пообедать *(p)*           | *pa-a-byé-dat'*            |
|                   | обедать *(i)*             | *a-byé-dat'*               |
| have dinner       | поужинать *(p)*           | *pa-óo-zhy-nat'*           |
|                   | ужинать *(i)*             | *óo-zhy-nat'*              |
| order             | заказать *(p)*            | *za-ka-záht'*              |
|                   | заказывать *(i)*          | *za-káh-zy-vat'*           |
| peel              | очистить *(p)*            | *a-chís-tit'*              |
|                   | чистить *(i)*             | *chís-tit'*                |
| pour              | налить *(p)*              | *na-lít'*                  |
|                   | лить *(i)*                | *lit'*                     |
| serve             | подать *(p)*              | *pa-dáht'*                 |
|                   | подавать *(i)*            | *pa-da-váht'*              |
| set the table     | накрыть на стол *(p)*     | *na-krýt' na stol*         |
|                   | накрывать на стол *(i)*   | *na-kry-váht' na stol*     |
| shop for food     | покупать *(i)*            | *pa-ku-páht' pra-dóok-ty*  |
|                   | продукты                 |                            |
| slice             | ломоть *(m)* (хлеба)      | *ló-mat' (klyé-ba)*        |
| • piece           | кусок                    | *ku-sók*                   |
| toast             | тост                     | *tost*                     |
| weigh             | весить *(i)*             | *vyé-sit'*                 |

## p. DESCRIBING FOOD AND DRINK

| appetizing        | аппетитный *(adj)*        | *a-pi-tít-nyj*             |
| • appetizingly    | аппетитно *(adv)*         | *a-pi-tít-na*              |
| bad               | плохой *(adj)*            | *pla-khój*                 |
|                   | нехороший *(adj)*         | *ni-kha-ró-shij*           |
| • badly           | плохо *(adv)*             | *pló-kha*                  |
|                   | нехорошо *(adv)*          | *ni-kha-ra-shó*            |
| baked             | печёный                  | *pi-chyó-nyj*              |
| bitter            | горький                  | *gór'-kij*                 |
| cheap             | дешёвый *(adj)*           | *di-shó-vyj*               |
| • cheaply         | дёшево *(adv)*            | *dyó-shy-va*               |
| cold              | холодный *(adj)*          | *kha-lód-nyj*              |
|                   | холодно *(adv)*           | *khó-lad-na*               |
| expensive         | дорогой *(adj)*           | *da-ra-gój*                |
| • expensively     | дорого *(adv)*            | *dó-ra-ga*                 |
| fried             | жареный                  | *zháh-ri-nyj*              |
| good              | хороший *(adj)*           | *kha-ró-shij*              |
| • well            | хорошо *(adv)*            | *kha-ra-shó*               |
| hot               | горячий *(adj)*           | *ga-ryáh-chij*             |
| • hotly           | горячо *(adv)*            | *ga-ri-chó*                |
| mild              | лёгкий *(adj)*            | *lyókh-kij*                |
| • mildly          | легко *(adv)*             | *likh-kó*                  |
| pleasant          | приятный                 | *pri-yáht-nyj (-nin'-kij)* |
|                   | (-ненький) *(adj)*        |                            |

| | | |
|---|---|---|
| • **pleasantly** | приятно *(adv)* | *pri-yáht-na* |
| **salty** | солёный *(adj)* | *sa-lyó-nyj* |
| | солёно *(adv)* | *sa-lyó-na* |
| **sharp** | острый | *óst-ryj* |
| **sour** | кислый | *kís-lyj* |
| **spicy** | пикантный *(adj)* | *pi-káhnt-nyj* |
| • **spicily** | пикантно *(adv)* | *pi-káhnt-na* |
| **sweet** | сладкий *(adj)* | *sláht-kij* |
| • **sweetly** | сладко *(adv)* | *sláht-ka* |
| **tasty** | вкусный *(adj)* | *fkóos-nyj* |
| • **tastily** | вкусно *(adv)* | *fkóos-na* |
| **vegetarian** *(adj)* | вегетарианский *(m)* | *vi-gi-ta-ri-áhn-skij* |
| | вегетарианское *(n)* | *vi-gi-ta-ri-áhn-ska-ye* |
| | вегетарианская *(f)* | *vi-gi-ta-ri-áhn-ska-ya* |
| **with ice** | со льдом | *sa l'dom* |

## 25. SHOPPING AND ERRANDS

### a. GENERAL VOCABULARY

| | | |
|---|---|---|
| **art gallery** | картинная галерея | *kar-tín-na-ya ga-li-ryé-ya* |
| **bag** | сумка | *sóom-ka* |
| | мешок [-шки *(pl)*] | *mi-shók (-shki)* |
| **bill** | счёт | *shchot* |
| **buy online** | купить *(p)* он-лайн | *ku-pít' an-láhjn* |
| | покупать *(i)* | *pa-ku-páht'* |
| **buy, purchase** | купить *(p)* | *ku-pít'* |
| | покупать *(i)* | *pa-ku-páht'* |
| **carryall, netlike bag** | авоська | *a-vós'-ka* |
| **cash register** | касса | *káh-sa* |
| • **cashier** | кассир *(m)* | *ka-sír* |
| | кассирша *(f)* | *ka-sír-sha* |
| **change (money)** | сдача | *sdáh-cha* |
| **cost** | стоимость *(f)* | *stó-i-mast'* |
| • **cost** | стоить *(i)* | *stó-it'* |
| • **How much does it cost?** | Сколько это стоит? | *skól'-ka éh-ta stó-it* |
| **counter** | прилавок | *pri-láh-vak* |
| **customer** | покупатель *(m)* | *pa-ku-páh-til'* |
| | покупательница *(f)* | *pa-ku-páh-til'-ni-tsa* |
| | клиент (-ка) | *kli-yént (-ka)* |
| **department (of store)** | отдел | *at-dyél* |
| **department store** | универсальный магазин | *u-ni-vir-sáhl'-nyj ma-ga-zín* |
| **entrance** | вход | *fkhot* |
| **exit** | выход | *vý-khat* |
| **gift** | подарок | *pa-dáh-rak* |
| **look for something** | искать *(i)* что-нибудь | *is-káht' shtó-ni-but'* |

| | | |
|---|---|---|
| **package** | свёрток | *svyór-tak* |
| | пакет | *pa-kyét* |
| **pay** | заплатить *(p)* | *za-pla-tít'* |
| | платить *(i)* | *pla-tít'* |

*Expressions*

| | | |
|---|---|---|
| **To pay little for (something)** | = | Платить мало/недорого за (что-то) |
| **To pay much for (something)** | = | Платить много/дорого за (что-то) |
| **To pay someone back,** <br> **to settle a score** | = | Свести счёты |
| **To pay the bill** | = | Заплатить по счёту |

| | | |
|---|---|---|
| • **cash** | деньги | *dyén'-gi* |
| • **check** | чек | *chyek* |
| • **credit card** | кредитная карточка | *kri-dít-na-ya káhr-tach-ka* |
| **pay (buy) by check** | купить *(p)* чеком | *ku-pít' chyé-kam* |
| | покупать *(i)* | *pa-ku-páht'* |
| **price** | цена | *tsy-náh* |
| • **discount** | скидка | *skít-ka* |
| • **fixed price** | фиксированная цена | *fik-sí-ra-va-na-ya tsy-náh* |
| • **high** | высокая | *vy-só-ka-ya* |
| • **inexpensive** | недорогая | *ni-da-ra-gáh-ya* |
| • **low** | низкая | *nís-ka-ya* |
| • **price tag** | ярлык | *ir-lýk* |
| • **reduced price** | сниженная цена | *sní-zhy-na-ya tsy-náh* |
| **produce market** | рынок | *rý-nak* |
| **products *(pl)*,** <br> merchandise | товары *(pl)* | *ta-váh-ry* |
| **purchase** | покупка | *pa-kóop-ka* |
| **sale** | распродажа | *ras-pra-dáh-zha* |
| • **for sale** | на продажу | *na pra-dáh-zhu* |
| • **on sale** | на распродаже | *na ras-pra-dáh-zhy* |
| • **sell** | продать *(p)* | *pra-dáht'* |
| | продавать *(i)* | *pra-da-váht'* |
| **shop, store** | магазин | *ma-ga-zín* |
| • **shop** | идти, ходить *(i)* за | *it-tí, kha-dít' za* |
| | покупками | *pa-kóop-ka-mi* |
| • **closed** | закрыт | *za-krýt* |
| • **closing time** | время закрытия | *vryé-mya za-krý-ti-ya* |
| • **department** | отдел | *at-dyél* |
| • **open** | открыт | *at-krýt* |
| • **opening time** | время открытия | *vryé-mya at-krý-ti-ya* |
| • **store clerk** | служащий *(m)* | *slóo-zha-shchij* |
| | магазина | *ma-ga-zí-na* |
| | служащая *(f)* | *slóo-zha-shchi-ya* |
| | магазина | *ma-ga-zí-na* |

| • window | витрина | vit-rí-na |
| souvenir shop | сувенирный магазин | su-vi-nír-nyj ma-ga-zín |
| spend | потратить *(p)* | pa-tráh-tit' |
| | тратить *(i)* | tráh-tit' |
| street market | толкучка | tal-kóoch-ka |
| take | взять *(p)* | vzyaht' |
| | брать *(i)* | braht' |
| • take back | вернуть *(p)* | vir-nóot' |
| | возвращать *(i)* | vaz-vra-shcháht' |

## b. HARDWARE

| battery | батарейка | ba-ta-ryéj-ka |
| cable | трос, кабель *(m)* | tros, káh-bil' |
| clamp | зажим | za-zhým |
| | скрепа | skryé-pa |
| drill | сверло | svir-ló |
| • electrical | электрическое | y-lik-trí-chis-ka-ye |
| file | напильник | na-píl'-nik |
| flashlight | карманный фонарь *(m)* | kar-máhn-yj fa-náhr' |
| fuse | пробка | próp-ka |
| hammer | молоток | ma-la-tók |
| hardware store | скобяные товары | ska-bi-ný-i ta-váh-ry |
| insulation (tape) | изоляционная лента | i-zy-li-tsy-ó-na-ya lyén-ta |
| light bulb | (световая) лампочка | (svi-ta-váh-ya) láhm-pach-ka |
| • bulb | света | svyé-ta |
| • fluorescent | лампа дневного света | láhm-pa dniv-nó-va svyé-ta |
| • neon | неоновая | ni-ó-na-va-ya |
| mechanical *(adj)* | механический | mi-kha-ní-chis-kij |
| nail | гвоздь *(m)* | gvost' |
| outlet | розетка | ra-zyét-ka |
| plane | рубанок | ru-báh-nak |
| pliers | плоскогубцы *(pl)* | pla-ska-góop-tsy |
| plug | штепсель *(m)* | shtéhp-sil' |
| | вилка | víl-ka |
| plumbing | водопровод | va-da-pra-vót |
| punch | штамп | shtahmp |
| saw | пила | pi-láh |
| screw | винт | vint |
| | болт | bolt |
| screwdriver | отвёртка | at-vyórt-ka |
| shovel | лопата | la-páh-ta |
| tool | инструмент | in-stru-myént |
| transformer | трансформатор | trans-far-máh-tar |
| wire | проволока | pró-va-la-ka |
| | провод | pró-vat |
| wrench | гаечный ключ | gáh-ich-nyj klyuch |

## c. STATIONERY

| | | |
|---|---|---|
| **adhesive tape** | клейкая лента | *klyéj-ka-ya lyén-ta* |
| **ballpoint pen** | шариковая ручка | *sháh-ri-ka-va-ya róoch-ka* |
| **briefcase** | портфель *(m)* | *part-fyél'* |
| **envelope** | конверт | *kan-vyért* |
| **marker** | фломастер | *fla-máhs-tir* |
| **notepad** | блокнот | *blak-nót* |
| **paper** | бумага | *bu-máh-ga* |
| **pen** | ручка | *róoch-ka* |
| **pencil** | карандаш | *ka-ran-dáhsh* |
| **sheet of paper** | лист бумаги | *list bu-máh-gi* |
| **staple** | скобка | *skóp-ka* |
| **stapler** | стейплер | *stéhjp-lyer* |
| **stationery store** | писчебумажный | *pis-chi-bu-máhzh-nyj* |
| | магазин | *ma-ga-zín* |
| **string** | верёвка | *vi-ryóf-ka* |
| | бечёвка | *bi-chyóf-ka* |
| **writing pad** | блокнот | *blak-nót* |

## d. PHOTO AND CAMERA

| | | |
|---|---|---|
| **button** | кнопка | *knóp-ka* |
| **camera** | фотоаппарат | *fo-ta-a-pa-ráht* |
| • **camcorder** | видеокамера | *vi-di-a-káh-mi-ra* |
| • **movie camera** | киноаппарат | *ki-na-a-pa-ráht* |
| **camera shop** | фототовары | *fo-ta-ta-váh-ry* |
| **compact flash (card)** | компакт флэш | *kam-páhkt fléhsh* |
| **digital camera** | цифровой фотоаппарат | *tsyf-ra-vój fá-ta-a-pa-ráht* |
| | цифровая камера | *tsyf-ra-váh-ya káh-mi-ra* |
| **digital photography** | цифровая фотография | *tsyf-ra-váh-ya* |
| | | *fa-ta-gráh-fi-ya* |
| **exposure** | экспозиция | *yks-pa-zí-tsy-ya* |
| **enlargement** | увеличение | *u-vi-li-chyé-ni-ye* |
| **film** | плёнка | *plyón-ka* |
| • **roll of film** | катушка | *ka-tóosh-ka* |
| **flash** | вспышка | *vspýsh-ka* |
| **lens** | линза | *lín-za* |
| **memory card** | карта памяти | *káhr-ta páh-mi-ti* |
| **photo, picture** | фотография | *fa-ta-gráh-fi-ya* |
| | фотокарточка | *fa-ta-káhr-tach-ka* |
| • **clear (good)** | хорошая | *kha-ró-sha-ya* |
| • **color picture** | цветная | *tsvit-náh-ya* |
| | фотография | *fa-ta-gráh-fi-ya* |
| • **focus** | фокус | *fó-kus* |
| • **in black and white** | чернобелая | *chir-na-béh-la-ya* |
| • **out of focus** | не в фокусе | *ni f fó-ku-si* |

| | | |
|---|---|---|
| • **take a picture** | снять (что-то) *(p)* | *snyaht' (shtó-ta)* |
| | снимать (что-то) *(i)* | *sni-máht' (shtó-ta)* |
| • **The picture turned out badly** | Фотография плохо получилась | *fa-ta-gráh-fi-ya pló-kha pa-lu-chí-las'* |
| • **The picture turned out well** | Фотография хорошо получилась | *fa-ta-gráh-fi-ya kha-ra-shó pa-lu-chí-las'* |
| **"red eye"** | "красные глаза" *(pl)* | *kráhs-ny-i glá-za* |
| **resolution** | разрешение | *raz-ri-shéh-ni-ye* |
| **sharpness** | резкость | *ryés-kast'* |
| **screen** | экран | *yk-ráhn* |
| **slide** | диапозитив | *di-a-pa-zi-tíf* |
| **telephoto lens** | увеличительная линза | *u-vi-li-chí-til'-na-ya lín-za* |
| **timer** | таймер | *táhj-mir* |
| • **self-timer** | автотаймер | *áhf-ta-táhj-mir* |
| **wide angle** | широкий угол | *shy-ró-kij oó-gal* |
| **zoom** | зум | *zoom* |
| **zoom lens** | зум линза | *zoom lín-za* |

### e. TOBACCO

| | | |
|---|---|---|
| **cigar** | сигара | *si-gáh-ra* |
| **cigarette** | сигарета | *si-ga-ryé-ta* |
| • **half filled with tobacco** | папироса | *pa-pi-ró-sa* |
| **lighter** | зажигалка | *za-zhy-gáhl-ka* |
| **match** | спичка | *spích-ka* |
| **pipe** | трубка | *tróop-ka* |
| **tobacco** | табак | *ta-báhk* |
| **tobacco products** | табачные товары | *ta-báhch-ny-i ta-váh-ry* |

### f. COSMETICS AND TOILETRIES

| | | |
|---|---|---|
| **blade** | лезвие | *lyéz-vi-ye* |
| **brush** | щётка | *shchyót-ka* |
| **cologne** | одеколон | *a-di-ka-lón* |
| **comb** | расчёска | *ra-shchyós-ka* |
| **cosmetics shop** | косметические товары | *kas-mi-tí-chis-ki-i ta-váh-ry* |
| **cream** | крем | *krehm* |
| **curler** | бигуди *(coll)* | *bi-gu-dí* |
| **deodorant** | деодорант | *di-ó-da-rant* |
| **electric razor** | электрическая бритва | *y-lik-trí-chis-ka-ya brít-va* |
| **face powder** | пудра для лица | *póod-ra dlya li-tsáh* |
| **hair dryer** | сушилка для волос | *su-shýl-ka dlya va-lós* |
| | фен | *fyen* |
| **lipstick** | губная помада | *gub-náh-ya pa-máh-da* |
| **lotion** | лосьон | *las'-yón* |

| makeup | косметика | *kas-myé-ti-ka* |
| mascara | тушь *(f)* для ресниц | *toosh dlya ris-níts* |
| nail polish | лак для ногтей | *lahk dlya nak-tyéj* |
| • nail polish remover | ацетон | *a-tsy-tón* |
| perfume | духи *(pl)* | *du-khí* |
| perfume shop | парфюмерия | *par-fyu-myé-ri-ya* |
| razor | бритва | *brít-va* |
| shampoo | шампунь *(m)* | *sham-póon'* |
| shaving cream | крем для бритья | *krehm dlya brit'-yáh* |
| soap | мыло | *mý-la* |
| talcum powder | тальк | *tahl'k* |
| tampon | тампон | *tam-pón* |

## g. LAUNDRY

| button | пуговица | *póo-ga-vi-tsa* |
| clean | чистый | *chís-tyj* |
| clothes | одежда | *a-dyézh-da* |
| • clothes basket | корзина (-нка) для белья | *kar-zí-na (-nka) dlya bil'-yáh* |
| • underclothes | бельё | *bil'-yó* |
| clothespin | прищепка | *pri-shchyép-ka* |
| detergent | стиральный порошок | *sti-ráhl'-nyj pa-ra-shók* |
| dirty | грязный | *gryáz-nyj* |
| dry cleaner | химчистка | *khim-chíst-ka* |
| hole | дыра (-рка) | *dy-ráh (-rka)* |
| iron | утюг | *u-tyúk* |
| • iron | гладить *(i)* | *gláh-dit'* |
| laundry room | прачечная | *práh-chish-na-ya* |
| laundromat | автоматическая прачечная | *av-to-ma-tí-chis-ka-ya práh-chish-na-ya* |
| mend | починить *(p)* | *pa-chi-nít'* |
| | чинить *(i)* | *chi-nít'* |
| pocket | карман | *kar-máhn* |
| sew | зашить *(p)* | *za-shýt'* |
| | шить *(i)* | *shyt'* |
| sleeve | рукав | *ru-káhf* |
| spot, stain | пятно | *pit-nó* |
| starch | крахмал | *krahk-máhl* |
| stitch | стежок | *sti-zhók* |
| • stitch | простегать *(p)* | *pra-sti-gáht'* |
| | стегать *(i)* | *sti-gáht'* |
| wash | стирка *(coll)* | *stír-ka* |
| zipper | молния | *mól-ni-ya* |

## h. PHARMACY AND DRUGSTORE

| | | |
|---|---|---|
| **antibiotic** | антибиотик | *an-ti-bi-ó-tik* |
| **aspirin** | пирамидон | *pi-ra-mi-dón* |
| | аспирин | *as-pi-rín* |
| **Band-Aid** | липкий пластырь *(m)* | *líp-kij pláhs-tyr'* |
| **birth-control pills** | противозачаточные | *pra-ti-va-za-* |
| | таблетки | *cháh-tach-ny-ye* |
| | | *tab-lyét-ki* |
| **condom** | презерватив | *pri-zir-va-tíf* |
| **cotton wool** | вата | *váh-ta* |
| **drug** | лекарство | *li-káhr-stva* |
| **drugstore/ pharmacy** | аптека | *ap-tyé-ka* |
| **hand lotion** | крем для рук | *krehm dlya rook* |
| **injection** | укол | *u-kól* |
| **insulin** | инсулин | *in-su-lín* |
| **medicine** | лекарство/ | *li-káhr-stva/* |
| | медикамент | *mi-di-ka-myént* |
| **ointment** | мазь *(f)* | *mahs'* |
| **penicillin** | пенициллин | *pi-ni-tsy-lín* |
| **petroleum jelly** | вазелин | *va-zi-lín* |
| **pharmaceutical** | фармацевтический | *far-ma-tsyf-tí-chis-kij* |
| **pharmacist** | аптекарь *(m)* | *ap-tyé-kar'* |
| | аптекарша *(f)* | *ap-tyé-kar-sha* |
| **pill** | таблетка | *tab-lyét-ka* |
| **powder** | порошок | *pa-ra-shók* |
| **prescription** | рецепт | *ri-tséhpt* |
| **sodium carbonate** | углекислый натрий | *ug-li-kís-lyj náht-rij* |
| **syrup** | сироп | *si-róp* |
| **tablet** | таблетка | *tab-lyét-ka* |
| **thermometer** | термометр | *tir-mó-mitr* |
| **tincture of iodine** | настойка йода | *na-stój-ka jó-da* |
| **tissue** | салфетка | *sal-fyét-ka* |
| **toothbrush** | зубная щётка | *zub-náh-ya shchyót-ka* |
| **toothpaste** | зубная паста | *zub-náh-ya páh-sta* |
| **vitamin** | витамин | *vi-ta-mín* |

## i. JEWELRY

| | | |
|---|---|---|
| **amber** | янтарь *(m)* | *in-táhr'* |
| **artificial** | искусственный | *is-kóost-vi-nyj* |
| **bracelet** | браслет | *bras-lyét* |
| **brooch** | брошь (-шка) *(f)* | *brosh* |
| **carat** | карат | *ka-ráht* |

| chain | цепь (цепочка) *(f)* | *tsehp' (tsy-póch-ka)* |
| diamond | бриллиант | *bri-li-áhnt* |
| earring | серьга | *sir'-gáh* |
| emerald | изумруд | *i-zum-róot* |
| false | фальшивый | *fal'-shý-vyj* |
| fix, repair | починить *(p)* | *pa-chi-nít'* |
| | чинить *(i)* | *chi-nít'* |
| gold | золото | *zó-la-ta* |
| jewel | драгоценный камень *(m)* | *dra-ga-tséh-nyj káh-min'* |
| jeweler | ювелир | *yu-vi-lír* |
| jewelry | драгоценности *(pl)* | *dra-ga-tséh-nas-ti* |
| • genuine | настоящие *(pl)* | *nas-ta-yáh-shchi-ye* |
| necklace | ожерелье | *a-zhy-ryél'-i* |
| opal | опал | *a-páhl* |
| pearl | жемчужина | *zhym-chóo-zhy-na* |
| precious | драгоценный | *dra-ga-tséh-nyj* |
| ring | кольцо | *kal'-tsó* |
| ruby | рубин | *ru-bín* |
| sapphire | сапфир | *sap-fír* |
| silver | серебро | *si-ri-bró* |
| topaz | топаз | *ta-páhs* |
| watch, clock | часы *(pl)* | *chi-sý* |
| • alarm clock | будильник | *bu-díl'-nik* |
| • dial | циферблат | *tsy-fîr-bláht* |
| • hand | стрелка | *stryél-ka* |
| • spring | пружина | *pru-zhý-na* |
| • watchband | ремешок для часов | *ri-mi-shók dlya chi-sóf* |
| • wind | завести *(p)* | *za-vis-tí* |
| | заводить *(i)* | *za-va-dít'* |

*Expressions*

| **Not everything that shines is gold** | = Не всё золото, что блестит |
| **To mark time** (To watch the clock) | = На часы смотреть |
| **To mask something** (To cover with gold) | = Позолотить |
| **To pay a bribe** (To cover one's hand with gold) | = Позолотить руку |
| **To promise a rose garden** (To promise golden mountains) | = Обещать золотые горы |

## j. MUSIC

| | | |
|---|---|---|
| **alternative music** | альтернативная музыка | *al'-tyr-na-tív-na-ya moo-zy-ka* |
| **cassette** | кассета | *ka-syé-ta* |
| **classical music** | классическая музыка | *kla-sí-chis-ka-ya móo-zy-ka* |
| **compact disc** | компактный диск | *kam-páhkt-nyj disk* |
| **composer** | композитор | *kam-pa-zí-tar* |
| **concert** | концерт | *kan-tséhrt* |
| **dance music** | танцевальная музыка | *tan-tsy-váhl'-na-ya móo-zy-ka* |
| **download music** | скачать *(p)* музыку скачивать *(i)* | *ska-cháht' móo-zy-ku skáh-chi-vat'* |
| **folk song** | народная песня | *na-ród-na-ya pyés'-nya* |
| **heavy metal** | хэви-метал | *khéh-vi-myé-tal* |
| **iPod** | айпод | *áhj-pad* |
| **jazz** | джаз | *dzhahs* |
| **karaoke** | караоке | *ka-ra-ó-ke* |
| **MP3 player** | эмпи три/Мп3 плеер | *éhm-pi trí/éhm-pi-trí plyé-ir* |
| **music** | музыка | *móo-zy-ka* |
| **rap** | рэп | *rehp* |
| **rock** | рок (-н-ролл) | *rók, rak-yn-ról* |
| **singer** | певец *(m)* певица *(f)* | *pi-vyéts pi-ví-tsa* |
| **song** | песня | *pyés-nya* |
| **tape** | плёнка | *plyón-ka* |
| • **recording** | запись *(f)* | *záh-pis'* |

*Expressions*

| | |
|---|---|
| **He is generous, a good-hearted person (He has a golden soul)** | = У него душа золотая |
| **I am happy/excited (My soul is singing)** | = У меня душа поёт |

## k. CLOTHING

| | | |
|---|---|---|
| **articles of clothing** | предметы одежды | *prid-myé-ty a-dyézh-dy* |
| **bathing suit** | плавки *(for males)* купальник *(for females)* | *pláhf-ki ku-páhl'-nik* |
| **belt** | пояс *(for females)* ремень *(for males) (m)* | *pó-yas ri-myén'* |
| **beret** | берет | *bi-ryét* |
| **blouse** | блузка | *blóos-ka* |

| bra | лифчик | *líf-chik* |
| | бюстгальтер | *byust-gáhl'-tir* |
| cap | кепка | *kyép-ka* |
| clothing store | магазин одежды | *ma-ga-zín a-dyézh-dy* |
| coat | пальто *(indecl)* | *pal-tó* |
| dress | платье | *pláht'-ye* |
| fashion | мода | *mó-da* |
| fur coat | меховое пальто *(indecl)* | *mi-kha-vó-ye pal'-tó* |
| | шуба | *shóo-ba* |
| glove | перчатка | *pir-cháht-ka* |
| handkerchief | носовой платок | *na-sa-vój pla-tók* |
| hat | шапка | *sháhp-ka* |
| | шляпа | *shlyáh-pa* |
| jacket | куртка/жакет | *kóort-ka/zha-kyét* |
| men's shop/ clothing | магазин мужской одежды | *ma-ga-zín muzh-skój a-dyézh-dy* |
| mitten | рукавица | *ru-ka-ví-tsa* |
| nightgown | ночная рубашка | *nach-náh-ya ru-báhsh-ka* |
| pajamas | пижама | *pi-zháh-ma* |
| pants | штаны | *shta-ný* |
| panty | трусики *(pl)* | *tróo-si-ki* |
| pantyhose | колготки *(pl)* | *kal-gót-ki* |
| raincoat | плащ | *plahshch* |
| | дождевик | *dazh-di-vík* |
| scarf | шарф | *shahrf* |
| shawl | шаль *(f)* | *shahl'* |
| shirt | рубашка | *ru-báhsh-ka* |
| shorts | трусы | *tru-sý* |
| size | размер | *raz-myér* |
| skirt | юбка | *yúp-ka* |
| slip | комбинация | *kam-bi-náh-tsi-ya* |
| suit | костюм | *kas-tyúm* |
| sweater | свитер | *sví-tyr* |
| T-shirt | майка | *máhj-ka* |
| tie | галстук | *gáhls-tuk* |
| trench coat | пыльник | *pýl'-nik* |
| trousers | брюки | *bryú-ki* |
| underwear | бельё *(coll)* | *bil'-yó* |
| vest | жилет | *zhy-lyét* |
| women's shop/ clothing | магазин женской одежды | *ma-ga-zín zhéhn-skaj a-dyézh-dy* |

## l. DESCRIBING CLOTHING

| beautiful | красивый | *kra-sí-vyj* |
| big | большой | *bal'-shój* |
| cotton | хлопчатобумажный | *khlap-cháh-ta-bu-máhzh-nyj* |

| | | |
|---|---|---|
| elegant | элегантный | *y-li-gáhnt-nyj* |
| fabric | материал | *ma-ti-ri-áhl* |
| in the latest style/ fashion | по последней моде | *pa pas-lyéd-nij mó-di* |
| leather | кожа *(n)* | *kó-zha* |
| | кожаный *(adj)* | *kó-zhy-nyj* |
| linen | лён *(n)* | *lyon* |
| | льняной *(adj)* | *l'-ni-nój* |
| loose | свободный | *sva-bód-nyj* |
| • fit loosely | сидеть *(i)* свободно | *si-dyét' sva-bód-na* |
| nylon | нейлоновый | *nij-ló-na-vyj* |
| plaid | клетчатый | *klyét-chi-tyj* |
| polyester | полиэфир | *pa-li-y-fír* |
| silk | шёлковый | *shyól-ka-vyj* |
| small | маленький | *máh-lin'-kij* |
| striped | полосатый | *pa-la-sáh-tyj* |
| tight | тесный | *tyés-nyj* |
| • narrow | узкий | *óos-kij* |
| ugly | некрасивый | *ni-kra-sí-vyj* |
| wool | шерстяной | *shyr-sti-nój* |

*Expressions*

| | | |
|---|---|---|
| **Clothes (slang) (Rags)** | = | Тряпки |
| **Devil may care** (To put one's cap on over one's ear) | = | Надеть кепку набекрень |
| **Someone who follows all the latest fashions** | = | Модник *(m)*, модница *(f)* |

## m. CLOTHING: ACTIVITIES

| | | |
|---|---|---|
| lengthen | удлинить *(p)* | *u-dlí-nit'* |
| | удлинять *(i)* | *u-dli-nyáht'* |
| put on | одеть *(p)* | *a-dyét'* |
| | надеть *(p)* | *na-dyét'* |
| shorten | укоротить *(p)* | *u-ka-ra-tít'* |
| | укорачивать *(i)* | *u-ka-ráh-chi-vat'* |
| take in | заузить *(p)* | *za-óo-zit'* |
| | зауживать *(i)* | *za-óo-zhy-vat'* |
| take off | снять *(p)* | *snyaht'* |
| | снимать *(i)* | *sni-máht'* |

| | | |
|---|---|---|
| **tighten** | затянуть *(p)* | *za-ti-nóot'* |
| | затягивать *(i)* | *za-tyáh-gi-vat'* |
| **try on** | примерить *(p)* | *pri-myé-rit'* |
| | померить *(p)* | *pa-myé-rit'* |
| | мерять *(i)* | *myé-rit'* |
| **undress (take off)** | снять *(p)* | *snyaht'* |
| | снимать *(i)* | *sni-máht'* |
| | раздеться *(p)* | *raz-dyét'-tsa* |
| | раздеваться *(i)* | *raz-di-váht'-tsa* |
| **wear** | носить *(i)* | *na-sít'* |
| **widen** | расширить *(p)* | *rash-shý-rit'* |
| | расширять *(i)* | *ra-shy-ryáht'* |
| **widen clothes** | расставить *(p)* | *ra-stáh-vit'* |
| | расставлять *(i)* | *ra-stav-lyáht'* |

## n. FOOTWEAR

| | | |
|---|---|---|
| **boot** | сапог | *sa-pók* |
| **pair** | пара | *páh-ra* |
| **shoe** | туфель *(sg, m)* | *tóo-fíl'* |
| | туфли *(pl)* | *tóof-li* |
| | ботинок *(sg)* | *ba-tí-nak* |
| | ботинки *(pl)* | *ba-tín-ki* |
| **shoe store** | обувной магазин | *a-buv-nój ma-ga-zín* |
| **shoelace** | шнурок | *shnu-rók* |
| **size** | размер | *raz-myér* |
| **slippers** | тапки, тапочки *(pl)* | *táhp-ki, táh-pach-ki* |
| **sock** | носок *(sg)* | *na-sók* |
| | носки *(pl)* | *nas-kí* |
| **stocking** | чулок *(sg)* | *chu-lók* |
| | чулки *(pl)* | *chul-kí* |
| **tennis shoes** | кроссовки | *kra-sóf-ki* |

## o. BOOKS

| | | |
|---|---|---|
| **audiobook** | аудиокнига | *áh-u-di-o-kní-ga* |
| **book** | книга | *kní-ga* |
| • **best-seller** | бест-селлер | *byest-syé-lyer* |
| • **hard cover** | в твёрдой обложке | *f tvyór-daj ab-lósh-kye* |
| • **paperback** | в мягкой обложке | *v myáh-kaj ab-lósh-kye* |
| **bookstore** | книжный магазин | *knízh-nyj ma-ga-zín* |
| **comics** | комиксы | *kó-mik-sy* |
| **dictionary** | словарь *(m)* | *sla-váhr'* |
| **encyclopedia** | энциклопедия | *yn-tsy-kla-pyé-di-ya* |
| **fiction** | беллетристика | *bi-lit-rís-ti-ka* |

| | | |
|---|---|---|
| **guidebook** | путеводитель *(m)* | *pu-ti-va-dí-til'* |
| **magazine** | журнал | *zhur-náhl* |
| **mystery** | детективный роман | *dy-tyk-tív-nyj ra-máhn* |
| **newspaper** | газета | *ga-zyé-ta* |
| **novel** | роман | *ra-máhn* |
| **poetry** | поэзия | *pa-éh-zi-ya* |
| **reference book** | справочник | *spráh-vach-nik* |
| **romance** | роман | *ra-máhn* |
| **science fiction** | научная фантастика | *na-óoch-na-ya fan-táhs-ti-ka* |
| **technical reference** | технический справочник | *tikh-ní-chis-kij spráh-vach-nik* |
| **textbook** | учебник | *u-chyéb-nik* |

## 26. BANKING AND COMMERCE

| | | |
|---|---|---|
| **account** | счёт | *shchyot* |
| • close an account | закрыть *(p)* счёт | *za-krýt' shchyot* |
| | закрывать *(i)* | *za-kry-váht'* |
| • open an account | открыть *(p)* счёт | *at-krýt' shchyot* |
| | открывать *(i)* | *at-kry-váht'* |
| **account balance** | состояние счёта | *sas-ta-yáh-ni-ye shchyó-ta* |
| **advertisement** | реклама | *rik-láh-ma* |
| **ATM** | банкомат | *ban-ka-maht* |
| • cash dispenser | раздатчик наличных | *raz-dáht-chik na-lích-nykh* |
| **bank** | банк | *bahnk* |
| • head office | главное отделение | *gláhv-na-ye at-di-lyé-ni-ye* |
| • work in a bank | работать *(i)* в банке | *ra-bó-tat' v báhn-ki* |
| **bankbook** | банковская книжка | *báhn-kaf-ska-ya knísh-ka* |
| | сберегательная книжка | *sbi-ri-gáh-til'-na-ya knísh-ka* |
| **bank rate** | банковская ставка процента | *báhn-kaf-ska-ya stáhf-ka pra-tséhn-ta* |
| • fixed | фиксированная | *fik-sí-ra-va-na-ya* |
| • variable | переменная | *pi-ri-myé-na-ya* |
| **bankrupt** *(n)* | банкрот | *bank-rót* |
| | несостоятельный должник | *ni-sas-ta-yáh-til'-nyj dalzh-ník* |
| **bar code** | бар-код | *báhr-kót* |
| | штрих-код | *shtríkh-kót* |
| **bill/bank note** | банкнота | *bank-nó-ta* |
| • dollar | доллар | *dó-lar* |
| • large bill | большая банкнота | *bal'-sháh-ya bank-nó-ta* |
| • ruble | рубль *(m)* | *roobl'* |
| **budget** | бюджет | *byud-zhéht* |

| | | |
|---|---|---|
| **business** | бизнес | *bíz-nis* |
| **cash** | наличные (деньги) | *na-lích-ny-i (dyén'-gi)* |
| • **cash** | получить *(p)* деньги по чеку | *pa-lu-chít' dyén'-gi pa chyé-ku* |
| | получать *(i)* | *pa-lu-cháht'* |
| **cash card** | наличная карточка | *na-lích-na-ya káhr-tych-ka* |
| **cashier, teller** | кассир (-ша) | *ka-sír (-sha)* |
| **check** | чек | *chyek* |
| • **checkbook** | чековая книжка | *chyé-ka-va-ya knísh-ka* |
| **coin** | монета | *ma-nyé-ta* |
| **cost** | стоимость | *sto-i-mast'* |
| **coupon, voucher** | купон | *ku-pón* |
| **credit** | кредит | *kri-dít* |
| • **credit card** | кредитная карточка | *kri-dít-na-ya káhr-tach-ka* |
| **currency** | валюта | *va-lyúh-ta* |
| • **hard currency** | твёрдая валюта | *tvyór-da-ya va-lyúh-ta* |
| **current account** | текущий счёт | *ti-kóo-shchij shchyot* |
| **customer** | покупатель *(m)* (-ница) | *pa-ku-páh-til' (-ni-tsa)* |
| | клиент (-ка) | *kli-yént (-ka)* |
| **debt** | долг | *dolk* |
| **deposit** | вклад | *vklahd* |
| • **deposit** | вложить *(p)* | *vla-zhýt'* |
| | вкладывать *(i)* | *vkláh-dy-vat'* |
| **discount** | скидка | *skít-ka* |
| **employee (bank)** | служащий (-ая) (банка) | *slóo-zha-shchij (-a-ya) (báhn-ka)* |
| **endorse (sign)** | подписать *(p)* | *pat-pi-sáht'* |
| | подписывать *(i)* | *pat-pí-sy-vat'* |
| **enter (key)** | ввести *(p)* | *vvis-tí* |
| | вести *(i)* | *vis-tí* |
| **euro** | евро | *yév-ra* |
| **exchange** | обмен | *ab-myén* |
| • **exchange** | обменять *(p)* | *ab-mi-nyaht'* |
| | менять *(i)* | *mi-nyáht'* |
| **exchange rates (currency)** | курс обмена (валюты) | *koors ab-myéna (va-lyú-ty)* |
| **expiration date (valid until)** | действительно до... | *di-ství-til'-na da* |
| **income** | доход, заработок | *da-khót, záh-ra-ba-tak* |
| **insurance** | страховка | *stra-khóf-ka* |
| **interest** | проценты *(pl)* | *pra-tséhn-ty* |
| • **interest rate** | процентная ставка | *pra-tséhnt-na-ya stáhf-ka* |
| **invest** | вложить *(p)* | *vla-zhýt'* |
| | вкладывать *(i)* | *fkláh-dy-vat'* |

| | | |
|---|---|---|
| • investment | вложение | vla-zhéh-ni-ye |
| | капиталовложение | ka-pi-ta-la-vla-zhéh-ni-ye |
| key | клавиша | kláh-vi-sha |
| key pad | клавиатура | kla-vi-a-tóo-ra |
| kopeck | копейка | ka-pyéj-ka |
| limit (cash/withdrawal) | лимит | li-mít |
| line | очередь (f) | ó-chi-rit' |
| • stand in line | стоять в очереди (i) | sta-yáht' v ó-chi-ri-di |
| loan | заём | za-yóm |
| • get a loan | взять (p) взаём | vzyaht' vza-yóm |
| | брать (i) | braht' |
| | одолжить (p) | a-dal-zhýt' |
| | одалживать (i) | a-dáhl-zhy-vat' |
| loose change | мелочь (f) | myé-lach |
| manager | заведующий (-ая) | za-vyé-du-yu-shchij (-a-ya) |
| | менеджер | myé-nad-zhyr |
| marketing | маркетинг | máhr-ki-tink |
| money | деньги (pl) | dyén'-gi |
| motto | девиз | di-vís |
| multifunctional card (banking/ATM) | многофункциональная карточка | mno-ga-funk-tsy-a-náhl'-na-ya káhr-tych-ka |
| office | офис | ó-fis |
| owner | владелец (m) | vla-dyé-lits |
| | владелица (f) | vla-dyé-li-tsa |
| pay | платить (i) | pla-tít' |
| • pay off | уплатить (p) | u-pla-tít' |
| | выплатить (p) | vý-pla-tit' |
| • payment | оплата | a-pláh-ta |
| | платёж | pla-tyósh |
| PIN (personal identification number) | личный код/личный (идентификационный) номер | lích-nyj kot/lích-nyj (i-din-ti-fi-ka-tsy-ón-nyj) nó-mir |
| • input (n) | набор (n) | na-bór |
| plastic card (plastic) | пластиковая карточка | pláhs-ti-ka-va-ya káhr-tych-ka |
| pound (U.K.) | фунт | foont |
| private bank | частные банк | cháhs-nyj bahnk |
| receipt | квитанция | kvi-táhn-tsy-ya |
| safe | сейф | syejf |
| • safe deposit box | сейфовый ящик | syéj-fa-vyj yáh-shchik |
| salary | зарплата | zar-pláh-ta |
| save | сберечь (p) | sbi-ryéch |
| | сберегать (i) | sbi-ri-gáht' |
| | отложить (p) | at-la-zhýt' |
| | откладывать (i) | at-kláh-dy-vat' |
| • savings | сбережения (pl) | sbi-ri-zhéh-ni-ya |

| sign | подписать *(p)* | *pat-pi-sáht'* |
|------|----------------|----------------|
|  | подписывать *(i)* | *pat-pí-sy-vat'* |
| • signature | подпись *(f)* | *pót-pis'* |
| state bank | государственные банк | *ga-su-dáhr-stvi-nyj bahnk* |
| stock | сток | *stok* |
|  | акция | *áhk-tsy-ya* |
| stock market | биржа | *bír-zha* |
| trade (buying-selling) | купля-продажа | *kóop-lya-pra-dáh-zha* |
| transfer *(n)* (money) | перевод *(n)* (денег) | *pi-ri-vót (dyé-nik)* |
| traveler's check | дорожный чек | *da-rózh-nyj chyek* |
| withdraw | снять со счёта *(p)* | *snyaht' sa shchyó-ta* |
|  | снимать со счёта *(i)* | *sni-máht' sa shchyó-ta* |
| • withdrawal | снятие со счёта | *snyáh-ti-ye sa shchyó-ta* |

## 27. REAL ESTATE

| application | заявка | *za-yáhf-ka* |
|-------------|--------|-------------|
| (loan, rental, etc.) |  |  |
| appraiser (company) | оценочная компания | *a-tséh-nach-na-ya kam-páh-ni-ya* |
| backyard | задний двор | *záhd-nij dvor* |
| bank fees *(pl)* | банковские сборы *(pl)* | *báhn-kaf-ski-i sbó-ry* |
| block house | блокированный дом | *bla-ki-ró-va-nyj dom* |
| (townhouse) |  |  |
| broker | брокер | *bró-kir* |
| buyer (of an apartment) | покупатель квартиры | *pa-ku-páh-til' kvar-tí-ry* |
| ceiling | потолок | *pa-ta-lók* |
| collateral (for loan) | залог | *za-lók* |
| commission | комиссия | *ka-mí-si-yah* |
| common room | общая комната | *óp-shchya-ya kóm-na-ta* |
| (the commons) |  |  |
| contract form | бланк договора | *blahnk da-ga-vó-ra* |
| cottage | коттедж/дача | *ka-téhdzh/dáh-cha* |
| country home | загородный дом | *záh-ga-rad-nyj dom* |
| credit | кредит | *kri-dít* |
| • credit rating | кредитоспособность | *kri-dí-ta-spa-sób-nast'* |
| driveway | въезд | *v'-yést* |
|  | подъезд | *pad'-yést* |
| duplex | дуплекс | *dóop-liks* |
| entrance | вход | *fkhot* |
| • back door | задний вход | *záhd-nij fkhot* |
| • front door | парадный вход | *pa-ráhd-nyj fkhot* |
| fenced *(adj)* | огороженный *(adj)* | *a-ga-ró-zhy-nyj* |
| floor (of a room) | пол | *pol* |
| floor (level) | этаж | *y-táhzh* |
| • first floor | первый этаж | *pyér-vyj y-táhzh* |
| • second floor | второй этаж | *fta-rój y-táhzh* |
| • third floor | третий этаж | *tryé-tij y-táhzh* |
| • mezzanine | мансарда | *man-sáhr-da* |

| floor plan (apartment) | планировка квартиры | *pla-ni-róf-ka kvar-tí-ry* |
|---|---|---|
| flower bed | клумба | *kloóm-ba* |
| heating | отопление | *a-tap-lyé-ni-ye* |
| installment payment | рассрочка платежа | *ras-sróch-ka pla-ti-zhah* |
| insurance | страхование | *stra-kha-váh-ni-ye* |
| | страховка *(slang)* | *stra-khóf-ka* |
| landlord | арендодатель | *a-rin-da-dáh-til'* |
| lease (term) | срок аренды | *srok a-ryén-dy* |
| • long-term (lease) | длительный срок | *dlí-til'-nyj srok* |
| lender (creditor) | кредитор | *kri-dí-tor* |
| loan | ссуда | *ssóo-da* |
| location | расположение | *ras-pa-la-zhéh-ni-ye* |
| lot | земельный участок | *zi-myél'-nyj u-cháhs-tak* |
| monthly payment | ежемесячная плата | *í-zhy-myé-sich-na-ya pláh-ta* |
| mortgage | ипотека | *i-pa-tyé-ka* |
| | ссуда на жильё | *ssoó-da na zhyl'-yó* |
| mortgage loan | ипотечный кредит | *i-pa-tyéch-nyj kri-dít* |
| parking (spot/place) | парковочное место | *par-kó-vach-na-ye myés-ta* |
| | парковка *(slang)* | *par-kóf-ka* |
| • underground parking | подземная автостоянка | *pat-zyém-na-ya ahv-ta-sta-yáhn-ka* |
| parking garage | гаражный комплекс | *ga-ráhzh-nyj kómp-liks* |
| percentage rate | процентная ставка | *pra-tséhnt-na-ya stáhf-ka* |
| place of residence | место проживания | *myés-ta pra-zhi-váh-ni-ya* |
| population | население | *na-si-lyé-ni-ye* |
| porch | крыльцо | *kryl'-tso* |
| price | цена | *tsy-náh* |
| proximity | близость | *blí-zast'* |
| refinancing | рефинансирование | *ri-fi-nan-sí-ra-va-ni-ye* |
| rent *(v)* (to someone) | здать *(p)* комнату/дом | *sdáht' kóm-na-tu/dom* |
| | здавать *(i)* | *sda-váht'* |
| rent *(v)* (from someone) | снять *(p)* комнату/дом | *snyáht' kóm-na-tu/dom* |
| | снимать *(i)* | *sni-máht'* |
| | заарендовать *(p)* | *za-a-rin-da-váht'* |
| | арендовать *(i)* | *a-rin-da-váht'* |
| rental *(n, adj)* | аренда | *a-ryén-da* |
| real estate | жилая недвижимость | *zhy-láh-ya nid-vi-zhý-mast'* |
| real estate agency | агентство недвижимости | *a-gyént-stva nid-vi-zhý-mas-ti* |
| residence (place) | жильё | *zhyl'-yó* |
| reduction (of payment) | снижение платы | *sni-zhéh-ni-ye pláh-ty* |
| sectional home | секционный дом | *sik-tsy-ón-nyj dom* |
| secure building | охраняемый дом | *akh-ra-nyáh-i-myj dom* |
| seller (of an apartment) | продавец квартиры | *pra-da-vyéts kvar-tí-ry* |

| separate | отдельный *(m)* | *at-dyél'-nyj* |
| | отдельное *(n)* | *at-dyél'-na-ye* |
| | отдельная *(f)* | *at-dyél'-na-ya* |
| sign a lease /sale | заключить *(p)* договор | *za-klyu-chít' da-ga-vór* |
|   (agreement) | заключать *(i)* | *za-klyu-cháht'* |
| size | размер | *raz-myér* |
| square meter | квадратный метр | *kvad-ráht-nyj myetr* |
| | (abbreviation: кв.м ) | |
| stair | лестница | *lyés-ni-tsa* |
| subsidy | субсидия | *sup-sí-di-ya* |
| tax | налог | *na-lók* |
| tenant | арендатор | *a-rin-dáh-tar* |
| title (right of | титул (право | *tí-tul (práh-va* |
|   ownership) | собственности) | *sóp-s-vi-nas-ti)* |
| tower | башня | *báhsh-nya* |
| townhouse | таунхаус | *táh-un-háh-us* |
| view | вид | *vit* |
| virtual tour | виртуальный тур | *vir-tu-áhl'-nyj toor* |
| village (subdivision) | посёлок | *pa-syó-lak* |
| water supply | водоснабжение | *va-do-snab-zhéh-ni-ye* |
| window | окно | *ak-nó* |

## 28. GAMES AND SPORTS

### a. GAMES, HOBBIES, AND PHYSICAL FITNESS

| billiards | биллиард | *bi-li-áhrt* |
| • billiard ball | биллиардный шар | *bi-li-áhrd-nyj shahr* |
| • billiard table | биллиардный стол | *bi-li-áhrd-nyj stol* |
| • cue | кий | *kij* |
| • cushion | борт | *bort* |
| • pocket (net) | луза | *lóo-za* |
| checkers | шашки *(pl)* | *sháhsh-ki* |
| • checkerboard | шашечная доска | *sháh-shych-na-ya das-káh* |
| • checker piece | шашка | *sháhsh-ka* |
| chess | шахматы *(pl)* | *sháhkh-ma-ty* |
| • bishop | офицер | *a-fi-tséhr* |
| • chessboard | шахматная доска | *sháhkh-mat-na-ya das-káh* |
| • king | король *(m)* | *ka-ról'* |
| • knight | конь *(m)* | *kon'* |
| • pawn | пешка | *pyésh-ka* |
| • queen | королева | *ka-ra-lyé-va* |
| • rook | ладья | *lad'-yáh* |

| coin | монета | *ma-nyé-ta* |
|---|---|---|
| • coin collecting | собирание монет | *sa-bi-ráh-ni-ye ma-nyét* |
| dice | игральные кости | *ig-ráhl'-ny-i kós-ti* |
| domino | домино | *da-mi-nó* |
| • domino players | доминошники *(pl)* | *da-mi-nósh-ni-ki* |
| game | игра | *ig-ráh* |
| hobby | любимое занятие | *lyu-bí-ma-ye za-nyáh-ti-ye* |
| instrument | инструмент | *in-stru-myént* |
| • play (an instrument) | играть *(i)* (на инструменте) | *ig-ráht' (na in-stru-myén-te)* |
| jog | бегать *(i)* | *byé-gat'* |
| • jogging | беганье | *byé-gan'-ye* |
| play (a game) | играть *(i)* в... | *ig-ráht' v* |
| play cards | играть *(i)* в карты | *ig-ráht' f káhr-ty* |
| practice a sport | заняться *(p)* спортом | *zah-nyáht'-sah spór-tam* |
| | заниматься *(i)* | *zah-ni-máht'-sah* |
| stamp | марка | *máhr-ka* |
| • stamp collecting | филателия | *fi-la-téh-li-ya* |

**b. SPORTS**

| amateur | любитель *(m)* | *lyu-bí-til'* |
|---|---|---|
| | любительница *(f)* | *lyu-bí-til'-ni-tsa* |
| athlete | атлет *(m&f)* | *at-lyét* |
| ball | мяч | *myahch* |
| baseball | бейсбол | *byejs-ból* |
| basketball | баскетбол | *bas-kit-ból* |
| bicycle racing | велосипедные гонки *(pl)* | *vi-la-si-pyéd-ny-ye gón-ki* |
| boxing | бокс | *boks* |
| • boxing gloves | боксёрские перчатки *(pl)* | *bak-syór-ski-ye pir-cháht-ki* |
| • boxing ring | боксёрский ринг | *bak-syór-skij rink* |
| car racing | автомобильные гонки *(pl)* | *av-ta-ma-bíl'-ny-ye gón-ki* |
| catch | ловить *(i)* | *la-vít'* |
| | поймать *(p)* | *paj-máht'* |
| coach | тренер *(m&f)* | *tryé-nir* |
| competition | соревнование | *sa-riv-na-váh-ni-ye* |
| | состязание | *sas-ti-záh-ni-ye* |
| diving | дайвинг | *dáhj-vink* |
| downhill skiing | горнолыжный спорт | *gar-na-lýzh-nyj sport* |
| • downhill skis *(pl)* | горные лыжи *(pl)* | *gór-ny-i lý-zhy* |
| • downhill (skiing) slope | горнолыжная трасса | *gar-na-lýzh-na-ya tráh-sa* |
| exercise room | тренажёрный зал | *tri-na-zhór-nyj zahl* |
| fencing | фехтование | *fikh-ta-váh-ni-ye* |
| field | поле | *pó-li* |

| | | |
|---|---|---|
| **fitness center/club** | фитнесс центр/клуб | *fít-nys tsehntr/kloop* |
| **football** | регби | *réhg-bi* |
| **game** | игра, матч | *ig-ráh, máhtch* |
| **goal** | ворота *(pl)* | *va-ró-ta* |
| **golf** | гольф | *gol'f* |
| **gymnasium** | спортивный зал | *spar-tív-nyj zahl* |
| **gymnastics** | гимнастика | *gim-náhs-ti-ka* |
| **helmet** | шлем | *shlyem* |
| **hit** | удар | *u-dáhr* |
| **hockey** | хоккей | *kha-kyéj* |
| • **hockey rink** | хоккейный каток | *kha-kyéj-nyj ka-tók* |
| • **hockey stick** | хоккейная клюшка | *kha-kyéj-na-ya klyúsh-ka* |
| • **puck** | шайба | *sháhj-ba* |
| • **skate** | конек *(sg)* | *ka-nyók* |
| | коньки *(pl)* | *kan'-kí* |
| **horseback riding** | катание на лошадях | *ka-táh-ni-ye na la-sha-dyáhkh* |
| **horse track** | конная трасса | *kón-na-ya tráh-sa* |
| **kick** | удар (ногой) | *u-dáhr (na-gój)* |
| **mountain climbing** | скалолазание | *ska-la-láh-zyn'-ye* |
| • **knapsack** | рюкзак | *ryuk-záhk* |
| • **rope** | верёвка | *vi-ryóf-ka* |
| • **snow goggles** | защитные очки *(pl)* | *za-shchít-ny-i ach-kí* |
| **net** | сеть *(f)* | *syet'* |
| **pass** | передача | *pi-ri-dáh-cha* |
| | пас | *pahs* |
| **penalty shot** | штрафной удар | *shtraf-nój u-dáhr* |
| **ping-pong** | пинг-понг | *pink-pónk* |
| **play** | игра | *ig-ráh* |
| • **player** | игрок *(m&f)* | *ig-rók* |
| **point** | очко *(sg)* | *ach-kó* |
| | очки *(pi)* | *ach-kí* |
| **professional player** | профессиональный игрок | *pra-fi-si-a-náhl'-nyj ig-rók* |
| **race** | пробег | *pra-byék* |
| | гонки *(pl)* | *gón-ki* |
| • **horse racing** | скачки *(pl)* | *skáhch-ki* |
| **rafting** | сплав на плотах | *splahf na pla-táhkh* |
| **referee** | судья *(m&f)* | *sud'-yáh* |
| **run** | бег | *byek* |
| **score** | счёт | *shchyot* |
| • **draw, tie** | ничья *(indecl)* | *nich'-yáh* |
| • **draw** | играть *(i)* вничью | *ig-ráht' vnich-yú* |
| • **lose** | проиграть *(p)* | *pra-ig-ráht'* |
| | проигрывать *(i)* | *pra-íg-ry-vat'* |
| • **loss** | проигрыш | *pró-ig-rysh* |
| • **win** | выиграть *(p)* | *vý-ig-rat'* |
| | выигрывать *(i)* | *vy-íg-ry-vat'* |

| | | |
|---|---|---|
| skate | кататься *(i)* на коньках | *ka-táh-tsa na kan'-káhkh* |
| • figure skating | фигурное катание | *fi-góor-na-ye ka-táh-ni-ye* |
| • roller skate | кататься *(i)* на роликах | *ka-táh-tsa na ró-li-kakh* |
| • speed skating | беговое катание | *bi-ga-vó-ye ka-táh-ni-ye* |
| skiing | катание на лыжах | *ka-táh-ni-ye na lý-zhakh* |
| • cross-country skiing | ходить *(i)* на лыжах | *kha-dít' na lý-zhakh* |
| | идти *(i)* | *it-tí* |
| • skis | лыжи | *lý-zhy* |
| • slalom | слалом | *sláh-lam* |
| • water skiing | катание на водных лыжах | *ka-táh-ni-ye na vód-nykh lý-zhakh* |
| soccer | футбол | *fud-ból* |
| • corner | угол | *óo-gal* |
| • goalkeeper | вратарь *(m)* | *vra-táhr'* |
| • goal kick | удар на ворота | *u-dáhr na va-ró-ta* |
| • header | удар головой | *u-dáhr ga-la-vój* |
| • penalty kick | штрафной удар | *shtraf-nój u-dáhr* |
| sport | спорт | *sport* |
| • sports competition | спортивное состязание | *spar-tív-na-ye sas-ti-záh-ni-ye* |
| • sports fan | спортивный болельщик (-ица) | *spar-tív-nyj ba-lyél'-shchik (-i-tsa)* |
| sports center/club | спортивный центр/клуб | *spar-tív-nyj tsehntr/kloop* |
| sports facility | спортивное учреждение | *spar-tív-na-ye uch-rizh-dyé-ni-ye* |
| stadium | стадион | *sta-di-ón* |
| swim | плыть *(p)* | *plyt'* |
| | плавать *(i)* | *pláh-vat'* |
| • swimming | плавание | *pláh-va-ni-ye* |
| team | команда | *ka-máhn-da* |
| tennis | теннис | *téh-nis* |
| • racket | ракетка | *ra-kyét-ka* |
| terrain course | терренкур | *ti-rin-kóor* |
| throw | заброс | *zab-rós* |
| ticket | билет | *bi-lyét* |
| track | трек | *trehk* |
| track and field | лёгкая атлетика | *lyókh-ka-ya at-lyé-ti-ka* |
| vitamin | витамин | *vi-ta-mín* |
| • multivitamins *(pl)* | мультивитамины *(pl)* | *móol'-ti-vi-ta-mí-ny* |
| volleyball | волейбол | *va-li-ból* |
| • net | сеть *(f)* | *syet'* |
| | сетка | *syét-ka* |
| • men's team | мужская команда | *mush-skáh-ya ka-máhn-da* |
| • women's team | женская команда | *zhéhn-ska-ya ka-máhn-da* |
| water polo | поло | *pó-la* |
| weight lifting | поднятие тяжестей | *pad-nyáh-ti-ye tyáh-zhys-tij* |
| wrestling | борьба | *bar'-báh* |
| yoga | йога | *jó-ga* |

## 29. THE ARTS

### a. CINEMA

| | | |
|---|---|---|
| **actor** | актёр | *ak-tyór* |
| **actress** | актриса | *akt-rí-sa* |
| **aisle** | проход | *pra-khót* |
| **box office** | билетная касса | *bi-lyét-na-ya káh-sa* |
| **lobby** | вестибюль *(m)* | *vis-ti-byúl'* |
| | фойе | *faj-yé* |
| **movie, film** | фильм, кинофильм | *film, ki-na-fíl'm* |
| • **horror movie** | фильм ужасов | *fílm óo-zha-sav* |
| • **make a movie** | снять *(p)* кинофильм | *snyaht' ki-na-fíl'm* |
| | снимать *(i)* | *sni-máht'* |
| • **porno movie** | порнографический фильм | *par-na-gra-fí-chis-kij fíl'm* |
| • **premiere** | премьера | *prim'-yé-ra* |
| **movie director** | директор картины *(m&f)* | *di-ryék-tar kar-tí-ny* |
| **movie star** | звезда экрана *(m&f)* | *zviz-dáh yk-ráh-na* |
| **movie theater** | кинотеатр | *ki-na-tyáhtr* |
| **row** | ряд | *ryaht* |
| **screen** | экран | *yk-ráhn* |
| • **wide screen** | широкий экран | *shy-ró-kij yk-ráhn* |
| **seat** | место | *myés-ta* |
| **soundtrack** | музыка из фильма | *móo-zy-ka is fíl'-ma* |

### b. ART, SCULPTURE, AND ARCHITECTURE

| | | |
|---|---|---|
| **architect** | архитектор *(m&f)* | *ar-khi-tyék-tar* |
| • **architecture** | архитектура | *ar-khi-tik-tóo-ra* |
| • **blueprint** | синька | *sín'-ka* |
| **art** | искусство | *is-kóost-va* |
| • **art exposition** | художественная экспозиция | *khu-dó-zhyst-vi-na-ya yks-pa-zí-tsy-ya* |
| • **art gallery** | художественная галерея | *khu-dó-zhyst-vi-na-ya ga-li-ryé-ya* |
| • **art museum** | музей искусств | *mu-zyéj is-kóostv* |
| **art salon** | художественный салон | *khu-dó-zhyst-vi-nyj sa-lón* |
| **artist** | художник (-ца) | *khu-dózh-nik (-tsa)* |
| **brush** | кисть *(f)* | *kist'* |
| **copy** | копия | *kó-pi-ya* |

| drawing | рисунок | ri-sóo-nak |
|---|---|---|
| • pencil drawing | карандашный рисунок | ka-ran -dáhsh-nyj ri-sóo-nak |
| easel, tripod | мольберт | mal'-byért |
| etching | гравюра/офорт | gra-vyú-ra/a-fórt |
| exhibition | выставка | výs-taf-ka |
| fresco painting | фреска | fryés-ka |
| gravure | гравюра | gra-vyú-ra |
| landscape | пейзаж | pij-záhsh |
| masterpiece | шедевр | shy-déhvr |
| monument | монумент | ma-ny-myént |
| museum | музей | mu-zyéj |
| • museum hall | музейный зал | mu-zyéj-nyj zahl |
| original | оригинал | a-ri-gi-náhl |
| paint | краска | kráhs-ka |
| • oil paint | масляная краска (масло) | máhs-li-na-ya kráhs-ka (máhs-la) |
| • painter | художник (-ца) | khu-dózh-nik (-tsa) |
| • painting | картина | kar-tí-na |
| palette | палета | pa-lyé-ta |
| pastel | пастель (f) | pas-téhl' |
| portrait | портрет | part-ryét |
| • group portrait | групповой портрет | gru-pa-vój part-ryét |
| relief | рельеф | ril'-yéf |
| sculptor | скульптор (m&f) | skóol'p-tar |
| • sculpture | скульптура | skul'p-tóo-ra |
| still life | натюрморт | na-tyur-mórt |
| watercolor | акварель (f) | ak-va-ryél' |

## c. MUSIC AND DANCE

| accordion | аккордеон | a-kar-di-ón |
|---|---|---|
| ballet | балет | ba-lyét |
| • ballet dancer | балерун (m) | ba-li-róon |
| | балерина (f) | ba-li-rí-na |
| classical music | классическая музыка | kla-sí-chis-ka-ya móo-zy-ka |
| composer | композитор (m&f) | kam-pa-zí-tar |
| • composition | сочинение | sa-chi-nyé-ni-ye |
| concert | концерт | kan-tséhrt |
| dance | танец | táh-nits |
| • dance | танцевать (i) | tan-tsy-váht' |
| • dancer | танцовщик (m) | tan-tsaf-shchík |
| | танцовщица (f) | tan-tsaf-shchí-tsa |
| folk dance | народный танец | na-ród-nyj táh-nits |
| folk music | народная музыка | na-ród-na-ya móo-zy-ka |
| guitar | гитара | gi-táh-ra |
| • guitarist | гитарист (-ка) | gi-ta-ríst (-ka) |

| | | |
|---|---|---|
| **harmonica** | губная гармоника | *gub-náh-ya gar-mó-ni-ka* |
| **harmony** | гармония | *gar-mó-ni-ya* |
| **harp** | арфа | *áhr-fa* |
| **instrument** | инструмент | *in-stru-myént* |
| • play an instrument | играть *(i)* на инструменте | *ig-ráht' na in-stru-myén-te* |
| **jazz** | джаз | *dzhahs* |
| **keyboard instruments** | клавиатурные инструменты *(pl)* | *kla-vi-a-tóor-ny-ye ins-tru-myén-ty* |
| • grand piano | рояль *(m)* | *ra-yáhl'* |
| • harpsichord | клавесин | *kla-vi-sín* |
| • organ | орган | *ar-gáhn* |
| • pianist | пианист (-ка) | *pi-a-níst (-ka)* |
| • piano | пианино | *pi-a-ní-na* |
| **light music** | лёгкая музыка | *lyókh-ka-ya móo-zy-ka* |
| **mandolin** | мандолина | *man-da-lí-na* |
| **modern dance** | современный танец | *sav-ri-myé-nyj táh-nits* |
| **music** | музыка | *móo-zy-ka* |
| • musician, player | музыкант (-ша) | *mu-zy-káhnt (-sha)* |
| **note** | нота | *nó-ta* |
| **opera** | опера | *ó-pi-ra* |
| **operetta** | оперетта | *a-pi-ryé-ta* |
| **orchestra** | оркестр | *ar-kyéstr* |
| • conductor | дирижёр *(m&f)* | *di-ri-zhór* |
| **percussion instruments** | ударные инструменты | *u-dáhr-ny-ye in-stru-myén-ty* |
| • cymbals | тарелки *(pl)* | *ta-ryél-ki* |
| • drum | барабан | *ba-ra-báhn* |
| • timpani | тимпан | *tim-páhn* |
| **rhythm** | ритм | *ritm* |
| **rock** | рок (-н-ролл) | *rok, rak-yn-ról* |
| **show** | выступление | *vys-tup-lyé-ni-ye* |
| **song** | песня | *pyés-nya* |
| • sing | спеть *(p)* | *spyet'* |
| | петь *(i)* | *pyet'* |
| • singer | певец, певица | *pi-vyéts, pi-ví-tsa* |
| **stringed instruments** | струнные инструменты | *stróo-ny-ye in-stru-myén-ty* |
| • bass viol | контрабас | *kant-ra-báhs* |
| • bow | смычок | *smy-chók* |
| • cello | виолончель *(f)* | *vi-a-lan-chyél'* |
| • double bass | двойной бас | *dvaj-nój bahs* |
| • string | струна | *stru-náh* |
| • violin | скрипка | *skríp-ka* |
| • violin quartet | скрипичный квартет | *skri-pích-nyj kvar-tyét* |
| **symphony** | симфония | *sim-fó-ni-ya* |
| **wind instruments** | духовые инструменты *(pl)* | *du-kha-vý-ye in-stru-myén-ty* |

| • bagpipes | волынка | *va-lýn-ka* |
| • bassoon | фагот | *fa-gót* |
| • clarinet | кларнет | *klar-nyét* |
| • flute | флейта | *flyéj-ta* |
| • horn | рожок | *ra-zhók* |
| • oboe | гобой | *ga-bój* |
| • saxophone | саксофон | *sak-sa-fón* |
| • trombone | тромбон | *tram-bón* |
| • trumpet | труба | *tru-báh* |
| • tuba | туба | *tóo-ba* |

*FOCUS: Well-known Russian Composers*

| Peter Chaikovsky (1840-1893) | *Swan Lake* (ballet) |
| Sergei Prokofief (1891-1953) | *Love for Three Oranges* (opera) |
| Nikolai Rimski-Korsakov (1844-1908) | *Scheherazade* (opera) |
| Dmitri Shostakovich (1906-1975) | *October* Symphony |
| Igor Stravinsky (1882-1971) | *Petrushka* (opera) |

*FOCUS: Well-known Russian Ballet Dancers and Choreographers*

| George Balanchine (1904-1983) | Vaslav Nijinsky (1890-1950) |
| Mikhail Baryshnikov (1948- ) | Rudolf Nureyev (1938-1992) |
| Sergei Diaghilev (1872-1929) | Anna Pavlova (1885-1941) |

## d. LITERATURE

| **autobiography** | автобиография | *af-ta-bi-a-gráh-fi-ya* |
| **biography** | биография | *bi-a-gráh-fi-ya* |
| **chapter** | глава | *gla-váh* |
| **character** | персонаж | *pir-sa-náhsh* |
| **criticism** | критика | *krí-ti-ka* |
| • critical review | критическая статья | *kri-tí-chis-ka-ya stat'-yáh* |
| **essay** | очерк | *ó-chirk* |
| **fable** | басня | *báhs-nya* |
| **fairy tale** | волшебная сказка | *val-shéhb-na-ya skáhs-ka* |
| • folktale | народная сказка | *na-ród-na-ya skáhs-ka* |
| **fiction** | беллетристика | *bi-lit-rís-ti-ka* |
| | художественная литература | *khu-dó-zhyst-vi-na-ya li-ti-ra-tóo-ra* |

| genre | жанр | *zhahnr* |
|---|---|---|
| literature | литература | *li-ti-ra-tóo-ra* |
| myth | миф | *mif* |
| • mythology | мифология | *mi-fa-ló-gi-ya* |
| novel | роман | *ra-máhn* |
| novella | повесть *(f)* | *pó-vist* |
| plot | сюжет | *syu-zhéht* |
| poet | поэт *(m)*, поэтесса *(f)* | *pa-éht, pa-y-téh-sa* |
| poetry | поэзия | *pa-éh-zi-ya* |
| preface | предисловие | *pri-dis-ló-vl-ye* |
| prose | проза | *pró-za* |
| short story | короткий рассказ | *ka-rót-kij ras-káhs* |
| style | стиль *(m)* | *stil'* |
| theme | тема | *tyé-ma* |
| work | работа | *ra-bó-ta* |
| writer | писатель *(m)* | *pi-sáh-til'* |
|  | писательница *(f)* | *pi-sáh-til'-ni-tsa* |

*FOCUS: Well-known Russian Poets and Writers*

| Ivan Bunin (1870-1953) | *The Village* |
|---|---|
| Fyodor Dostoyevskij (1821-1881) | *Crime and Punishment* |
| Boris Pasternak (1890-1960) | *Doctor Zhivago* |
| Alexander Pushkin (1799-1837) | *Eugene Onegin* |
| Alexander Solzhenitsyn (1918-2008) | *The Gulag Archipelago* |
| Leo Tolstoy (1828-1910) | *War and Peace* |

## e. THEATER

| act | акт | *ahkt* |
|---|---|---|
| • act | играть *(i)* (роль) | *ig-ráht' rol'* |
| actor | актёр | *ak-tyór* |
| • actress | актриса | *akt-rí-sa* |
| • leading actor | ведущий актёр | *vi-dóo-shchij ak-tyór* |
| applause | аплодисменты *(pl)* | *ap-la-dis-myén-ty* |
| • applaud | аплодировать *(i)* | *ap-la-dí-ra-vat'* |
| audience (spectators) | зрители *(pl)* | *zrí-ti-li* |
| audience (listeners) | слушатели *(pl)* | *slóo-sha-ti-li* |
| comedian | комедийный актёр *(m)* | *ka-mi-díj-nyj ak-tyór* |
|  | комедийная актриса *(f)* | *ka-mi-díj-na-ya akt-rí-sa* |
| comedy | комедия | *ka-myé-di-ya* |
| curtain | занавес | *záh-na-vyes* |
| drama | драма | *dráh-ma* |
| hero | герой | *gi-rój* |

| | | |
|---|---|---|
| **heroine** | героиня | *gi-ra-í-nya* |
| **intermission** | антракт | *ant-ráhkt* |
| **playwright** | драматург *(m&f)* | *dra-ma-tóorg* |
| **plot** | сюжет | *syu-zhéht* |
| **program** | программка | *prag-ráhm-ka* |
| **scene** | картина | *kar-tí-na* |
| **scenery** | декорация | *di-ka-ráh-tsy-ya* |
| **theater** | театр | *tyahtr* |
| • **lobby** | вестибюль *(m)* | *vis-ti-byúl'* |
| | фойе | *faj-yé* |
| **tragedy** | трагедия | *tha-gyé-di-ya* |
| **stage** | сцена | *stséh-na* |

*FOCUS: Well-known Russian Playwrights*

| | |
|---|---|
| **Anton Chekhov (1860-1904)** | *Three Sisters* |
| **Nikolay Gogol (1809-1852)** | *Dead Souls* |
| **Maxim Gorki (1868-1936)** | *The Lower Depths* |
| **Vladimir Mayakovsky (1893-1930)** | *Mystery-Bouffe* |

## 30. HOLIDAYS AND GOING OUT

### a. HOLIDAYS AND SPECIAL OCCASIONS

| | | |
|---|---|---|
| **anniversary** | годовщина | *ga-daf-shchí-na* |
| **birthday** | день *(m)* рождения | *dyen' razh-dyé-ni-ya* |
| **Christmas** | Рождество | *razh-di-stvó* |
| **Easter** | Пасха | *páhs-kha* |
| • **Eastern Orthodox Easter** | Православная Пасха | *pra-va-sláhv-na-ya páhs-kha* |
| **engagement** | обручение | *ab-ru-chyé-ni-ye* |
| **First of May** | Первое мая | *pyér-va-ye máh-ya* |
| **holiday** | праздник | *práhz-nik* |
| **New Year's Day** | Новогодний день | *na-va-gód-nij dyen'* |
| **New Year's Eve** | канун Нового года | *ka-nóon nó-va-va gó-da* |
| **parade** | парад | *pa-ráht* |
| **vacation** | отпуск | *ót-pusk* |
| • **break** | каникулы *(pl)* | *ka-ní-ku-ly* |
| • **take a vacation** | взять *(p)* отпуск | *vzyaht' ót-pusk* |
| | брать *(i)* | *braht'* |
| **Victory Day, May 9** | День Победы, Девятое Мая | *dyen' pa-byé-dy, dye-vyáh-ta-ye máh-ya* |
| **wedding** | свадьба | *sváht'-ba* |
| **Women's Day** | Женский день | *zhéhn-skij dyen'* |

*FOCUS: Last Czars, Revolutions, and Political Figures*

---

Alexander II (ruled 1855-1881)
Alexander III (ruled 1881-1894)
Nicholas II (ruled 1894-1917)
The Bloody Revolution — 1905
The February Revolution — March 1917
The October Revolution — November 1917
Vladimir Lenin (1870-1924)
Joseph Stalin (1879-1953)
Leon Trotsky (1879-1940)
Nikita Khrushchev (1894-1971)
Mikhail Gorbachev (1931-   )
Boris Yeltsin (1931-2007)
Vladimir Putin (1952-   )
The collapse of the Soviet Union–August-December, 1991
Formation of the Commonwealth of Independent States (CIS) - December 8, 1991
- CIS Members: Armenia, Azerbaijan, Belarus, Georgia, Kazakhstan, Kyrgyzstan, Moldova, Russia, Tajikistan, Ukraine, and Uzbekistan.

---

## b. GOING OUT

| dance | танец | *táh-nits* |
|---|---|---|
| • dance | танцевать *(i)* | *tan-tsy-váht'* |
| • go dancing | идти танцевать *(i)* | *it-tí tan-tsy-váht'* |
| disco | дискотека | *dis-ka-tyé-ka* |
| drop by | заскочить *(p)* | *za-ska-chít'* |
| | забежать *(p)* | *za-bi-zháht'* |
| gather (group) | собраться *(p)* | *sab-ráh-tsa* |
| | собираться *(i)* | *sa-bi-ráh-tsa* |
| go out | пойти куда-нибудь *(p)* | *paj-tí ku-dáh-ni-but'* |
| have fun | веселиться *(i)* | *vi-si-lí-tsa* |
| party | вечеринка | *vi-chi-rín-ka* |
| remain | остаться *(p)* | *a-stáh-tsa* |
| | оставаться *(i)* | *a-sta-váh-tsa* |
| return | вернуться *(p)* | *vir-nóo-tsa* |
| | возвратиться *(p)* | *vaz-vra-tí-tsa* |
| | возвращаться *(i)* | *vaz-vra-shcháh-tsa* |
| visit | посетить *(p)* | *pa-si-tít'* |
| | посещать *(i)* | *pa-si-shcháht'* |
| • come to tea | прийти *(p)* на чашку чая | *pri-tí na cháhsh-ku cháh-ya* |
| | приходить *(i)* | *pri-kha-dít'* |
| • come to visit | прийти в гости *(p)* | *pri-tí v gós-ti* |
| | (при-)ходить в гости *(i)* | *pri-kha-dít' v gós-ti* |

## c. SPECIAL GREETINGS

| All the best! (good-bye) | Всего наилучшего! | *fsi-vó na-i-lóot-shy-va* |
|---|---|---|
| Best of luck! | Желаю удачи! | *zhy-láh-yu u-dáh-chi* |
| Best wishes! | Наилучшие пожелания! | *na-i-lóot-shy-i pa-zhy-láh-ni-ya* |
| Congratulations! | Поздравляю! | *paz-drav-lyáh-yu* |
| Happy Birthday! | С днём рождения! | *s dnyom razh-dyé-ni-ya* |
| Happy Easter! | Счастливой Пасхи! | *shchis-lí-vaj páhs-khi* |
| | Христос Воскресе! | *khris-tós vask-ryé-sye* |
| Happy New Year! | С Ноым годом! | *s nó-vym gó-dam* |
| Merry Christmas! | Счастливого Рождества! | *shchis-lí-va-va razh-dist-váh* |

---

## TRAVEL

---

*31. CHOOSING A DESTINATION*

**a. AT THE TRAVEL AGENCY**

| | | |
|---|---|---|
| **abroad** | заграницу *(adv)* | *za-gra-ní-tsu* |
| **brochure** | брошюра | *bra-shóo-ra* |
| **center (of town)** | центр (города) | *tsehntr (gó-ra-da)* |
| **charter flight** | фрахтованный рейс | *frakh-tó-va-nyj ryejs* |
| **city** | город | *gó-rat* |
| • **capital city** | столица | *sta-lí-tsa* |
| **class** | класс | *klahs* |
| • **business class** | служебный класс | *slu-zhéhb-nyj klahs* |
| • **first class** | первый класс | *pyér-vyj klahs* |
| • **tourist class** | туристический класс | *tu-ris-tí-chis-kij klahs* |
| **continent** | континент | *kan-ti-nyént* |
| **country** | страна | *stra-náh* |
| **exchange rate** | курс обмена | *koors ab-myé-na* |
| **excursion** | экскурсия | *yks-kóor-si-ya* |
| **hotel** | гостиница | *gas-tí-ni-tsa* |
| **immunization** | прививка | *pri-víf-ka* |
| **insurance** | страховка | *stra-khóf-ka* |
| **nation** | страна | *stra-náh* |
| **outskirts** | окраины *(pl)* | *ak-ráh-i-ny* |
| **passport** | паспорт | *páhs-part* |
| **see** | видеть *(i)* | *ví-dit'* |
| | смотреть *(i)* | *smat-ryét'* |
| **ticket** | билет | *bi-lyét* |
| • **buy a ticket** | купить *(p)* билет | *ku-pít' bi-lyét* |
| • **by ship** | на пароходе | *na pa-ra-khó-di* |
| | пароходом | *pa-ra-khó-dam* |
| • **by plane** | на самолёте | *na sa-ma-lyó-ti* |
| | самолётом | *sa-ma-lyó-tam* |
| • **by train** | на поезде | *na pó-iz-di* |
| | поездом | *pó-iz-dam* |
| • **return ticket** | обратный билет | *ab-ráht'-nyj bi-lyét* |
| **tourist** | турист | *tu-ríst* |
| **travel** | путешествие | *pu-ti-shéhst-vi-ye* |
| • **travel agency** | туристическое агентство | *tu-ris-tí-chis-ka-ye a-gyént-stva* |
| **trip, journey** | поездка | *pa-yést-ka* |
| • **Have a nice trip!** | Счастливого пути! | *shchis-lí-va-va pu-tí* |
| • **take a trip** | поехать *(p)* | *pa-yé-khat'* |
| | ехать *(i)* | *yé-khat'* |

## b. COUNTRIES AND CONTINENTS

| | | |
|---|---|---|
| **Africa** | Африка | *áhf-ri-ka* |
| **America** | Америка | *a-myé-ri-ka* |
| • **Central America** | Центральная Америка | *tsint-ráhl'-na-ya a-myé-ri-ka* |
| • **Latin America** | Латинская Америка | *la-tíns-ka-ya a-myé-ri-ka* |
| • **North America** | Северная Америка | *syé-vir-na-ya a-myé-ri-ka* |
| • **South America** | Южная Америка | *yúzh-na-ya a-myé-ri-ka* |
| **Armenia** | Армения | *ar-myé-ni-ya* |
| **Asia** | Азия | *áh-zi-ya* |
| **Australia** | Австралия | *ahf-stráh-li-ya* |
| **Austria** | Австрия | *áhfst-ri-ya* |
| **Azerbaijan** | Азербайджан | *a-zyr-baj-dzháhn* |
| **Bulgaria** | Болгария | *bal-gáh-ri-ya* |
| **Belgium** | Бельгия | *byél'-gi-ya* |
| **Belarus** | Белорусь *(f)* | *bi-la-róos'* |
| **Brazil** | Бразиль *(f)* | *bra-zíl'* |
| **Canada** | Канада | *ka-náh-da* |
| **China** | Китай | *ki-táhj* |
| **Commonwealth of Independent States (CIS)** | Содружество Независимых Государств (СНГ) | *sad-róo-zhyst-va ni-za-ví-si-mykh ga-su-dáhrstf (es-ehn-geh)* |
| **Czech Republic** | Чехия | *chyé-khi-ya* |
| **Denmark** | Дания | *dáh-ni-ya* |
| **Egypt** | Египет | *i-gí-pit* |
| **England** | Англия | *áhng-li-ya* |
| **Estonia** | Эстония | *ys-tó-ni-ya* |
| **Europe** | Европа | *iv-ró-pa* |
| **Finland** | Финляндия | *fin-lyáhn-di-ya* |
| **France** | Франция | *fráhn-tsy-ya* |
| **Georgia** | Грузия | *gróo-zi-ya* |
| **Germany** | Германия | *gir-máh-ni-ya* |
| **Holland** | Голландия | *ga-láhn-di-ya* |
| **India** | Индия | *ín-di-ya* |
| **Iran** | Иран | *i-ráhn* |
| **Ireland** | Ирландия | *ir-láhn-di-ya* |
| **Israel** | Израиль *(m)* | *iz-ráh-il'* |
| **Italy** | Италия | *i-táh-li-ya* |
| **Japan** | Япония | *i-pó-ni-ya* |
| **Kazakhstan** | Казахстан | *ka-zakh-stáhn* |
| **Kenya** | Кения | *kyé-ni-ya* |
| **Korea** | Корея | *ka-ryé-ya* |
| **Kyrgyzstan** | Кыргызстан | *kyr-gys-stáhn* |
| **Latvia** | Латвия | *láht-vi-ya* |

| | | |
|---|---|---|
| **Lithuania** | Литва | *lit-váh* |
| **Mexico** | Мексика | *myék-si-ka* |
| **Moldova** | Молдова | *mal-dó-va* |
| **Norway** | Норвегия | *nahr-vyé-gi-ya* |
| **Poland** | Польша | *pól'-sha* |
| **Russia** | Россия | *ra-sí-ya* |
| **Slovakia** | Словакия | *sla-váh-ki-ya* |
| **Soviet Union** | Советский Союз | *sa-vyéts-kij sa-yús* |
| **(1922-1991)** | | |
| **Spain** | Испания | *is-páh-ní-ya* |
| **Sweden** | Швеция | *shvyé-tsy-ya* |
| **Switzerland** | Швейцария | *shvij-tsáh-ri-ya* |
| **Tajikistan** | Таджикистан | *tad-zhy-ki-stáhn* |
| **Turkey** | Турция | *tóor-tsy-ya* |
| **Turkmenistan** | Туркменистан | *turk-mi-ni-stáhn* |
| **Ukraine** | Украина | *uk-ra-í-na* |
| **United States** | Соединённые | *sa-i-di-nyó-ny-ye shtáh-ty* |
| | Штаты | |
| **Uzbekistan** | Узбекистан | *uz-bi-ki-stáhn* |

## c. A FEW CITIES

| | | |
|---|---|---|
| **Berlin** | Берлин | *bir-lín* |
| **Helsinki** | Хельсинки | *khyél'-sin-ki* |
| **Kiev** | Киев | *kí-if* |
| **London** | Лондон | *lón-dan* |
| **Milan** | Милан | *mi-láhn* |
| **Minsk** | Минск | *minsk* |
| **Moscow** | Москва | *mask-váh* |
| **Munich** | Мюнхен | *myún-khin* |
| **Novosibirsk** | Новосибирск | *na-va-si-bírsk* |
| **Paris** | Париж | *pa-rísh* |
| **Prague** | Прага | *práh-ga* |
| **Rome** | Рим | *rim* |
| **Sofia** | София | *sa-fí-ya* |
| **St. Petersburg** | (Санкт-) Петербург | *(sáhnkt-) pi-tir-bóork* |

## d. NATIONALITIES AND LANGUAGES

Nationalities are given in their masculine form with the feminine form in parentheses ( ). Languages are given below the nationalities and indented.

| | | |
|---|---|---|
| **American** | американец (-нка) | *a-mi-ri-káh-nits (-nka)* |
| • **English** | английский | *ang-lís-kij* |

| | | |
|---|---|---|
| **Arab** | араб (-ка) | *a-ráhp (-k )* |
| • **Arabic** | арабский | *a-ráhps-kij* |
| **Australian** | австралиец (-йка) | *af-stra-lí-its (-jka)* |
| • **English** | английский | *ang-lís-kij* |
| **Austrian** | австриец (-йка) | *afst-rí-its (-jka)* |
| • **German** | немецкий | *ni-myéts-kij* |
| **Belgian** | бельгиец (-йка) | *bil'-gí-its (-jka)* |
| • **Flemish** | фламандский | *fla-máhnts-kij* |
| • **French** | французский | *fran-tsóos-kij* |
| **Brazilian** | бразилец (-лка) | *bra-zí-lits (-lka)* |
| • **Portuguese** | португальский | *par-tu-gáhl's-kij* |
| **Canadian** | канадец (-дка) | *ka-náh-dits (-tka)* |
| • **English** | английский | *ang-lís-kij* |
| • **French** | французский | *fran-tsóos-kij* |
| **Chinese** | китаец (-таянка) | *ki-táh-its (-ta-yáhn-ka)* |
| • **Chinese** | китайский | *ki-táhj-skij* |
| **Dane** | датчанин (-чанка) | *dat-cháh-nin (-cháhn-ka)* |
| • **Danish** | датский | *dáhts-kij* |
| **Dutch** | голландец (-дка) | *ga-láhn-dits (-tka)* |
| • **Dutch** | голландский | *ga-láhnt-skij* |
| **English** | англичанин (-нка) | *ang-li-cháh-nin (-nka)* |
| • **English** | английский | *ang-lís-kij* |
| **French** | француз (-женка) | *fran-tsóos (-zhyn-ka)* |
| • **French** | французский | *fran-tsóos-kij* |
| **German** | немец (немка) | *nyé-mits (nyém-ka)* |
| • **German** | немецкий | *ni-myéts-kij* |
| **Irish** | ирландец (-дка) | *ir-láhn-dits (-tka)* |
| • **English** | английский | *ang-lís-kij* |
| **Israeli** | израильтянин (-нка) | *iz-ra-il'-tyáh-nin (-nk )* |
| • **Hebrew** | иврит | *iv-rít* |
| **Italian** | итальянец (-нка) | *i-tal'-yáh-nits (-nka)* |
| • **Italian** | итальянский | *i-tal'-yáhn-skij* |
| **Japanese** | японец (-нка) | *i-pó-nits (-nk )* |
| • **Japanese** | японский | *i-pón-skij* |
| **Norwegian** | норвежец (-жка) | *nar-vyé-zhyts (-shka)* |
| • **Norwegian** | норвежский | *nar-vyésh-skij* |
| **Pole** | поляк (полячка) | *pa-lyáhk (pa-lyách-ka)* |
| • **Polish** | польский | *pól'-skij* |
| **Portuguese** | португалец (-лка) | *par-tu-gáh-lits (-lka)* |
| • **Portuguese** | португальский | *par-tu-gáhl's-kij* |
| **Russian** | русский (-ая) | *róos-kij (-a-ya)* |
| • **Russian** | русский | *róos-kij* |
| **Spaniard** | испанец (-нка) | *is-páh-nits (-nka)* |
| • **Spanish** | испанский | *is-páhn-skij* |
| **Swede** | швед (-ка) | *shvyet (-ka)* |
| • **Swedish** | шведский | *shvyét-skij* |

## 32. PACKING AND GOING THROUGH CUSTOMS

| | | |
|---|---|---|
| bag | сумка | *sóom-ka* |
| baggage, luggage | багаж | *ba-gáhsh* |
| • hand luggage | ручной багаж | *ruch-nój ba-gáhsh* |
| border | граница | *gra-ní-tsa* |
| carry | носить *(i)* | *na-sít'* |
| | нести *(p)* | *nis-tí* |
| customs | таможня | *ta-mózh-nya* |
| • customs officer | таможенник (-ица) | *ta-mó-zhy-nik (-i-tsa)* |
| declare | назвать *(p)* | *naz-váht'* |
| | называть *(i)* | *na-zy-váht'* |
| • declaration | декларация | *dik-la-ráh-tsy-ya* |
| Do you have anything to declare? | У вас есть что-нибудь, подлежащее обложению пошлиной? | *u vahs yest' shtó-ni-but' pad-li-zháh-shchi-ye ab-la-zhéh-ni-yu pósh-li-noj* |
| documents | документы | *da-ku-myén-ty* |
| duty | пошлина | *pósh-li-na* |
| | тариф | *ta-ríf* |
| foreign currency | иностранная валюта | *i-nast-ráh-na-ya va-lyú-ta* |
| foreigner | иностранец (-нка) | *i-nast-ráh-nits (-nka)* |
| form (to fill out) | анкета | *an-kyé-ta* |
| identification papers | удостоверение личности | *u-das-ta-vi-ryé-ni-ye lích-nas-ti* |
| import | ввоз | *vvos* |
| | импорт | *ím-part* |
| knapsack | рюкзак | *ryuk-záhk* |
| pack (one's bags/ luggage) | упаковать(-ся) *(p)* | *u-pa-ka-váht' (-tsa)* |
| | паковать(-ся) *(i)* | *pa-ka-váht' (-tsa)* |
| passport | паспорт | *páhs-part* |
| passport control | паспортный контроль *(m)* | *páhs-part-nyj kant-ról'* |
| • tariff | тариф | *ta-ríf* |
| • visa | виза | *ví-za* |
| suitcase | чемодан | *chi-ma-dáhn* |
| weight | вес | *vyes* |
| • heavy | тяжёлый | *ti-zhó-lyj* |
| • light | лёгкий | *lyókh-kij* |
| • maximum | максимальный | *mak-si-máhl'-nyj* |

## 33. TRAVELING BY AIR

### a. AT THE TERMINAL

| airline | авиакомпания | *ah-vi-a-kam-páh-ni ya* |
|---|---|---|
| airport | аэропорт | *a-y-ra-pórt* |
| arrival | приезд | *pri-yést* |
| boarding | посадка | *pa-sáht-ka* |
| • boarding pass | посадочный талон | *pa-sáh-dach-nyj ta-lón* |
| business class | служебный класс | *slu-zhéhb-nyj klahs* |
| check-in | регистрация | *ri-gist-ráh-tsy-ya* |
| | регистрироваться *(i)* | *ri-gist-rí-ra-va-tsa* |
| connection | пересадка | *pi-ri-sáht-ka* |
| departure | отъезд | *at'-yést* |
| departure by air | отлёт | *at-lyót* |
| economy class | экономичный класс | *y-ka-na-mích-nyj klahs* |
| first class | первый класс | *pyér-vyj klahs* |
| flight | рейс | *ryejs* |
| gate | ворота *(pl)* | *va-ró-ta* |
| information desk | справочное бюро | *spráh-vach-na-ye byu-ró* |
| lost and found | бюро находок | *byu-ró na-khó-dak* |
| tourist class | туристический класс | *tu-ris-tí-chis-kij klahs* |

### b. FLIGHT INFORMATION

| canceled | отменён | *at-mi-nyón* |
|---|---|---|
| early | ранний *(adj)* | *ráhn-ij* |
| | рано *(adv)* | *ráh-na* |
| late | поздний *(adj)* | *póz-nij* |
| | поздно *(adv)* | *póz-na* |
| on time | во время | *vó vrye-mya* |
| The flight is canceled | Полёт отменён | *pa-lyót at-mi-nyón* |

### c. ON THE PLANE

| airplane | самолёт | *sa-ma-lýot* |
|---|---|---|
| aisle | проход | *pra-khót* |
| copilot | второй пилот | *fta-rój pi-lót* |
| crew | экипаж | *y-ki-páhsh* |
| flight attendant | стюард (-есса) | *styu-árt (styu-ar-déh-sa)* |
| headphones | наушники | *na-óosh-ni-ki* |
| land | приземлиться *(p)* | *pri-zim-lí-tsa* |
| | приземляться *(i)* | *pri-zim-lyáh-tsa* |

| | | |
|---|---|---|
| **lavatory** | туалет | *tu-a-lyét* |
| | уборная | *u-bór-na-ya* |
| **life jacket** | спасательный жилет | *spa-sáh-til'-nyj zhy-lyét* |
| **passenger** | пассажир (-ка) | *pa-sa-zhýr (-ka)* |
| **place** | место | *myés-ta* |
| **runway** | лётная дорожка | *lyót-na-ya da-rósh-ka* |
| **seat** | сидение | *si-dyé-ni-ye* |
| • **seat belt** | привязной ремень *(m)* | *pri-viz-nój ri-myén'* |
| • **buckle up** | застегнуть *(p)* (ремень) | *zas-tig-nóot' ri-myén'* |
| | застёгивать *(i)* | *zas-tyó-gi-vat'* |
| **sit down** | сесть *(p)* | *syest'* |
| | садиться *(i)* | *sa-dí-tsa* |
| **takeoff** | взлёт | *vzlyot* |
| | вылет | *vý-lit* |
| • **takeoff** | взлететь *(p)* | *vzli-tyét'* |
| | взлетать *(i)* | *vzli-táht'* |
| **tray** | поднос | *pad-nós* |
| **turbulence** | болтанка | *bal-táhn-ka* |
| **wheel, landing gear** | шасси | *sha-sí* |
| **window** | окно | *ak-nó* |
| **wing** | крыло | *kry-ló* |

*34. ON THE ROAD*

a. **VEHICLES**

| | | |
|---|---|---|
| **ambulance** | машина скорой помощи | *ma-shý-na skó-raj pó-ma-shchi* |
| **automobile** | автомобиль *(m)* | *af-ta-ma-bíl'* |
| **bicycle** | велосипед | *vi-la-si-pyét* |
| • **brake** | тормоз | *tór-mas* |
| • **chain** | цепь *(f)* | *tsehp'* |
| • **handlebar** | руль *(m)* | *rool'* |
| • **pedal** | педаль *(f)* | *pi-dáhl'* |
| • **seat** | сидение | *si-dyé-ni-ye* |
| • **spoke** | спица | *spí-tsa* |
| • **tire** | шина | *shý-na* |
| **bus** | автобус | *af-tó-bus* |
| • **streetcar, tram** | трамвай | *tram-váhj* |
| • **trolley** | троллейбус | *tra-lyéj-bus* |
| **car** | машина | *ma-shý-na* |

| | | |
|---|---|---|
| • rent a car | взять *(p)* | *vzyaht'* |
| | брать *(i)* машину на | *braht' ma-shý-nu na* |
| • sports car | прокат | *pra-káht* |
| | спортивная машина | *spar-tív-na-ya ma-shý-na* |
| minivan | миниавтобус | *mi-ni-af-tó-bus* |
| take in tow | брать *(i)* на буксир | *braht' na buk-sír* |
| taxi | такси | *tak-sí* |
| tow a car | тянуть *(i)* | *ti-nóot* |
| | тащить *(i)* (машину) | *ta-shchít' (ma-shý-nu)* |
| | на буксире | *na buk-sí-ri* |
| trailer | прицеп | *pri-tséhp* |
| truck | грузовик | *gru-za-vík* |
| • fire truck | пожарная машина | *pa-zháhr-na-ya ma-shý-na* |
| • garbage truck | мусорный грузовик | *móo-sar-nyj gru-za-vík* |
| • tanker | цистерна | *tsys-téhr-na* |
| van | автобус | *af-tó-bus* |
| vehicle | машина | *ma-shý-na* |

## b. DRIVING: PEOPLE AND DOCUMENTS

| | | |
|---|---|---|
| driver | водитель *(m)* | *va-dí-til'* |
| | водительница *(f)* | *va-dí-til'-ni-tsa* |
| • car driver | водитель *(m)* | *va-dí-til' ma-shý-ny* |
| | машины | |
| | водительница *(f)* | *va-dí-til'-ni-tsa* |
| • driver's license | водительские права | *va-dí-til'-ski-ye pra-váh* |
| insurance | страховка | *stra-khóf-ka* |
| militia | милиция | *mi-lí-tsy-ya* |
| • direct traffic | руководить *(i)* | *ru-ka-va-dít'* |
| | движением | *dvi-zhéh-ni-yem* |
| • militiaman | милиционер *(m&f)* | *mi-li-tsy-a-nyér* |
| ownership papers | свидетельство о | *svi-dyé-til'st-va a vla-dyé-* |
| | владении | *ni-i (ma-shý-naj)* |
| | (машиной) | |
| passenger | пассажир (-ка) | *pa-sa-zhýr (-ka)* |
| pedestrian | пешеход (-ница) | *pi-shy-khót (-ni-tsa)* |

## c. DRIVING: ADDITIONAL VOCABULARY

| | | |
|---|---|---|
| accident | авария | *a-váh-ri-ya* |
| back up | пробка (в движении) | *próp-ka (v dvi-zhéh-ni-i)* |
| (city) block | квартал | *kvar-táhl* |
| brake | тормоз (-а) | *tór-mas (tar-ma-záh)* |
| bridge | мост | *most* |
| (street) corner | (уличный) угол | *(óo-lich-nyj) óo-gal* |

| | | |
|---|---|---|
| curve | извилина | *iz-ví-li-na* |
| • curved road | извилистая дорога | *iz-ví-lis-ta-ya da-ró-ga* |
| distance | расстояние | *ras-ta-yáh-ni-ye* |
| drive | водить машину *(i)* | *va-dít' ma-shý-nu* |
| | вести *(i)* | *vis-tí* |
| fine | штраф | *shtrahf* |
| gas station | бензозаправочная станция | *bin-za-zap-ráh-vach-na-ya stáhn-tsy-ya* |
| • check the oil | проверить *(p)* масло | *pra-vyé-rit' máhs-la* |
| | проверять *(i)* | *pra-vi-ryáht'* |
| • fix, repair | починить *(p)* | *pa-chi-nít'* |
| | чинить *(i)* | *chi-nít'* |
| • full tank | полный бак | *pól-nyj bahk* |
| • gas | бензин | *bin-zín* |
| • leaded gas | этилированный бензин | *y-ti-li-ró-va-nyj bin-zín* |
| • mechanic | механик | *mi-kháh-nik* |
| • self-service | самообслуживание | *sa-ma-ap-slóo-zhy-va-ni-ye* |
| • tools | инструменты *(pl)* | *ins-tru-myén-ty* |
| • unleaded gas | неэтилированный бензин | *ni-y-ti-li-ró-va-nyj bin-zín* |
| gear | скорость *(от)* | *skó-rast'* |
| | передача | *pi-ri-dáh-cha* |
| • change gears | переключить *(p)* скорость *(f)* | *pi-ri-klyú-chit' skó-rast'* |
| | переключать *(i)* | *pi-rik-lyu-cháht'* |
| go forward | проехать *(p)* вперёд | *pra-yé-khat' fpi-ryót* |
| | ехать *(i)* | *yé-khat'* |
| go through a red light | проехать *(p)* на красный свет | *pra-yé-khat' na kráhs-nyj svyet* |
| | ехать *(i)* | *yé-khat'* |
| highway | шоссе | *sha-séh* |
| intersection | перекрёсток | *pi-rik-ryós-tak* |
| lane (traffic) | полоса | *pa-la-sáh* |
| park | поставить *(p)* машину | *pa-stáh-vit' ma-shý-nu* |
| | ставить *(i)* | *stáh-vit'* |
| | парковаться *(i)* | *par-ka-váh-tsa* |
| • parking | парковка, стоянка | *par-kóf-ka, sta-yáhn-ka* |
| • parking zone | парковочная зона | *par-kó-vach-na-ya zó-na* |
| pass | обогнать *(p)* | *a-bag-náht'* |
| | обгонять *(i)* | *ab-ga-nyáht'* |
| pedestrian crossing | пешеходный переход | *pi-shy-khód-nyj pi-ri-khót* |
| private transportation | личный транспорт | *lích-nyj tráhns-part* |
| public transportation | общественный транспорт | *ab-shchyést-vi-nyj tráhns-part* |
| ramp | скат | *skaht* |

| | | |
|---|---|---|
| **road** | дорога | *da-ró-ga* |
| **rush hour** | час-пик | *cháhs-pík* |
| **shuttle bus (route taxi)** | маршрутное такси | *marsh-róot-na-ye tak-sí* |
| **sidewalk** | тротуар | *tra-tu-áhr* |
| **signal** | сигнал | *sig-náhl* |
| **speed** | скорость *(f)* | *skó-rast'* |
| • **speed up** | увеличить *(p)* скорость *(f)* | *u-vi-lí-chit' skó-rast'* |
| | увеличивать *(i)* | *u-vi-lí-chi-vat'* |
| • **slow down** | снизить *(p)* скорость | *sní-zit' skó-rast'* |
| | снижать *(i)* | *sni-zháht'* |
| **start (the car)** | завести *(p)* (машину) | *za-vis-tí ma-shý-nu* |
| | заводить *(i)* | *za-va-dít'* |
| **traffic** | дорожное движение | *da-rózh-na-ye dvi-zhéh-ni-ye* |
| **traffic light** | светофор | *svi-ta-fór* |
| **tunnel** | туннель *(m)* | *tu-néhl* |
| **turn** | поворот | *pa-va-rót* |
| • **turn left** | повернуть *(p)* налево | *pa-vir-nóot' na-lyé-va* |
| | поворачивать *(i)* | *pa-va-ráh-chi-vat'* |
| • **turn right** | повернуть *(p)* направо | *pa-vir-nóot' na-práh-va* |
| | поворачивать *(i)* | *pa-va-ráh-chi-vat'* |

## d. ROAD SIGNS

| | | |
|---|---|---|
| **Bicycle Path** | Велосипедная дорожка | *vi-la-si-pyéd-na-ya da-rósh-ka* |
| **Emergency Lane** | Аварийный ряд | *a-va-ríj-nyj ryaht* |
| **Exit** | Выезд | *vý-yest* |
| **Intersection** | Перекрёсток | *pi-rik-ryós-tak* |
| **Merge** | Сливающееся движение | *sli-váh-yu-shchi-i-sya dvi-zhéh-ni-ye* |
| **No Entry** | Въезд запрещён | *v'yezd za-pri-shchyón* |
| **No Left Turn** | Поворот налево запрещён | *pa-va-rót na-lyé-va za-pri-shchyón* |
| **No Parking** | Стоянка запрещена | *sta-yáhn-ka za-pri-shchi-náh* |
| **No Passing** | Обгон воспрещён Нет обгона | *ab-gón vas-pri-shchyón nyet ab-gó-na* |
| **No Right Turn** | Поворот направо запрещён | *pa-va-rót na-práh-va za-pri-shchyón* |
| **No Stopping** | Не стоять *(i)* | *ni sta-yáht'* |
| **No vehicles allowed** | Движение запрещено | *dvi-zhéh-ni-ye za-pri-shchi-nó* |

Разворот запрещён/
No U-turn

Обгон запрещён/
No passing

Таможня/Border
crossing

Светофорное
регулирование/
Traffic signal ahead

Ограничение
максимальной
скорости/Speed limit

Круговое движение/
Traffic circle ahead

Ограничеие
минимальной
скорости/Minimum
speed limit

Движение налево/
All traffic turns left

Конец зоны
запрещения
обгоня/End of no
passing zone

Выезд на дорогу
с односторонним
движением/One way

Направление
объезда/Detour

Прочие опасности/
Danger ahead

Автомагистраль/
Expressway

Конец
автомагистрали/
Expressway ends

Железнодорожный переезд
со шлагбаумом/Guarded
railway crossing

Уступите дорогу/Yield

Движение без остановки
запрещено/Stop

Главная дорога/
Right of way

Пересечение равнозначных
дорог/Dangerous
intersection ahead

Автозаправочная
станция/Service
station ahead

Место стоянки/
Parking

Движение
запрещено/No
vehicles allowed

Опасные повороты/
Dangerous curves

Пешеходный
переход/Pedestrian
crossing

Преимущество
встречного
движения/Oncoming
traffic has right of way

Движение на
велосипедах
запрещено/No
bicycles allowed

Стоянка запрещена/
No parking

Въезд запрещён/
No entry

Поворот налево
запрещён/No left turn

| **No U-Turn** | Разворот запрещён | *raz-va-rót za-pri-shchyón* |
| **One Way** | Одностороннее движение | *ad-na-sta-ró-ni- ye dvi-zhéh-ni-ye* |
| **Passing Lane** | Ряд для обгона | *ryaht dlya ab-gó-na* |
| **Pedestrian Crosswalk** | Пешеходный переход | *pi-shy-khód-nyj pi-ri-khót* |
| **Speed Limit** | Ограничение скорости | *ag-ra-ni-chyé-ni-ye skó-ras-ti* |
| **Stop** | Стоп | *stop* |
| **Underpass** | Подземный переход | *pad-zyém-nyj pi-ri-khót* |
| **Work in Progress** | Дорожные работы | *da-rózh-ny-ye ra-bó-ty* |
| **Yield** | Уступать *(i)* дорогу | *us-tu-páht' da-ró-gu* |

### e. THE CAR

| **air conditioner** | кондиционер | *kan-di-tsy-a-nyér* |
| **battery** | батарея | *ba-ta-ryé-ya* |
| | аккумулятор | *a-ku-mu-lyáh-tar* |
| **body** | кузов | *kóo-zaf* |
| **brake** | тормоз *(-a)* | *tór-mas (tar-ma-záh)* |
| **bumper** | бампер | *báhm-pir* |
| **carburetor** | карбюратор | *kar-byu-ráh-tar* |
| **choke** | дроссель *(m)* | *dró-sil'* |
| **clutch** | сцепление/муфта | *stsyp-lyé-ni-ye/móof-ta* |
| **dashboard** | приборная доска | *pri-bór-na-ya das-káh* |
| **door** | дверь *(f)* | *dvyer'* |
| **fender** | крыло | *kry-ló* |
| **filter** | фильтр | *fil'tr* |
| **gas pedal** | газовая педаль *(f)* | *gáh-za-va-ya pi-dáhl'* |
| **gas tank** | бензобак | *bin-za-báhk* |
| **gearshift** | переключение передач | *pi-ri-klyú-chye-ni-ye pi-ri-dáhch* |
| **glove compartment** | перчаточное отделение | *pir-cháh-tach-na-ye at-di-lyé-ni-ye* |
| **handle** | ручка/рукоятка | *róoch-ka/ru-ka-yáht-ka* |
| **hazard flashes** | мигайка | *mi-gáhj-ka* |
| **heater** | обогреватель *(m)* | *a-bag-ri-váh-til'* |
| **hood** | капот | *ka-pót* |
| **horn** | гудок | *gu-dók* |
| **horsepower** | лошадиная сила | *la-sha-dí-na-ya sí-la* |
| **license plate** | номерной знак | *na-mir-nój znahk* |
| **lights** | фары *(pl)* | *fáh-ry* |
| • **high beam** | дальнего света | *dáhl'-ni-va svyé-ta* |
| • **low beam** | ближнего света | *blízh-ni-va svyé-ta* |
| **motor** | мотор | *ma-tór* |

| | | |
|---|---|---|
| • **fan** | вентилятор | *vin-ti-lyáh-tar* |
| • **gas pump** | бензоколонка | *bin-za-ka-lón-ka* |
| • **generator** | генератор | *gi-ni-ráh-tar* |
| • **piston** | поршень *(m)* | *pór-shyn'* |
| • **shaft** | приводной вал | *pri-vad-nój vahl* |
| • **spark plug** | пробка | *próp-ka* |
| **muffler** | глушитель *(m)* | *glu-shý-til'* |
| **oil** | масло | *máhs-la* |
| **power brake** | механический тормоз | *mi-kha-ní-chis-kij tór-mas* |
| **power steering** | механическое управление | *mi-kha-ní-chis-ka-ye up-rav-lyé-ni-ye* |
| **radiator** | радиатор | *ra-di-áh-tar* |
| **rear window** | заднее окно | *záhd-ni-ye ak-nó* |
| **rearview mirror** | зеркало заднего вида | *zyér-ka-la záhd-ni-va ví-da* |
| **roof** | крыша | *krý-sha* |
| **seat** | сидение | *si-dyé-ni-ye* |
| • **seat belt** | привязной ремень *(m)* | *pri-viz-nój ri-myén'* |
| **side mirror** | боковое зеркало | *ba-ka-vó-ye zyér-ka-la* |
| **speedometer** | спидометр | *spi-dó-mitr* |
| **steering wheel** | руль *(m)* | *rool'* |
| **tire** | шина | *shý-na* |
| **transmission** | коробка передач | *ka-róp-ka pi-ri-dáhch* |
| **trunk** | багажник | *ba-gáhzh-nik* |
| **turn signal** | поворотный сигнал | *pa-va-rót-nyj sig-náhl* |
| **vent** | отдушина | *at-dóo-shy-na* |
| **wheel** | колесо | *ka-li-só* |
| **window** | окно машины | *ak-nó ma-shý-ny* |
| **windshield** | ветровое стекло | *vit-ra-vó-ye stik-ló* |
| • **windshield wiper** | дворник | *dvór-nik* |

## 35. TRAIN, BUS, TROLLEY, AND SUBWAY

| | | |
|---|---|---|
| **bus, van** | автобус | *af-tó-bus* |
| **bus driver** | водитель *(m)* автобуса | *va-dí-til' af-tó-bu-sa* |
| **bus station, depot** | автобусный вокзал | *af-tó-bus-nyj vak-záhl* |
| **compartment** | купе | *ku-péh* |
| **conductor** | кондуктор | *kan-dóok-tar* |
| **connection** | пересадка | *pi-ri-sáht-ka* |
| **dining car** | вагон-ресторан | *va-gón-ris-ta-ráhn* |
| **direct train** | прямой поезд | *pri-mój pó-ist* |
| **express train** | курьерский поезд | *kur'-yérs-kij pó-ist* |

| | | |
|---|---|---|
| • leave, depart | отправиться *(p)* | *at-práh-vi-tsa* |
| | отправляться *(i)* | *at-prav-lyáh-tsa* |
| • miss the train | опоздать на поезд *(p)* | *a-paz-dáht' na pó-ist* |
| | опаздывать *(i)* | *a-páhz-dy-vat'* |
| local train | пригородный поезд | *prí-ga-rad-nyj pó-ist* |
| newsstand | газетный киоск | *ga-zyét-nyj ki-ósk* |
| porter | носильщик | *na-síl'-shchik* |
| railroad | железная дорога | *zhy-lyéz-na-ya da-ró-ga* |
| schedule | расписание | *ras-pi-sáh-ni-ye* |
| • early | рано *(adv)* | *ráh-na* |
| • late | поздно *(adv)* | *póz-na* |
| • on time | во время *(adv)* | *vó vrye-mya* |
| seat | место/сидение | *myés-ta/si-dyé-ni-ye* |
| • first class | первый класс | *pyér-vyj klahs* |
| • business class | пассажирский класс | *pa-sa-zhýr-skij klahs* |
| • coach | второй класс | *fta-rój klahs* |
| station | вокзал | *vak-záhl* |
| stop | остановка | *as-ta-nóf-ka* |
| subway (metro) | метро *(indecl)* | *mit-ró* |
| • cashier | кассир | *ka-sír* |
| • Caution! | Осторожно! | *as-ta-rózh-na* |
| • drop a token | бросить *(p)* жетон | *bró-sit' zhy-tón* |
| | бросать *(i)* | *bra-sáht'* |
| • platform | платформа | *plat-fór-ma* |
| • subway station | станция метро | *stáhn-tsy-ya mit-ró* |
| • The doors are closing! | Двери закрываются! | *dvyé-ri za-kry-váh-yu-tsa* |
| • window | касса | *káh-sa* |
| take the train | поехать *(p)* на поезде | *pa-yé-khat' na pó-iz-di* |
| | сесть *(p)* на поезд | *syest' na pó-ist* |
| ticket | билет | *bi-lyét* |
| • buy a ticket | купить *(p)* билет | *ku-pít' bi-lyét* |
| • ticket window | билетная касса | *bi-lyét-na-ya káh-sa* |
| track | рельс | *ryel's* |
| train | поезд | *pó-ist* |
| • The train is departing! | Поезд отправляется! | *pó-ist at-prav-lyáh-i-tsa* |
| • train station | железнодорожная станция | *zhy-liz-na-da-rózh-na-ya stáhn-tsy-ya* |
| • wait for | ждать *(i)* | *zhdaht'* |

*36. HOTELS AND MOTELS*

## a. LODGING

| | | |
|---|---|---|
| **check-in, registration** | регистрация | *rye-gist-ráh-tsy-ya* |
| **check-out time** | время освобождения комнат | *vryé-mya as-va-bazh-dyé-ni-ya kóm-nat* |
| **hostel (dormitory)** | общежитие | *ap-shchi-zhý-ti-ye* |
| **hotel** | гостиница | *gas-tí-ni-tsa* |
| • **central hotel** | центральная гостиница | *tsynt-ráhl'-na-ya gas-tí-ni-tsa* |
| • **hotel for foreigners** | гостиница для иностранцев | *gas-tí-ni-tsa dlya i-nast-ráhn-tsef* |
| • **hotel on the outskirts** | гостиница на окраине | *gas-tí-ni-tsa na ak-ráh-i-ni* |
| **motel** | мотель *(m)* | *ma-téhl'* |

## b. STAYING IN HOTELS

| | | |
|---|---|---|
| **bellhop** | коридорный | *ka-ri-dór-nyj* |
| **bill** | счёт | *shchyot* |
| • **ask for the bill** | попросить *(p)* счёт | *pap-ra-sít' shchyot* |
| | просить *(i)* | *pra-sít'* |
| **breakfast** | завтрак | *záhft-rak* |
| • **breakfast included** | включая завтрак | *fklyu-cháh-ya záhft-rak* |
| **call for a taxi** | вызвать *(p)* такси | *výz-vat' tak-sí* |
| | вызывать *(i)* | *vy-zy-váht'* |
| **complain** | пожаловаться *(p)* | *pa-zháh-la-va-tsa* |
| | жаловаться *(i)* | *zháh-la-va-tsa* |
| • **complaint** | жалоба | *zháh-la-ba* |
| **concierge** | дежурный (-ая) | *di-zhóor-nyj (-a-ya)* |
| **doorman** | швейцар | *shvij-tsáhr* |
| **elevator** | лифт | *lift* |
| **entrance** | вход | *fkhot* |
| **exit** | выход | *vý-khat* |
| **floor (level)** | этаж | *y-táhsh* |
| **garage** | гараж | *ga-ráhsh* |
| **hotel clerk** | служащий гостиницы | *slóo-zha-shchij gas-tí-ni-tsy* |
| **identification** | удостоверение личности | *u-das-ta-vi-ryé-ni-ye lích-nas-ti* |
| **key** | ключ | *klyuch* |

| | | |
|---|---|---|
| • give back the room key before leaving | вернуть *(p)* ключ к комнате перед отъездом | *vir-nóot' klyuch k kóm-na-ti pí-rid at'-yéz-dam* |
| lobby | вестибюль *(m)* | *vis-ti-byúl'* |
| • main door | главный вход | *gláhv-nyj fkhot* |
| • side door | боковая дверь *(f)* | *ba-ka-váh-ya dvyer'* |
| luggage | багаж | *ba-gáhsh* |
| • luggage rack | багажная полка | *ba-gáhzh-na-ya pól-ka* |
| maid | горничная *(f)* | *gór-nich-na-ya* |
| manager | заведующий | *za-vyé-du-yu-shchij* |
| message (note) | записка | *za-písk-ka* |
| passport | паспорт | *páhs-part* |
| pay | заплатить *(p)* | *zap-la-tít'* |
| | платить *(i)* | *pla-tít'* |
| • cash | деньги *(pl)* | *dyén'-gi* |
| • check | чек | *chyek* |
| • credit card | кредитная карточка | *kri-dít-na-ya káhr-tach-ka* |
| • traveler's check | дорожный чек | *da-rózh-nyj chyek* |
| pool | бассейн | *ba-syéjn* |
| porter | носильщик | *na-síl'-shchik* |
| • give the porter a tip | дать *(p)* носильщику на чай (чаевые) | *daht' na-síl'-shchi-ku na chahj (cha-y-vý-i)* |
| | давать *(i)* | *da-váht'* |
| price | цена | *tsy-náh* |
| • How much is a single room? | Сколько стоит комната на одного? | *skól'-ka stó-it kóm-na-ta na ad-na-vó* |
| • How much is a double room? | Сколько стоит комната на двоих? | *skól'-ka stó-it kóm-na-ta na dva-íkh* |
| receipt | квитанция | *kvi-táhn-tsy-ya* |
| reservation | броня | *bra-nyáh* |
| • reserve | забронировать *(p)* | *zab-ra-ní-ra-vat'* |
| | бронировать *(i)* | *bra-ní-ra-vat'* |
| room | комната | *kóm-na-ta* |
| • Do you have a vacant room? | У вас есть *(pol)* свободная комната? | *vahs yest' sva-bód-na-ya kóm-na-ta* |
| • double room | комната на двоих | *kóm-na-ta na dva-íkh* |
| • have baggage taken to one's room (upstairs) | послать *(p)* багаж наверх | *pas-láht' ba-gáhsh na-vyérkh* |
| | посылать *(i)* | *pa-sy-láht'* |
| • room with bath | комната с ванной | *kóm-na-ta s váh-naj* |
| • room with two beds | комната с двумя кроватями | *kóm-na-ta s dvu-myáh kra-váh-ti-mi* |

| • single room | комната на одного | *kóm-na-ta na ad-na-vó* |
| services | обслуживание | *ap-slóo-zhy-va-ni-ye* |
| stairs | лестница *(sg)* | *lyést-ni-tsa* |
| view | вид (из окна) | *vit (iz ak-náh)* |
| wake up | разбудить *(p)* | *raz-bu-dít'* |
| | будить *(i)* | *bu-dít'* |

## c. THE HOTEL ROOM

| armchair | кресло | *kryés-la* |
| balcony | балкон | *bal-kón* |
| • sliding door | раздвижная дверь *(f)* | *raz-dvizh-náh-ya dvyer'* |
| bathroom | ванная (комната) | *váh-na-ya (kóm-na-ta)* |
| bathtub | ванна | *váh-na* |
| bed | кровать *(f)* | *kra-váht'* |
| • double bed | двойная кровать *(f)* | *dvaj-náh-ya kra-váht'* |
| bedside table | ночной столик | *nach-nój stó-lik* |
| blanket | одеяло | *a-di-yáh-la* |
| chest of drawers, dresser | комод | *ka-mót* |
| closet | шкаф | *shkahf* |
| curtain | занавес (-ка) | *záh-na-vyes (za-na-vyés-ka)* |
| faucet | кран | *krahn* |
| lamp | лампа | *láhm-pa* |
| lights | свет *(sg)* | *svyet* |
| • current | ток | *tok* |
| • switch | выключатель *(m)* | *vy-klyu-cháh-til'* |
| | переключатель *(m)* | *pi-ri-klyu-cháh-til'* |
| • switch off | потушить *(p)* | *pa-tu-shýt'* |
| | выключить *(p)* | *výk-lyu-chit'* |
| • switch on | включить *(p)* | *fklyu-hít'* |
| | включать *(i)* | *fklyu-cháht'* |
| mirror | зеркало | *zyér-ka-la* |
| pillow | подушка | *pa-dóosh-ka* |
| radio | радио | *ráh-di-a* |
| shampoo | шампунь *(m)* | *sham-póon'* |
| sheet | простыня | *pras-ty-nyáh* |
| shower | душ | *doosh* |
| sink | раковина | *ráh-ka-vi-na* |
| • cold water | холодная вода | *kha-lód-na-ya va-dáh* |
| • hot water | горячая вода | *ga-ryáh-chi-ya va-dáh* |
| soap bar | кусок мыла | *ku-sók mý-la* |
| table | стол | *stol* |
| telephone | телефон | *ti-li-fón* |

| | | |
|---|---|---|
| **television set** | телевизор | *ti-li-ví-zar* |
| **thermostat** | термостат | *tir-ma-státh* |
| **toilet** | туалет | *tu-a-lyét* |
| | унитаз | *u-ni-táhs* |
| • **toilet paper** | туалетная бумага | *tu-a-lyét-na-ya bu-máh-ga* |
| **towel** | полотенце | *pa-la-tyén-tsy* |
| • **bath towel** | купальное | *ku-páhl'-na-ye* |
| | полотенце | *pa-la-tyén-tsy* |

*37. ON VACATION*

**a. TOURISM**

| | | |
|---|---|---|
| **beach** | пляж | *plyahzh* |
| **business center** | бизнесс центр | *bíz-nis tsehntr* |
| **conference hall** | конференц-зал | *káhn-fi-rintz-záhl* |
| **cottage** | коттедж | *ka-téhdsh* |
| **cruise** | морское путешествие | *mar-skó-ye pu-ti-shéhst-vi-ye* |
| | круиз | *kru-ís* |
| **disco** | дискотека | *dis-ka-tyé-ka* |
| **eco-tourism** | эко-туризм | *y-ka-tu-rízm* |
| **excursion** | экскурсия | *yks-koór-si-ya* |
| • **helicopter excursion** | облёт на вертолёте | *ab-lyot na vir-ta-lyó-ti* |
| **exhibit** | выставка | *výs-taf-ka* |
| **festival** | фестиваль | *fis-ti-váhl'* |
| **fishing** | рыбалка | *ry-báhl-ka* |
| **guidebook** | путеводитель | *pu-ti-va-dí-til'* |
| **guide (tour)** | гид | *git* |
| • **guide-interpreter** | гид-переводчик | *gít-pi-ri-vót-chik* |
| **hiking** | пешая прогулка | *pyé-sha-ya pra-góol-ka* |
| **honeymoon (trip)** | свадебное | *sváh-dib-na-ye* |
| | путешествие | *pu-ti-shéhst-vi-ye* |
| **lake** | озеро | *ó-zi-ra* |
| **massage** | массаж | *ma-sáhsh* |
| **mineral spring** | минеральный источник | *mi-ni-ráhl'-nyj is-tóch-nik* |
| **mountain bicycle** | горный велосипед | *gór-nyj vi-la-si-pyét* |
| **nightclub** | ночной клуб | *nach-nój kloop* |
| **relax** *(v)* | расслабиться *(p)* | *ras-sláh-bi-tsa* |
| | расслабляться *(i)* | *ras-sla-blyáh-tsa* |
| **rent** *(v)* | взять *(p)*/брать *(i)*/ | *vzyaht'/braht'/* |
| | взимать *(i)* на прокат | *vzi-máht' na pra-káht* |
| • **bicycle** | велосипед | *vi-la-si-pyét* |
| • **(row) boat** | лодку | *lót-ku* |
| **resort** *(n)* | курорт | *ku-rórt* |
| **safari** | сафари | *sa-fáh-ri* |
| **sauna** | сауна | *sáh-u-na* |
| **spa** | спа | *spah* |

| spa resort | курорт спа | *ku-rórt spah* |
| take a trip | совершить | *sa-vir-shýt'* |
| | путешествие | *pu-ti-shéhst-vi-ye* |
| tour | тур | *toor* |
| tourism | туризм | *tu-rízm* |
| travel agency | туристическое | *tu-ris-tí-chis-ka-ye* |
| | агентство | *a-gyént-stva* |
| voyage | рейс | *ryejs* |
| walking tour | пешеходная прогулка | *pi-shy-khód-na-ya* |
| | | *pra-goól-ka* |
| water park | водные аттракционы | *vód-ny-ye at-rak-tsy-ó-ny* |
| (water attractions) | *(pl)* | |
| (whitewater) rafting | рафтинг/сплав | *ráhf-tink/splahf na* |
| | на плоту | *pla-tóo* |

## b. SIGHTSEEING

| amphitheater | амфитеатр | *am-fi-ti-áhtr* |
| art gallery | художественная | *khu-dó-zhyst-vi-na-ya* |
| | галерея | *ga-li-ryé-ya* |
| avenue | проспект | *pras-pyékt* |
| basilica | базилика | *ba-zí-li-ka* |
| bell tower | колокольня | *ka-la-kól'-nya* |
| bridge | мост | *most* |
| castle | замок | *záh-mak* |
| cathedral | кафедральный | *ka-fid-ráhl'-nyj sa-bór* |
| | собор | |
| cemetery | кладбище | *kláht-bi-shchi* |
| church | церковь *(f)* | *tséhr-kaf'* |
| city | город | *gó-rat* |
| • center of the city | центр города | *tsehntr gó-ra-da* |
| city map | карта города | *káhr-ta gó-ra-da* |
| corner | угол | *óo-gal* |
| • on the corner | на углу | *na ug-lóo* |
| guide | гид | *git* |
| intersection | перекрёсток | *pi-rik-ryós-tak* |
| kiosk | киоск | *ki-ósk* |
| mausoleum | мавзолей | *mav-za-lyéj* |
| monument | памятник | *páh-mit-nik* |
| • historic | исторический | *is-ta-rí-chis-kij* |
| monument | памятник | *páh-mit-nik* |
| museum | музей | *mu-zyéj* |
| park | парк | *pahrk* |
| park bench | парковая скамья | *páhr-ka-va-ya skam'-yáh* |
| | (скамейка) | *(ska-myéj-ka)* |
| pay for parking | платить *(i)* за | *pla-tít' za sta-yáhn-ku* |
| | стоянку | |

| | | |
|---|---|---|
| pedestrian crosswalk | пешеходный переход | *pi-shy-khód-nyj pi-ri-khót* |
| (public) garden | парк | *pahrk* |
| | сад | *saht* |
| (public) notice | объявление | *ab'-iv-lyé-ni-ye* |
| (public) washroom | туалет | *tu-a-lyét* |
| | уборная | *u-bór-na-ya* |
| railway crossing | железнодорожный переход | *zhy-liz-na-da-rózh-nyj pi-ri-khót* |
| sidewalk | тротуар | *tra-tu-áhr* |
| square | площадь *(f)* | *pló-shchat'* |
| street | улица | *óo-li-tsa* |
| • street sign | уличный знак | *óo-lich-nyj znahk* |
| • the name of the street | название улицы | *naz-váh-ni-ye óo-li-tsy* |
| • What is this street called? | Как эта улица называется? | *kahk éh-ta óo-li-tsa na-zy-váh-i-tsa* |
| synagogue | синагога | *si-na-gó-ga* |
| take an excursion | пойти *(p)* на экскурсию | *paj-tí na yks-kóor-si-yu* |
| | идти *(i)* | *it-tí* |
| temple | храм | *khrahm* |
| tower | башня | *báhsh-nya* |
| traffic light | светофор *(sg)* | *svi-ta-fór* |
| water fountain | фонтан | *fan-táhn* |

## c. GETTING OUT OF THE CITY

| | | |
|---|---|---|
| beach | пляж | *plyahzh* |
| | побережье | *pa-bi-ryézh-ye* |
| • sunburn | солнечный ожог | *sól-nich-nyj a-zhók* |
| • suntan | загар | *za-gáhr* |
| • suntan (v) | загореть *(p)* | *za-ga-ryét'* |
| | загорать *(i)* | *za-ga-ráht'* |
| boat | лодка | *lót-ka* |
| brook | ручей | *ru-chyéj* |
| camp | бивуак | *bi-vu-áhk* |
| canoe | байдарка | *baj-dáhr-ka* |
| cruise | морское путешествие | *mars-kó-ye pu-ti-shéhst-vi-ye* |
| fish | рыба | *rý-ba* |
| • fish | поймать *(p)* рыбу | *paj-máht' rý-bu* |
| | ловить *(i)* рыбу | *la-vít' rý-bu* |
| in the country (nature) | на природе | *na pri-ró-di* |
| in the mountains | в горах | *v ga-ráhkh* |
| knapsack | рюкзак | *ryuk-záhk* |

| | | |
|---|---|---|
| lake | озеро | *ó-zi-ra* |
| mountain climbing | скалолазание | *ska-la-láh-za-ni-ye* |
| pond | пруд | *proot* |
| river | река | *ri-káh* |
| sea | море | *mó-ri* |
| skiing | катание на лыжах | *ka-táh-ni-ye na lý-zhakh* |
| • ski trail | пролыжина | *pra-lý-zhy-na* |
| sleeping bag | спальный мешок | *spáhl'-nyj mi-shók* |
| tent | палатка | *pa-láht-ka* |
| trip | поездка | *pa-yést-ka* |
| vacation | отпуск | *ót-pusk* |
| vacation break | каникулы *(pl)* | *ka-ní-ku-ly* |

## d. ASKING FOR DIRECTIONS

| | | |
|---|---|---|
| across | через | *chyé-ris* |
| ahead | вперёд, впереди | *fpi-ryót, fpi-ri-dí* |
| approach | подойти *(p)* к | *pa-daj-tí k* |
| | идти *(i)* к, в | *it-tí k, v* |
| at the end of | в конце | *f kan-tséh* |
| at the top of | на вершине | *na vir-shý-ni* |
| back | назад | *na-záht* |
| behind | сзади | *zzáh-di* |
| Can you tell me where...? | Скажите, пожалуйста, где...? *(pol)* | *ska-zhý-ri pa-zháh-lu-sta gdye* |
| | Скажи... *(fam)* | *ska-zhý* |
| cross (over) | перейти *(p)* | *pi-rij-tí* |
| | переходить *(i)* | *pi-ri-kha-dít'* |
| • cross the street | перейти *(p)* улицу | *pi-rij-tí óo-li-tsu* |
| down | вниз | *vnis* |
| enter | войти *(p)* | *vaj-tí* |
| | входить *(i)* | *fkha-dít'* |
| everywhere | всюду/везде | *fsyú-du/viz-dyé* |
| exit, go out | выйти *(p)* | *výj-ti* |
| | выходить *(i)* | *vy-kha-dít'* |
| far (from) | далеко *(от)* | *da-li-kó (at)* |
| follow | (по-) следовать *(i)* | *(pa-) slyé-da-vat'* |
| go | идти, ходить *(i)* | *it-tí kha-dít'* |
| here | здесь | *zdyés'* |
| in front of | перед | *pyé-rit* |
| inside | в, внутри | *v, vnoot-rí* |
| near | около, возле | *ó-ka-la, vóz-li* |
| outside | снаружи | *sna-róo-zhy* |
| straight ahead | прямо вперёд | *pryáh-ma fpi-ryót* |

| there | там | *tahm* |
| through | через | *chyé-ris* |
| to the east | на восток | *na vas-tók* |
| to the left | налево | *na-lyé-va* |
| to the north | на север | *na syé-vir* |
| to the right | направо | *nap-ráh-va* |
| to the south | на юг | *na yúk* |
| to the west | на запад | *na záh-pat* |
| toward | к, ко | *k, ka* |
| turn | повернуть *(p)* | *pa-vir-nóot'* |
|  | поворачивать *(i)* | *pa-va-ráh-chi-vat'* |

*Expressions*

| Can you show me...<br>on the map? | = Не могли бы вы показать<br>мне ... на карте? *(pol)*<br>Не мог бы ты ... *(fam, m)*<br>Не могла бы ты ... *(fam, f)* |
| Get off at the next stop | = Сойди/-те *(fam/pol)*<br>на следующей остановке |
| How do you get to...? | = Как пройти (проехать) к...? |
| How far is it from here to...? | = Сколько отсюда до...? |
| Where/When do I need to get off? | = Где мне нужно сойти?<br>Когда мне нужно сойти? |
| Would you happen to know<br>where... is located? | = Не знаете ли вы, где<br>находится...? *(pol)*<br>Не знаешь ли ты, где<br>находится...? *(fam)* |

# SCHOOL AND WORK

*38. SCHOOL*

## a. TYPES OF SCHOOLS AND GRADES

| conservatory | музыкальная школа | *mu-zy-káhl'-na-ya shkó-la* |
|---|---|---|
| day | день *(m)* | *dyen'* |
| • the first day of school | первый день *(m)* школы | *pyér-vyj dyen' shkó-ly* |
| day care, kindergarten | детский сад | *dyéts-kij saht* |
| elementary school | начальная школа | *na-cháhl'-na-ya shkó-la* |
| grade | класс | *klahs* |
| • first grade | первый класс | *pyér-vyj klahs* |
| • second grade | второй класс | *fta-rój klahs* |
| high school | средняя школа | *sryéd-ni-ya shkó-la* |
| higher education (school) | высшая школа | *vý-sha-ya shkó-la* |
| institute | институт | *ins-ti-tóot* |
| night school | вечерняя школа | *vi-chyér-ni-ya shkó-la* |
| specialized school | специальная школа | *spi-tsáhl'-na-ya shkó-la* |
| technical school | техникум | *tyéch-ni-kum* |
| vocational school | школа трудового обучения | *shkó-la tru-da-vó-va a-bu-chyé-ni-ya* |
| university | университет | *u-ni-vir-si-tyét* |
| vacation (break) | каникулы *(pl)* | *ka-ní-ku-ly* |
| year | год | *got* |
| • school year | школьный год | *shkól'-nyj got* |

## b. THE CLASSROOM

| assignment book | дневник | *dniv-ník* |
|---|---|---|
| atlas | атлас | *áht-las* |
| ballpoint pen | шариковая ручка | *sháh-ri-ka-va-ya róoch-ka* |
| book | книга | *kní-ga* |
| book bag | книжная сумка | *knízh-na-ya sóom-ka* |
| bookcase | книжный шкаф | *knízh-nyi shkahf* |
| chalk | мел | *myel* |
| chalkboard | доска | *das-káh* |
| • erase the chalkboard | вытереть *(p)* доску | *vý-ti-rit' dóhs-ku* |
| | вытирать *(i)* | *vy-ti-ráht'* |

| | | |
|---|---|---|
| compass | циркуль *(m)* | *tsýr-kul'* |
| desk (student's) | парта | *páhr-ta* |
| desk (teacher's) | учительский стол | *u-chí-til's-kij stohl* |
| dictionary | словарь *(m)* | *sla-váhr'* |
| encyclopedia | энциклопедия | *yn-tsyk-la-pyé-di-ya* |
| eraser | ластик | *láhs-tik* |
| film projector | кинопроектор | *ki-na-pra-éhk-tar* |
| ink | чернила *(pl)* | *chir-ní-la* |
| magazine | журнал | *zhur-náhl* |
| map | карта | *káhr-ta* |
| notebook | тетрадь *(f)* | *tit-ráht'* |
| paper | бумага | *bu-máh-ga* |
| pen | ручка | *róoch-ka* |
| pencil | карандаш | *ka-ran-dáhsh* |
| • lead | грифель *(m)* | *grí-fil'* |
| • sharpen a pencil | отточить *(p)* карандаш | *a-ta-chít' ka-ran-dáhsh* |
| | оттачивать *(i)* | *a-táh-chi-vat'* |
| record player | проигрыватель *(m)* | *pra-íg-ry-va-til'* |
| ruler | линейка | *li-nyéj-ka* |
| school bag | школьная сумка | *shkól'-na-ya sóom-ka* |
| sketch pad | блокнот для рисования | *blak-nót dlya ri-sa-váh-ni-ya* |
| tack | кнопка | *knóp-ka* |
| tape recorder | магнитофон | *mag-ni-ta-fón* |
| textbook | учебник | *u-chyéb-nik* |
| wall map | стенная карта | *sti-náh-ya káhr-ta* |

## c. SCHOOL AREAS

| | | |
|---|---|---|
| auditorium | аудитория | *a-u-di-tó-ri-ya* |
| canteen, cafeteria | столовая | *sta-ló-va-ya* |
| classroom | классная комната | *kláhs-na-ya kóm-na-ta* |
| gymnasium | спортивный зал | *spar-tív-nyj zahl* |
| hallway | коридор | *ka-ri-dór* |
| laboratory | лаборатория | *la-ba-ra-tó-ri-ya* |
| language lab | лингафонный кабинет | *lin-ga-fón-yj ka-bi-nyét* |
| library | библиотека | *bib-li-a-tyé-ka* |
| principal's office | кабинет директора | *ka-bi-nyét di-ryék-ta-ra* |
| professor's office | кабинет профессора | *ka-bi-nyét pra-fyé-sa-ra* |
| school yard | школьный двор | *shkól'-nyj dvor* |
| teacher's lounge | учительская (комната) | *u-chí-til's-ka-ya (kóm-na-ta)* |

### d. SCHOOL PEOPLE

| | | |
|---|---|---|
| assistant | помощник *(m&f)* | *pa-mósh-nik* |
| • assistant principal | завуч *(m&f)* | *záh-vuch* |
| class (of students) | класс | *klahs* |
| elementary school | начальная школа | *na-cháhl'-na-ya shkó-la* |
| high school | средняя школа | *sryéd-ni-ya shkó-la* |
| janitor | уборщик *(m)* (-щица) *(f)* | *u-bór-shchik (u-bór-shchi-tsa)* |
| librarian | библиотекарь (-рша) | *bib-li-a-tyé-kar' (-rsha)* |
| president of a university | ректор *(m&f)* университета | *ryék-tar u-ni-vir-si-tyé-ta* |
| principal | директор *(m&f)* | *di-ryék-tar* |
| professor | профессор *(m&f)* | *pra-fyé-sar* |
| pupil | ученик (-ница) | *u-chi-ník (-ní-tsa)* |
| schoolmate | школьный товарищ *(m&f)* | *shkól'-nyj ta-váh-rishch* |
| secretary | секретарь *(m)* (-рша) *(f)* | *sik-ri-táhr' (-rsha)* |
| student | студент (-ка) | *stu-dyént (-ka)* |
| teacher | учитель *(m)* | *u-chí-til'* |
| | учительница *(f)* | *u-chí-til'-ni-tsa* |
| • college teacher | преподаватель (-ница) | *pri-pa-da-váh-til' (-ni-tsa)* |
| technician | техник *(m&f)* | *tyékh-nik* |

### e. SCHOOL SUBJECTS

| | | |
|---|---|---|
| algebra | алгебра | *áhl-gib-ra* |
| anatomy | анатомия | *a-na-tó-mi-ya* |
| anthropology | антропология | *ant-ra-pa-ló-gi-ya* |
| archeology | археология | *ar-khi-a-ló-gi-ya* |
| architecture | архитектура | *ar-khi-tik-tóo-ra* |
| arithmetic | арифметика | *a-rif-myé-ti-ka* |
| art (drawing) | рисование | *ri-sa-váh-ni-ye* |
| astronomy | астрономия | *ast-ra-nó-mi-ya* |
| biology | биология | *bi-a-ló-gi-ya* |
| botany | ботаника | *ba-táh-ni-ka* |
| calculus | высшая математика | *vý-sha-ya ma-ti-máh-ti-ka* |
| chemistry | химия | *khí-mi-ya* |
| computer science | кибернетика | *ki-bir-néh-ti-ka* |
| drafting | черчение | *chir-chyé-ni-ye* |
| economics | экономика | *y-ka-nó-mi-ka* |

| engineering (sciences) | инженерное дело | yn-zhy-nyér-na-ye dyé-la |
| foreign language | иностранный язык | i-nast-ráh-nyj y-zýk |
| • English | английский | ang-lís-kij |
| • French | французский | fran-tsóos-kij |
| • German | немецкий | ni-myéts-kij |
| geography | география | gi-ag-ráh-fi-ya |
| geology | геология | gi-a-ló-gi-ya |
| geometry | геометрия | gi-a-myét-ri-ya |
| history | история | is-tó-ri-ya |
| • history of art | история искусств *(pl)* | is-tó-ri-ya is-kóostf |
| humanities | гуманитарные науки *(pl)* | gu-ma-ni-táhr-ny-ye na-óo-ki |
| law | законоведение | za-ka-na-vyé-di-ni-ye |
| literature | литература | li-ti-ra-tóo-ra |
| mathematics | математика | ma-ti-máh-ti-ka |
| medicine | медицина | mi-di-tsý-na |
| music | музыка | móo-zy-ka |
| natural sciences | естественные науки *(pl)* | is-tyést-vi-ny-i na-óo-ki |
| philosophy | философия | fi-la-só-fi-ya |
| physics | физика | fí-zi-ka |
| psychology | психология | psi-kha-ló-gi-ya |
| sociology | социология | sa-tsy-a-ló-gi-ya |
| statistics | статистика | sta-tís-ti-ka |
| subject | предмет | prid-myét |
| trigonometry | тригонометрия | tri-ga-na-myét-ri-ya |
| zoology | зоология | za-a-ló-gi-ya |

## f. ADDITIONAL SCHOOL VOCABULARY

| answer | ответ | at-vyét |
| • answer | ответить *(p)* | ai-vyé-tit' |
| | отвечать *(i)* | at-vi-cháht' |
| • brief, short | краткий (короткий) | kráht-kij (ka-rót-kij) |
| • long | длинный | dlí-nyj |
| • right | правильный | práh-vil'-nyj |
| • wrong | неправильный | ni-práh-vil'-nyj |
| assignment (homework) | домашнее задание | da-máhsh-ni-ye za-dáh-ni-ye |
| attend school | ходить *(i)* в школу | kha-dít' f shkó-lu |
| | посещать *(i)* | pa-si-shcháht' |
| be absent | отсутствовать *(i)* | at-sóot-stva-vat' |
| be present | присутствовать *(i)* | pri-sóot-stva-vat' |
| class | класс | klahs |

| | | |
|---|---|---|
| • lesson | урок | *u-rók* |
| • skip a class | пропустить *(p)* класс | *pra-pus-tít' klahs* |
| | пропускать *(i)* | *pra-pus-káht'* |
| • skip school | прогулять *(p)* школу | *pra-gu-lyáht' shkó-lu* |
| (play hooky) | прогуливать *(i)* | *pra-góo-li-vat'* |
| • There is no class | Сегодня занятия *(pl)* | *si-vód-nya za-nyáh-ti-ya* |
| today | не состоятся | *ni sas-ta-yáh-tsa* |
| • Today's lecture is | Сегодняшняя | *si-vód-nish-ni-ya* |
| canceled | лекция отменена | *lyék-tsy-ya at-mi-ni-náh* |
| composition | сочинение | *sa-chi-nyé-ni-ye* |
| copy | переписать *(p)* | *pi-ri-pi-sáht'* |
| | переписывать *(i)* | *pi-ri-pí-sy-vat'* |
| course | курс | *koors'* |
| • take a course | прослушать *(p)* курс | *pras-lóo-shat' koors* |
| | прослушивать *(i)* | *pras-lóo-shy-vat'* |
| dictation | диктант | *dik-táhnt* |
| diploma | диплом | *dip-lóm* |
| • get a diploma | получить *(p)* диплом | *pa-lu-chít' dip-lóm* |
| | получать *(i)* | *pa-lu-cháht'* |
| • high school | аттестат зрелости | *a-tis-táht zryé-las-ti* |
| diploma | | |
| • university | университетский | *u-ni-vir-si-tyéts-kij* |
| diploma | диплом | *dip-lóm* |
| draw | рисовать *(i)* | *ri-sa-váht'* |
| • drawing | рисование | *ri-sa-váh-ni-ye* |
| education | образование | *ab-ra-za-váh-ni-ye* |
| • educated | образованный *(m)* | *ab-ra-zó-va-nyj* |
| • get an education | получить *(p)* | *pa-lu-chít'* |
| | образование | *ab-ra-za-váh-ni-ye* |
| | получать *(i)* | *pa-lu-cháht'* |
| • uneducated | необразованный | *ni-ab-ra-zó-va-nyj* |
| error, mistake | ошибка | *a-shýp-ka* |
| • make a mistake | сделать *(p)* ошибку | *sdyé-lat' a-shýp-ku* |
| | делать *(i)* | *dyé-lat'* |
| essay | очерк/сочинение | *ó-chirk/sa-chi-nyé-ni-ye* |
| exam, test | экзамен | *yk-záh-min* |
| • entrance exams | вступительные | *fstu-pí-til'-ny-i* |
| | экзамены *(pl)* | *yk-záh-mi-ny* |
| • oral exam | устный экзамен | *óos-nyi yk-záh-min* |
| • pass an exam | выдержать *(p)* | *vý-dir-zhat' yk-záh-min* |
| | экзамен | |
| | выдерживать *(i)* | *vy-dyér-zhy-vat'* |
| • take an exam | сдавать *(i)* экзамен | *sda-váht' yk-záh-min* |
| • written exam | письменный | *pís'-mi-nyj yk-záh-min* |
| | экзамен | |
| exercise | упражнение | *up-razh-nyé-ni-ye* |

| | | |
|---|---|---|
| **explanation** | объяснение | *a-b'is-nyé-ni-ye* |
| • explain | объяснить *(p)* | *a-b'-is-nít'* |
| | объяснять *(i)* | *a-b'-is-nyáht'* |
| **fail an exam** | завалить *(p)* экзамен | *za-va-lít' yk-záh-min* |
| | заваливать *(i)* | *za-váh-li-vat'* |
| **field (of study)** | область *(f)* | *ób-last'* |
| | отрасль *(f)* | *ót-rasl'* |
| **give/hand back** | вернуть *(p)* | *vir-nóot* |
| | возвращать *(i)* | *vaz-vra-shcháht'* |
| **grade, mark** | отметка | *at-myét-ka* |
| | оценка | *a-tséhn-ka* |
| **grammar** | грамматика | *gra-máh-ti-ka* |
| **learn** | учить *(i)* | *u-chít'* |
| | изучать *(i)* | *i-zu-cháht'* |
| • learn by heart/ | выучить *(p)* | *vý-u-chit' na-i-zóost'* |
| memorize | наизусть | |
| | выучивать *(i)* | *vy-óo-chi-vat'* |
| **lecture** | лекция | *lyék-tsy-ya* |
| • lecture | читать *(i)* лекцию | *chi-táht' lyék-tsy-yu* |
| **listen to** | слушать *(i)* | *slóo-shat'* |
| **notes** | конспекты | *kans-pyék-ty* |
| • take notes | сделать *(p)* записи | *sdyé-lat' záh-pi-si* |
| | делать *(i)* записи | *dyé-lat' záh-pi-si* |
| **problem** | задача | *za-dáh-cha* |
| • solve a problem | решить *(p)* задачу | *ri-shýt' za-dáh-chu* |
| | решать *(i)* | *ri-sháht'* |
| **question** | вопрос | *vap-rós* |
| • answer a | ответить *(p)* на | *at-vyé-tit' na vap-rós* |
| question | вопрос | |
| | отвечать *(i)* | *at-vi-cháht'* |
| • ask a question | спросить *(p)* | *sprah-sít'* |
| | спрашивать *(i)* | *spráh-shy-vat'* |
| | задать *(p)* вопрос | *za-dáht' vap-rós* |
| | задавать *(i)* | *za-da-váht'* |
| **read** | прочитать *(p)* | *pra-chi-táht'* |
| | читать *(i)* | *chi-táht'* |
| • reading | чтение | *chtyé-ni-ye* |
| **registration** | регистрация | *ri-gist-ráh-tsy-ya* |
| **repeat** | повторить *(p)* | *paf-ta-rít'* |
| | повторять *(i)* | *paf-ta-ryáht'* |
| **roll call** | перекличка | *pi-rik-lích-ka* |
| **school** | школа | *shkó-la* |
| • finish school | кончить *(p)* школу | *kóhn-chit' shkó-lu* |
| | кончать *(i)* | *kan-cháht'* |
| • go to school | идти в школу *(i)* | *it-tí f shkó-lu* |
| | ходить в школу *(i)* | *kha-dít' f shkó-lu* |

| study | учиться *(i)* | u-chí-tsa |
| | изучать *(i)* | i-zu-cháht' |
| take (study) mathematics | изучать *(i)* математику | i-zu-cháht' ma-ti-máh-ti-ku |
| take Russian | изучать *(i)* русский язык | i-zu-cháht' róos-kij i-zýk |
| teach | преподавать *(i)* | pri-pa-da-váht' |
| | учить/обучать *(i)* | u-chít'/a-bu-cháht' |
| thesis (diploma project) | дипломный проект | dip-lóm-nyj pra-éhkt |
| type | напечатать *(p)* | na-pi-cháh-tat' |
| | печатать *(i)* | pi-cháh-tat' |
| • typist | машинистка | ma-shy-níst-ka |
| understand | понять *(p)* | pa-nyáht' |
| | понимать *(i)* | pa-ni-máht' |
| write | написать *(p)* | na-pi-sáht' |
| | писать *(i)* | pi-sáht' |

*39. WORK*

## a. JOBS AND PROFESSIONS

| accountant | бухгалтер *(m&f)* | bu-gáhl-tir |
| | счетовод *(m&f)* | shchi-ta-vót |
| actor | актёр | ak-tyór |
| actress | актриса | akl-rí-sa |
| architect | архитектор *(m&f)* | ar-khi-tyék-tar |
| baker | пекарь *(m&f)* | pyé-kar' |
| barber | парикмахер *(m)* | pa-rik-máh-khir |
| biologist | биолог *(m&f)* | bi-ó-lak |
| bricklayer | каменщик (-ица) | káh-min-shchik (-i-tsa) |
| bus driver | водитель *(m&f)* автобуса | va-di-til' af-tó-bu-sa |
| businessman (-woman) | бизнесмен (-ка) | biz-nis-myén (-ka) |
| butcher | мясник | mis-ník |
| carpenter | столяр/плотник | sta-lyáhr/plót-nik |
| construction worker | строительный рабочий | stra-í-til'-nyj ra-bó-chij |
| cook | повар *(m&f)* | pó-var |
| dentist | зубной врач *(m&f)* | zub-nój vrahch |
| doctor | врач *(m&f)* | vrahch |
| editor | редактор *(m&f)* | ri-dáhk-tar |
| electrician | электрик/ монтёр | y-lyékt-rik/man-tyór |

| engineer | инженер *(m&f)* | yn-zhy-nyér |
| entrepreneur | предприниматель | prit-pri-ni-máh-til' |
| | (-ница) | (-ni-tsa) |
| factory worker | рабочий (-ая) | ra-bó-chij (-a-ya) |
| | фабрики | fáhb-ri-ki |
| farmer | фермер (-ша) | fyér-mir (-sha) |
| firefighter | пожарный | pa-zháhr-nij |
| hairdresser | парикмахер *(m)* | pa-rik-máh-khir |
| | парикмахерша *(f)* | pa-rik-máh-khir-sha |
| janitor | уборщик (-щица) | u-bór-shchik (-shchi-tsa) |
| job | работа/труд | ra-bó-ta/troot |
| journalist | журналист (-ка) | zhur-na-líst (-ka) |
| lawyer | адвокат *(m&f)* | ad-va-káht |
| mathematician | математик *(m&f)* | ma-ti-máh-tik |
| mechanic | механик | mi-kháh-nik |
| musician | музыкант *(m&f)* | mu-zy-káhnt |
| nurse | медицинская сестра | mi-di-tsýn-ska-ya sist-ráh |
| | медсестра | mit-sist-ráh |
| occupation | занятие | za-nyáh-ti-ye |
| painter (artist) | художник (-ница) | khu-dózh-nik (-ni-tsa) |
| painter (walls) | маляр | ma-lyáhr |
| pharmacist | фармацевт *(m&f)* | far-ma-tséhft |
| | аптекарь *(m)* (-рша) | ap-tyé-kar' (-rsha) |
| physicist | физик *(m&f)* | fí-zik |
| pilot | лётчик | lyót-chik |
| | пилот | pi-lót |
| plumber | слесарь | slyé-sar' |
| police officer | милиционер | mi-li-tsy-a-nyér |
| priest | священник | svi-shchyé-nik |
| profession | профессия | pra-fyé-si-ya |
| • professional | профессиональный | pra-fi-si-a-náhl'-nyj |
| | работник *(m&f)* | ra-bót-nik |
| professor | профессор *(m&f)* | pra-fyé-sar |
| prostitute | проститутка | pras-ti-tóot-ka |
| psychiatrist | психиатр | psi-khi-áhtr |
| psychologist | психолог *(m&f)* | psi-khó-lak |
| repairman | монтёр (-ша) | man-tyór (-sha) |
| scientist | учёный *(m)* (-ная) | u-chyó-nyj (-na-ya) |
| secretary | секретарь *(m)* | sik-ri-táhr' |
| | секретарша *(f)* | sik-ri-táhr-sha |
| soldier | солдат (-ка) | sal-dáht (-ka) |
| surgeon | хирург *(m&f)* | khi-róork |
| tailor | портной *(m)* | part-nój |
| teacher (school) | учитель *(m)* | u-chí-til' |
| | учительница *(f)* | u-chí-til'-ni-tsa |

| teacher (university) | преподаватель *(m)* | *pri-pa-da-váh-til'* |
| | преподавательница *(f)* | *pri-pa-da-váh-til'-ni-tsa* |
| technician | техник | *tyékh-nik* |
| typist | машинистка *(f)* | *ma-shy-níst-ka* |
| writer | писатель *(m)* | *pi-sáh-til'* |
| | писательница *(f)* | *pi-sáh-til'-ni-tsa* |

*Expressions*

| Patience and hard work can overcome anything | = Терпение и труд всё перетрут |
| To work hard enough for ten people | = Работать за десятерых |
| To work very hard (To work like an ox) | = Работать, как вол |
| To work with the sweat on one's brow | = Работать в поте лица |
| Work can wait (Work won't run away) | = Работа не убежит |

## b. INTERVIEWING FOR A JOB

| address | адрес | *áhd-ris* |
| • street | улица | *óo-li-tsa* |
| • number (of the house) | номер дома | *nó-mir dó-ma* |
| • city | город | *gó-rat* |
| • zip code | почтовый индекс | *pach-tó-vyj ín-dyks* |
| age | возраст | *vóz-rast* |
| citizenship | гражданство | *grazh-dáhnst-va* |
| date and place of birth | дата и место рождения | *dáh-ta i myés-ta razh-dyé-ni-ya* |
| education | образование | *ab-ra-za-váh-ni-ye* |
| • elementary school | начальная школа | *na-cháhl'-na-ya shkó-la* |
| • high school | средняя школа | *sryéd-ni-ya shkó-la* |
| • higher education | высшее образование | *výsh-y-ye ab-ra-za-váh-ni-ye* |
| marital status | семейное положение | *si-myéj-na-ye pa-la-zhéh-ni-ye* |
| • married | женат (-ый) *(m)* | *zhy-náht (-tyj)* |
| | замужем (-жняя) *(f)* | *záh-mu-zhym (za-móozh-ni-ya)* |

| | | |
|---|---|---|
| • single | неженат (-ый), | *ni-zhy-náht (-tyi)* |
| | холост (-ой) *(m)* | *khó-last (kha-las-tój)* |
| | незамужняя *(f)* | *ni-za-móozh-ni-ya* |
| name | имя | *í-mya* |
| • first name | имя | *í-mya* |
| • signature | подпись *(f)* | *pót-pis'* |
| • surname, family name | фамилия | *fa-mí-li-ya* |
| nationality | национальность *(f)* | *na-tsy-a-náhl'-nast'* |
| place of employment | место работы | *myés-ta ra-bó-ty* |
| profession | профессия | *pra-fyé-si-ya* |
| sex | пол | *pol* |
| • male | мужской | *mush-skój* |
| • female | женский | *zhéhns-kij* |
| telephone number | номер телефона | *nó-mir ti-li-fó-na* |

## c. THE OFFICE

| | | |
|---|---|---|
| adhesive tape | клейкая лента | *klyéj-ka-ya lyén-ta* |
| appointment | деловая | *di-la-váh-ya* |
| | встреча/свидание | *fstryé-cha/svi-dáh-ni-ye* |
| briefcase | портфель *(m)* | *part-fyél'* |
| calendar | календарь *(m)* | *ka-lin-dáhr'* |
| chair | стул | *stool* |
| computer | компьютер | *kamp'-yú-tar* |
| | вычислительная | *vy-chis-lí-til'-na-ya* |
| | машина | *ma-shý-na* |
| • keyboard | клавиатура | *kla-vi-a-tóo-ra* |
| • mouse | мышь *(f)* | *mysh* |
| • printer | принтер | *prín-tyr* |
| • screen | экран | *yk-ráhn* |
| desk | письменный стол | *pís'-mi-nyj stohl* |
| file (folder) | папка | *páhp-ka* |
| filing card | карточка | *káhr-tach-ka* |
| paper | бумага | *bu-máh-ga* |
| • sheet of paper | лист бумаги | *list bu-máh-gi* |
| | листы бумаги *(pl)* | *lis-tý bu-máh-gi* |
| pen | ручка | *róoch-ka* |
| pencil | карандаш | *ka-ran-dáhsh* |
| photocopier | копировальная | *ka-pi-ra-váhl'-na-ya* |
| | машина | *ma-shý-na* |
| ruler | линейка | *li-nyéj-ka* |
| scissors | ножницы *(pl)* | *nózh-ni-tsy* |
| staple | скобка | *skóp-ka* |
| stapler | стейплер | *stéhjp-lir* |

| | | |
|---|---|---|
| tack | кнопка | *knóp-ka* |
| telephone | телефон | *ti-li-fón* |
| typewriter | пишущая машинка | *pí-shu-shcha-ya ma-shýn-ka* |
| wastepaper basket | корзина (-нка) для бумаг | *kar-zí-na (-nka) dlya bu-máhk* |
| word processor | текстовой редактор | *tik-sta-vój ri-dáhk-tar* |

## d. ADDITIONAL WORK VOCABULARY

| | | |
|---|---|---|
| advertisement | объявление/реклама | *a-b'-iv-lyé-ni-ye/ rik-láh-ma* |
| boss | начальник | *na-cháhl'-nik* |
| career | карьера | *kar'-yé-ra* |
| colleague | коллега *(m&f)* | *ka-lyé-ga* |
| company | компания/фирма | *kam-páh-ni-ya/fír-ma* |
| contract | договор/контракт | *da-ga-vór/kant-ráhkt* |
| earn | заработать *(p)* | *za-ra-bó-tat'* |
| | зарабатывать *(i)* | *za-ra-báh-ty-vat'* |
| employee | работник | *ra-bót-nik* |
| | служащий | *slóo-zha-shchij* |
| employer | наниматель *(m)* | *na-ni-máh-til'* |
| | работодатель *(m)* | *ra-ba-ta-dáh-til'* |
| employment agency | трудовое агентство | *tru-da-vó-ye a-gyénst-va* |
| factory | фабрика | *fáhb-ri-ka* |
| fire | уволить *(p)* | *u-vó-lit'* |
| | освободить *(p)* от обязанностей | *as-va-ba-dít' at a-byáh-za-nas-tij* |
| hire | нанять *(p)* | *na-nyáht'* |
| | нанимать *(i)* | *na-ni-máht'* |
| manager | заведующий | *za-vyé-du-yu-shchij* |
| market | рынок | *rý-nak* |
| office | контора | *kan-tó-ra* |
| plant | завод | *za-vót* |
| retirement | пенсия | *pyén-si-ya* |
| • retire | уйти *(p)* на пенсию | *uj-tí na pyén-si-yu* |
| | уходить *(i)* | *u-kha-dít'* |
| unemployment | безработица | *biz-ra-bó-ti-tsa* |
| wage, salary | заработок | *záh-ra-ba-tak* |
| | зарплата | *zarp-láh-ta* |
| work | работа | *ra-bó-ta* |
| • work | работать *(i)* | *ra-bó-tat'* |
| work associate | сослуживец *(m)* | *sas-lu-zhý-vits* |
| | сослуживица *(f)* | *sas-lu-zhý-vi-tsa* |

# EMERGENCIES

## 40. REPORTING AN EMERGENCY

### a. FIRE

| | | |
|---|---|---|
| alarm | тревога | *tri-vó-ga* |
| ambulance | машина скорой помощи | *ma-shý-na skó-raj pó-ma-shchi* |
| building | здание | *zdáh-ni-ye* |
| burn | ожог | *a-zhók* |
| • burn (oneself) | обжечься *(p)* | *ap-zhéhch-sya* |
| call the fire department | вызвать *(p)* пожарную команду | *výz-vat' pa-zháhr-nu-yu ka-máhn-du* |
| | вызывать *(i)* | *vy-zy-váht'* |
| catch fire | загореться *(p)* | *za-ga-ryé-tsa* |
| danger | опасность *(f)* | *a-páhs-nast'* |
| destroy | разрушить *(p)* | *raz-róo-shyt'* |
| | разрушать *(i)* | *raz-ru-sháht'* |
| emergency exit | запасной выход | *za-pas-nój vý-khat* |
| • fire exit | пожарный выход | *pa-záhr-nyj vý-khat* |
| escape, get out | бежать *(p)* | *bi-zháht'* |
| extinguish, put out | погасить *(p)* | *pa-ga-sít'* |
| | потушить *(p)* | *pa-tu-shýt'* |
| fire | пожар | *pa-zháhr* |
| | огонь *(m)* | *a-gón'* |
| • be on fire | гореть *(i)* | *ga-ryét'* |
| | быть в огне *(i)* | *byt' v ag-nyé* |
| • Fire! | Пожар! | *pa-zháhr* |
| • fire alarm | пожарная тревога | *pa-zháhr-na-ya tri-vó-ga* |
| • fire extinguisher | огнетушитель *(m)* | *ag-ni-tu-shý-til'* |
| • fire hose | пожарный шланг | *pa-zháhr-nyj shlahnk* |
| • fire hydrant | пожарный кран | *pa-zháhr-nyj krahn* |
| • fire truck | пожарная машина | *pa-zháhr-na-ya ma-shý-na* |
| fireproof | огнестойкий | *ag-ni-stój-kij* |
| | несгораемый | *nis-ga-ráh-i-myj* |
| first aid | скорая помощь *(f)* | *skó-ra-ya pó-mashch* |
| flame | пламя | *pláh-mya* |
| get out | выходить *(i)* | *vy-kha-dít'* |
| • Everybody out! | Все наружу! | *fsye na-róo-zhu* |
| help | помощь *(f)* | *pó-mashch* |
| • Help! | На помощь! | *na pó-mashch* |
| | Помогите! | *pa-ma-gí-ti* |

| | | |
|---|---|---|
| • give help | помочь *(p)* | pa-móch |
| | помогать *(i)* | pa-ma-gáht' |
| ladder | лестница | lyés-ni-tsa |
| protect | защитить *(p)* | za-shchi-tít' |
| | защищать *(i)* | za-shchi-shcháht' |
| rescue | спасти *(p)* | spas-tí |
| | спасать *(i)* | spa-sáht' |
| shout | крик | krik |
| • shout | крикнуть *(p)* | krík-nut' |
| | кричать *(i)* | kri-cháht' |
| siren | сирена | si-ryé-na |
| smoke | дым | dym |
| victim | жертва | zhéhrt-va |

## b. ROBBERY AND ASSAULT

| | | |
|---|---|---|
| argue | ссориться *(i)* / ругаться *(i)* | só-ri-tsa/ru-gáh-tsa |
| arrest | арест | a-ryést |
| • arrest | арестовать *(p)* | a-ris-ta-váht' |
| | арестовывать *(i)* | a-ris-tó-vy-vat' |
| assault | нападение | na-pa-dyé-ni-ye |
| Come (here) quickly! | Идите *(pol)* сюда скорей! | i-dí-ti syu-dáh ska-rýej |
| | Иди *(fam)* | i-dí |
| crime | преступление | pris-tup-lyé-ni-ye |
| • crime wave | волна преступлений | val-náh pris-tup-lyé-nij |
| • criminal | преступный | pris-tóop-nyj |
| description | описание | a-pi-sáh-ni-ye |
| detective | следователь *(m)* | slyé-da-va-til' |
| fight | драка | dráh-ka |
| firearm | огнестрельное оружие | ag-nist-ryél'-na-ye a-róo-zhy-ye |
| gun | ружьё | ruzh'-yó |
| handcuffs | наручники *(pl)* | na-róoch-ni-ki |
| injure, wound | поранить *(p)* | pa-ráh-nit' |
| | ранить *(i)* | ráh-nit' |
| • injury, wound | рана | ráh-na |
| kill | убить *(p)* | u-bít' |
| | убивать *(i)* | u-bi-váht' |
| • murderer | убийца | u-bíj-tsa |
| knife | нож | nosh |
| • switchblade | финский нож | fín-skij nosh |
| machine gun | автомат | af-ta-máht |
| murder | убийство | u-bíjst-va |

| | | |
|---|---|---|
| **pickpocket** | карманщик | *kar-máhn-shchik* |
| **pistol** | пистолет | *pis-ta-lyét* |
| **police** | милиция | *mi-lí-tsy-ya* |
| • **call the police** | позвать *(p)* милицию | *paz-váht' mi-lí-tsy-yu* |
| | звать *(i)* | *zvaht'* |
| • **police officer** | милиционер | *mi-li-tsy-a-nyér* |
| **rape** | изнасилование | *iz-na-sí-la-va-ni-ye* |
| • **rape** | изнасиловать *(p)* | *iz-na-sí-la-vat'* |
| **revolver** | револьвер | *ri-val'-vyér* |
| **rifle** | ружьё | *ruzh'-yó* |
| | винтовка | *vin-tóf-ka* |
| **robber** | грабитель | *gra-bí-til'* |
| • **armed robbery** | ограбление с | *ag-rab-lyé-ni-ye s* |
| | применением | *pri-mi-nyé-ni-yem* |
| | оружия | *a-róo-zhy-ya* |
| • **rob** | ограбить *(p)* | *ag-ráh-bit'* |
| | грабить *(i)* | *gráh-bit'* |
| • **robbery** | грабёж | *gra-byósh* |
| | ограбление | *ag-rab-lyé-ni-ye* |
| **shoot** | выстрелить *(p)* | *výs-tri-lit'* |
| | стрелять *(i)* | *stri-lyáht'* |
| **steal** | украсть *(p)* | *uk-ráhst'* |
| | воровать *(i)* | *vu-ra-váht'* |
| **thief** | вор | *vor* |
| • **Stop thief!** | Остановите *(pl)* | *as-ta-na-ví-ti vó-ra* |
| | вора! | |
| **weapon** | оружие | *a-róo-zhy-ye* |
| • **armed** | вооружённый | *va-a-ru-zhó-nyj* |

## c. TRAFFIC ACCIDENTS

| | | |
|---|---|---|
| **accident** | несчастный случай | *ni-shcháhs-nyi slóo-chahj* |
| • **automobile accident** | авария | *a-váh-ri-ya* |
| **ambulance** | машина скорой | *ma-shý-na skó-raj* |
| | помощи | *pó-ma-shchi* |
| • **call an ambulance** | вызвать скорую | *výz-vaht' skó-ru-yu* |
| | помощь | *pó-mashch* |
| **be run over (by a car)** | попасть под машину | *pa-páhst' pad ma-shý-nu* |
| **bleed** | кровоточить *(i)* | *kra-va-tó-chit'* |
| • **bleeding** | кровотечение | *kra-va-ti-chyé-ni-ye* |
| • **blood** | кровь *(f)* | *krof'* |
| **break a bone** | сломать *(p)* кость | *sla-máht' kost'* |
| **bump** | шишка | *shýsh-ka* |

| collide | столкнуться *(p)* | *stalk-nóo-tsa* |
| | сталкиваться *(i)* | *stáhl-ki-va-tsa* |
| • collision | столкновение | *stalk-na-vyé-ni-ye* |
| crash | крушение | *kru-shéh-ni-ye* |
| • crash | разбиться *(p)* | *raz-bí-tsa* |
| | разбиваться *(i)* | *raz-bi-váh-tsa* |
| doctor | врач | *vrahch* |
| | доктор | *dók-tar* |
| • get a doctor | позвать *(p)* врача | *paz-váht' vra-cháh* |
| | звать *(i)* | *zváht'* |
| first aid | первая помощь *(f)* | *pyér-va-ya pó-mashch* |
| • antiseptic | антисептическое средство | *an-ti-syp-tí-chis-ka-ye sryét-stva* |
| • bandage | повязка | *pa-vyáhs-ka* |
| • gauze | бинт | *bint* |
| • scissors | ножницы | *nózh-ni-tsy* |
| • splint | шина | *shý-na* |
| • tincture of iodine | настойка йода | *nas-tój-ka jóh-da* |
| Help! | Помогите! | *pa-ma-gí-ti* |
| hospital | больница | *bal'-ní-tsa* |
| • x rays | рентген | *rin-gyén* |
| injury, wound | рана | *ráh-na* |
| police | милиция | *mi-lí-tsy-ya* |
| • call the police | вызвать *(p)* милицию | *výz-vat' mi-lí-tsy-yu* |
| shock | состояние шока | *sas-ta-yáh-ni-ye shó-ka* |

*41. MEDICAL CARE*

a. THE DOCTOR

| ache | боль *(f)* | *bol'* |
| acne | угри *(pl)* | *ug-rí* |
| allergy | аллергия | *a-lir-gí-ya* |
| appendicitis | аппендицит | *a-pin-di-tsít* |
| • appendix | аппендикс | *a-pyén-diks* |
| appointment (with the doctor) | запись *(f)* (к врачу) | *záh-pis' (k vra-chóo)* |
| artery | артерия | *ar-téh-ri-ya* |
| arthritis | артрит | *art-rít* |
| aspirin | аспирин | *as-pi-rín* |
| | пирамидон | *pi-ra-mi-dón* |
| bandage | перевязка | *pi-ri-vyáhs-ka* |
| | повязка | *pa-vyáhs-ka* |

| | | |
|---|---|---|
| • bandage | перевязать *(p)* | *pi-ri-vi-záht'* |
| | перевязывать *(i)* | *pi-ri-vyáh-zy-vat'* |
| blood | кровь *(f)* | *krof'* |
| • blood pressure | кровяное давление | *kra-vi-nó-ye dav-lyé-ni-ye* |
| bone | кость *(f)* | *kost'* |
| brain | мозг | *mosk* |
| bronchitis | бронхит | *bran-khít* |
| cancer | рак | *rahk* |
| cataract | катаракта | *ka-ta-ráhk-ta* |
| cold | простуда | *pras-tóo-da* |
| convalesce | выздороветь *(p)* | *výz-da-ra-vit'* |
| | выздоравливать *(i)* | *vyz-da-ráhv-li-vat'* |
| • convalescence | выздоровление | *vyz-da-rav-lyé-ni-ye* |
| • Get well soon! | Желаю скорого | *zhy-láh-yu skóh-ra-va* |
| | выздоровления! | *vyz-da-rav-lyé-ni-ye* |
| cough | кашель *(m)* | *káh-shyl'* |
| • cough | кашлять *(i)* | *káhsh-lit'* |
| cure | излечение | *iz-li-chyé-ni-ye* |
| | средство | *sryét-stva* |
| • cure | вылечить *(p)* | *vý-li-chit'* |
| | вылечивать *(i)* | *vy-lyé-chi-vat'* |
| dandruff | перхоть *(f)* | *pyér-khat'* |
| digestive system | пищеварительные | *pi-shchi-va-rí-til'-ny-ye* |
| | органы *(pl)* | *ór-ga-ny* |
| • anus | задний проход | *záhd-nij pra-khót* |
| • defecate | иметь *(i)* стул | *i-myét' stool* |
| • rectum | прямая кишка | *pri-máh-ya kish-káh* |
| • stomach | желудок | *zhy-lóo-dak* |
| | живот | *zhy-vót* |
| • I have a stomachache | У меня живот болит | *mi-nyáh zhy-vót ba-lít* |
| doctor | врач | *vrahch* |
| | доктор | *dók-tar* |
| • at the doctor's | у врача | *vra-cháh* |
| doctor's visit | посещение врача | *pa-si-shchyé-ni-ye vra-cháh* |
| examine (medically) | осмотреть *(p)* | *as-mat-ryét'* |
| | осматривать *(i)* | *as-máht-ri-vat'* |
| eye doctor | глазной врач | *glaz-nój vrahch* |
| • contact lenses | контактные линзы | *kan-táhkt-ny-i lín-zy* |
| • eyeglasses | очки | *ach-kí* |
| • sight | зрение | *zryé-ni-ye* |
| feel | чувствовать *(i)* | *chóost-va-vat'* |
| • feel bad | плохо себя | *pló-kha si-byáh* |
| | чувствовать *(i)* | *chóost-va-vat'* |

| | | |
|---|---|---|
| • feel well | хорошо себя чувствовать *(i)* | *kha-ra-shó si-byáh chóost-va-vat'* |
| • How do you feel? | Как вы себя чувствуете? *(pol)* | *kahk vy si-byáh chóost-vy-i-ti* |
| | Как ты себя чувствуешь? *(fam)* | *kahk ty si-byáh chóost-vy-ish* |
| • I feel weak | У меня слабость | *u mi-nyáh sláh-bast'* |
| fever | жар | *zhahr* |
| | высокая температура | *vy-só-ka-ya tim-pi-ra-tóo-ra* |
| flu | грипп | *grip* |
| headache | головная боль *(f)* | *ga-lav-náh-ya bol'* |
| • I have a headache | У меня голова болит | *mi-nyáh ga-la-váh ba-lít* |
| health | здоровье | *zda-róv'-ye* |
| • healthy | здоровый *(m)* | *zda-ró-vyj* |
| heart | сердце | *syér-tsy* |
| • heart attack | инфаркт | *in-fáhrkt* |
| hurt | боль *(f)* | *bol'* |
| infection | инфекция | *in-fyék-tsy-ya* |
| injection | укол | *u-kól* |
| itch | чесаться *(i)* | *chi-sáh-tsa* |
| look after | ухаживать *(i)* | *u-kháh-zhy-vat'* |
| lymphatic glands | лимфатические железы *(pl)* | *lim-fa-tí-chis-ki-i zhéh-li-zy* |
| medical instruments | медицинские инструменты | *mi-di-tsýn-ski-i in-stru-myén-ty* |
| • electrocardiograph | электрокардиограф | *y-lyekt-ra-kar-di-a-gráhf* |
| • stethoscope | стетоскоп | *sty-tas-kóp* |
| • syringe | шприц | *shprits* |
| • thermometer | термометр | *tir-mó-mitr* |
| medicine (drug) | лекарство | *li-káhrst-va* |
| menstruation | менструация | *min-stru-áh-tsy-ya* |
| muscle | мышца | *mýsh-tsa* |
| nerves | нервы *(pl)* | *nyér-vy* |
| • nervous system | нервная система | *nyérv-na-ya sis-tyé-ma* |
| nurse | медицинская сестра | *mi-di-tsýn-ska-ya sist-ráh* |
| | медсестра | *mit-sist-ráh* |
| operation | операция | *a-pi-ráh-tsy-ya* |
| • operating room | операционная | *a-pi-ra-tsy-ó-na-ya* |
| ophthalmologist | глазной врач | *glaz-nój vrahch* |
| pain | боль *(f)* | *bol'* |
| patient | пациент | *pa-tsy-éhnt* |
| | больной | *bal'-nój* |
| pill | таблетка | *tab-lyét-ka* |
| pimple | прыщ | *pryshch* |

| | | |
|---|---|---|
| pneumonia | воспаление лёгких | *vas-pa-lyé-ni-ye lyókh-kikh* |
| pregnant | беременная | *bi-ryé-mi-na-ya* |
| prescription | рецепт | *ri-tséhpt* |
| pulse | пульс | *pool's* |
| respiratory system | дыхательные органы | *dy-kháh-til'-ny-ye ór-ga-ny* |
| • bad breath | запах изо рта | *záh-pakh i-za rtah* |
| • breath | дыхание | *dy-kháh-ni-ye* |
| • breathe | дышать *(i)* | *dy-sháht'* |
| • lung | лёгкое | *lyókh-ka-ye* |
| • nostril | ноздря | *nazd-ryáh* |
| • out of breath | задохнуться *(p)* | *za-dakh-nóo-tsa* |
| | задыхаться *(i)* | *za-dy-kháh-tsa* |
| rheumatism | ревматизм | *riv-ma-tízm* |
| sedative | успокоительное | *us-pa-ka-í-til'-na-ye* |
| sick | болен *(m)*, больна *(f)* | *bó-lin, bal'-náh* |
| | больной *(m)*, больная *(f)* | *bal'-nój, bal'-náh-ya* |
| • get sick | заболеть *(p)* | *za-ba-lyét'* |
| | заболевать *(i)* | *za-ba-li-váht'* |
| • sickness, disease | болезнь *(f)* | *ba-lyézn'* |
| sneeze | чих | *chikh* |
| • sneeze | чихнуть *(p)* | *chikh-nóot'* |
| | чихать *(i)* | *chi-kháht'* |
| (I have a) sore back | (У меня) спина болит | *(u mi-nyáh) spi-náh ba-lít* |
| (I have) a sore/stiff neck | Мне надуло в шею | *mnye na-dóo-la f shéh-yu* |
| • My neck doesn't turn | У меня шея не поворачивается | *u mi-nyáh shéh-ya ni pa-va-ráh-chi-va-i-tsa* |
| specialist | специалист | *spi-tsy-a-líst* |
| suffer | страдать *(i)* | *stra-dáht'* |
| suppository | (слабительная) свеча | *(sla-bí-til'-na-ya) svyéch-ka* |
| surgeon | хирург | *khi-róork* |
| • surgery | операция | *a-pi-ráh-tsy-ya* |
| swollen | распух (-ший) | *ras-póokh (-shyj)* |
| tablet | таблетка | *tab-lyét-ka* |
| temperature | температура | *tim-pi-ra-tóo-ra* |
| • take one's temperature | измерить *(p)* температуру | *iz-myé-rit' tim-pi-ra-tóo-ru* |
| | мерить *(i)* | *myé-rit'* |
| throat | горло | *gór-la* |
| • sore throat (hurts) | горло болит *(i)* | *gór-la ba-lít* |

| | | |
|---|---|---|
| **throw up, vomit** | вырвать *(p)* | *výr-vat'* |
| | вырывать *(i)* | *vy-ry-váht'* |
| • **I am nauseated** | Меня тошнит | *mi-nyáh tash-nít* |
| **tonsils** | аденоиды *(pl)* | *a-dy-nó-i-dy* |
| **treatment** | курс лечения | *koors li-chyé-ni-ya* |
| **urinary system** | мочеводные органы | *ma-chi-vód-ny-ye ór-ga-ny* |
| • **kidney** | почка | *póch-ka* |
| • **urinate** | мочиться *(i)* | *ma-chí-tsa* |
| **vein** | вена | *vyé-na* |

## b. THE DENTIST

| | | |
|---|---|---|
| **anesthesia** | анестезия | *a-nys-ty-zí-ya* |
| **appointment** | запись *(f)* | *záh-pis'* |
| **bridge** | мост | *most* |
| **cavity** | дупло | *dup-ló* |
| **clean, brush** | чистить *(i)* | *chís-tit'* |
| **crown** | коронка | *ka-rón-ka* |
| • **install a crown** | поставить *(p)* коронку | *pas-táh-vit' ka-rón-ku* |
| | ставить *(i)* | *stáh-vit'* |
| **dentist** | зубной врач | *zub-nój vrahch* |
| • **at the dentist's** | у зубного врача | *u zub-nó-va vra-cháh* |
| • **dentist's chair** | кресло | *kryés-la* |
| • **dentist's office** | зубной кабинет | *zub-nój ka-bi-nyét* |
| **denture, false teeth** | вставные зубы | *fstav-ný-i zóo-by* |
| **drill** | бормашина | *bor-ma-shý-na* |
| • **drill** | сверлить *(i)* | *svir-lít'* |
| **examine** | проверить *(p)* | *pra-vyé-rit'* |
| | проверять *(i)* | *pra-vi-ryáht'* |
| **extract, pull** | удалить *(p)* | *u-da-lít'* |
| | удалять *(i)* | *u-da-lyáht'* |
| • **extraction** | удаление | *u-da-lyé-ni-ye* |
| **filling** | пломба | *plóm-ba* |
| **mouth** | рот | *rot* |
| • **gums** | дёсны *(pl)* | *dyós-ny* |
| • **jaw** | челюсть *(f)* | *chyé-lyust'* |
| • **lip** | губа | *gu-báh* |
| • **Open your mouth** | Откройте *(pol)* рот | *atk-rój-ti rot* |
| | Открой *(fam)* рот | *atk-rój rot* |
| • **palate** | нёбо | *nyó-ba* |
| • **tongue** | язык | *i-zýk* |
| **needle** | игла | *ig-láh* |
| **office hours** | часы *(pl)* приёма | *chi-sý pri-yó-ma* |

| root | корень *(m)* | *kó-rin'* |
| • root canal | коренной канал | *ka-ri-nój ka-náhl* |
| tooth | зуб | *zoop* |
| • canine | клык | *klyk* |
| • incisor | передний зуб | *pi-ryéd-nij zoop* |
| • molar | коренной зуб | *ka-ri-nój zoop* |
| • wisdom tooth | зуб мудрости | *zoop móod-ras-ti* |
| toothache | зубная боль *(f)* | *zub-náh-ya bol'* |
| • I have a toothache | У меня зубная боль | *u mi-nyáh zub-náh-ya bol'* |
| • My tooth hurts | У меня зуб болит | *u mi-nyáh zoop ba-lít* |
| toothbrush | зубная щётка | *zub-náh-ya shchyót-ka* |
| toothpaste | зубная паста | *zub-náh-ya páhs-ta* |
| x ray | рентген | *rin-gyén* |

## 42. LEGAL MATTERS

| accusation | обвинение | *ab-vi-nyé-ni-ye* |
| • accuse | обвинить *(p)* | *ab-vi-nít'* |
| | обвинять *(i)* | *ab-vi-nyáht'* |
| • accused (person) | обвинённый (-ая) | *ab-vi-nyó-nyj (-a-ya)* |
| address oneself to | обратиться *(p)* к | *ab-ra-tí-tsa k* |
| | обращаться *(i)* к | *ab-ra-shcháh-tsa k* |
| admit | признаться *(p)* | *priz-náh-tsa* |
| | признаваться *(i)* | *priz-na-váh-tsa* |
| • admit guilt | признать *(p)* вину | *priz-náht' vi-nóo* |
| | признавать *(i)* | *priz-na-váht'* |
| agree | согласиться *(p)* | *sag-la-sí-tsa* |
| | соглашаться *(i)* | *sag-la-sháh-tsa* |
| appeal | подать *(p)* | *pa-dáht'* |
| | кассационную жалобу | *ka-sa-tsyón-nu-yu zháh-la-bu* |
| | подавать *(i)* | *pa-da-váht'* |
| • appeal the verdict | обжаловать *(p)* приговор | *ab-zháh-la-vat' pri-ga-vór* |
| charge | обвинение | *ab-vi-nyé-ni-ye* |
| • charge | предъявить *(p)* обвинение | *prid'-i-vít' ab-vi-nyé-ni-ye* |
| | предъявлять *(i)* | *prid'-iv-lyáht'* |
| chief officer (of militia) | командный офицер | *ka-máhnd-nyj a-fi-tséhr* |
| controversy | спор | *spohr* |
| | полемика | *pa-lyé-mi-ka* |
| convince, persuade | убедить *(p)* | *u-bi-dít'* |
| | убеждать *(i)* | *u-bizh-dáht'* |

| | | |
|---|---|---|
| contraband | контрабанда | *kan-tra-báhn-da* |
| court | суд | *soot* |
| • courthouse | здание суда | *zdáh-ni-ye su-dáh* |
| • courtroom | зал суда | *zahl su-dáh* |
| debate | обсуждение | *ab-suzh-dyé-ni-ye* |
| • debate, discuss | обсудить *(p)* | *ab-su-dít'* |
| | обсуждать *(i)* | *ab-suzh-dáht'* |
| defend oneself | защититься *(p)* | *za-shchi-tí-tsa* |
| | защищаться *(i)* | *za-shchi-shcháh-tsa* |
| disagree | разойтись *(p)* во мнении | *ra-zaj-tís' va mnyé-ni-i* |
| | расходиться *(i)* | *ras-kha-dí-tsa* |
| guilt | вина | *vi-náh* |
| • guilty | виновен *(m)* | *vi-nó-vin* |
| | виновна *(f)* | *vi-nóv-na* |
| innocence | невиновность *(f)* | *ni-vi-nóv-nast'* |
| • innocent | невиновен *(m)* | *ni-vi-nó-vin* |
| | невиновна *(f)* | *ni-vi-nóv-na* |
| investigator | следователь | *sli-da-va-tyél'* |
| jail, prison | тюрьма | *tyur'-máh* |
| judge | судья *(m&f)* | *sud'-yáh* |
| • judge | судить *(i)* | *su-dít'* |
| justice | справедливость *(f)* | *spra-vid-lí-vast'* |
| law | закон | *za-kón* |
| | законодательство | *za-ka-na-dáh-til'-stva* |
| | по закону | *pa za-kó-nu* |
| • civil law | гражданское законодательство | *grazh-dáhn-ska-ye za-ka-na-dáh-til'-stva* |
| • criminal law | уголовное право | *u-ga-lóv-na-ye práh-va* |
| • lawful, legal | законный | *za-kó-nyj* |
| • unlawful, illegal | незаконный *(adj)* | *ni-za-kó-nyj* |
| lawsuit | иск | *isk* |
| | дело | *dyé-la* |
| lawyer | юрист | *yu-ríst* |
| litigate | судиться *(i)* | *su-dí-tsa* |
| magistrate | мировой судья *(m&f)* | *mi-ra-vój sud'-yáh* |
| plea | заявление | *za-iv-lyé-ni-ye* |
| • plea for mercy | ходатайство о помиловании | *kha-dáh-taj-stva a pa-mí-la-va-ni-i* |
| • plead guilty | признать *(p)* себя виновным *(m)* (-ной) | *priz-náht' si-byáh vi-nóv-nym (-noj)* |
| | признавать *(i)* | *priz-na-váht'* |
| • plead not guilty | не признать *(p)* себя виновным *(m)* | *ni priz-náht' si-byáh vi-nóv-nym* |
| | признавать *(i)* | *priz-na-váht'* |
| police department (station) | отделение милиции | *at-di-lyé-ni-ye mi-lí-tsy-i* |

| | | |
|---|---|---|
| **public prosecutor** | народный обвинитель *(m&f)* | *na-ród-nyj ab-vi-ní-til'* |
| **right, privilege** | право | *práh-va* |
| **sentence** | приговор | *pri-ga-vór* |
| • **pass sentence** | вынести приговор | *vý-nis-ti pri-ga-vór* |
| • **prison sentence** | приговор к тюрьме | *pri-ga-vór k tyur'-myé* |
| • **serve a sentence** | отбыть *(p)* срок наказания | *at-být' srok na-ka-záh-ni-ya* |
| | отбывать *(i)* | *at-by-váht'* |
| **sue** | подать *(p)* в суд на... | *pa-dáht' f soot na* |
| | подавать *(i)* | *pa-da-váht'* |
| **summons** | вызов | *vý-zaf* |
| **trial** | судебный процесс | *su-dyéb-nyj pra-tséhs* |
| • **be on trial** | быть *(i)* под судом | *byt' pat su-dóm* |
| • **put someone on trial** | предать *(p)* суду | *pri-dáht' su-dóo* |
| | предавать *(i)* | *pri-da-váht'* |
| **verdict** | решение суда | *ri-shéh-ni-ye su-dáh* |
| • **guilty** | виновен *(m)* | *vi-nó-vin* |
| | виновна *(f)* | *vi-nóv-na* |
| • **not guilty** | невиновен *(m)* | *ni-vi-nó-vin* |
| | невиновна *(f)* | *ni-vi-nóv-na* |
| **witness** | свидетель *(m)* (-ница) *(f)* | *svit-dyé-til' (-ni-tsa)* |
| **eyewitness** | очевидец *(m)* (-дица) *(f)* | *a-chi-ví-dits (-di-tsa)* |
| • **for the defense** | свидетель *(m)* защиты | *svit-dyé-til' za-shchí-ty* |
| • **for the prosecution** | свидетель *(m)* обвинения | *svit-dyé-til' ab-vi-nyé-ni-ya* |

*Expressions*

| | | |
|---|---|---|
| **There is no doubt about it** | = | В этом нет никакого сомнения |
| **This matter/case is subject to discussion** | = | Это дело подлежит обсуждению |

## THE CONTEMPORARY WORLD

### 43. SCIENCE AND TECHNOLOGY

| | | |
|---|---|---|
| **astronaut** | космонавт | *kas-ma-náhft* |
| **atom** | атом | *áh-tam* |
| • **electron** | электрон | *y-likt-rón* |
| • **neutron** | нейтрон | *nijt-rón* |
| • **proton** | протон | *pra-tón* |
| • **quantum theory** | квантовая теория | *kváhn-ta-va-ya ti-ó-ri-ya* |
| **compact disc** | компактный диск | *kam-páhkt-nyj disk* |
| **fax machine** | телефакс | *ti-li-fáhks* |
| **laser** | лазер | *láh-zyr* |
| • **laser beam** | лазерный луч | *láh-zyr-nyj looch* |
| **microwave** | микроволна | *mik-ra-val-náh* |
| **missile** | ракета | *ra-kyé-ta* |
| • **launch pad** | платформа для запуска (ракет) | *plat-fór-ma dlya záh-pus-ka (ra-kyét)* |
| **monorail** | однорельсовая железная дорога | *ad-na-ryél'-sa-va-ya zhy-lyéz-na-ya da-ró-ga* |
| **nuclear industry** | ядерная промышленность (f) | *yáh-dir-na-ya pra-mýsh-li-nast'* |
| • **nuclear energy** | ядерная энергия | *yáh-dir-na-ya y-néhr-gi-ya* |
| • **nuclear fuel** | ядерное топливо | *yáh-dir-na-ye tóp-li-va* |
| • **nuclear reactor** | ядерный реактор | *yáh-dir-nyi ri-áhk-tar* |
| **robot** | робот | *ró-bat* |
| **satellite** | спутник | *spóot-nik* |
| **scientific research** | научное исследование | *na-óoch-na-ye is-lyé-da-va-ni-ye* |
| **space flight** | космический полёт | *kas-mí-chis-kij pa-lyót* |
| • **lunar module** | лунный отсек | *lóon-yj at-syék* |
| • **space shuttle** | космический челнок | *kas-mí-chis-kij chil-nók* |
| **telecommunication** | телесвязь (f) | *ti-li-svyáhs'* |
| • **teleconferencing** | телеконференция | *ti-li-kan-fi-ryén-tsy-ya* |
| **telex machine** | телекс | *tye-líks* |

## 44. POLITICS

|  |  |  |
|---|---|---|
| **area (geographical)** | округ | *ók-rug* |
| **army** | армия | *áhr-mi-ya* |
| **assembly** | собрание | *sab-ráh-ni-ye* |
| | ассамблея | *a-samb-lyé-ya* |
| **association** | общество | *óp-shchist-va* |
| | объединение | *ab'-i-di-nyé-ni-ye* |
| | ассоциация | *a-sa-tsy-áh-tsy-ya* |
| **authority** | полномочие | *pal-na-mó-chi-ye* |
| **body (political)** | орган | *ór-gan* |
| **budget** *(n)* | бюджет | *bjud-zhéht* |
| **centralized** *(adj)* | централизованный *(m)* | *tsyn-tra-li-zó-va-nyj* |
| | централизованное *(n)* | *tsyn-tra-li-zó-va-na-ye* |
| | централизованная *(f)* | *tsyn-tra-li-zó-va-na-ya* |
| **committee** | комитет | *ka-mi-tyét* |
| **communism** | коммунизм | *ka-mu-nízm* |
| • **Communist** | коммунист | *ka-mu-níst* |
| **Congress of People's Deputies** | Съезд Народных Депутатов | *s'yezt na-ród-nykh di-pu-táh-taf* |
| **conservative** | консервативный | *kan-sir-va-tív-nyj* |
| **Constitution (of Russia)** | Конституция (России) | *kan-sti-toó-tsy-ya (ra-sí-i)* |
| **council** | совет | *sa-vyét* |
| **corruption** | коррупция | *ka-rúp-tsy-ya* |
| **democracy** | демократия | *di-mak-ráh-ti-ya* |
| • **democrat** | демократ | *di-mak-ráht* |
| • **democratic** | демократический | *di-mak-ra-tí-chis-kij* |
| **Duma** | Дума | *dóo-ma* |
| **deputy** | депутат | *di-pu-táht* |
| **development (improvement)** | развитие | *raz-ví-ti-ye* |
| **economy** | экономика | *y-ka-nó-mi-ka* |
| **elect** | выбрать *(p)* | *výb-rat'* |
| | выбирать *(i)* | *vy-bi-ráht'* |
| • **elections** | выборы | *vý-ba-ry* |
| **elected body** | выборный орган | *vý-bar-nyj ór-gan* |
| **faction** | фракция | *fráhk-tsy-ya* |
| **Federal Assembly** | Федеральное Собрание | *fi-di-ráhl'-na-ye sab-ráh-ni-ye* |
| **Federation Council** | Совет Федерации | *sa-vyét fi-di-ráh-tsy-i* |
| • **upper house** | высшая палата | *výs-sha-ya pa-láh-ta* |
| • **lower house** | нижняя палата | *niz-ni-ya pa-láh-ta* |
| **fraud** | обман/мошенничество | *ab-máhn/ma-shéh-ni-chist-va* |
| **function** | функция | *foónk-tsy-ya* |

| govern | управлять *(i)* | *up-rav-lyáht'* |
|---|---|---|
| • government | правительство | *pra-ví-til'st-va* |
| head of state | глава правительства | *gla-váh pra-ví-til'-st-va* |
| • head *(v)* a | возглавить *(p)* | *vaz-gláh-vit'* |
| government | возглавлять *(i)* | *vaz-glav-lyáht'* |
| | правительство | *pra-ví-til'-st-va* |
| ideology | идеология | *i-di-a-ló-gi-ya* |
| inflation | инфляция | *inf-lyáh-tsy-ya* |
| labor/trade union | профсоюз | *praf-sa-yús* |
| law | закон | *za-kón* |
| leader | лидер | *lí-dir* |
| legislation | законодательство | *za-ka-na-dáh-til'-st-va* |
| • legislative *(adj)* | законодательный *(m)* | *za-ka-na-dáh-til'-nyj* |
| | законодательное *(n)* | *za-ka-na-dáh-til'-na-ye* |
| | законодательная *(f)* | *za-ka-na-dáh-til'-na-ya* |
| liberal | либеральный | *li-bi-ráhl'-nyj* |
| local authorities | местные власти | *myés-ny-i vláhs-ti* |
| lose elections | проиграть *(p)* | *pra-i-gráht'* |
| | проигрывать *(i)* | *pra-í-gry-vat'* |
| | выборы | *vý-ba-ry* |
| majority | большинство | *bal'-shyn-stvó* |
| mayor | мэр | *mehr* |
| minister | министр | *mi-nístr* |
| minority | меньшинство | *min'-shyn-stvó* |
| monarchy | монархия | *ma-náhr-khi-ya* |
| • czar | царь *(m)* | *tsahr'* |
| • czarina | царица | *tsa-rí-tsa* |
| • heir to the throne | наследник престола | *nas-lyéd-nik pris-tó-la* |
| opposition (political) | оппозиция | *a-pa-zí-tsy-ya* |
| parliament | парламент | *par-láh-mint* |
| • elected | выборный | *vý-bar-nyj* |
| representative | представитель *(m)* | *prit-sta-ví-til'* |
| | депутат | *di-pu-láht* |
| • assembly of | собрание/конгресс | *sab-ráh-ni-ye/kang -ryés* |
| representatives | представителей | *prit-sta-ví-ti-lyej* |
| • president of the | президент | *pri-zi-dyént ris-póob-li-ki* |
| republic | республики | |
| • right to vote | право голоса | *práh-va gó-la-sa* |
| • universal | избирательное | *iz-bi-ráh-til'-na-ye* |
| suffrage | право | *práh-va* |
| parliamentary | парламентские | *par-láh-mints-ki-i vý-ba-ry* |
| elections | выборы | |
| party in power | партия власти | *páhr-ti-ya vláhs-ti* |
| party list | партийный список | *par-tíj-nyj spí-sak* |
| peace | мир | *mir* |
| policy | политика | *pa-lí-ti-ka* |
| politics | политика | *pa-lí-ti-ka* |
| • political party | политическая | *pa-li-tí-chis-ka-ya* |
| | партия | *páhr-ti-ya* |

| | | |
|---|---|---|
| • political power | политическая власть *(f)* | *pa-li-tí-chis-ka-ya vlahst'* |
| • politician | политический деятель *(m)* | *pa-li-tí-chis-kij dyé-i-til'* |
| president | президент | *pri-zi-dyént* |
| protest | протест | *pra-tyést* |
| referendum | референдум | *ri-fi-ryén-dum* |
| reform | реформа | *ri-fór-ma* |
| region | регион | *ri-gi-ón* |
| republic | республика | *ris-póob-li-ka* |
| revolt | восстание | *vas-táh-ni-ye* |
| • revolution | революция | *ri-va-lyú-tsy-ya* |
| Russian Federation | Российская Федерация | *ra-síj-ska-ya fi-di-ráh-tsy-ya* |
| socialism | социализм | *sa-tsy-a-lízm* |
| • socialist | социалист | *sa-tsy-a-líst* |
| sovereign democracy | суверенная демократия | *su-vi-ryé-na-ya di-mak-rah-ti-ya* |
| state | государство | *ga-su-dáhrst-va* |
| • head of state | глава государства | *gláh-va ga-su-dáhrst-va* |
| State Assembly | Государственная Дума | *ga-su-dáhr-stvi-na-ya dóo-ma* |
| • chair (person) | председатель думы | *prid-si-dáh-til' dóo-my* |
| strike | забастовка | *za-bas-tóf-ka* |
| • go on strike | пойти *(p)* на забастовку | *paj-tí na za-bas-tóf-ku* |
| | идти *(i)* | *it-tí* |
| third world | третий мир | *tryé-tij mir* |
| • developing countries | развивающиеся страны | *raz-vi-váh-yu-shchi-i-sya stráh-ny* |
| vote | голос | *gó-las* |
| • vote | голосовать *(i)* | *ga-la-sa-váht'* |
| war | война | *vaj-náh* |
| • state of war | состояние войны | *sas-ta-yáh-ni-ye vaj-ný* |
| welfare | благосостояние | *bla-ga-sas-ta-yáh-ni-ye* |
| | социальное обеспечение | *sa-tsy-áhl'-na-ye a-bis-pi-chyé-ni-ye* |
| win elections | выиграть *(p)* | *vý-ig-rat'* |
| | выигрывать *(i)* выборы | *vy-íg-ry-vat' vy-ba-ry* |

## 45. CONTROVERSIAL ISSUES

### a. THE ENVIRONMENT

| | | |
|---|---|---|
| air pollution | загрязнение воздуха | *zag-riz-nyé-ni-ye vóz-du-kha* |
| bacteria | бактерия | *bak-téh-ri-ya* |

| conservation | сохранение | *sakh-ra-nyé-ni-ye* |
| consumption | потребление | *pat-rib-lyé-ni-ye* |
| ecosystem | экосистема | *y-ka-sis-tyé-ma* |
| energy | энергия | *y-néhr-gi-ya* |
| • energy crisis | энергетический кризис | *y-nyr-gi-tí-chis-kij krí-zis* |
| • energy source | источник энергии | *is-tóch-nik y-néhr-gi-i* |
| • energy waste | потеря, растрата энергии | *pa-tyé-rya, rast-ráh-ta y-néhr-gi-i* |
| environment | окружающая среда | *ak-ru-zháh-yu-shchi-ya sri-dáh* |
| food chain | пищевая цепь *(f)* | *pi-shchi-váh-ya tsehp'* |
| fossil fuel | ископаемое топливо | *ys-ka-páh-i-ma-ye tóp-li-va* |
| geothermal energy | геотермическая энергия | *gi-a-tir-mí-chis-ka-ya y-néhr-gi-ya* |
| microbe | микроб | *mik-róp* |
| natural resources | полезные ископаемые | *pa-lyéz-ny-ye is-ka-páh-i-my-ye* |
| petroleum | нефть *(f)* | *nyeft'* |
| pollution | загрязнение среды | *zag-ríz-nyé-ni-ye sri-dý* |
| radiation | радиация | *ra-di-áh-tsy-ya* |
| • radioactive waste | радиоактивные отходы | *ra-di-a-ak-tív-ny-ye at-khó-dy* |
| solar cell | солнечный элемент | *sól-nich-nyj y-li-myént* |
| solar energy | солнечная энергия | *sól-nich-na-ya y-néhr-gi-ya* |
| thermal energy | тепловая энергия | *tip-la-váh-ya y-néhr-gi-ya* |
| water pollution | загрязнение воды | *zag-riz-nyé-ni-ye va-dý* |
| wind energy | энергия ветра | *y-néhr-gi-ya vyét-ra* |

## b. SOCIETY

| abortion | аборт | *a-bórt* |
| • fetus | плод, зародыш | *plot, za-ró-dysh* |
| AIDS | СПИД (синдром приобретённого иммунодефицита) | *spit (sind-róm pri-ab-ri-tyó-na-va i-móo-na-di-fi-tsy-ta)* |
| bodily fluids *(pl)* | жидкости организма *(pl)* | *zhýt-kas-ti ar-ga-níz-ma* |
| blood transfusion | переливание крови | *pi-ri-li-váh-ni-ye kró-vi* |
| casino | игорный дом | *í-gar-nyj dom* |
| censorship | цензура | *tsyn-zóo-ra* |
| chemical weapon | химическое оружие | *khi-mí-chis-ka-ye a-róo-zhy-ye* |
| class (socioeconomic) | класс | *klahs* |
| • lower class | низший класс | *nís-shyj klahs* |
| • lower-middle class | низший средний класс | *nís-shyj sryéd-nij klahs* |

| | | |
|---|---|---|
| • middle class | средний класс | *sryéd-nij klahs* |
| • underclass | андеркласс | *áhn-dar-kláhs* |
| • upper class | верхний класс | *vyérkh-nij klahs* |
| • upper-middle class | верхний средний класс | *vyérkh-nij sryéd-nij klahs* |
| • working class | рабочий класс | *ra-bó-chij klahs* |
| danger | опасность | *a-páhs-nast'* |
| drug | наркотик | *nar-kó-tik* |
| • drug addiction | наркомания | *nar-ka-máh-ni-ya* |
| • drug user | потребитель *(m)* наркотиков | *pat-ri-bí-til'* *nar-kó-ti-kaf* |
| | потребительница *(f)* | *pat-ri-bí-til'-ni-tsa* |
| | наркопотребитель *(m)* | *náhr-ka-pat-ri-bí-til'* |
| | наркопотребительница *(f)* | *náhr-ka-pat-ri-bí-til'-ni-tsa* |
| • sell drugs | продать *(p)* наркотики | *pra-dáht' nar-kó-ti-ki* |
| | продавать *(i)* | *pra-da-váht'* |
| • take drugs | принять *(p)* наркотики | *pri-nyáht' nar-kó-ti-ki* |
| | принимать *(i)* | *pri-ni-máht'* |
| epidemic | эпидемия | *y-pi-dyé-mi-ya* |
| erotica | эротика | *y-ró-ti-ka* |
| family planning | планирование семьи | *pla-ní-ra-va-ni-ye sim'-yí* |
| feminism | феминизм | *fi-mi-nízm* |
| • feminist | феминист (-ка) | *fi-mi-níst (-ka)* |
| genitals *(pl)* | половые органы *(pl)* | *pa-la-vý-ye ór-ga-ny* |
| heterosexual *(adj)* | гетеросексуальный *(adj) (m)* | *gí-ti-ra-sik-su-áhl'-nyj* |
| | гетеросексуальная *(adj) (f)* | *gí-ti-ra-sik-su-áhl'-na-ya* |
| HIV | ВИЧ (-инфекция) (вирус иммунодефицита человека) | *vich (-in-fyék-tsy-ya) (ví-rus i-moó-na-di-fi-tsý-ta chi-la-vyé-ka)* |
| homosexuality | гомосексуализм | *ga-ma-sik-su-a-lízm* |
| • homosexual | гомосексуалист | *ga-ma-sik-su-a-líst* |
| • lesbian | лесбиянка | *lis-bi-yáhn-ka* |
| | лесбийский *(adj)* | *lis-bís-kij* |
| illness | заболевание | *za-ba-li-váh-ni-ye* |
| • chronic | хроническое | *khra-ní-chis-ka-ye* |
| infection | инфекция | *in-fyék-tsy-ya* |
| liposuction | липоотсасывание | *lí-pa-at-sáh-sy-va-ni-ye* |
| morality | мораль *(f)* | *ma-ráhl'* |
| | нравственность *(f)* | *nráhfst-vi-nast'* |
| nuclear weapon | ядерное оружие | *yáh-dir-na-ye a-róo-zhy-ye* |
| • antinuclear protest | протест против ядерных установок | *pra-tyést pró-tif yáh-dir-nykh us-ta-nó-vak* |

| | | |
|---|---|---|
| • **atomic bomb** | атомная бомба | *áh-tam-na-ya bóm-ba* |
| **nudism** | нудизм | *nóo-dizm* |
| **poor** *(n & adj)* | бедняк *(n) (m)* | *bid-nyáhk* |
| | беднячка *(n) (f)* | *bid-nyáhch-ka* |
| | бедный *(adj) (m)* | *byéd-nyj* |
| | бедная *(adj) (f)* | *byéd-na-ya* |
| **pornography** | порнография | *par-na-gráh-fi-ya* |
| • **porno** | порно | *pór-na* |
| • **hard** | жёсткое (порно) | *zhóst-ka-ye (pór-na)* |
| • **soft** | лёгкое (порно) | *lyókh-ka-ye (pór-na)* |
| **prostitution** | проституция | *pras-ti-tóo-tsy-ya* |
| **racism** | расизм | *ra-sízm* |
| **rich** *(n & adj)* | богач *(n) (m)* | *ba-gáhch* |
| | богачка *(n) (f)* | *ba-gáhch-ka* |
| | богатый *(adj) (m)* | *ba-gáh-tyj* |
| | богатая *(adj) (f)* | *ba-gáh-ta-ya* |
| **poverty** | бедность | *byéd-nast'* |
| **sex** | секс | *sehks* |
| **sexual act** | сексуальный/ | *sik-su-áhl'-nyj/pa-la-vój* |
| | половой акт | *ahkt* |
| • **contact** | контакт | *kan-táhkt* |
| **sexual orientation** | сексуальная | *sik-su-áhl'-na-ya* |
| | ориентация | *a-ri-in-táh-tsy-ya* |
| **sexual relationship** | сексуальное | *sik-su-áhl'-na-ye* |
| | отношение | *at-na-shéh-ni-ye* |
| | половые | *pa-la-vý-ye* |
| | отношения *(pl)* | *at-na-shéh-ni-ya* |
| **sexually-transmitted disease (venereal disease)** | венерическое заболевание | *vi-ni-rí-chis-ka-ye za-ba-li-váh-ni-ye* |
| **street drugs** *(pl)* | уличные наркотики *(pl)* | *óo-lich-ny-ye nar-kó-ti-ki* |
| **underage/minor** *(n)* | несовершеннолетний *(m)* | *ni-sa-vir-shy-na-lyét-nij* |
| | несовершеннолетняя *(f)* | *ni-sa-vir-shy-na-lyét-nya-ya* |
| **unemployment** | безработица | *biz-ra-bó-ti-tsa* |
| **virus** | вирус | *ví-rus* |

## c. EXPRESSING YOUR OPINION

| | | |
|---|---|---|
| **As a matter of fact...** | На самом деле... | *na sáh-mam dyé-li* |
| **As it seems to me...** | Как мне кажется... | *kahk mnye káh-zhy-tsa* |
| **As I understand it...** | Как я понимаю... | *kahk yah pa-ni-máh-yu* |
| **By the way...** | Кстати... | *kstáh-ti* |
| | Между прочим... | *myézh-du pró-chim* |
| **For example...** | Например... | *na-pri-myér* |
| **I believe that...** | Я считаю, что... | *yah shchi-táh-yu shto* |

| I can (only) say that... | Я (только) могу сказать, что... | *yah (tól'-ka) ma-góo ska-záht' shto* |
|---|---|---|
| I don't know (if)... | Я не знаю... | *yah ni znáh-yu* |
| I doubt that (in)... | Я сомневаюсь (в)... | *yah sam-ni-váh-yus' (v)* |
| I'm afraid that... | Я боюсь, что... | *yah ba-yús' shto* |
| In my point of view... | С моей точки зрения... | *s ma-yéj tóch-ki zryé-ni-ya* |
| In this/that case... | В этом/том случае... | *v éh-tam/tom slóo-chi-ye* |
| I think that... | Я думаю, что... | *yah dóo-ma-yu shto* |
| I would like (want) to say that... | Я хочу сказать, что... | *yah kha-chóo ska-záht' shto* |
| I'm not sure that... | Я не уверен (-a), что... | *yah ni u-vyé-rin (-a) shto* |
| I suppose... | Я полагаю... | *yah pa-la-gáh-yu* |
| In conclusion... | В заключение... | *v zak-lyu-chyé-ni-ye* |
| In other words... | Другими словами... | *dru-gí-mi sla-váh-mi* |
| In my opinion... | По моему мнению... | *pa ma-i-móo mnyé-ni-yu* |
| In my (point of) view... | С моей точки зрения... | *s ma-yéj tóch-ki zryé-ni-ya* |
| It seems (to me) that... | Мне кажется, что... | *mnye káh-zky-tsa shto* |
| It's clear that... | Ясно, что... | *yáhs-na shto* |
| There is no doubt that... | Нет(никакого) сомнения, что... | *nyet (ni-ka-kó-va) sam-nyé-ni-ya shto* |
| Therefore... | Поэтому... | *pa-éh-ta-mu* |

*Expressions*

| Man proposes but God disposes | = Человек полагает, а Бог (Господь) располагает |
|---|---|
| Measure twice but cut only once | = Два раза отмерь, один раз отрежь |
| The advisor gets kicked first | = Советчика первого бьют |
| Two heads are better than one | = Одна голова-хорошо, а две-лучше |
| What do you suggest/propose? | = Что вы предлагаете? *(pol)*<br>Что ты предлагаешь? *(fam)* |

# ENGLISH-RUSSIAN WORD FINDER

This alphabetical listing of all the English words in *Russian Vocabulary* will enable you to find the information you need quickly and efficiently. If all you want is the Russian equivalent and/or pronunciation of an entry word, you will find it here. If you also want usage aids or closely associated words and phrases, use the reference number(s) and letter(s) to locate the section(s) in which the entry appears. This is especially important for words that have multiple meanings.

Adjectives are presented in the masculine singular form.

Expressions and road signs start with a capital letter.

Although most verbs are given both in the perfective and imperfective aspects in the main body of the text, only one aspect was selected for inclusion in the Word Finder.

| | | | |
|---|---|---|---|
| **a little** | немного/немножко | *ni-mnó-ga/ni-mnó-shka* | 3c |
| **a lot, much** | много | *mnó-ga* | 3c |
| **abbreviation** | сокращение | *sak-ra-shchyé-ni-ye* | 19d |
| **abdomen** | живот | *zhy-vót* | 12a |
| **abortion** | аборт | *a-bórt* | 45b |
| **about** | о, около | *o, ó-ka-la* | 8d |
| **above, over** | над | *naht* | 8d |
| **above** | вверху | *vvir-khoó* | 3d |
| **above zero** | выше ноля | *vý-shy na-lyáh* | 6c |
| **abroad** | заграница | *zag-ra-ní-tsa* | 19f, 31a |
| **academic year** | учебный год | *u-chéb-nyj got* | 5b |
| **accept** | принимать | *pri-ni-máht'* | 21b |
| **acceptable** | приемлемый | *pri-yém-li-myj* | 21b |
| **accident (mechanical)** | авария | *a-váh-ri-ya* | 34c |
| **accident (human)** | несчастный случай | *ni-shcháhs-nyj slóo-chahj* | 40c |
| **accordion** | аккордеон | *a-kar-di-ón* | 29c |
| **account** | счёт | *shchyot* | 26 |
| **account balance** | состояние счёта | *sas-ta-yáh-ni-ye shchyó-ta* | 26 |
| **accountant** | бухгалтер *(m&f)*, счетовод *(m&f)* | *bu-gáhl-tir, schi-ta-vót* | 39a |
| **accusation** | обвинение | *ab-vi-nyé-ni-ye* | 42 |
| **accusative** | винительный | *vi-ní-til'-nyj* | 8a |
| **ache** | боль *(f)* | *bol'* | 41a |
| **acid** | кислота | *kis-la-táh* | 13c |
| **acne** | угри *(pl)* | *ug-rí* | 41a |
| **acquaintance** | знакомый | *zna-kó-myj* | 10b, 16b |
| **across** | напротив, через | *na-pró-tif, chyé-ris* | 3d, 37d |
| **act** | играть (роль) | *ig-ráht' (rol')* | 29e |
| **activate** | активировать *(i)* | *ak-ti-ví-ra-vat'* | 19a |

| active | активный | *ak-tív-nyj* | 11e |
| actively | активно | *ak-tív-na* | 11e |
| actor | актёр | *ak-tyór* | 29a, 29e, 39a |
| actress | актриса | *akt-rí-sa* | 29a, 29e, 39a |
| actually | действительно, на самом деле | *dist-ví-til'-na, na sáh-mam dyé-li* | 17b |
| adaptable | гибкий | *gíp-kij* | 11e |
| add (quantity) | добавлять | *da-ba-vlyáht'* | 3c |
| add | сложить | *sla-zhýt'* | 1e |
| address | адрес | *áhd-res* | 11f, 19f, 39b |
| address book | адресная книжка | *áhd-ris-na-ya knísh-ka* | 19a |
| address (e-mail) | адрес | *áhd-ris* | 19a |
| address oneself to | обращаться к | *ab-ra-shcháh-tsa k* | 42 |
| addressee | адресат | *ad-ri-sáht* | 19f |
| adhesive tape | клейкая лента | *klyéj-ka-ya lyén-ta* | 19e, 25c, 39c |
| adjective | прилагательное | *pri-la-gáh-til'-na-ye* | 8a |
| admit | признаваться | *priz-na-váh-tsa* | 42 |
| adult | взрослый | *vzrós-lyj* | 11b |
| adventure | приключение | *prik-lyu-chyé-ni-ye* | 20a |
| adverb | наречие | *na-ryé-chi-ye* | 8a |
| advertisement | объявление | *ab'-iv-lyé-ni-ye* | 20a |
| | реклама | *rik-láh-ma* | 2b, 39d |
| advice | совет | *sa-vyét* | 17a |
| advise, to | советовать | *sa-vyé-ta-vat'* | 17a |
| affection | привязанность *(f)* | *pri-vyáh-zan-nast'* | 21a |
| affectionate | ласковый | *láhs-ka-vyj* | 21a |
| Africa | Африка | *áhf-ri-ka* | 31b |
| after | после | *pós-li* | 4e |
| afternoon | вторая половина дня | *fta-ráh-ya pa-la-ví-na dnyah* | 4a |
| again | опять, снова | *a-pyáht', snó-va* | 4e |
| age | возраст | *vóz-rast* | 11b, 39b |
| aggressive | агрессивный | *ag-ri-sív-nyj* | 11e |
| aggressiveness | агрессивность *(f)* | *ag-ri-sív-nast'* | 11e |
| agnostic | агностик | *ag-nós-tik* | 11d |
| agree | соглашаться | *sag-la-sháh-tsa* | 21a, 22b, 42 |
| agriculture | сельское хозяйство | *syél'-ska-ye kha-zyáhjst-va* | 14a |
| ahead, forward | вперёд | *fpi-ryót* | 3d |
| AIDS | СПИД (синдром приобретённого иммунодефицита) | *spit (sind-róm pri-ab-ri-tyó-na-va i-móo-na-di-fí-tsy-ta)* | 45b |
| air | воздух | *vóz-dukh* | 6a, 13b, 13c, 37d |
| air conditioner | кондиционер | *kan-di-tsy-a-nyér* | 23e, 34e |
| air conditioning | кондиционирование воздуха | *kan-di-tsy-a-ní-ra-va-ni-ye vóz-du-kha* | 23e |

| air pollution | загрязнение воздуха | *zag-riz-nyé-ni-ye vóz-du-kha* | 45a |
| airline | авиакомпания | *ah-vi-a-kam-páh-ni-ya* | 33a |
| airmail | авиапочта | *a-vi-a-póch-ta* | 19f |
| airplane | самолёт | *sa-ma-lyót* | 33c |
| airport | аэропорт | *a-y-ra-pórt* | 33a |
| aisle | проход | *pra-khót* | 29a, 33c |
| alarm | тревога | *tri-vó-ga* | 40a |
| alarm clock | будильник | *bu-díl'-nik* | 4d, 25i |
| albatross | альбатрос | *al'-bat-rós* | 15b |
| alder | ольха | *al'-kháh* | 14c |
| algebra | алгебра | *áhl-gib-ra* | 1f, 38e |
| all, everyone | все | *fsye* | 3c |
| all, every | весь *(m)*, | *vyés', fsyo, fsyah* | 8b |
| | всё *(n)*, вся *(f)* | | |
| All the best! | Всего хорошего!, | *fsi-vó kha-ró-shy-va,* | 16c |
| | Всего наилучшего! | *fsi-vó na-i-lóoch-shy-va* | 30c |
| allergy | аллергия | *a-lir-gí-ya* | 41a |
| alligator | аллигатор | *a-li-gáh-tar* | 15c |
| almost, nearly | почти | *pach-tí* | 3c |
| along | по | *pa* | 8d |
| alphabet | алфавит | *al-fa-vít* | 8a |
| alphabetical order | алфавитный порядок | *al-fa-vít-nyj pa-ryáh-dak* | 8a |
| already | уже | *u-zhéh* | 4e |
| alternative music | альтернативная | *al'-tyr-na-tív-na-ya* | 25j |
| | музыка | *moó-zy-ka* | |
| although | хотя | *kha-tyáh* | 8h |
| altruism | альтруизм | *al'-tru-ízm* | 11e |
| altruist | альтруист | *al'-tru-íst* | 11e |
| altruistic | альтруистичный | *al'-tru-is-tích-nyj* | 11e |
| always | всегда, постоянно | *fsig-dáh, pas-ta-yáh-na* | 4e |
| AM (amplitude | АМ (амплитудная | *am-pli-tóod-na-ya* | 20e |
| modulation) | модуляция) | *ma-du-lyáh-tsi-ya* | |
| amateur | любитель *(m)*, | *lyu-bí-til',* | |
| | любительница *(f)* | *lyu-bí-til'-ni-tsa* | 28b |
| amber | янтарь *(m)* | *in-táhr'* | 25i |
| ambulance | машина скорой | *ma-shý-na skó-raj* | 40a, 40c |
| | помощи | *pó-ma-shchi* | |
| America | Америка | *a-myé-ri-ka* | 31b |
| American | американец (-нка) | *a-mi-ri-káh-nits (-nka)* | 31d |
| among, between | между | *myézh-du* | 3d, 8d |
| anatomy | анатомия | *a-na-tó-mi-ya* | 38e |
| and | и | *i* | 8h |
| anesthesia | анестезия | *a-nys-ty-zí-ya* | 41b |
| anger | гнев | *gnyef* | 11d |
| angle | угол | *óo-gal* | 2b |
| angry | сердитый, | *sir-dí-tyj,* | 11e, |
| | гневный | *gnyév-nyj* | 21a |
| animal | животное | *zhy-vót-na-ye* | 15a |
| animation | анимация | *a-ni-máh-tsy-ya* | 20d |
| animated gif | гиф-анимация | *gíf-a-ni-máh-tsy-ya* | 20d |
| ankle | щиколотка | *shchí-ka-lat-ka* | 12a |

| anniversary | годовщина | *ga-dav-shchí-na* | 11c, 30a |
| announce | объявлять | *ab'-i-vlyát'* | 17a |
| announcement | объявление | *ab'-iv-lyé-ni-ye* | 17a |
| answer | ответ | *at-vyét* | 9, 17a, 38f |
| answer, to | отвечать | *at-vye-cháht'* | 9, 17a, 38f |
| answer a question | отвечать на вопрос | *at-vye-cháht' na vap-rós* | 38f |
| answering machine | автоответчик | *av-ta-at-vyét-chik* | 18a |
| ant | муравей | *mu-ra-vyéj* | 15d |
| Antarctic Circle | Южный полярный круг | *yúzh-nyj pa-lyáhr-nyj krook* | 13e |
| Antarctic Ocean | Антарктический океан | *an-tark-tí-chis-kij a-ki-áhn* | 13b |
| antenna | антенна | *an-téh-na* | 20e |
| anthropology | антропология | *ant-ra-pa-ló-gí-ya* | 38e |
| antibiotic | антибиотик | *an-ti-bi-ó-tík* | 25h |
| antiseptic | антисептическое средство | *an-ti-syp-tí-chis-ka-ye sryét-stva* | 40c |
| anus | задний проход | *záhd-nij pra-khót* | 41a |
| anxiety | беспокойство озабоченность *(f)* | *bis-pa-kój-stva, a-za-bó-chi-nast'* | 21a |
| anxious | озабоченный неспокойный | *a-za-bó-chi-nyj, ni-spa-kój-nyj* | 21a |
| apartment | квартира | *kvar-tí-ra* | 23g |
| appeal | подавать кассационную жалобу | *pa-da-váht' ka-sa-tsyón-nu-yu zháh-la-bu* | 42 |
| appeal the verdict | обжаловать приговор | *ab-zháh-la-vat' pri-ga-vór* | 42 |
| appendicitis | аппендицит | *a-pin-di-tsít* | 41a |
| appendix | аппендикс | *a-pyén-diks* | 41a |
| appendix (supplement) | приложение | *pri-la-zhéh-ni-ye* | 20a |
| appetizer | закуска | *za-kóos-ka* | 24g |
| appetizing | аппетитный | *a-pi-tít-nyj* | 24p |
| applaud | аплодировать | *ap-la-dí-ra-vat'* | 29e |
| applause | аплодисменты *(pl)* | *ap-la-dis-myén-ty* | 29e |
| apple | яблоко | *yáhb-la-ka* | 14d, 24f |
| apple tree | яблоня | *yáhb-la-nya* | 14c |
| application (loan, rental, etc.) | заявка | *za-yáhf-ka* | 27 |
| appointment (with the doctor) | запись *(f)* (к врачу) | *záh-pis' (k vra-chóo)* | 41a, 41b |
| appraiser (company) | оценочная компания | *a-tséh-nach-na-ya kam-páh-ni-ya* | 27 |
| approach | подойти к | *pa-daj-tí k* | 37d |
| approval | одобрение | *a-dab-ryé-ni-ye* | 21b |
| approve | одобрять | *a-dab-ryáht'* | 21b |
| approximately | приблизительно | *pri-bli-zí-til'-na* | 3c |

| apricot | абрикос | *ab-ri-kós* | 14d, 24f |
|---|---|---|---|
| April | апрель *(m)* | *ap-ryél'* | 5b |
| Arab | араб (-ка) | *a-ráhp (-ka)* | 31d |
| Arabic | арабский | *a-ráhps-kij* | 31d |
| archeology | археология | *ar-khi-a-ló-gi-ya* | 38e |
| archipelago | архипелаг | *ar-khi-pi-lákh* | 13b |
| architect | архитектор *(m&f)* | *ar-khi-tyék-tar* | 29b, 39a |
| architecture | архитектура | *ar-khi-tik-tóo-ra* | 29b, 38e |
| Arctic Circle | Северный полярный круг | *syé-vir-nyj pa-lyáhr-nyj krook* | 13e |
| Arctic | Арктика | *áhrk-ti-ka* | 13b |
| area | площадь *(f)* | *pló-shchit'* | 3a |
| area (geographical) | округ | *ók-rug* | 44 |
| area code | код города | *kot gó-ra-da* | 18b |
| argue (to reason) | спорить, утверждать | *spó-rit', ut-vir-zhdáht'* | 17a |
| argue (to dispute) | ссориться/ругаться | *só-ri-tsa/ ru-gá-tsa* | 40b |
| argument | спор | *spor* | 17a |
| arithmetic | арифметика | *a-rif-myé-ti-ka* | 1f, 38e |
| arm | рука | *ru-káh* | 12a |
| armchair | кресло | *kryés-la* | 23c, 36c |
| armed | вооружённый | *va-a-ru-zhó-niy* | 40b |
| Armenia | Армения | *ar-myé-ni-ya* | 31b |
| army | армия | *áhr-mi-ya* | 44 |
| arrest | арест | *a-ryést* | 40b |
| arrest, to | арестовывать | *a-ris-tóh-vy-vat'* | 40b |
| arrival | приезд | *pri-yést* | 33a |
| arrive | приехать | *pri-yé-khat'* | 3e |
| arrogance | нахальство | *na-kháhl'-stva* | 11e |
| arrogant | нахальный | *na-kháhl'-nyj* | 11e |
| art | искусство | *is-kóost-va* | 29b |
| art (drawing) | рисование | *ri-sa-váh-ni-ye* | 38e, 38f |
| art gallery | картинная галерея | *kar-tín-na-ya ga-li-ryé-ya* | 25a |
| art museum | музей искусств | *mu-zyéj is-kóostv* | 29b |
| art salon | художественный салон | *khu-dó-zhyst-vi-nyj sa-lón* | 29b |
| artery | артерия | *ar-téh-ri-ya* | 41a |
| arthritis | артрит | *art-rít* | 41a |
| artichoke | артишок | *ar-ti-shók* | 14e, 24e |
| article | статья | *stat'-yáh* | 20a |
| artificial | искусственный | *is-kóost-ví-nyj* | 13d, 25i |
| artist | художник (-ница) | *khu-dózh-nik (-ni-tsa)* | 29b |
| as if | как будто | *kahk bóo-ta* | 8h |
| as soon as | как только | *kahk tól'-ka* | 4e, 8h |
| ash | ясень *(m)* | *yáh-sin'* | 14c |
| Asia | Азия | *áh-zi-ya* | 31b |
| ask a question | задавать вопрос | *za-da-váht' vap-rós* | 17a, 38f |
| ask for something | просить что-нибудь (что-то) | *pra-sít' shtó-ni-but' (shtó-ta)* | 9 |
| ask someone | спрашивать (у) кого-нибудь | *sprá-shi-vat' ka-vó-ni-but'* | 9, 17a, 38f |
| asparagus | спаржа | *spáhr-zha* | 14e, 24e |

| | | | |
|---|---|---|---|
| **aspect** | вид | *vit* | 8a |
| **aspirin** | пирамидон, аспирин | *pi-ra-mi-dón, as-pi-rín* | 25h, 40b, 41a |
| **assault** | нападение | *na-pa-dyé-ni-ye* | 40b |
| **assembly** | собрание, ассамблея | *sab-ráh-ni-ye, a-samb-lyé-ya* | 44 |
| **assignment (homework)** | домашнее задание | *da-máhsh-ni-ye za-dáh-ni-ye* | 38f |
| **assistant** | помощник *(m&f)* | *pa-mósh-nik* | 38d |
| **association** | общество, объединение, ассоциация | *óp-shchist-va, ab'-i-di-nyé-ni-ye, a-sa-tsy-áh-tsy-ya* | 44 |
| **assure** | уверить | *u-vyé-rit'* | 21a |
| **asterisk** | звёздочка (знак) | *zvyóz-dach-ka (znak)* | 19d |
| **astronaut** | космонавт | *kas-ma-náhft* | 43 |
| **astronomy** | астрономия | *ast-ra-nó-mi-ya* | 13a, 38e |
| **at** | на, в | *nah, v* | 8d |
| **at home** | дома | *dó-ma* | 23f |
| **at night** | ночью | *nóch'-yu* | 4a |
| **At what time?** | В какое время?, В котором часу? | *f ka-kó-ye vryé-mya?, f ka-tó-ram chah-sóo?* | 4b 4b |
| **atheism** | атеизм | *a-ty-ízm* | 11d |
| **atheist** | атеист *(m&f)* | *a-ty-íst* | 11d |
| **athlete** | атлет *(m&f)* | *at-lyét* | 28b |
| **Atlantic Ocean** | Атлантический океан | *at-lan-tí-chis-kij a-ki-áhn* | 13b |
| **atlas** | атлас | *áht-las* | 20a, 38b |
| **ATM** | банкомат | *ban-ka-máht* | 26 |
| **atmosphere** | атмосфера | *at-mas-fyé-ra* | 6a, 13b |
| **atom** | атом | *áh-tam* | 13c, 43 |
| **attachment** | приложение | *pri-la-zhé-ni-ye* | 19a |
| **attend school** | посещать школу | *pa-si-shcháht' shkó-lu* | 38f |
| **attic** | чердак | *chir-dáhk* | 23a |
| **attitude** | отношение | *at-na-shéh-ni-ye* | 21a |
| **attractive** | привлекательный | *pri-vli-káh-til'-nyj* | 11a |
| **audience (listeners)** | слушатели *(pl)* | *slóo-sha-ti-li* | 29e |
| **audience (spectators)** | зрители *(pl)* | *zrí-ti-li* | 29e |
| **audiobook** | аудиокнига | *áh-u-di-o-kní-ga* | 25o |
| **audio equipment** | звуковое оборудование | *zvu-ka-vó-ye a-ba-róo-da-va-ni-ye* | 20e |
| **auditorium** | аудитория | *a-u-di-tó-ri-ya* | 38c |
| **August** | август | *áhv-gust* | 5b |
| **aunt** | тётя | *tyó-tya* | 10a |
| **Australia** | Австралия | *ahf-stráh-li-ya* | 31b |
| **Australian** | австралиец (-йка) | *af-stra-lí-its (-jka)* | 31d |
| **Austria** | Австрия | *áhfst-ri-ya* | 31b |
| **Austrian** | австриец (-йка) | *afst-rí-its (-jka)* | 31d |
| **authentic** | настоящий, подлинный | *nas-ta-yáh-shchij, pód-li-nyj* | 13d |
| **author** | автор *(m&f)* | *áhf-tar* | 20a |
| **authority** | полномочие | *pal-na-mó-chi-ye* | 44 |

| autobiography | автобиография | *af-ta-bi-a-gráh-fi-ya* | 29d |
| automobile | автомобиль *(m)* | *af-ta-ma-bíl'* | 34a |
| automobile accident | авария | *a-váh-ri-ya* | 40c |
| avarice, greed | жадность | *zháhd-nast'* | 11e |
| avaricious | жадный | *zháhd-nyj* | 11e |
| avenue | проспект | *pras-pyékt* | 37b |
| average | среднее *(n)* | *sryéd-ni-ye* | 1f |
| away | от | *at* | 3d |
| awful | ужасный | *u-zháhs-nyj* | 6a |
| axis | ось *(f)* | *os'* | 2b |
| Azerbaijan | Азербайджан | *a-zyr-baj-dzháhn* | 31b |

## B

| baby | ребёнок, младенец | *ri-byó-nak, mla-dyé-nits* | 11b |
| bachelor | холостяк | *kha-la-styáhk* | 11c |
| back, backward | назад | *na-záht* | 3d, 37b |
| back | спина | *spi-náh* | 12a |
| back door | задний вход | *záhd-nij fkhot* | 27 |
| backyard | задний двор | *záhd-nij dvor* | 27 |
| bacteria | бактерия | *bak-téh-ri-ya* | 45a |
| bad | плохой, нехороший | *pla-khój, ni-kha-ró-shij* | 24p |
| badly | плохо | *pló-kha* | 16a |
| bag | сумка, мешок | *sóom-ka, mi-shók* | 23d, 25a, 32 |
| baggage, luggage | багаж | *ba-gáhsh* | 32, 36b |
| baked | печёный | *pi-chyó-nyj* | 24p |
| baker | пекарь *(m&f)* | *pyé-kar'* | 39a |
| bakery | булочная | *bóo-lach-na-ya* | 24n |
| balcony | балкон | *bal-kón* | 23a, 36c |
| bald | лысый | *lý-syj* | 12d |
| ball | мяч | *myahch* | 28b |
| ballet | балет | *ba-lyét* | 29c |
| ballet dancer | балерун *(m),* балерина *(f)* | *ba-li-róon, ba-li-rí-na* | 29c |
| banana | банан | *ba-náhn* | 14d, 24f |
| Band-Aid | липкий пластырь | *líp-kij pláhs-tyr'* | 25h |
| bandage | повязка | *pa-vyáhs-ka* | 40c, 41a |
| | перевязка | *pi-ri-vyáhs-ka* | |
| bank | банк | *bahnk* | 26 |
| bank fees *(pl)* | банковские сборы *(pl)* | *báhn-kaf-ski-i sbó-ry* | 27 |
| bank rate | банковская ставка | *báhn-kaf-ska-ya stáhf-ka* | 26 |
| bankbook | банковская книжка | *báhn-kaf-ska-ya knísh-ka* | 26 |
| bankrupt *(n)* | банкрот, несостоятельный, должник | *bank-rót, ni-sas-ta-yáh-til'-nyj, dalzh-ník* | 26 |
| baptism | крестины *(pl)* | *kris-tí-ny* | 11d |
| bar | бар | *bahr* | 23d |
| bar code | бар-код, штрих-код | *báhr-kót, shtríkh-kót* | 26 |
| bar stool | барный стул | *báhr-nyj stool* | 23d |
| barbeque | барбекю (also -кью) | *bar-bi-kyú (also -k'yu)* | 23d |
| barber | мужской парикмахер | *muzh-skój pa-rik-máh-khir* | 12d, 39a |
| barber shop | парикмахерская | *pa-rik-máh-khir-ska-ya* | 12d |

| bark | кора | *ka-ráh* | 14c |
| barley | ячмень *(m)* | *ich-myén'* | 24i |
| barn | сарай | *sa-ráhj* | 15a |
| barometer | барометр | *ba-ró-mitr* | 6c |
| barrel | бочка | *bóch-ka* | 23d |
| baseball | бейсбол | *byejs-ból* | 28b |
| basement | подвал | *pad-váhl* | 23a |
| basket | корзина (-нка) | *kar-zí-na (-nka)* | 23d |
| basketball | баскетбол | *bas-kit-ból* | 28b |
| bass viol | контрабас | *kant-ra-báhs* | 29c |
| bassoon | фагот | *fa-gót* | 29c |
| bat | летучая мышь *(f)* | *li-tóo-cha-ya mysh* | 15a |
| bathing suit | плавки *(for males),* | *pláhf-ki,* | 25k |
| | купальник *(for females)* | *ku-páhl'-nik* | |
| bathroom | ванная (комната) | *váh-na-ya (kóm-na-ta)* | 23b, 36c |
| bathtub | ванна | *váhn-a* | 23a, 36c |
| battery | батарейка, | *ba-ta-ryéj-ka,* | 20b, 25b, |
| | аккумулятор, | *a-ku-mu-lyáh-tar,* | 34e |
| | аккумуляторная | *a-ku-mu-lyáh-tar-na-ya* | 18a, |
| | батарея | *ba-ta-ryé-ya* | 20b |
| bay | бухта | *bóokh-ta* | 13b |
| be absent | отсутствовать | *at-sóot-stva-vat'* | 38f |
| be acquainted | быть знакомым | *byt' zna-kó-mym* | 10b |
| be afraid | бояться, опасаться *(i)* | *ba-yáh-tsa, a-pa-sáh-tsa* | 21a |
| be ashamed | стыдиться | *sty-dí-tsa* | 21a |
| be born | родиться | *ra-dí-tsa* | 11c |
| be called | называть | *na-zy-váht'* | 11f |
| Be careful! | Осторожно! | *as-ta-rózh-na* | 21c |
| be enemies, to | враждовать | *vrazh-da-váht'* | 10b |
| be hungry | быть голодным *(m)*, | *byt' ga-lód-nym,* | 24o |
| | быть голодной *(f)* | *byt' ga-lód-naj* | |
| be interested in | интересоваться | *in-ti-ri-sa-váh-tsa* | 22b |
| be late, to | опоздать | *a-paz-dáht'* | 4e |
| be located | находиться, быть | *na-kha-dí-tsa,* | 13e |
| | расположенным | *byt' ras-pa-ló-zhyn-ym* | |
| be pregnant | беременная | *bi-ryé-mi-na-ya* | 11c |
| be present | присутствовать | *pri-sóot-stva-vat'* | 38f |
| be run over (by a car) | попасть под машину | *pa-páhst' pad ma-shý-nu* | 40c |
| Be seated! | Садитесь! *(polite)* | *sa-dí-tis'* | 16b |
| be thirsty | хотеть пить | *kha-tyét' pit'* | 24o |
| beach | берег/пляж | *byé-rik/plyahzh* | 13b, 37a, 37c |
| beak | клюв | *klyuf* | 15b |
| bean | боб | *bop* | 14e, 24e |
| bear | медведь *(m)* | *mid-vyét'* | 15a |
| beard | борода | *ba-ra-dáh* | 12a |
| beast | зверь *(m)* | *zvyer'* | 15d |
| beautician | косметичка *(f)* | *kas-mi-tích-ka* | 12d |
| beautiful | красивый *(adj)* | *kra-sí-vyj* | 11a, 25l |
| beauty | красота | *kra-sa-táh* | 11a |
| because | потому что | *pa-ta-móo shta* | 8h |

| become | стать | *staht'* | 4e |
|---|---|---|---|
| become acquainted | знакомиться | *zna-kó-mi-tsa* | 10b |
| become engaged | обручиться | *a-bru-chí-tsa* | 11c |
| become old | постареть | *pa-sta-ryét'* | 11b |
| become sick | заболеть | *za-ba-lyét'* | 11a |
| become weak | ослабеть | *a-sla-byét'* | 11a |
| bed | кровать *(f)* | *kra-váht'* | 23c, 36c |
| bedbug | клоп | *klop* | 15d |
| bedroom | спальня | *spáhl-nya* | 23b |
| bee | пчела | *pchi-láh* | 15d |
| beef | говядина | *ga-vyáh-di-na* | 24c |
| beer | пиво | *pí-va* | 24k |
| beet | свёкла | *svyók-la* | 14e, 24e |
| before, in front | до, перед | *da, pyé-rid* | 4e, 8d |
| begin | начать | *na-cháht'* | 4e |
| beginning | начало | *na-cháh-la* | 4e |
| behind | за, сзади | *za, zzáh-di* | 8d, 37d |
| beige | бежевый | *byé-zhy-vyj* | 7a |
| Belarus | Белорусь *(f)* | *bi-la-róos'* | 31b |
| Belgian | бельгиец (-йка) | *bil'-gí-its (-jka)* | 31d |
| Belgium | Бельгия | *byél'-gi-ya* | 31b |
| belief | вера | *vyé-ra* | 11d |
| believe | верить | *vyé-rit'* | 22b |
| bellhop | коридорный | *ka-ri-dór-nyj* | 36b |
| beloved | любимый | *lyu-bí-myj* | 11e |
| below zero | ниже ноля | *ní-zhy na-lyáh* | 6c |
| belt | пояс *(for females)*, | *pó-yas,* | 25k |
| | ремень *(for males) (m)* | *ri-myén'* | |
| benevolent | доброжелательный | *da-bra-zhe-láh-til'-nyj* | 11e |
| Berlin | Берлин | *bir-lín* | 31c |
| Best wishes! | Наилучшие | *na-i-lóoch-shy-ye* | 16c, 30c |
| | пожелания! | *po-zhy-láh-ni-ya* | |
| between, among | между | *myézh-du* | 8d |
| beyond | за | *za* | 3d |
| bicycle | велосипед | *vi-la-si-pyét* | 33a, 37a |
| bicycle racing | велосипедные | *vi-la-si-pyéd-ny-ye* | 28b |
| | гонки *(pl)* | *gón-ki* | |
| big, large | большой | *bal'-shój* | 3c, 251 |
| bill, check | счет | *shchot* | 24m, |
| | | | 25a, 36b |
| bill/bank note | банкнота | *bank-nó-ta* | 26 |
| billiards | биллиард | *bi-li-áhrt* | 28a |
| biography | биография | *bi-a-gráh-fi-ya* | 29d |
| biologist | биолог *(m&f)* | *bi-ó-lak* | 39a |
| biology | биология | *bi-a-ló-gi-ya* | 38e |
| birch | берёза | *bi-ryó-za* | 14c |
| birth | рождение | *razh-dyé-ni-ye* | 11c |
| birth-control pills | противозачаточные | *pra-ti-va-za-cháh-tach-* | 25h |
| | таблетки | *ny-ye tab-lyét-ki* | |
| birthday | день рождения *(m)* | *dyen' razh-dyé-ni-ya* | 11c, 30a |
| bitter | горький | *gór-kij* | 24p |

| black | чёрный | *chyór-nyj* | 7a |
| black-and-white *(printer)* | черный-белый *(adj) (m)* | *chór-nyj-byé-lyj* | 20b |
| blanket | одеяло | *a-di-yáh-la* | 23d, 36c |
| bleed | кровоточить | *kra-va-tó-chit'* | 40c |
| bleeding | кровотечение | *kra-va-ti-chyé-ni-ye* | 40c |
| blender | блендер | *blyén-dir* | 23d |
| blind | слепой | *sli-pój* | 12c |
| blindness | слепота | *sli-pa-táh* | 12c |
| blizzard | буран | *bu-ráhn* | 6a |
| block house (townhouse) | блокированный дом | *bla-ki-ró-va-nyj dom* | 27 |
| blog | блог | *blok* | 20d |
| blond | блондин *(m),* блондинка *(f)* | *blan-dín,* *blan-dín-ka* | 11a |
| blood | кровь *(f)* | *krof'* | 12a, 40c, 41a |
| blood pressure | кровяное давление | *kra-vi-nó-ye dav-lyé-ni-ye* | 41a |
| blood transfusion | переливание крови | *pi-ri-li-váh-ni-ye kró-vi* | 45b |
| bloom | расцвести (за-) | *ras-tsvis-tí* | 14a |
| bloom | цветок *(sg),* цветы/цветки *(pl)* | *tsvi-tók,* *tsvi-tý/tsvit-kí* | 14a |
| blouse | блузка | *blóoz-ka* | 25k |
| blue | синий | *sí-nij* | 7a |
| blueberry | черника | *chir-ní-ka* | 14d, 24f |
| boarding | посадка | *pa-sáht-ka* | 33a |
| boarding pass | посадочный талон | *pa-sáh-dach-nyj ta-lón* | 33a |
| boat | лодка | *lót-ka* | 37b |
| bodily fluids *(pl)* | жидкости организма *(pl)* | *zhýt-kas-ti ar-ga-níz-ma* | 45b |
| body | тело | *tyé-le* | 11a |
| | *(of car)* kuzov | *kóo-zaf* | 34e |
| body (political) | орган | *ór-gan* | 44 |
| body (text) | текст | *tyekst* | 19d |
| boil (food) | варить | *va-rít'* | 24b |
| boil (water) | кипятить | *ki-pi-tít'* | 24b |
| boiled | варёный, кипячёный | *va-ryó-nyj, ki-pi-chyó-nyj* | 24b |
| bold face | жирный шрифт | *zhýr-nyj shrift* | 20b |
| bologna | докторская колбаса | *dók-tar-ska-ya kal-ba-sáh* | 24c |
| bone | кость *(f)* | *kost'* | 12a, 41a |
| book | книга | *kní-ga* | 20a, 25o, 38b |
| bookcase | книжный шкаф | *knízh-nyj shkháf* | 23c, 38b |
| bookstore | книжный магазин | *knízh-nyj ma-ga-zín* | 25o |
| boot | сапог | *sa-pók* | 25n |
| border | граница | *gra-ní-tsa* | 13e, 32 |
| boredom | скука | *skóo-ka* | 21a |
| boring | скучный | *skóoch-nyj* | 21a |
| borscht | борщ | *borshch* | 24g |
| boss | начальник | *na-cháhl'-nik* | 39d |

| botanical | ботанический | *ba-ta-ní-chis-kij* | 14a |
|---|---|---|---|
| botany | ботаника | *ba-táh-ni-ka* | 14a, 38e |
| both | оба, обе | *ó-ba, ó-bi* | 3c |
| bottle | бутылка | *bu-týl-ka* | 23d, 241 |
| boulevard | бульвар | *bul'-váhr* | 11f |
| bouquet | букет | *bu-kyét* | 14b |
| bowl | миска | *mís-ka* | 241 |
| box (large), case | ящик | *yáh-shchik* | 23d |
| box (small) | коробка | *ka-róp-ka* | 23d |
| box office | билетная касса | *bi-lyét-na-ya káh-sa* | 29a |
| boxing | бокс | *boks* | 28b |
| boy | мальчик | *máhl'-chik* | 11a |
| bra | лифчик, бюстгальтер | *líf-chik, byust-gáhl'-tir* | 25k |
| bracelet | браслет | *bras-lyét* | 25i |
| bracket | скобка | *skóp-ka* | 19d |
| brain | мозг | *mosk* | 12a, 41a |
| brake | тормоз | *tór-mas* | 34a, 34c, 34e |
| branch | ветка | *vyét-ka* | 14a |
| Brazil | Бразиль (f) | *bra-zíl'* | 31b |
| Brazilian | бразилец (-лка) | *bra-zí-lits (-lka)* | 31d |
| bread | хлеб (coll) | *khlyep* | 24i |
| break | каникулы (pl) | *ka-ní-ku-ly* | 30a, 37c, 38a |
| break a bone | сломать (p) кость | *sla-máht' kost'* | 40c |
| breakfast | завтрак | *záhft-rak* | 24a, 36b |
| breast, chest | грудь (f) | *grood'* | 12a |
| breath | дыхание | *dy-kháh-ni-ye* | 41a |
| breathe | дышать | *dy-sháht'* | 12b |
| bricklayer | каменщик (-щица) | *káh-min-shchik (-shchi-tsa)* | 39a |
| bridge | мост | *most* | 34c, 37b, 41b |
| brief | короткий, краткий | *ka-rót-kij, kráht-kij* | 4e, 38f |
| briefcase | портфель (m) | *part-fyél'* | 25c, 39c |
| briefly speaking | короче говоря, короче | *ka-ró-chi ga-va-ryáh, ka-ró-chi* | 17b |
| bright | яркий | *yáhr-kij* | 7b |
| broker | брокер | *bró-kir* | 27 |
| bronchitis | бронхит | *bran-khít* | 41a |
| bronze | бронза | *brón-za* | 13c |
| brooch | брошь (f) | *brosh* | 25i |
| brook | ручей | *ru-chéj* | 37c |
| broom | веник, метла | *vyé-nik, mit-láh* | 23d |
| brother | брат | *braht* | 10a |
| brother-in-law | зять (m) | *zyaht'* | 10a |
| brown | коричневый | *ka-rích-ni-vyj* | 7a |
| browser | браузер | *bráh-u-zir* | 20b, 20d |
| browsing (n) | обзор | *ab-zór* | 20b |
| brunet | брюнет (m), брюнетка (f) | *bryu-nyét, bryu-nyét-ka* | 11a |

| brush, comb one's hair *(pl)* | расчёсывать волосы | *ras-chóh-sy-vat' vó-la-sy* | 12d |
| brush (artist's) | кисть *(f)* | *kist* | 29b |
| brush | щётка | *shchyót-ka* | 12d, 25f |
| buckle up | застегнуть (ремень) | *zas-tig-nóot' ri-myén'* | 33c |
| bud | бутон | *bu-tón* | 14a |
| Buddhism | буддизм | *bud-ízm* | 11d |
| budget | бюджет | *byut-zhéht* | 26, 44 |
| buffalo | бизон | *bi-zón* | 15a |
| buffer | буфер | *bóo-fir* | 20b |
| bug | букашка/насекомое | *bu-káhsh-ka/ na-si-kó-ma-ye* | 15d |
| build | строить | *stró-it'* | 23f |
| building | здание | *zdáh-ni-ye* | 40a |
| bulb | луковица | *lóo-ka-vi-tsa* | 14a |
| Bulgaria | Болгария | *bal-gáh-ri-ya* | 31b |
| bull | бык | *byk* | 15a |
| bump | шишка | *shýsh-ka* | 40c |
| bumper | бампер | *báhm-pir* | 34e |
| burn | ожог | *a-zhók* | 40a |
| bus, van | автобус | *af-tó-bus* | 35 |
| bus driver | водитель *(m)* автобуса | *va-dí-til' af-tó-bu-sa* | 35, 39a |
| bus station, depot | автобусный вокзал | *af-tó-bus-nyj vak-záhl* | 35 |
| business | бизнес | *bíz-nis* | 26 |
| business center | бизнесс центр | *bíz-nis tsehntr* | 37a |
| business lunch | бизнис ланч | *bíz-nis lánch* | 24a |
| businessman (woman) | бизнесмен (-ка) | *biz-nis-myén (-ka)* | 39a |
| but | но, а | *no, ah* | 8h |
| butcher | мясник | *mis-ník* | 39a |
| butcher shop | мясной магазин | *mis-nój ma-ga-zín* | 24n |
| butter | масло | *máhs-la* | 24h |
| butterfly | бабочка | *báh bach-ku* | 15d |
| buttock | ягодица | *yá-ga-di-tsa* | 12a |
| button | пуговица | *póo-ga-vi-tsa* | 25g |
| button (key) | кнопка | *knóp-ka* | 18a, 20b, 25d |
| buy online | купить *(p)* он-лайн, покупать *(i)* | *ku-pít' an-láhjn, pa-ku-páht'* | 25a |
| buyer (of an apartment) | покупатель квартиры | *pa-ku-páh-til' kvar-tí-ry* | 27 |
| buy, purchase | покупать | *pa-ku-páht'* | 23f, 25a |
| by the way | кстати, между прочим | *kstáh-ti, myézh-du pró-chim* | 17b |
| byte | байт | *bahjt* | 20b |

## C

| cabbage | капуста | *ka-póos-ta* | 14e, 24e |
| cabinet (wall) | настенный шкаф | *nas-tyén-nyj shkahf* | 23d |
| cable | кабель *(m)*, трос | *káh-bil', tros* | 18a, 25b |
| cafeteria | кафетерий/столовая | *ka-fi-téh-rij/sta-ló-va-ya* | 24m |
| cake | кекс | *kyeks* | 24g |
| calculator | калькулятор | *kal'-ku-lyáh-tyr* | 23d |

| calculus | высшая математика | *vý-sha-ya ma-ti-máh-ti-ka* | 38e |
| calendar | календарь *(m)* | *ka-lin-dáhr'* | 5b, 23d, |
| | | | 39c |
| call (on the phone) | звонить | *zva-nít'* | 17a |
| call (someone) | звать | *zvaht'* | 17a |
| call the fire | вызвать пожарную | *výz-vat' pa-zháhr-nu-yu* | 40a |
| department | команду | *ka-máhn-du* | |
| calm | спокойный | *spa-kój-nyj* | 11e |
| calmness | покой *(m)* | *pa-kój* | 11e |
| camcorder | видеокамера | *vi-di-a-káh-mi-ra* | 25d |
| camel | верблюд | *virb-lyút* | 15a |
| camera | фотоаппарат | *fo-ta-pa-ráht* | 25d |
| camp | бивуак | *bi-vu-áhk* | 37c |
| Can you tell me? *(pol)* | Скажите, | *ska-zhý-ti pa-zháh-lus-ta* | 9 |
| | пожалуйста... | | |
| Canada | Канада | *ka-náh-da* | 31b |
| Canadian | канадец (-дка) | *ka-náh-dits (-tka)* | 31d |
| canceled | отменён | *at-mi-nyón* | 33b |
| cancer | рак | *rahk* | 41a |
| candle | свеча | *svi-cháh* | 11d |
| canine | клык | *klyk* | 41b |
| canoe | байдарка | *baj-dáhr-ka* | 37c |
| cantaloupe | дыня | *dýn-ya* | 24f |
| canteen, cafeteria | столовая | *sta-ló-va-ya* | 38c |
| cap | кепка | *kyép-ka* | 25k |
| capacity | ёмкость *(f)* | *yóm-kast'* | 3c |
| capital | столица | *sta-lí-tsa* | 13e, 31a |
| capital letter | большая буква | *bal'-sháh-ya bóok-va* | 19d |
| car racing | автомобильные | *av-ta-ma-bíl'-ny-ye* | 28b |
| | гонки *(pl)* | *gón-ki* | |
| carbon | углерод | *ug-li-rót* | 13c |
| carbonated water | газированная вода | *ga-zi-ró-va-na-ya va-dáh* | 24k |
| carburetor | карбюратор | *kar-byu-ráh-tar* | 34e |
| career | карьера | *kar'-yé-ra* | 11f, 39d |
| carnation | гвоздика | *gvaz-dí-ka* | 14b |
| carp | карп | *kahrp* | 15c |
| carpenter | столяр/плотник | *sta-lyáhr/plót-nik* | 39a |
| carpet, rug | ковёр | *kav-yór* | 23c |
| carrot | морковь *(f)* | *mar-kóf'* | 14e, 24e |
| carry | носить | *na-sít'* | 32 |
| carryall, netlike bag | авоська | *a-vós-ka* | 25a |
| case | падеж | *pa-dyésh* | 8a |
| cash | наличные (деньги) | *na-lích-ny-i (dyén-gi)* | 26 |
| cash, to | получить деньги по | *pa-lu-chít' dyén'-gi pa* | 26 |
| | чеку | *chyé-ku* | |
| cash card | наличная карточка | *na-lích-na-ya káhr-tych-ka* | 26 |
| cash dispenser | раздатчик наличных | *raz-dáht-chik na-lích-nykh* | 26 |
| cash register | касса | *káh-sa* | 25a |
| cashier, teller | кассир *(m),* | *ka-sír,* | 25a, 26, |
| | кассирша *(f)* | *ka-sír-sha* | 35 |
| casino | игорный дом | *í-gar-nyj dom* | 45b |

| | | | |
|---|---|---|---|
| cassette tape | кассета | *ka-syé-ta* | 20e, 25j |
| castle | замок | *záh-mak* | 37b |
| cat | кот *(m)*, кошка *(f)* | *kot, kósh-ka* | 15a |
| cataract | катаракта | *ka-ta-ráhk-ta* | 41a |
| catch | поймать | *paj-máht'* | 28b |
| catch a chill (cold) | простудиться | *pras-tu-dí'-tsa* | 6b |
| catch fire | загореться | *za-ga-ryé-tsa* | 40a |
| caterpillar | гсуеница | *gu-si-ní-tsa* | 15d |
| catfish | сом | *som* | 15c |
| cathedral | кафедральный собор | *ka-fid-ráhl-nyj sa-bór* | 11d, 37b |
| Catholicism | католичество | *ka-ta-lí-chist-vo* | 11d |
| cauliflower | цветная капуста | *tsvit-náh-ya ka-póos-ta* | 14e, 24e |
| Caution! | Осторожно! | *as-ta-rózh-na* | 35 |
| caviar | икра | *ik-ráh* | 24d |
| cavity | дупло | *dup-ló* | 41b |
| cc | скопировать *(p)*, | *ska-pí-ra-vat',* | 19a |
| | копировать *(i)* | *ka-pí-ra-vat'* | |
| cedar | кедр | *kyedr* | 14c |
| ceiling | потолок | *pa-ta-lók* | 23a, 27 |
| celery | сельдерей | *sil'-di-ryéj* | 14e, 24e |
| cell | клетка | *klyét-ka* | 14a |
| cell phone | сотовый телефон, | *so-tó-vyj ti-li-fón,* | 18a |
| | сотовик, | *sa-tó-vik,* | |
| | мобильный телефон, | *ma-bíl'-nyj ti-li-fón,* | |
| | мобильник | *ma-bíl'-nik* | |
| cellar | погреб | *pó-grib* | 23b |
| cello | виолончель *(f)* | *vi-a-lan-chyél'* | 29c |
| Celsius | Цельсий | *tséhl'-sij* | 6c |
| cemetery | кладбище | *kláht-bi-shchi* | 37b |
| censorship | цензура | *tsyn-zóo-ra* | 45b |
| center (of town) | центр (города) | *tséhntr (gó-ra-da)* | 31a, 37b |
| centimeter | сантиметр | *san-ti-myétr* | 3a |
| Central America | Центральная | *tsint-ráhl'-na-ya* | 31b |
| | Америка | *a-myé-ri-ka* | |
| centralized *(adj)* | централизованный *(m)*, | *tsyn-tra-li-zó-va-nyj,* | 44 |
| | централизованное *(n)*, | *tsyn-tra-li-zó-va-na-ye,* | |
| | централизованная *(f)* | *tsyn-tra-li-zó-va-na-ya* | |
| century | век (века *pl)* | *vyek (vi-káh)* | 4c |
| chain | цепь (цепочка) *(f)* | *tséhp' (tsy-póch-ka)* | 25i, 34a |
| chair | стул | *stool* | 23c, 39c |
| chair (person) | председатель думы | *prid-si-dáh-til' dóo-my* | 44 |
| chalk | мел | *myel* | 38b |
| chalkboard | доска | *das-káh* | 38b |
| champagne | шампанское | *sham-páhns-ka-ye* | 24k |
| change (money) | сдача | *sdáh-cha* | 25a |
| channel (canal) | канал | *ka-náhl* | 13b |
| channel (TV) | канал | *ka-náhl* | 20b |
| chapter | глава | *gla-váh* | 29d |
| character | символ | *sím-val* | 19a |
| character (person) | персонаж | *pir-sa-náhsh* | 29d |

| character (disposition) | характер | kha-ráhk-tir | 11e |
|---|---|---|---|
| characteristic | характеристика | kha-rak-ti-rís-ti-ka | 11e |
| charge | обвинение | ab-vi-nyé-ni-ye | 42 |
| charge | предъявить (p) | prid'-i-vit | 42 |
| | предъявлять (i) | prid'-iv-lyáht' | |
| | обвинение | ab-vi-nyé-ni-ye | |
| charge | зарядить (p), | za-ri-dít', | 18a, |
| | заряжать (i) | za-ri-zháht' | 20b |
| charter flight | фрахтованный рейс | frakh-tó-va-nyj ryejs | 31a |
| chat | болтать, | bal-táht', | |
| | трепаться (colloquial) | tri-páh-tsa | 17a |
| chat | чат, беседа | chyet, bi-syé-da | 20d |
| chat room | комната для бесед | kóm-na-ta dlyah bi-syét | 20d |
| cheap | дешёвый | di-shó-vyj | 24p |
| cheaply | дёшево | dyó-shy-va | 24p |
| check | чек | chyek | 25a, 26, |
| | | | 36b |
| check the oil | проверить масло | pra-vyé-rit' máhs-la | 34c |
| check-in | регистрация, | ri-gist-ráh-tsy-ya, | |
| | регистрироваться | ri-gist-rí-ra-va-tsa | 33a, 36a |
| check-out time | время освобождения | vré-myah as-va-bazh- | 36a |
| | комнат | dyé-ni-ya kóm-nat | |
| checkbook | чековая книжка | chyé-ka-va-ya knísh-ka | 26 |
| checkers | шашки (pl) | sháhsh-ki | 28a |
| cheek | щека | shchi-káh | 12a |
| cheese | сыр | syr | 24h |
| chemical | химический | khi-mí-chis-kij | 13c |
| chemical weapon | химическое оружие | khi-mí-chis-ka-ye | 45b |
| | | a-róo-zhy-ye | |
| chemistry | химия | khí-mi-ya | 13c, 38e |
| cherry | вишня (coll) | vísh-nya | 14d, 24f |
| cherry tree | вишня | vísh-nya | 14c |
| chess | шахматы (pl) | sháhkh-ma-ty | 28a |
| chest of drawers/ | комод | ka-mót | 23c, 36c |
| dresser | | | |
| chestnut | каштан | kash-táhn | 14d |
| chicken | цыплёнок, | tsyp-lyó-nak, | 15b, |
| | курица | kóo-ri-tsa | 24c |
| chief officer | начальник милиции | na-cháhl'-nik mi-lí-tsi-i | 42 |
| (of militia) | | | |
| chimney | труба | tru-báh | 23c |
| chin | подбородок | pad-ba-ró-dak | 12a |
| China | Китай | ki-táhj | 31b |
| Chinese | китаец (-таянка) | ki-táh-its (-ta-yáhn-ka) | 31d |
| Chinese | китайский | ki-táhj-skij | 31d |
| chlorine | хлор | khlor | 13c |
| chlorophyll | хлорофилл | khl -ra-fíl | 14a |
| choke | дроссель (m) | dró-sil' | 34e |
| Christian | христианин | khris-ti-áh-nin | 11d |
| Christianity | христианство | khris-ti-áhn-stvo | 11d |

| Christmas | Рождество (Христово) | razh-dist-vó (khris-tó-va) | 5e, 30a |
|---|---|---|---|
| chum | приятель *(m)*, приятельница *(f)* | pri-yáh-til', pri-yáh-til'-ni-tsa | 10b |
| church | церковь *(f)* | tséhr-kaf' | 11d, 37b |
| cigar | сигара | si-gáh-ra | 25e |
| cigarette | сигарета | si-ga-ryé-ta | 25e |
| cinnamon | корица | ka-rí-tsa | 24j |
| circle | круг | krook | 2a |
| citizenship | гражданство | grazh-dáhnst-va | 39a |
| citrus | цитрус | tsýt-rus | 14d |
| city, town | город | gó-rod | 11f, 13e, 31a, 37b, 39b |
| clam | моллюск | ma-lyúsk | 15d, 24d |
| clamp | зажим, скрепа | za-zhým, skryé-pa | 25b |
| clarinet | кларнет | klar-nyét | 29c |
| class | класс | klahs | 38f, 45b |
| classroom | классная комната | kláhs-na-ya kóm-na-ta | 38c |
| clause | предложение | prid-la-zhéh-ni-ye | 8a |
| clean, to; brush, to | чистить | chis-tít' | 12d, 23f, 41b |
| clean | чистый *(adj)*, чисто *(adv)* | chís-tyj, chís-ta | 11a, 25g |
| clean oneself | очиститься | a-chis-tít-tsa | 12d |
| clear (weather) | ясно | yáhs-na | 6a |
| clear the table | убрать со стола | u-bráht' sa sta-láh | 23f, 24o |
| clerk | служащий (-ая) | sló-zha-shchij (-a-ya) | 19f, 25a, 36b |
| click *(n)* | щелчок | shchil-chók | 20b |
| click *(v)* | щёлкнуть *(p)*, щёлкать *(i)* | shchyólk-nut', shchyól-kat' | 20b |
| climate | климат | klí-mat | 6a |
| clip | скрепка | skryép-ka | 19e |
| clock | часы *(pl)* | chi-sý | 4d, 25i |
| closed | закрыт | za-krýt | 25a |
| closet | чулан, шкаф | chu-láhn, shkahf | 23b, 36c |
| closing (ending) | заключение | zak-luy-chyé-ni-ye | 19d |
| clothes | одежда | a-dyézh-da | 25g |
| clothes hanger | вешалка | vyé-shyl-ka | 23d |
| cloud | облако *(sg)*, облака *(pl)* | ób-la-ka, ab-la-káh | 13b, 6a |
| clove | гвоздика | gvaz-dí-ka | 24j |
| clutch | сцепление/муфта | stsyp-lyé-ni-ye/móof-ta | 34e |
| co-op | кооператив | ka-a-pi-ra-tíf | 23g |
| co-pilot | второй пилот | fta-rój -lót | 33c |
| coach | тренер *(m&f)* | tryé-nir | 28b |
| coarse (person) | грубый *(adj)* | gróo-byj | 11a |
| coarsely | грубо *(adv)* | gróo-ba | 11a |
| coast | побережье | pa-bi-ryézh'-ye | 13b |
| coat | пальто *(indecl)* | pal'-tó | 25k |

| cockroach | таракан | *ta-ra-káhn* | 15d |
| codfish | треска | *tris-káh* | 15c, 24d |
| coffee | кофе | *kó-fi* | 24k |
| coffee-maker | кофеварка | *ka-fi-váhr-ka* | 23d |
| coffee pot | кофейник | *ka-fyéj-nik* | 23d |
| cognac | коньяк | *kan'-yáhk* | 24k |
| coin | монета | *ma-nyé-ta* | 26, 28a |
| coin collecting | коллекционирование монет | *ka-lik-tsi-a-ní-ra-va-ni-ye ma-nyét* | 28a |
| cold (sickness) | простуда | *pras-tóo-da* | 41a |
| cold | холод | *khó-lad* | 6a |
| cold | холодно *(adv)* | *khó-lad-na* | 6a, 24p |
| cold | холодный *(adj)* | *kha-lód-nyj* | 24p |
| collateral (for loan) | залог | *za-lók* | 27 |
| colleague | коллега *(m&f)* | *ka-lyé-ga* | 10b, 39d |
| collect call | звонить за счёт вызываемого | *zva-nít' za shchyot vy-zy-váh-i-ma-va* | 18b |
| college teacher | преподаватель (-ница) | *pri-pa-da-váh-til' (-ni-tsa)* | 38d, 39a |
| collide | сталкиваться | *stáhl-ki-va-tsa* | 40a |
| collision | столкновение | *stalk-na-vyé-ni-ye* | 40c |
| cologne | одеколон | *a-di-ka-lón* | 25f |
| colon | двоеточие | *dva-i-tó-chi-ye* | 19d |
| color | цвет | *tsvyet* | 7c |
| color | цветной *(adj) (m)* | *tsvit-nój* | 20b |
| colored pencil | цветной карандаш | *tsvit-nój ka-ran-dáhsh* | 7c |
| comb | гребень *(m)*, гребёнка *(f)*, расчёска | *gryé-bin', grí-byón-ka, ra-shchyós-ka* | 12d, 25f |
| come | прийти | *prij-tí* | 3e |
| come back | вернуться | *vir-nóo-tsa* | 3e |
| come from | приехать из | *pri-yé-khat' iz* | 11f |
| Come in! | Войдите! | *vaj-dí-ti* | 16b |
| come to visit | прийти в гости | *pri-tí v gós-ti* | 30b |
| comedian | комедийный актёр *(m)*, комедийная актриса *(f)* | *ka-mi-díj-nyj ak-tyór, ka-mi-díj-na-ya akt-rí-sa* | 29e |
| comedy | комедия | *ka-myé-di-ya* | 20a, 29e |
| comet | комета | *ka-myé-ta* | 13a |
| comics | комиксы | *kó-mik-sy* | 20a, 25o |
| comma | запятая | *za-pi-táh-ya* | 19d |
| commission | комиссия | *ka-mí-si-yah* | 27 |
| committee | комитет | *ka-mi-tyét* | 44 |
| common room (the commons) | общая комната | *óp-shchya-ya kóm-na-ta* | 27 |
| Commonwealth of Independent States (CIS) | Содружество Независимых Государств (СНГ) | *sad-róo-zhyst-va ni-za-ví-si-mykh ga-su-dáhrstf (es-ehn-geh)* | 31b |
| communication | связь *(f)*, сообщение | *svyahs', sa-ap-shchyé-ni-ye* | 17a |

| communism | коммунизм | *ka-mu-nízm* | 44 |
| compact disc | компактный диск | *kam-páhkt-nyj disk* | 20e, 25j, 43 |
| compact flash (card) | компакт флэш | *kam-páhkt fléhsh* | 25d |
| company | компания/фирма | *kam-páh-ni-ya/fír-ma* | 39d |
| compare | сравнивать | *srav-ni-váht'* | 17a |
| comparison | сравнение | *srav-nyé-ni-ye* | 8a, 17a |
| compartment | купе | *ku-péh* | 35 |
| compass | циркуль *(m)* | *tsýr-kul'* | 38b |
| compatible | совместимый | *sav-mis-tí-myj* | 20b |
| complain | жаловаться | *zháh-la-va-tsa* | 21a, 36b |
| complaint | жалоба | *zháh-la-ba* | 21a, 36b |
| complicated | сложный | *slózh-nyj* | 22a |
| composer | композитор | *kam-pa-zí-tar* | 25j, 29c |
| composition | сочинение | *sa-chi-néy-ni-ye* | 38f |
| compound | состав | *sas-táhf* | 13c |
| computer | компьютер, вычислительная машина | *kamp'-yú-tar, vy-chis-lí-til'-na-ya ma-shý-na* | 20b, 39c |
| computer science | кибернетика | *ki-bir-néh-ti-ka* | 20b, 38e |
| concept | понятие | *pa-nyáh-ti-ye* | 22a |
| concert | концерт | *kan-tséhrt* | 25j, 29c |
| concierge | дежурный (-ая) | *di-zhóor-nyj (-a-ya)* | 36b |
| conclude | заключить | *zak-lyu-chít'* | 17a |
| conclusion | заключение | *zak-lyu-chyé-ni-ye* | 17a |
| condom | презерватив | *pri-zir-va-tíf* | 25h |
| conductor (music) | дирижёр *(m&f)* | *di-ri-zhór* | 29c |
| conductor (driver) | кондуктор | *kan-dóok-tar* | 35 |
| cone | конус | *kó-nus* | 2a |
| conference hall | конференц-зал | *káhn-fi-rintz-záhl* | 37a |
| congratulate | поздравить | *pazd-ráh-vit'* | 17a |
| Congratulations! | Поздравляю тебя! *(fam)* | *paz-drav-lyáh-yu ti-byáh,* | |
| | Поздравляю вас! *(pol)* | *paz-drav-lyáh-yu vahs* | 16c |
| conjugation | спряжение | *spri-zhéh-ni-ye* | 8a |
| conjunction | союз | *sa-yús* | 8a |
| connect to the Internet | соединиться *(p)* с Интернет, соединяться *(i)* | *sa-i-di-ní-tsa s in-tyr-nyét, sa-i-di-nyáh-tsa* | 20d |
| connection | пересадка | *pi-ri-sáht-ka* | 33a, 35 |
| conscious | сознательный | *saz-náh-til'-nyj* | 22a |
| consciousness | сознание | *saz-náh-ni-ye* | 22a |
| conservation | сохранение | *sakh-ra-nyé-ni-ye* | 45 |
| conservative | консервативный | *kan-sir-va-tív-nyj* | 11e, 43 |
| conservatory | музыкальная школа | *mu-zy-káhl'-na-ya shkó-la* | 38a |
| consonant | согласная | *sag-láhs-na-ya* | 8a |
| Constitution (of Russia) | Конституция (России) | *kan-sti-toó-tsy-ya (ra-sí-i)* | 44 |
| construction worker | строительный рабочий | *stra-í-til'-nyj ra-bó-chij* | 39a |

| consumption | потребление | pat-rib-lyé-ni-ye | 45a |
| contact lenses | контактные линзы | kan-táhkt-ny-i lín-zy | 41a |
| contacts (list) | список контактов | spí-sak kan-táhk-tov | 18a, 20b |
| continent | континент | kan-ti-nyént | 13e, 31a |
| continue | продолжать (-ся) | pra-dal-zháht' (-tsa) | 4e |
| contraband | контрабанда | kan-tra-báhn-da | 42 |
| contract | договор/контракт | da-ga-vór/kant-ráhkt | 39d |
| contract form | бланк договора | blahnk da-ga-vó-ra | 27 |
| contrary | противоречивый | pra-ti-va-ri-chí-vyj | 11e |
| controversy | спор, полемика | spohr, pa-lyé-mi-ka | 42 |
| convalesce | выздоравливать | vyz-da-ráh-vli-vat' | 41a |
| conversation | разговор | raz-ga-vór | 17a |
| convince, persuade | убеждать | u-bi-zhdáht' | 22b, 42 |
| cook | повар (m&f) | pó-var | 39a |
| cook, to | готовить | ga-tó-vit' | 24b, 24o |
| cookie | куки | koó-ki | 20b |
| cookies | печенье (coll) | pi-chyén-ye | 24g |
| cool | прохладный | prakh-láhd-nyj | 6a |
| copper | медь (f) | myet' | 13c |
| copy | копия | kó-pi-ya | 29c |
| copy | скопировать (p) | ska-pí-ra-vat' | 20b |
| copy a file | копировать (i), | ska-pí-ra-vat' | 20b |
| | скопировать (p) файл | ska-pí-ra-vat' fahjl | |
| copy, to | переписывать | pi-ri-pí-sy-vat' | 38f |
| corn | кукуруза | ku-ku-róo-za | 14e, 24i |
| corner (street) | угол улицы | óo-gal óo-li-tsy | 34c |
| Correct? | Правильно? | práh-vil'-na | 17b |
| correspondence | переписка, письма (pl) | pi-ri-pís-ka, pís'-ma | 19f |
| corridor | коридор | ka-ri-dór | 23a |
| corruption | коррупция | ka-rúp-tsy-ya | 44 |
| cosmos | космос | kós-mas | 13a |
| cost | стоимость (f) | stó-í-mast' | 25a, 26 |
| cost, to | стоить | stó-it' | 24o, 25a |
| cottage | коттедж/дача | ka-téhdzh/dáh-cha | 27, 37a |
| cotton (processed) | хлопчатобумажный | khlap-cháh-ta-bu-máhzh-nyj | 25l |
| cotton (raw) | хлопок | khló-pak | 13c |
| cotton wool | вата | váh-ta | 25h |
| cottonwood | тополь (m) | tó-pol' | 14c |
| cough | кашель (m) | káh-shyl' | 41a |
| council | совет | sa-vyét | 44 |
| counter | прилавок | pri-láh-vak | 25a |
| country | страна | stra-náh | 11f, 13e, 31a |
| country home | загородный дом | záh-ga-rad-nyj dom | 27 |
| coupon, voucher | купон | ku-pón | 26 |
| courage | отвага | at-váh-ga | 11e |
| courageous | отважный, смелый | at-váhzh-nyj, smyé-lyj | 11e |
| courier | курьер | kur'-yér | 19f |
| course | курс | koors | 38f |
| court | суд | soot | 42 |

| | | | |
|---|---|---|---|
| **courteous** | вежливый | *vyézh-li-vyj* | 11e |
| **courtesy** | вежливость *(f)* | *vyézh-li-vast'* | 11e |
| **courthouse** | здание суда | *zdáh-ni-ye su-dáh* | 42 |
| **courtroom** | зал суда | *zahl su-dáh* | 42 |
| **cousin** | двоюродный брат *(m),* | *dva-yú-rad-nyj braht,* | |
| | двоюродная сестра *(f)* | *dva-yú-rad-na-ya* | 10a |
| | | *sist-ráh* | |
| **cover** | обложка | *ab-lósh-ka* | 20a |
| **cow** | корова | *ka-ró-va* | 15a |
| **crab** | краб | *krahp* | 15d |
| **crane** | журавль *(m)* | *zhu-ráhvl'* | 15a |
| **crash** | крушение | *kru-shéh-ni-ye* | 40c |
| **crash, to** | разбиться | *raz-bí-tsa* | 40c |
| **crazy, mad** | сумасшедший | *su-ma-shéht-shyj* | 11e |
| **cream (cosmetics)** | крем | *krehm* | 25f |
| **cream (dairy)** | сливки *(pl)* | *slíf-ki* | 24h |
| **create *(v)* a file** | создать *(p)* файл, | *saz-dáht' fahjl,* | 20b |
| | создавать *(i)* | *saz-da-váht'* | |
| **creating files *(pl)*** | создание файлов *(pl)* | *saz-dáh-ni-ye fáhjl-of* | 20b |
| **credit** | кредит | *kri-dít* | 26, 27 |
| **credit card** | кредитная карточка | *kri-dít-na-ya káhr-tach-ka* | 25a, 26, |
| | | | 36b |
| **credit rating** | кредитоспособность | *kri-dí-ta-spa-sób-nast'* | 27 |
| **crepe** | блин | *blin* | 24g |
| **crew** | экипаж | *y-ki-páhsh* | 33c |
| **crime** | преступление | *pris-tup-lyé-ni-ye* | 40b |
| **crime wave** | волна преступлений | *val-náh pris-tup-lyé-nij* | 40b |
| **criminal** | преступный | *pris-tóop-nyj* | 40b |
| **critical** | критический | *kri-tí-chis-kij* | 11e |
| **criticism** | критика | *krí-ti-ka* | 20a, 29d |
| **crocodile** | крокодил | *kra-ka-díl* | 15c |
| **chronic (illness)** | хроническое | *khra-ní-chis-ka-ye* | 45b |
| **cross (over)** | перейти улицу | *pi-rij-tí óo-li-tsu* | 37d |
| **cross-country skiing** | ходить на лыжах | *kha-dít' na lý-zhakh* | 28b |
| **crown** | коронка | *ka-rón-ka* | 41b |
| **cruise** | морское | *mar-skó-ye* | 37a, 37c |
| | путешествие | *pu-ti-shéhst-vi-ye* | |
| | круиз | *kru-ís* | 37a |
| **cry** | плакать | *pláh-kat'* | 11e, 21a |
| **crying** | плач | *plahch* | 21a |
| **cube** | куб | *koop* | 2a |
| **cubic** | кубический | *ku-bí-chis-kij* | 3a |
| **cucumber** | огурец (-рцы) *(pl)* | *a-gu-ryéts (a-gur-tsý)* | 14e, 24e |
| **cultivate** | обрабатывать, | *ab-ra-báh-ty-vat',* | 14a |
| | растить, выращивать | *ras-tít', vy-ráh-shchi-vat'* | |
| **cultured** | культурный | *kul'-tóor-nyj* | 11e |
| **cunning, crafty** | хитрый | *khít-ryj* | 11e |
| **cup** | чашка | *cháhsh-ka* | 23d, 24l |
| **cupboard** | шкаф | *shkahf* | 23b |
| **cure** | лечение | *li-chyé-ni-ye* | 41a |
| **cure, to** | вылечить | *vý-li-chit'* | 41a |
| **curiosity** | любопытство | *lyu-ba-pýt-stva* | 11e |

| curious | любопытный | *lyu-ba-pýt-nyj* | 11e |
| curler | бигуди *(coll)* | *bi-gu-dí* | 25f |
| curls | кудри *(pl)* | *kóod-ri* | 12d |
| curly-haired | кудрявый | *kud-ryáh-vyj* | 11a |
| currency | валюта | *va-lyú-ta* | 26 |
| current | ток | *tok* | 36c |
| current account | текущий счёт | *ti-kóo-shchij shchyot* | 26 |
| cursor | курсор | *kóor-sar* | 20b |
| curtain | занавесь *(f)* (-ка) | *záh-na-vis'* | 23c, 29e, |
|  |  | *(za-na-vés-ka)* | 36c |
| curve | извилина | *iz-ví-li-na* | 34c |
| customer | покупатель *(m)*, | *pa-ku-páh-til'*, | 25a, |
|  | покупательница *(f)*, | *pa-ku-páh-til'-ni-tsa,* | 26 |
|  | клиент (-ка) | *kli-yént (-ka)* |  |
| customs | таможня | *ta-mózh-nya* | 32 |
| cut one's hair | остричь волосы, | *a-strích vó-la-sy,* | 12d |
|  | постричься | *pa-strích-sya* |  |
| cut | резать (по-, на-) | *ryé-zat' (pa-, na-)* | 24o |
| cutlery, tableware | столовый прибор | *sta-ló-vyj pri-bór* | 24l |
| cutlet | котлета | *kat-lyé-ta* | 24g |
| cylinder | цилиндр | *tsy-líndr* | 2a |
| cymbals | тарелки *(pl)* | *ta-ryél-ki* | 29c |
| cypress | кипарис | *ki-pa-rís* | 14c |
| Czech Republic | Чехия | *chyé-khi-ya* | 31b |

**D**

| dad | папа *(m)* | *páh-pa* | 10a |
| daffodil | нарцисс | *nar-tsýs* | 14b |
| daily | ежедневно *(adv)* | *i-zhy-dnyév-na* | 4c |
| daisy | маргаритка | *mar-ga-rít-ka* | 14b |
| dance, to | танцевать | *tan-tsy-váht'* | 29c, 30b |
| dance | танец | *táh-nits* | 29c, 30b |
| dancer | танцовщик *(m)*, | *tan-tsaf-shchík,* | 29c |
|  | танцовщица *(f)* | *tan-tsaf-shchí-tsa* |  |
| dandruff | перхоть *(f)* | *pyér-khat'* | 41a |
| Dane | датчанин (-чанка) | *dat-cháh-nin (-cháhn-ka)* | 31d |
| danger | опасность *(f)* | *a-páhs-nast'* | 40a, 45b |
| Danish | датский | *dáhts-kij* | 31d |
| dark | тёмный *(adj)* | *tyóm-nyj* | 6a, 7b |
| dashboard | приборная доска | *pri-bór-na-ya das-káh* | 34e |
| data | данные | *dáhn-y-ye* | 20b |
| database | база данных | *báh-za dáh-nykh* | 20b |
| date (time) | дата | *dáh-ta* | 19d |
| date (fruit) | финик | *fí-nik* | 14d, 24f |
| date | свидание | *svi-dáh-ni-ye* | 10b |
| date and place of birth | дата и место | *dáh-ta i myés-ta* | 39b |
|  | рождения | *razh-dyé-ni-ya* |  |
| date and year of birth | день и год рождения | *dyen' i god razh-dyé-ni-ya* | 11f |
| dative | дательный | *dáh-til'-nyj* | 8a |
| daughter | дочь *(f)*/дочка | *doch/dóch-ka* | 10a |
| daughter-in-law | невестка | *ni-vyést-ka* | 10a |
| dawn | рассвет | *ras-vyét* | 4a |

| day | день *(m)* (дни *pl*) | *dyen' (dni)* | 4a, 4c, 38a |
| day care, kindergarten | детский сад | *dyéts-kij saht* | 38a |
| deaf | глухой | *glu-khój* | 12c |
| deafness | глухота | *glu-kha-táh* | 12c |
| Dear | Дорогой *(m)*, Дорогая *(f)* | *da-ra-gój*, *da-ra-gáh-ya* | 19c |
| Dear Madam | Дорогая гражданка, Дорогая госпожа | *da-ra-gáh-ya grazh-dáhn-ka*, *da-ra-gáh-ya gas-pa-zháh* | 19b |
| Dear Sir | Дорогой товарищ/ гражданин, Дорогой господин, Уважаемый | *da-ra-gój ta-váh-rishch/ grazh-da-nín*, *da-ra-gój gas-pa-dín*, *u-va-zháh-i-myj* | 19b |
| death | смерть *(f)* | *smyert'* | 11c |
| debate | обсуждение | *ab-suzh-dyé-ni-ye* | 42 |
| debate, to; discuss, to | обсудить *(p)*, обсуждать *(i)* | *ap-su-dít'*, *ap-suzh-dáht'* | 17a, 42 |
| debt | долг | *dolk* | 26 |
| decade | декада, десятилетка | *dy-káh-da, di-si-ti-lyét-ka* | 4c |
| December | декабрь *(m)* | *di-káh-bar'* | 5b |
| declaration | декларация | *dik-la-ráh-tsy-ya* | 32 |
| declare (to show) | называть | *na-zy-váht'* | 32 |
| declare (to announce) | объявлять | *ab'-iv-lyáht'* | 17a |
| declension | склонение | *skla-nyé-ni-ye* | 8a |
| decorated | украшенный | *u-kráh-shy-nyj* | 23c |
| decrease | уменьшение *(n)*, уменьшиться | *u-min-shéh-ni-ye*, *u-myén-shy-tsa* | 3c |
| deer | олень *(m)*, олениха *(f)* | *a-lyén', a-li-ní-kha* | 15a |
| defecate | иметь стул | *i-myét' stool* | 41a |
| defend oneself | защищаться | *za-shchi-shcháh-tsa* | 42 |
| definition | определение | *ap-ri-di-lyé-ni-ye* | 20a |
| degree | градус | *gráh-dus* | 2b, 6c |
| delete | удалить *(p)*, удалять *(i)* | *u-da-lít'*, *u-da-lyáht'* | 19a, 20b |
| delicatessen | магазин-кулинария | *ma-ga-zín-ku-li-ná-ri-ya* | 24n |
| democracy | демократия | *di-mak-ráh-ti-ya* | 44 |
| demonstrate | показывать | *pa-káh-zy-vat'* | 22b |
| Denmark | Дания | *dáh-ni-ya* | 31b |
| dense | плотный | *plót-nyj* | 3b |
| dentist | зубной врач *(m&f)* | *zub-nój vrahch* | 39a, 41b |
| denture, false teeth | вставные зубы | *fstav-ný-i zóo-by* | 41b |
| deny | отрицать | *at-ri-tsáht'* | 17d |
| deodorant | дезодорант | *di-ó-da-rant* | 12d, 25f |
| department (of store) | отдел | *at-dyél* | 25a |
| department store | универсальный магазин | *u-ni-vir-sáhl'-nyj ma-ga-zín* | 25a |
| departure | отъезд | *at'-yést* | 33a |
| deposit | вклад | *vklahd* | 26 |
| deposit, to | вложить | *vla-zhýt'* | 26 |
| depressed | подавленный, удручённый | *pa-dáhv-li-nyj*, *ud-ru-chyó-nyj* | 21a |
| depression | депрессия | *dip-ryé-si-ya* | 21a |

| | | | |
|---|---|---|---|
| deputy | депутат | *di-pu-táht* | 44 |
| describe | описать | *a-pi-sáht'* | 17a |
| description | описание | *a-pi-sáh-ni-ye* | 17a, 40b |
| desert | пустыня | *pus-tý-nya* | 13b |
| desk (student's) | парта | *páhr-ta* | 38b |
| desk (teacher's) | учительский стол | *u-chí-til's-kij stohl* | 38b |
| desperate | отчаянный | *at-cháh-i-nyj* | 21a |
| desperation | отчаяние | *at-cháh-i-ni-ye* | 21a |
| dessert | десерт, сладкое | *di-syért, sláht-ka-ye* | 24g |
| destroy | разрушить | *raz-róo-shyt'* | 40a |
| detective | следователь *(m)* | *slyé-da-va-til'* | 40b |
| detergent | стиральный порошок | *sti-ráhl-nyj pa-ra-shók* | 25g |
| detestable | отвратительный | *at-vra-tí-til'-nyj* | 21b |
| developing countries | развивающиеся страны | *raz-vi-váh-yuh-shchi-i-sya stráh-ny* | 44 |
| development (improvement) | развитие | *raz-ví-ti-ye* | 44 |
| dial | набирать (номер) | *na-bi-rát' (nó-mir)* | 18b |
| dialogue | диалог | *di-a-lók* | 20b |
| diamond | бриллиант | *bri-li-áhnt* | 25i |
| dice | игральные кости *(pl)* | *ig-ráhl'-ny-i kós-ti* | 28a |
| dictation | диктант | *dik-táhnt* | 38f |
| dictionary | словарь *(m)* | *sla-váhr'* | 20a, 25o, 38b |
| die | умирать | *u-mi-ráht'* | 11c |
| difference | разница | *ráhz-ni-tsa* | 1f |
| difficult | тяжёлый, трудный | *ti-zhó-lyj, tróod-nyj* | 11e, 22a |
| dig | рыть/копать | *ryt'/ka-pát'* | 14a |
| digestive system | пищеварительные органы *(pl)* | *pi-shchi-va-rí-til'-ny-ye ór-ga-ny* | 41a |
| digital camera | цифровой фотоаппарат, цифровая камера | *tsyf-ra-vój fá-ta-a-pa-ráht, tsyf-ra-váh-ya káh-mi-ra* | 25d |
| digital photography | цифровая фотография | *tsyf-ra-váh-ya fa-ta-gráh-fi-ya* | 25d |
| diligence | трудолюбие | *tru-da-lyú-bi-ye* | 11e |
| diligent | трудолюбивый | *tru-da-lyú-bi-vyj* | 11e |
| dill | укроп *(coll)* | *uk-róp* | 14e, 24e |
| dining car | вагон-ресторан | *va-gón-res-ta-ráhn* | 35 |
| dining room | столовая | *sta-ló-va-ya* | 23b |
| dinner | ужин | *óo-zhyn* | 24a |
| diploma | диплом | *dip-lóm* | 11f, 38f |
| diplomatic | дипломатичный | *dip-la-ma-tích-nyj* | 11e |
| directory | директория | *di-rik-tó-ri-ya* | 20b |
| dirty | грязный *(adj)*, грязно *(adv)* | *gryáz-nyj, gryáz-na* | 11a, 12d, 25g |
| disagree, to | разойтись во мнении | *ra-zaj-tís' va mnyé-ni-i* | 42 |
| disagree (not to agree) | не соглашаться | *ni sag-la-sháh-tsa* | 21a |
| disagreement | разногласие, расхождение | *raz-na-gláh-si-ye, ras-khazh-dyé-ni-ye* | 21a |
| disc player | дисковод | *dis-ka-vód* | 20e |

| disco | дискотека | *dis-ka-tyé-ka* | 37a |
| discontent | недовольный | *ni-da-vól'-nyj* | 11e |
| discount | скидка | *skít-ka* | 25a, 26 |
| discourse | обороты речи | *a-ba-ró-ty ryé-chi* | 8a |
| discourteous | грубый | *gróo-byj* | 11e |
| discussion | обсуждение | *ap-suzh-dyé-ni-ye* | 17a |
| disease | болезнь *(f)* | *ba-lyézn'* | 11a |
| disgust | отвращение | *at-vra-shchyé-ni-ye* | 21b |
| disgusting | отвратительный | *at-vra-tí-til'-nyj* | 21b |
| dishwasher | посудомоечная | *pa-sóo-da-mó-ich-na-ya* | 23d |
| | машина, | *ma-shý-na,* | |
| | посудомойка | *pa-su-da-mój-ka* | |
| dishes | посуда *(coll)* | *pa-sóo-da* | 23d |
| dishonest | нечестный, | *ni-chyés-nyj,* | 11e |
| | непорядочный | *ni-pa-ryáh-dach-nyj* | |
| disk | диск | *disk* | 20b |
| dislike | не нравиться | *ni nráh-vi-tsa* | 21b |
| display | дисплей | *dis-plyéj* | 18a |
| dissatisfaction | недовольство | *ni-da-vól'st-va* | 21a |
| dissatisfied | недовольный | *ni-da-vól'-nyj* | 21a |
| distance | расстояние | *ras-ta-yáh-ni-ye* | 34c |
| distribution list | список рассылки | *spí-sak ras-sýl-ki* | 19a |
| divide | разделить | *raz-di-lít'* | 1e |
| diving | дайвинг | *dáhj-vink* | 28b |
| divorce, to | развестись | *raz-vis-tís'* | 11c |
| divorce | развод | *raz-vód* | 11c |
| divorced | разведённый | *raz-vi-dyón-yj* | 11c |
| Do you have a vacant room? | У вас *(pol)* есть свободная комната? | *u vahs yest' sva-bód-na-ya kóm-na-ta* | 36b |
| doctor | врач *(m&f)*, | *vrahch*, | 39a, 41a, |
| | доктор | *dók-tar* | 40c |
| doctor's visit | посещение врача | *pa-si-shchyé-ni-ye vra-cháh* | 41a |
| documentary | документальный | *da-ku-min-táhl'-nyj* | 20b |
| | фильм | *fil'm* | |
| documents | документы | *da-ku-myén-ty* | 20b, 32 |
| dog | собака | *sa-báh-ka* | 15a |
| dollar | доллар | *dó-lar* | 26 |
| dolphin | дельфин | *dil'-fín* | 15c |
| domain | домен | *da-myén* | 20d |
| domino | домино | *da-mi-nó* | 28a |
| Don't mention it! | Не за что! | *nye za shta* | 16c |
| donkey | осёл | *a-syól* | 15a |
| door | дверь *(f)* | *dvyer'* | 23a, 34e |
| doorbell | звонок | *zva-nók* | 23a |
| doorman | швейцар | *shvij-tsáhr* | 36b |
| double-click *(n)* | двойной щелчок | *dvaj-nój shchil-chók* | 20b |
| double-click *(v)* | кликнуть/щёлкнуть | *klík-nut'/shchyólk-nut'* | 20b |
| | два раза | *dvah ráh-za* | |
| double room | комната на двоих | *kóm-na-ta na dva-íkh* | 36b |
| doubt | сомнение | *sam-nyé-ni-ye* | 22a |

| | | | |
|---|---|---|---|
| doubt, to | сомневаться | *sam-ni-váh-tsa* | 22b |
| dove, pigeon | голубь *(m)* | *gó-lup'* | 15b |
| down | вниз | *vnis* | 3d, 37d |
| downhill skiing | горнолыжный спорт | *gar-na-lýzh-nyj sport* | 28b |
| downhill skis *(pl)* | горные лыжи *(pl)* | *gór-ny-i lý-zhy* | 28b |
| downhill (skiing) slope | горнолыжная трасса | *gar-na-lýzh-na-ya tráh-sa* | 28b |
| download *(v)* | скачать *(p)*, скачивать *(i)* | *ska-cháht',* *skáh-chi-vat'* | 20d, 25j |
| download music | скачать *(p)* музыку | *ska-cháht' móo-zy-ku* | 25j |
| drafting | черчение | *chir-chyé-ni-ye* | 38e |
| drama | драма | *dráh-ma* | 20a, 29e |
| draw, tie | ничья *(indecl)* | *ních'-yah* | 28b |
| drawer | ящик | *yáh-shchik* | 23c |
| drawing | рисунок | *ri-sóo-nak* | 29b |
| dress | платье | *pláht'-ye* | 25k |
| drill (machine) | бормашина | *bor-ma-shý-na* | 41b |
| drill (manual) | сверло | *svir-ló* | 25b |
| drill, to | сверлить | *svir-lít'* | 41b |
| drink | напиток | *na-pí-tak* | 24k |
| drink, to | пить, выпить | *pit', vý-pit'* | 12b, 24o |
| drive (disk) | драйв | *drahjf* | 20b |
| drive a vehicle | водить машину | *va-dít' ma-shý-nu* | 34c |
| drive *(n)* | дисковод | *dis-ka-vót* | 20b |
| drive (go) | ехать, ездить | *yé-khat',* *yé-zdit'* | 3e |
| driver | водитель *(m)*, водительница *(f)* | *va-dí-til',* *va-dí-til'-ni-tsa* | 34b |
| driver's license | водительские права | *va-dí-til'-ski-ye pra-váh* | 34b |
| driveway | въезд, подъезд | *v'-yést, pad'-yést* | 27 |
| drizzle | мелкий дождь *(n, m)* | *myél-kij dozht'* | 6a |
| drizzle, to | моросить | *ma-ra-sít'* | 6a |
| drop (of rain) | капля (дождя) | *káhp-lya (dazh-dyáh)* | 6a |
| drop a token | бросить жетон | *bró-sit' zhy-tón* | 35 |
| drug (legal) | лекарство | *li-káhr-stva* | 25h |
| drug (illegal) | наркотик | *nar-kó-tik* | 45b |
| drug addiction | наркомания | *nar-ka-máh-ni-ya* | 45b |
| drug user | потребитель *(m)*, наркотиков, потребительница *(f)*, наркопотребитель *(m)*, наркопотребительница *(f)* | *pat-ri-bí-til',* *nar-kó-ti-kaf,* *pat-ri-bí-til'-ni-tsa,* *náhr-ka-pat-ri-bí-til',* *náhr-ka-pat-ri-bí-til'-ni-tsa* | 45b |
| drugstore/pharmacy | аптека | *ap-tyé-ka* | 25h |
| drum | барабан | *ba-ra-báhn* | 29c |
| drunk | пьяный | *p'yáh-nyj* | 24o |
| dry | сухой | *su-khój* | 6a |
| dry cleaner | химчистка | *khim-chíst-ka* | 25g |
| dryer (clothes) | сушильная машина, сушилка (для белья) | *su-shýl'-na-ya ma-shý-na,* *su-shýl-ka (dlyah bil'-yáh)* | 23d |
| dry oneself | вытереться | *vý-ti-ri-tsa* | 12d |

| | | | |
|---|---|---|---|
| dry the dishes | вытереть посуду | *vý-ti-rit' pa-sóo-du* | 23f |
| duck | утка *(f)*, селезень *(m)* | *óot-ka, syé-li-zin'* | 15b, 24c |
| due to (thanks to) | благодаря (тому) | *bla-ga-da-ryáh (ta-móo)* | 8h |
| dull | тусклый/мутный | *tóosk-lyj/móot-nyj* | 7b |
| Duma | Дума | *dóo-ma* | 44 |
| duplex | дуплекс | *dóop-liks* | 27 |
| during | в, во, в течение, | *v, va, f ti-chyé-ni-ye,* | 4e, 8d |
| | во время | *va vryé-mya* | |
| dustpan | совок | *sa-vók* | 23d |
| Dutch | голландец (-дка) | *ga-láhn-dits (-tka)* | 31d |
| Dutch | голландский | *ga-láhn-skij* | 31d |
| duty | лошлина, тариф | *pósh-li-na, ta-ríf* | 32 |
| DVD | дивиди | *di-vi-di* | 20e |
| DVD player | дивиди | *di-vi-di pra-íg-ry-va-tel'* | 20e |
| | проигрыватель | | |

## E

| | | | |
|---|---|---|---|
| eagle | орёл | *a-ryól* | 15b |
| ear | ухо | *óo-kha* | 12a |
| early | рано | *ráh-na* | 4e, 33b, 35 |
| earn | заработать | *za-ra-bó-tat'* | 39d |
| earring | серьга | *sir'-gáh* | 25i |
| Earth | Земля | *zim-lyáh* | 13a |
| earthquake | землетрясение | *zim-li-tri-syé-ni-ye* | 13b |
| easily | легко | *likh-kó* | 22a |
| east | восток | *vas-tók* | 3d |
| Easter | Пасха | *páhs-kha* | 5e, 11d, 30a |
| Eastern Orthodox | православный | *pra-va-sláhv-nyj* | 11d |
| easy | лёгкий | *lyókh-kij* | 22a |
| eat | есть | *yést'* | 12b |
| eccentric | эксцентричный | *yk-tsyn-trích-nyj* | 11e |
| eclipse | затмение | *zat-myé-ni-ye* | 13a |
| economics | экономика | *y-ka-nó-mi-ka* | 38e, 44 |
| ecosystem | экосистема | *y-ka-sis-tyé-ma* | 45a |
| eco-tourism | эко-туризм | *y-ka-tu-rízm* | 37a |
| edit *(v)* | отредактировать *(p)*, | *at-ri-dak-tí-ra-vat',* | 20b |
| | редактировать *(i)* | *ri-dak-tí-ra-vat'* | |
| editor | редактор *(m&f)* | *ri-dáhk-tar* | 20a, 39a |
| editorial | редакционная статья | *ri-dak-tsy-ó-na-ya stat'-yáh* | 20a |
| educated | образованный *(m)* | *ab-ra-zó-va-nyj* | 11e, 38f |
| education | образование | *ab-ra-za-váh-ni-ye* | 11e, 11f, 38f, 40b |
| eel | угорь *(m)* | *óo-gar'* | 15c, 24d |
| egg | яйцо | *ij-tsó* | 24h |
| eggplant | баклажан | *bak-la-zháhn* | 14e, 24e |
| egoism | эгоизм | *e-ga-ízm* | 11e |
| egotist | эгоист | *y-ga-íst* | 11e |
| egotistic | эгоистичный | *y-ga-is-tích-nyj* | 11e |
| Egypt | Египет | *i-gí-pet* | 31b |

| | | | |
|---|---|---|---|
| eight | восемь | *vó-sim'* | 1a |
| eighteen | восемнадцать | *va-sim-náh-tsat'* | 1a |
| eighth | восьмой | *vas'-mój* | 1b |
| eighty | восемьдесят | *vó-sem-di-sit* | 1a |
| elastic | эластичный | *y-las-tích-nyj* | 13d |
| elbow | локоть *(m)* | *ló-kat'* | 12a |
| elderly person | пожилой человек | *pa-zhy-lój chi-la-vyék* | 11b |
| elect | выбрать | *výb-rat'* | 44 |
| elected body | выборный орган | *vý-bar-nyj ór-gan* | 44 |
| electric current converter | конвертер | *kan-vyér-tyr* | 23d |
| electrical | электрический | *y-likt-rí-chis-kij* | 13c |
| electrician | электрик/монтёр | *y-lyékt-rik/man-tyór* | 39a |
| electricity | электричество | *y-likt-rí-chist-va* | 13c, 23e |
| electrocardiograph | электрокардиограф | *y-lyekt-ra-kar-di-a-gráhf* | 41a |
| electron | электрон | *y-likt-rón* | 43 |
| elegance | элегантность *(f)* | *y-li-gáhnt-nast'* | 11a |
| elegant | элегантный | *y-li-gáhnt-nyj* | 11a, 25l |
| element | элемент | *y-li-myént* | 13c |
| elementary school | начальная школа | *na-cháhl'-na-ya shkó-la* | 38a, 38d, 39b |
| elephant | слон | *slóhn* | 15a |
| elevator | лифт | *lift* | 23g, 36b |
| eleven | одиннадцать | *a-dí-na-tsat'* | 1a |
| e-mail | электронная почта | *i-lik-trón-a-ya póch-ta* | 19a |
| e-mail message | сообщение, письмо | *sa-ap-shchyé-ni-ye, pis'-mó* | 19a |
| emergency exit | запасной выход | *za-pas-nój vý-khat* | 40a |
| emphasis | ударение | *u-da-ryé-ni-ye* | 17a |
| emphasize | подчёркивать | *pat-chyór-ki-vat'* | 17a |
| employee (bank) | служащий (-ая) (банка) | *slóo-zha-shchij (-a-ya) (báhn-ka)* | 26 |
| employee | работник, служащий | *ra-bót-nik, slóo-zha-shchij* | 39d |
| employer | наниматель *(m)*, работодатель *(m)* | *na-ni-máh-til', ra-ba-ta-dáh-til'* | 39d |
| employment agency | трудовое агентство | *tru-da-vó-ye a-gyénst-va* | 39d |
| empty | пустой/порожний | *pus-tój/pa-rózh-nij* | 3c |
| empty *(adj)* file | пустая папка | *pus-táh-ya páhp-ka* | 20b |
| encourage | подбодрить | *pad-bad-rít'* | 21a |
| encouragement | поощрение | *pa-ashch-ryé-ni-ye* | 21a |
| encyclopedia | энциклопедия | *yn-tsy-kla-pyé-di-ya* | 20a, 25o, 38b |
| end, to; finish, to | кончать | *kan-cháht'* | 4e |
| end | конец | *ka-nyéts* | 4e |
| endorse (sign) | подписать | *pat-pi-sáht'* | 26 |
| enemy | враг | *vrahk* | 10b |
| energetic | энергичный | *y-nyr-gích-nyj* | 11e |
| energy | энергия | *y-néhr-gi-ya* | 11e, 13c |
| engaged | обручённый | *a-bru-chyó-nyj* | 11c |

| | | | |
|---|---|---|---|
| engagement | обручение | *a-bru-chyé-ni-ye* | 11c, 30a |
| engineer | инженер *(m&f)* | *yn-zhy-nyér* | 39a |
| engineering (sciences) | инженерное дело | *yn-zhy-nyér-na-ye dyé-la* | 38c |
| England | Англия | *áhng-li-ya* | 31b |
| enlargement | увеличение | *u-vi-li-chyé-ni-ye* | 25d |
| English (person) | англичанин (-нка) | *ang-li-cháh-nin (-nka)* | 31d |
| English | английский | *ang-lís-kij* | 31d, 38e |
| enough | достаточно *(adv)* | *das-táh-tach-na* | 3c |
| Enough! | Хватит! | *khváh-tit* | 21c |
| enter | войти | *vaj-tí* | 3e, 16b, |
| | входить | *fkha-dít'* | 37d |
| enter (key) | ввести *(p)*, вести *(i)* | *vvis-tí, vis-tí* | 26 |
| entire | целый *(adj)*, | *tséh-lyj,* | 3c |
| | целиком *(adv)* | *tsy-li-kóm* | |
| entrance | вход | *vkhot* | 23a, 25a, |
| | | | 36b |
| entrepreneur | предприниматель | *prit-pri-ni-máh-til'* | 39a |
| | (-ница) | *(-ni-tsa)* | |
| envelope | конверт | *kan-vyért* | 19e, 19f, |
| | | | 25c |
| envious | завистливый | *za-vís-li-vyj* | 11e |
| environment | окружающая среда | *ak-ru-zháh-yu-shcha-ya* | 13b |
| | | *sri-dáh* | |
| envy | зависть | *záh-vist'* | 11e |
| epidemic | эпидемия | *y-pi-dyé-mi-ya* | 45b |
| equation | уравнение | *u-rav-nyé-ni-ye* | 1f |
| equator | экватор | *yk-váh-tar* | 13e |
| erase the chalkboard | вытереть доску | *vý-ti-rit' dóhs-ku* | 38b |
| eraser | ластик, резинка | *láhs-tik, ri-zín-ka* | 19e, 38b |
| erotica | эротика | *y-ró-ti-ka* | 45b |
| error, mistake | ошибка | *a-shýp-ka* | 20b, 38f |
| eruption | извержение | *iz-vir-zhéh-ni-ye* | 13b |
| escape, get out | бежать | *bi-zháht'* | 40a |
| espresso-machine | кофеварка эспрессо | *ka-fi-váhr-ka yks-prýe-sa* | 23d |
| essay | очерк, сочинение | *óchirk, sa-chi-nyé-ni-ye* | 29d, 38f |
| Estonia | Эстония | *ys-tó-ni-ya* | 31b |
| euro | евро | *yév-ra* | 26 |
| Europe | Европа | *iv-r-ópa* | 31b |
| evening | вечер | *vyé-chir* | 4a |
| every, each | каждый | *kázh-dyj* | 3c |
| everything | всё | *fsto* | 3c |
| everywhere | всюду/везде | *fsyú-du/viz-dyé* | 37d |
| exam, test | экзамен | *yk-záh-min* | 38f |
| examine | проверить | *pra-vyé-rit'* | 41b |
| examine (medically) | осмотреть | *as-mat-ryét'* | 41a |
| exchange | обмен | *ab-myén* | 26 |
| exchange rates (currency) | курс обмена (валюты) | *koors ab-myé-na (va-lyú-ty)* | 26, 31a |
| exclamation mark | восклицательный знак | *vask-li-tsáh-til'-nyj zahnk* | 19d |
| excursion | экскурсия | *yks-kóor-si-ya* | 31a, 37a |

| | | | |
|---|---|---|---|
| excuse | извинение | *iz-vi-nyé-ni-ye* | 17a |
| excuse (yourself) | извиниться | *iz-vi-ní-tsa* | 17a |
| Excuse me! | Извини (меня)! *(fam)* | *iz-vi-ní (mi-nyáh)*, | |
| | Извините (меня) *(pol)* | *iz-vi-ní-ti (mi-nyáh)* | 16c |
| exercise | упражнение | *up-razh-nyé-ni-ye* | 38f |
| exercise room | тренажёрный зал | *tri-na-zhór-nyj zahl* | 28b |
| exhibit | выставка | *výs-taf-ka* | 37a |
| exhibition | выставка | *výs-taf-ka* | 20b, 29b |
| existence | существование | *su-shchi-stva-váh-ni-ye* | 22a |
| exit, go out | выйти | *výj-ti* | 37d |
| Exit (road sign) | Выезд | *vý-yest* | 34d |
| exit | выход | *vý-khat* | 25a, 36b |
| expensive | дорогой | *da-ra-gój* | 24p |
| expensively | дорого | *dó-ra-ga* | 24p |
| expiration date (valid until) | действительно до | *di-ství-til'-na da* | 26 |
| explain | объяснить | *ab-is-nít'* | 17a, 38f |
| explanation | объяснение | *ab'is-nyé-ni-ye* | 17a, 38f |
| exposure | экспозиция | *yks-pa-zí-tsy-ya* | 25d |
| express | выразить | *vý-ra-zit'* | 17a |
| expression | выражение | *vy-ra-zhéh-ni-ye* | 17a |
| extinguish, put out | погасить, потушить | *pa-ga-sít', pa-tu-shýt'* | 40a |
| extract, pull | удалить | *u-da-lít'* | 41b |
| extraction | удаление | *u-da-lyé-ni-ye* | 41b |
| eye | глаз | *glahs* | 12a |
| eye doctor | глазной врач | *glaz-nój vrahch* | 41a |
| eyebrow | бровь *(f)* | *brof'* | 12a |
| eyeglasses | очки | *ach-kí* | 41a |
| eyelash | ресница | *ris-ní-tsa* | 12a |
| eyelid | веко | *vyé-ka* | 12a |
| eyewitness | очевидец *(m)* | *a-chi-ví-dits* | 42 |
| | (-дица) *(f)* | *(-di-tsa)* | |

**F**

| | | | |
|---|---|---|---|
| fabric | материал | *ma-ti-ri-áhl* | 251 |
| face | лицо | *li-tsó* | 12a |
| faction | фракция | *fráhk-tsy-ya* | 44 |
| factory | фабрика | *fáhb-ri-ka* | 39d |
| factory worker | рабочий (-ая) | *ra-bó-chij (-a-ya)* | 39a |
| | фабрики | *fáhb-ri-ki* | |
| Fahrenheit | Фаренгейт | *fa-rin-gyéjt* | 6c |
| fail an exam | завалить экзамен | *za-va-lít' yk-záh-min* | 38f |
| fair-haired | светловолосый | *svit-la-va-ló-syj* | 11a |
| fairy tale | волшебная сказка | *val-shéhb-na-ya skáhs-ka* | 29d |
| faith, trust | доверие | *da-vyé-ri-ye* | 21a |
| faith | вера | *vyé-ra* | 11d |
| faithful | верный, преданный | *vyér-nyj, pryé-da-nyj* | 11e |
| fall (season) | осень *(f)* | *ó-sin'* | 5c |
| fall, to | упасть | *u-páhst'* | 3e |
| fall asleep | заснуть | *za-snóot'* | 12b |

| | | | |
|---|---|---|---|
| fall in love | влюбиться | *vlyu-bí-tsa* | 10b, 11c |
| family | семья | *si-m'yáh* | 10a |
| family name | фамилия | *fa-mí-li-ya* | 11f, 39b |
| family planning | планирование семьи | *pla-ní-ra-va-ni-ye sim'-yí* | 45b |
| fan | вентилятор | *vin-ti-lyáh-tar* | 34e |
| far (from) | далеко (от) | *da-li-kó (at)* | 3d, 37d |
| farm | ферма | *fyér-ma* | 15a |
| farmer | фермер | *fyér-mir* | 15a, 39a |
| farmland | пахотная земля | *páh-khat-na-ya zim-lyáh* | 13b |
| fashion | мода | *mó-da* | 25k |
| fast | быстро (adv) | *býst-ra* | 3d |
| fat | жирный | *zhýr-nyj* | 11a |
| father | отец | *a-tyéts* | 10a |
| father-in-law | свёкор | *svyó-kar* | 10a |
| faucet | кран | *krahn* | 23a, 36c |
| fax machine | телефакс | *ti-li-fáhks* | 18a |
| fear | боязнь (f), страх, опасение | *ba-yáhzn', strahkh, a-pa-syé-ni-ye* | 21a |
| feather | перо | *pi-ró* | 15b |
| February | февраль (m) | *fiv-ráhl'* | 5b |
| Federal Assembly | Федеральное Собрание | *fi-di-ráhl'-na-ye sab-ráh-ni-ye* | 44 |
| feel | чувствовать | *chóost-va-vat'* | 41a |
| feel bad | плохо себя чувствовать | *pló-kha si-byáh chóost-va-vat'* | 12b, 41a |
| feel well | хорошо себя чувствовать | *kha-ra-shó si-byáh chóost-va-vat'* | 12b, 41a |
| feeling | чувство | *chóost-va* | 21a |
| female | женский | *zhéhn-skij* | 11a |
| feminine | женский, женственный | *zhéhn-skij, zhéhn-stvi-nyj* | 8a, 11a |
| feminism | феминизм | *fi-mi-nízm* | 45b |
| fence | забор/ограда | *za-bór/ag-ráh-da* | 15a |
| fenced (adj) | огороженный (adj) | *a-ga-ró-zhy-nyj* | 27 |
| fencing | фехтование | *fikh-ta-váh-ni-ye* | 28b |
| fender | крыло | *kry-ló* | 34e |
| festival | фестиваль | *fis-ti-váhl'* | 37a |
| fever | жар, высокая температура | *zhahr, vy-só-ka-ya tim-pi-ra-tóo-ra* | 41a |
| fiancé, groom | жених | *zhy-níkh* | 10b, 11c |
| fiancée, bride | невеста | *ni-vyés-ta* | 10b, 11c |
| fiction | беллетристика, художественная литература | *bi-lit-rís-ti-ka, khu-dó-zhyst-vi-na-ya li-ti-ra-tóo-ra* | 20a, 25o, 29d |
| field | поле | *pó-li* | 13b, 28b |
| fifteen | пятнадцать | *pit-náh-tsat'* | 1a |
| fifth | пятый | *pyáh-tyj* | 1b |
| fifty | пятьдесят | *pi-di-syáht* | 1a |
| fig | инжир | *in-zhýr* | 24f |
| fight | драка | *dráh-ka* | 40b |

| file (electronic) | файл | *fahjl* | 20b, 43 |
| file (instrument) | напильник | *na-píl'-nik* | 25b |
| file (folder) | папка | *páhp-ka* | 20b, 39c |
| fillet | филе | *fi-lyé* | 24g |
| filling (dental) | пломба | *plóm-ba* | 41b |
| film | плёнка | *plyón-ka* | 25d |
| fitter | фильтр | *fil'tr* | 34e |
| fin | плавник | *plav-ník* | 15c |
| fine | хорошо | *kha-ra-shó* | 16a |
| finger | палец | *páh-lits* | 12a |
| finish school, graduate | кончить школу | *kón-chit' shkó-lu* | 11f, 38f |
| Finland | Финляндия | *fin-lyáhn-di-ya* | 31b |
| fire | пожар, огонь *(m)* | *pa-zháhr, a-gón'* | 40a |
| fire, to (a person) | уволить, освободить от обязанностей | *u-vó-lit', as-va-ba-dít' at a-byáh-za-nas-tij* | 39d |
| fire extinguisher | огнетушитель *(m)* | *ag-ni-tu-shý-til'* | 40a |
| fire pit (lit. garden fireplace) | садовый камин | *sa-dó-vyj ka-mín* | 23d |
| fire truck | пожарная машина | *pa-zháhr-na-ya ma-shý-na* | 40a |
| firearm | огнестрельное оружие | *ag-nist-ryél'-na-ye a-róo-zhy-ye* | 40b |
| firefighter | пожарный | *pa-zháhr-nij* | 39a |
| fireplace | камин | *ka-mín* | 23a |
| fireproof | огнестойкий, несгораемый | *ag-ni-stój-kij, nis-ga-ráh-i-myj* | 40a |
| firm | твёрдый | *tvyór-dyj* | 13d |
| firmly | твёрдо | *tvyór-da* | 13d |
| first | первый | *pyér-vyj* | 1b |
| first aid | скорая помощь *(f),* первая помощь *(f)* | *skó-ra-ya pó-mashch, pyér-va-ya pó-mashch* | 40a, 40c |
| first course | первое блюдо | *pyér-va-ye blyú-da* | 24g |
| first floor | первый этаж | *pyér-vyj y-táhzh* | 27 |
| first name | имя *(n)* | *í-mya* | 11f, 39b |
| First of May | Первое мая | *pyér-va-ye máh-ya* | 5e, 30a |
| fish | рыба | *rý-ba* | 15c, 24d, 24g, 37c |
| fish, to | поймать рыбу | *paj-máht' rý-bu* | 15c |
| fishing | рыбалка | *ry-báhl-ka* | 37a |
| fish store | рыбный магазин | *rýb-nyj ma-ga-zín* | 24n |
| fisherman | рыбак *(m),* рыбачка | *ry-báhk, ry-bách-ka* | 15c |
| fishing rod | удочка/удка | *óo-dach-ka/óot-ka* | 15c |
| fitness center/club | фитнесс центр/клуб | *fít-nys tsehntr/kloop* | 28b |
| five | пять | *pyaht'* | 1a |
| fix, repair | чинить | *chi-nít'* | 25i, 34c |
| flakes | хлопья *(pl)* | *khlóp'-ya* | 6a |
| flame | пламя | *pláh-mya* | 40a |
| flash | вспышка | *vspýsh-ka* | 25d |
| flash drive | флэш-брелок | *fléhsh-bri-lók* | 20b |
| flashlight | карманный фонарь *(m)* | *kar-máhn-yj fa-náhr* | 25b |

| | | | |
|---|---|---|---|
| flatter | льстить | *l'stit'* | 21a |
| flattery | лесть *(f)* | *lyest'* | 21a |
| flea | блоха | *bla-kháh* | 15d |
| Flemish | фламандский | *fla-máhnts-kij* | 31d |
| flight | полёт, рейс | *pa-lyót, ryejs* | 15b, 33a |
| flight attendant | стюард (-есса) | *styu-áhrt (styu-ar-déh-sa)* | 33c |
| floor (level) | этаж | *y-táhzh* | 23a, 27, 36b |
| floor (of a room) | пол | *pol* | 23a, 27 |
| floor plan (apartment) | планировка квартиры | *pla-ni-róf-ka kvar-tí-ry* | 27 |
| flounder | камбала | *kám-ba-la* | 15c, 24d |
| flour | мука | *mu-káh* | 24i |
| flower | цветок *(sg)*, цветы *(pl)* | *tsvi-tók, tsvi-tý* | 14a, 14b |
| flower bed | клумба | *kloóm-ba* | 27 |
| flu | грипп | *grip* | 41a |
| flute | флейта | *flyéj-ta* | 29c |
| fly, to | летать/лететь | *li-táht'/li-tyét'* | 15b |
| fly | муха | *móo-kha* | 15d |
| FM (frequency modulation) | ФМ (частотная модуляция) | *chas-tót-na-ya ma-du-lyáh-tsi-ya* | 20e |
| focus | фокус | *fó-kus* | 25d |
| fog | туман | *tu-máhn* | 6a |
| foliage | листва *(coll)* | *list-váh* | 14a |
| folk music | народная музыка | *na-ród-na-ya móo-zy-ka* | 29c |
| folk song | народная песня | *na-ród-na-ya pyés'-nya* | 25j |
| font | фонт, шрифт | *font, shrift* | 20b, 43 |
| food | еда/пища | *i-dáh/pí-shcha* | 24a |
| food chain | пищевая цепь *(f)* | *pi-shchi-váh-ya tsehp'* | 45a |
| food processor | кухонный комбайн | *ku khón-nyj kum-báhjn* | 23d |
| fool | дурак | *du-ráhk* | 11e |
| foolish | дурацкий | *du-ráhts-kij* | 11e |
| foot, leg | нога | *na-gáh* | 12a |
| football | регби | *réhg-bi* | 28b |
| footnote | сноска | *snós-ka* | 20a |
| for | для | *dlyah* | 8d |
| for | на | *na* | 4e |
| For example... | Например... | *na-pri-mýer* | 45c |
| for sale | на продажу | *na pra-dáh-zhu* | 25a |
| for what | зачем | *za-chyém* | 8g |
| forum | форум | *fo-rum* | 20d |
| forecast | предсказать погоду | *prit-ska-záht' pa-gó-du* | 6c |
| forehead | лоб | *lop* | 12a |
| foreign language | иностранный язык | *i-nast-ráh-nyj i-zýk* | 38e |
| foreigner | иностранец (-нка) | *i-nast-ráh-nits (-nka)* | 32 |
| forest, woods | лес *(sg)*, леса *(pl)* | *lyes, li-sáh* | 13b |
| forget | забыть | *za-být'* | 22b |
| fork | вилка | *víl-ka* | 23d, 241 |
| form (to fill out) | анкета | *an-kyé-ta* | 32 |
| format | формат | *far-máht* | 19a |
| forty | сорок | *só-rak* | 1a |

| forward | форвард, | *fór-vard,* | 19a |
| | переслать *(p)*, | *pi-ris-láht',* | |
| | пересылать *(i)* | *pi-ri-sy-láht'* | |
| **fossil fuel** | ископаемое топливо | *is-ka-páh-ye-ma-ye tóp-li-va* | 13c |
| **fountain** | фонтан | *fan-táhn* | 37b |
| **four** | четыре | *chi-tý-ri* | 1a |
| **fourteen** | четырнадцать | *chi-týr-na-tsat'* | 1a |
| **fourth** | четвёртый | *chit-vyór-tyj* | 1b |
| **fox** | лиса | *li-sáh* | 15a |
| **fraction** | дробь *(f)* | *drop'* | 1d |
| **France** | Франция | *fráhn-tsy-ya* | 31b |
| **fraud** | обман/мошенничество | *ab-máhn/ma-shéh-ni-chist-va* | 44 |
| **freeze** | замёрзнуть | *za-myórz-nut'* | 6a |
| **French** | француз (-женка) | *fran-tsóos (-zhyn-ka)* | 31d |
| **French** | французский | *fran-tsóos-kij* | 31d, 38e |
| **frequent** | частый *(adj)* | *cháhs-tyj* | 4e |
| **frequently** | часто *(adv)* | *cháhs-ta* | 4e |
| **Friday** | пятница | *pyáht-ni-tsa* | 5a |
| **fried** | жареный | *zháh-ri-nyj* | 24p |
| **fried eggs** | яичница | *i-ýsh-ni-tsa* | 24g |
| **friend** | друг/товарищ *(m&f)* | *drook/ta-váh-rishch* | 10b |
| **friendly** | дружелюбный, | *dru-zhy-lyúb-nyj,* | 11e |
| | приветливый | *pri-vyét-li-vyj* | |
| **friendship** | дружба | *dróozh-ba* | 10b |
| **frog** | лягушка | *li-góosh-ka* | 15c |
| **from** | из, от | *is, at* | 3d, 8d |
| **front door** | парадный вход | *pa-ráhd-nyj fkhot* | 27 |
| **fruit** | фрукт | *frookt* | 14d, 24f |
| **fruit tree** | фруктовое дерево *(sg)*, | *fruk-tó-va-ye dyé-ri-va,* | 14c |
| | фруктовые деревья *(pl)* | *fruk-tó-vy-ye di-ryév'-ya* | |
| **fry** | жарить | *zháh-rit'* | 24b |
| **fuel** | топливо | *tóp-li-va* | 13c |
| **full** | полный | *pól-nyj* | 3c |
| **fun, enjoyment** | забава/потеха | *za-báh-va/pa-tyé-kha* | 21a |
| **function** | функция | *fóonk-tys-ya* | 20b, 44 |
| **funny** | смешной | *smish-nój* | 11e |
| **furniture** | мебель *(f, coll)* | *myé-bil'* | 23c |
| **fuse** | пробка | *próp-ka* | 25b |
| **future** | будущее | *bóo-du-shchi-ye* | 4e |

## G

| **galaxy** | галактика | *ga-láhk-ti-ka* | 13a |
| **game** | игра, матч | *ig-ráh, máhtch* | 28a, 28b |
| **garage** | гараж | *ga-ráhzh* | 23a, 36b |
| **garden** | сад | *saht* | 14e, 23a, 37b |
| **garlic** | чеснок *(coll)* | *chis-nók* | 14e, 24j |
| **gas** | газ | *gahs* | 13c, 23e |
| **gas pump** | бензоколонка | *bin-za-ka-lón-ka* | 34e |

| gas station | бензозаправочная станция | *bin-za-zap-ráh-vach-na-ya stáhn-tsy-ya* | 34c |
|---|---|---|---|
| gas tank | бензобак | *bin-za-báhk* | 34e |
| gasoline | бензин | *bin-zín* | 13c, 34c |
| gather, reap | пожать/собрать | *pa-zháht'/sab-ráht'* | 14a |
| gather (group) | собраться | *sab-ráh-tsa* | 30b |
| gear shift | переключение передач | *pi-ri-klyú-cheh-ni-ye pi-ri-dáhch* | 34e |
| gender | род | *rot* | 8a, 11a |
| generally | вообще | *va-ap-shchyé* | 21c |
| generator | генератор | *gi-ni-ráh-tar* | 34e |
| generosity | щедрость | *shchyéd-rast'* | 11e |
| generous | щедрый | *shchyéd-ryj* | 11e |
| genitals | половые органы *(pl)* | *pa-la-vý-ye ór-ga-ny* | 12a, 45b |
| genitive | родительный | *ra-dí-til'-nyj* | 8a |
| gentle | мягкий | *myáhk-kij* | 11e |
| Gentlemen | Товарищи, Граждане | *ta-váh-ri-shchi, gráhzh-da-ni* | 19b |
| geographical | географический | *gi-ag-ra-fí-chis-kij* | 13e |
| geography | география | *gi-ag-ráh-fi-ya* | 13e, 38e |
| geology | геология | *gi-a-ló-gi-ya* | 38e |
| geometry | геометрия | *gi-a-myét-ri-ya* | 2b, 38e |
| Georgia | Грузия | *gróo-zi-ya* | 31b |
| geothermal energy | геотермическая энергия | *gi-a-tir-mí-chis-ka-ya y-néhr-gi-ya* | 45a |
| German (person) | немец (немка) | *nyé-mits (nyém-ka)* | 31d |
| German | немецкий | *ni-myéts-kij* | 31d, 38e |
| Germany | Германия | *gir-máh-ni-ya* | 31b |
| get married (for men) | жениться | *zhy-ní-tsa* | 11c |
| get married (for women) | выйти замуж | *výj-ti záh-muzh* | 11c |
| get out | выходить | *vy-kha-dít'* | 40a |
| get up, rise | подняться | *pad-nyáht'-tsa* | 3e |
| get up | встать | *fstaht'* | 12b |
| gift | подарок | *pa-dáh-rak* | 11c, 25a |
| gin | джин | *dzhyn* | 24k |
| giraffe | жираф | *zhy-ráhf* | 15a |
| girl | девочка | *dyé-vach-ka* | 11a |
| give (a gift) | подарить | *pa-dar-rít'* | 11c |
| give birth | родить | *ra-dít'* | 11c |
| give help | помочь | *pa-móch* | 40a |
| gland | железа | *zhy-li-záh* | 12a |
| glass (drinking) | стакан | *sta-káhn* | 23d, 24l |
| globe | земной шар, глобус | *zim-nój shahr,* (model) *gló-bus* | 13e |
| glove | перчатка | *pir-cháht-ka* | 25k |
| glove compartment | перчаточное отделение | *pir-cháh-tach-na-ye at-di-lyé-ni-ye* | 34e |
| glue | клей | *klyej* | 19e |
| go | идти | *it-tí* | 3e |

| Go ahead! | Давай! *(fam)* | da-váhj | 17b |
| Go to hell! | Иди к чёрту! | i-dí k chyór-tu | 21c |
| go to sleep/go to bed | идти спать | it-tí spaht' | 12b |
| goat | козёл *(m)*, козлиха *(f)* | ka-zyól, kaz-lí-kha | 15a |
| God | Бог | bok or bokh | 11d |
| gold | золото | zó-la-ta | 13c |
| gold *(adj)* | золотой | za-la-tój | 7a, 25i |
| goldfish | золотая рыбка | za-la-táh-ya rýp-ka | 15c |
| golf | гольф | gol'f | 28b |
| good | хороший | kha-ró-shij | 11e, 24p |
| Good afternoon! | Добрый день! | dób-ryj dyen' | 16a |
| Good evening! | Добрый вечер! | dób-ryj vyé-chir | 16a |
| Good luck! | Желаю удачи! | zhy-láh-yu u-dáh-chi | 16c |
| Good morning! | Доброе утро! | dób-ra-ye óot-ra | 16a |
| Good night! | Спокойной ночи! | spa-kój-naj nó-chi | 16a |
| Good-bye! | До свидания! | da svi-dáh-ni-ya | 16a |
| goose | гусь *(m)*, гусыня *(f)* | goos', gu-sý-nya | 15b |
| goulash | гуляш | gu-lyáhsh | 24g |
| government | правительство | pra-ví-til'st-va | 44 |
| grade, mark | отметка | at-myét-ka | 38f |
| grade | класс | klahs | 38a |
| graduate (from institute, university) | кончить (институт, университет) | kón-chit' (in-sti-tóot, u-ni-vyer-si-tyét) | 11f |
| grain | зерно | zir-nó | 14a, 24i |
| gram | грамм | grahm | 3a |
| grammar | грамматика | gra-máh-ti-ka | 8a, 38f |
| grand piano | рояль *(m)* | ra-yáhl' | 29c |
| granddaughter | внучка | vnóoch-ka | 10a |
| grandfather | дед/дедушка *(m)* | dyet/dyé-dush-ka | 10a |
| grandmother | бабка/бабушка *(f)* | báhp-ka/báh-bush-ka | 10a |
| grandson | внук | vnook | 10a |
| grapefruit | грейпфрут | gryéjp-fróot | 24f |
| grapes | виноград *(coll)*, виноградина *(sg)* | vi-nag-ráht, vi-nag-ráh-di-na | 14d, 24f |
| grass | трава | tra-váh | 13b, 14e |
| gravitation | притяжение | pri-ti-zhéh-ni-ye | 13a |
| gray | серый | syé-ryj | 7a |
| gray-haired | седоволосый | si-da-va-ló-syj | 11b |
| green | зелёный | zi-lyó-nyj | 7a |
| greenhouse | теплица | tip-lí-tsa | 14a |
| greet | приветствовать | pri-vyét-stva-vat' | 16a |
| grill | гриль | gril' | 23d |
| grocery store | продуктовый магазин, гастроном | pra-duk-tó-vyj ma-ga-zín, gast-ra-nóm | 24n |
| grow up | вырасти | vý-ras-ti | 11b |
| guide (tour) | гид | git | 37a, 37b |
| guide-interpreter | гид-переводчик | gít-pi-ri-vót-chik | 37a |
| guidebook | путеводитель *(m)* | pu-ti-va-dí-til' | 25o, 37a |
| guilt | вина | vi-náh | 42 |
| guitar | гитара | gi-táh-ra | 29c |
| gulf | залив | za-líf | 13b |

| gums | дёсны *(pl)* | *dyós-ny* | 41b |
| gun | ружьё | *rush'-yó* | 40b |
| gymnasium | спортивный зал | *spar-tív-nyj zahl* | 28b, 38c |
| gymnastics | гимнастика | *gim-náhs-ti-ka* | 28b |

## H

| habit | привычка | *pri-vých-ka* | 11e |
| hail | град | *graht* | 6a |
| hair | волос(ы) *(m)* | *vó-las(-y)* | 12a |
| hair dryer | сушилка для волос, фен | *su-shýl-ka dlya va-lós, fyen* | 12d, 25f |
| hair spray | лак для волос | *lahk dlya va-lós* | 12d |
| hairdresser | женский парикмахер *(m)*/парикмахерша *(f)* | *zhéhn-skij pa-rik-máh-khir/pa-rik-máh-khir-sha* | 12d, 39a |
| half | пол-, половина | *pol-, pa-la-ví-na* | 3c |
| hallway | коридор | *ka-ri-dór* | 23a, 38c |
| ham | ветчина | *vi-chi-náh* | 24c |
| hammer | молоток | *ma-la-tók* | 25b |
| handcuffs | наручники *(pl)* | *na-róoch-ni-ki* | 40b |
| handkerchief | носовой платок | *na-sa-vój pla-tók* | 25k |
| handle | ручка/рукоятка | *róoch-ka/ru-ka-yáht-ka* | 34e |
| handlebar | руль *(m)* | *rool'* | 34a |
| handset | телефонная трубка | *ti-li-fó-na-ya tróop-ka* | 18a |
| hang up | повесить трубку | *pa-vyé-sit' tróop-ku* | 18b |
| happen, occur | случаться | *slu-cháh-tsa* | 4e |
| happiness | счастье | *shcháhs-ti-ye* | 11e, 21a |
| happy, lucky | счастливый | *shchis-lí-vyj* | 11e, 21a |
| Happy birthday! | С днём рождения! | *s dnyom razh-dyé-ni-ya* | 11c |
| Happy New Year! | С Новым годом! | *s nó-vym gó-dam* | 16c, 30c |
| hard drive | жесткий диск | *zhóst-kij disk* | 20b |
| hardware | техническое обеспечение | *tich-ní-chis-ka-ye a-his-pi-chyé-ni-ye* | 20b |
| hardware store | скобяные товары | *ska-bi-ný-i ta-váh-ry* | 25b |
| hare | заяц | *záh-its* | 15a |
| harmonica | губная гармоника | *gub-náh-ya gar-mó-ni-ka* | 29c |
| harmony | гармония | *gar-mó-ni-ya* | 29c |
| harp | арфа | *áhr-fa* | 29c |
| hat | шапка, шляпа | *sháhp-ka, shlyáh-pa* | 25k |
| hate | ненависть *(f)* | *nyé-na-vist'* | 11e, 21b |
| hate, detest | ненавидеть | *ni-na-ví-dit'* | 11e |
| hatred | ненависть *(f)* | *nyé-na-vist'* | 21b |
| have a good time | хорошо провести время | *kha-ra-shó pra-vis-tí vryé-mya* | 21a |
| Have a good trip! | Счастливого пути! | *shchis-lí-va-va pu-tí* | 16c, 31a |
| Have a happy birthday! | С днём рождения! | *s dnyóm razh-dyé-ni-ya* | 16c, 29c |
| have dinner | поужинать | *pa-óo-zhi-nat'* | 24o |
| have fun | веселиться | *vi-si-lí-tsa* | 21a, 30b |
| have lunch | пообедать | *pa-a-byé-dat'* | 24o |
| hawk | ястреб | *yáhst-rip* | 15b |
| he | он | *on* | 8c |
| head | голова | *ga-la-váh* | 12a |

| head *(v)* a government | возглавить *(p),* | *vaz-gláh-vit',* | 44 |
|---|---|---|---|
| | возглавлять *(i),* | *vaz-glav-lyáht',* | |
| | правительство | *pra-ví-til'-st-va* | |
| head of state | глава правительства | *gla-váh pra-ví-til'-st-va* | 44 |
| headache | головная боль *(f)* | *ga-lav-náh-ya bol'* | 41a |
| headline | заголовок *(sg),* | *za-ga-ló-vak,* | 20a |
| | заголовки *(pl)* | *za-ga-lóf-ki* | |
| headphones | наушники | *na-óosh-ni-ki* | 20e, 33c |
| health | здоровье | *zda-róy'-ye* | 11a, 41a |
| healthy | здоровый *(m)* | *zda-ró-vyj* | 11a |
| hear | слышать | *slýsh-at'* | 12c |
| hearing | слух | *slookh* | 12c |
| heart | сердце | *syér-tse* | 12a, 41a |
| heart attack | инфаркт | *in-fáhrkt* | 41a |
| heat | теплота | *tip-la-táh* | 13c |
| heater | обогреватель *(m)* | *a-bag-ri-váh-til'* | 34e |
| heating | отопление | *a-tap-lyé-ni-ye* | 23e, 27 |
| heavily | тяжело | *ti-zhy-ló* | 11a |
| heavy | тяжёлый | *ti-zhó-lyj* | 3b, 11a, 13d, 32 |
| heavy metal (music) | хэви-метал | *khéh-vi-myé-tal* | 25j |
| Hebrew | иврит | *iv-rít* | 31d |
| height | рост | *rost* | 11a |
| Hello! | Здравствуйте! | *zdráhf-stvuj-ti* | 16a |
| Hello! | Алло, Аллё! | *a-ló, a-lyó* | 18b |
| help | помощь *(f)* | *pó-mashch* | 40a |
| Help! | На помощь!, | *na pó-mashch,* | 40a, 40c |
| | Помогите! | *pa-ma-gí-ti* | |
| Helsinki | Хельсинки | *khyél'-sin-ki* | 31c |
| helicopter excursion | облёт на вертолёте | *ab-lyot na vir-ta-lyó-ti* | 37a |
| hemisphere | полушарие | *pa-lu-sháh-ri-ye* | 13e |
| here | здесь | *zdyes'* | 3d, 37d |
| hero | герой | *gi-rój* | 29e |
| heroine | героиня | *gi-ra-í-nya* | 29e |
| herring | сельдь *(f)* (селёдка) | *syel'd' (si-lyót-ka)* | 15c, 24d, 24g |
| heterosexual *(adj)* | гетеросексуальный *(adj) (m),* | *gí-ti-ra-sik-su-áhl'-nyj,* | 45b |
| | гетеросексуальная *(adj) (f)* | *gí-ti-ra-sik-su-áhl'-na-ya* | |
| high school | средняя школа | *sryéd-ni-ya shkó-la* | 38a, 38d, 39b |
| high school (educational level) | среднее образование | *sryéd-ni-ye ab-ra-za-váh-ni-ye* | 11f |
| higher education | высшее образование | *výsh-shy-ye ab-ra-za-váh-ni-ye* | 11f |
| higher education (school) | высшая школа | *vý-sha-ya shkó-la* | 38a, 39b |
| highway | шоссе | *shy-séh* | 11f, 34c |
| hiking | пешая прогулка | *pyé-sha-ya pra-góol-ka* | 37a |
| hill | холм | *kholm* | 13b |

| Hindu | индус | *in-dóos* | 11d |
| hint | намёк | *na-myók* | 17a |
| hint, to | намекнуть | *na-mik-nóot'* | 17a |
| hip | бедро | *bid-ró* | 12a |
| hippopotamus | бегемот/гиппопотам | *bi-gi-mót/gi-pa-pa-táhm* | 15a |
| hire | нанять | *na-nyáht'* | 39d |
| history | история | *is-tó-ri-ya* | 38e |
| hit | удар | *u-dáhr* | 28b |
| HIV | ВИЧ (-инфекция) | *vich (-in-fyék-tsy-ya)* | 45b |
| | (вирус | *(ví-rus* | |
| | иммунодефицита | *i-moó-na-di-fi-tsý-ta* | |
| | человека) | *chi-la-vyé-ka)* | |
| hobby | любимое занятие | *lyu-bí-ma-ye za-nyáh-ti-ye* | 28a |
| hockey | хоккей | *kha-kyéj* | 28b |
| Hold the line | Подождите минуту! | *pa-dazh-dí-ti mi-nóo-tu* | 18b |
| (Wait a minute!) | | | |
| hole | дыра (-рка) | *dy-ráh (-rka)* | 25g |
| holiday | праздник | *práhz-nik* | 5a, 30a |
| Holland | Голландия | *ga-láhn-di-ya* | 31b |
| home page | домашняя страница | *da-máhsh-ni-ya stra-ní-tsa* | 20d |
| homosexuality | гомосексуализм | *ga-ma-sik-su-a-lízm* | 45b |
| honest | честный, | *chyés-nyj,* | 11e |
| | порядочный | *pa-ryáh-dach-nyj* | |
| honesty | честность *(f)* | *chyés-nast'* | 11e |
| honey | мёд | *myot* | 24j |
| honeymoon | медовый месяц | *mi-dó-vyj myé-sits* | 11c |
| honeymoon (trip) | свадебное | *sváh-dib-na-ye* | 37a |
| | путешествие | *pu-ti-shéhst-vi-ye* | |
| hood | капот | *ka-pót* | 34e |
| hook | крючок | *kryu-chók* | 15c |
| hope | надежда | *na-dyézh-da* | 21a |
| hope, to | надеяться | *na-dyé-i-tsa* | 21a |
| horizon | горизонт | *ga-ri-zónt* | 13b |
| horn (mechanical) | гудок | *gu-dók* | 34e |
| horn (organic) | рожок | *ra-zhók* | 29c |
| horror movie | фильм ужасов | *fílm óo-zha-sav* | 29a |
| horse | лошадь *(f)* | *ló-shat'* | 15a |
| horseback riding | катание на лошадях | *ka-táh-ni-ye na la-sha-dyáhkh* | 28b |
| horse racing | скачки *(pl)* | *skáhch-ki* | 28b |
| horse track | конная трасса | *kón-na-ya tráh-sa* | 28b |
| horsepower | лошадиная сила | *la-sha-dí-na-ya sí-la* | 34e |
| horticulture | садоводство | *sa-da-vót-stva* | 14a |
| hospital | больница | *bal'-ní-tsa* | 40c |
| hostel (dormitory) | общежитие | *ap-shchi-zhý-ti-ye* | 36a |
| hot | горячий | *ga-ryáh-chij* | 24p |
| hot cereal | каша | *káh-sha* | 24g |
| hot chocolate | какао | *ka-káh-o* | 24k |
| hot dog | сосиска | *sa-sís-ka* | 24g |
| hotel | гостиница | *gas-tí-ni-tsa* | 31a, 36a |
| hour | час | *chahs* | 4c |

| | | | |
|---|---|---|---|
| house | дом | *dom* | 23a |
| How are you? | Как дела? | *kakh di-láh* | 16a |
| how | как | *kahk* | 9 |
| How much | сколько | *skól'-ka* | 3c |
| How much does it cost? | Сколько это стоит? | *skól'-ka éh-ta stó-it* | 25a |
| How much is a single room? | Сколько стоит комната на одного?! | *skól'-ka stó-it kóm-na-ta na ad-na-vó* | 36b |
| How much? | Сколько | *skól'-ka* | 9 |
| How old are you? | Сколько вам лет? | *skól'-ka vahm lyet? (pol)* | 11b |
| | Сколько тебе лет? | *skól'-ka ti-byé let? (fam)* | |
| HTML | язык HTML, эйч-ти-эм-эл, хэтээмэл | *i-zyk kha-ta-am-éhl, éhjch-ti-am-éhl, kha-ta-am-éhl* | 20d |
| Hugs | Обнимаю | *ab-ni-máh-yu* | 19c |
| human | человек | *chi-la-vyék* | 11d, 15a |
| humanities | гуманитарные науки *(pl)* | *gu-ma-ni-táhr-ny-ye na-óo-ki* | 38e |
| humanity | человечество | *chi-la-vyé-chi-stva* | 11d |
| humid | влажно *(adv)* | *vlázh-na* | 6a |
| humidity | влажность *(f)* | *vlázh-nast'* | 6a |
| humor | юмор | *yú-mar* | 11e |
| hunger | голод | *gó-lad* | 12b |
| hungry | голодный | *ga-lód-nyj* | 12b |
| hunt | охотиться | *a-khó-ti-tsa* | 15a |
| hunter | охотник | *a-khót-nik* | 15a |
| hurricane | ураган | *u-ra-gáhn* | 6a |
| hurt | боль *(f)* | *bol'* | 41a |
| husband | муж | *moosh* | 10a, 11c |
| hydrogen | водород | *va-da-rót* | 13c |
| hyena | гиена | *gi-yé-na* | 15a |
| hygiene | гигиена | *gi-gi-yé-na* | 12d |
| hyphen | чёрточка | *chyór-tach-ka* | 19d |
| hypothesis | гипотеза | *gi-pó-ti-za* | 22a |

**I**

| | | | |
|---|---|---|---|
| I am cold | Мне холодно | *mnye khó-la-dna* | 12b |
| I am hot | Мне жарко | *mnye zháhr-ka* | 12b |
| I don't understand | Я не понимаю | *yah ni pa-ni-máh-yu* | 9 |
| I don't understand anything. | Я ничего не понимаю. | *yah ni-chi-vó ni pa-ni-máh-yu* | 21c |
| I | я | *yah* | 8c |
| I'm sorry! | Прости(те) меня, пожалуйста! | *pras-tí(ti) mi-nyáh pa-zháh-lus-ta* | 21c |
| I'm tired (of it)! | Мне надоело! | *mnye na-da-yé-la* | 21c |
| ice | лёд | *lyot* | 6a, 13b |
| ice cream | мороженое | *ma-ró-zhy-na-ye* | 24h |
| icon | икона | *i-kó-na* | 11d |
| | картинка | *kar-tín-ka* | 20b |
| idea | идея | *i-dyé-ya* | 22a |
| idealism | идеализм | *i-di-a-lízm* | 11e |
| idealist | идеалист | *i-di-a-líst* | 11e |

| idealistic | идеалистичный | *i-di-a-lis-tích-nyj* | 11e |
| identification | удостоверение личности | *u-das-ta-vi-ryé-ni-ye lích-nas-ti* | 11f |
| identification papers | удостоверение личности | *u-das-ta-vi-ryé-ni-ye lích-nas-ti* | 32, 36b |
| identify | удостоверить | *u-das-ta-vyé-rit'* | 17a |
| ideology | идеология | *i-di-a-ló-gi-ya* | 44 |
| idiot | идиот | *i-di-ót* | 11e |
| if | если | *yés-li* | 8h |
| ignorant | невежественный, неосведомлённый | *ni-vyé-zhyst-vi-nyj, ni-as-vi-dam-lyó-nyj* | 22a |
| illness | заболевание | *za-ba-li-váh-ni-ye* | 45b |
| illustration | иллюстрация, картинка | *i-lyust-rháh-tsy-ya, kar-tín-ka* | 20a |
| imagination | воображение | *va-ab-ra-zhéh-ni-ye* | 11e, 22a |
| imagine | вообразить | *va-ab-ra-zít'* | 22b |
| imam | имам | *i-máhm* | 11d |
| immunization | прививка | *pri-víf-ka* | 31a |
| impatient | нетерпеливый | *ni-tir-pi-lí-vyj* | 11e |
| imperfective | несовершенный | *ni-sa-vir-shéh-nyj* | 8a |
| impersonal | безличный | *biz-lích-nyj* | 8a |
| import | ввоз, импорт | *vvos, ím-part* | 32 |
| impractical | непрактичный | *ni-prak-tích-nyj* | 11e |
| impudence | наглость *(f)* | *náhg-last'* | 11e |
| impudent | наглый | *náhg-lyj* | 11e |
| in | в, внутри | *v, vnut-rí* | 8d |
| in | в | *v/f* | 3d |
| in an hour | через час | *chí-ris chahs* | 4e |
| in front of | перед | *pyé-rit* | 3d, 37d |
| in love | влюблённый | *vlyub-lyó-nyj* | 10b, 11c |
| In other words... | Другими словами... | *dru-gí-mi sla-váh-mi* | 45c |
| in the evening | вечером *(adv)* | *vyé-chi-ram* | 4a |
| in the middle | в середине | *f si-ri-dí-ni* | 3d |
| in the morning | утром *(adv)* | *óot-ram* | 4a |
| In this/that case... | В этом/том случае... | *v éh-tam/tom slóo-chi-ye* | 45c |
| incisor | передний зуб | *pi-ryéd-nij zoop* | 41b |
| income | доход, заработок | *da-khót, záh-ra-ba-tak* | 26 |
| increase | увеличение *(n)*, увеличиться *(p)*, увеличиваться *(i)* | *u-vi-li-chyé-ni-ye, u-vi-lí-chi-tsa, u-vi-lí-chi-va-tsa* | 3c |
| indecisive | нерешительный | *ni-ri-shý-til'-nyj* | 11e |
| independent | независимый | *ni-za-ví-si-myj* | 11e |
| index | указатель *(m)* | *u-ka-záh-tíl'* | 20a |
| India | Индия | *ín-di-ya* | 31b |
| Indian Ocean | Индийский океан | *in-díjs-kij a-ki-áhn* | 13b |
| indicate, point out | указать | *u-ka-záht'* | 17a |
| indication | указание, признак | *u-ka-záh-ni-ye, príz-nak* | 17a |
| indifference | безразличие | *biz-raz-lí-chi-ye* | 21a |
| indifferent | безразличный | *biz-raz-lích-nyj* | 11e, 21a |
| individualist | индивидуалист | *in-di-vi-du-a-líst* | 11e |
| industry | промышленность *(f)* | *pra-mýsh-li-nast'* | 13c |

| | | | |
|---|---|---|---|
| I-net | И-Нет | *i-nyét* | 20d |
| infection | инфекция | *in-fyék-tsy-ya* | 41a, 45b |
| inflation | инфляция | *inf-lyáh-tsy-ya* | 44 |
| inform | проинформировать | *pra-in-far-mí-ra-vat'* | 17a |
| information | справочное (бюро) | *spráh-vach-na-ye (byu-ró)* | 18b |
| information desk | справочное бюро | *sráh-vach-na-ye byu-ró* | 33a |
| injection | укол | *u-kól* | 25h, 41a |
| injure, wound | поранить | *pa-ráh-nit'* | 40b |
| injury, wound | рана | *ráh-na* | 40b |
| ink | чернила *(pl)* | *chir-ní-la* | 19e, 38b |
| inkjet (printer) | струйный *(adj) (m)*, | *stróoj-nyj,* | 20b |
| | чернильный *(adj) (m)* | *chir-níl'-nyj* | |
| innocence | невинность *(f)*, | *ni-ví-nast',* | 11e, |
| | невинновность *(f)* | *ni-vi-nóv-nast'* | 42 |
| innocent | невинный | *ni-ví-nyj* | 11e |
| inorganic | неорганический | *ni-ar-ga-ní-chis-kij* | 13c |
| input | набор *(n)* | *na-bór* | 26 |
| insect | насекомое | *na-si-kó-ma-ye* | 15d |
| insert | вставить *(p)*, | *fstáh-vit',* | 20b |
| | вставлять *(i)* | *fstav-lyáht'* | |
| inside | в, внутри | *v, vnut-rí* | 3d, 37c |
| installment payment | рассрочка платежа | *ras-sróch-ka pla-ti-zhah* | 27 |
| instant | мгновение | *mgna-vyé-ni-ye* | 4c |
| institute | институт | *ins-ti-tóot* | 38a |
| instrument | инструмент | *in-stru-myént* | 28a, 29c |
| instrumental | творительный | *tva-rí-til'-nyj* | 8a |
| insulin | инсулин | *in-su-lín* | 25h |
| insurance | страхование | *stra-kha-váh-ni-ye* | 27 |
| | страховка *(slang)* | *stra-khóf-ka* | 26, 31a, |
| | | | 34b |
| integrated circuit | микросхема | *mik-ra-skhyé-ma* | 20b |
| intelligent | умный | *óom-nyj* | 11e |
| intelligentsia | интеллигенция | *in-ti-li-gyén-tsy-ya* | 11e |
| intercom | интерком | *in-tir-kóm* | 18a |
| interest | проценты *(pl)* | *pra-tséhn-ty* | 26 |
| interest rate | процентная ставка | *pra-tséhnt-na-ya stáhf-ka* | 26 |
| interesting | интересный | *in-ti-ryés-nyj* | 22a |
| interestingly | интересно | *in-ti-ryés-na* | 22a |
| interface | интерфейс | *in-tyr-féhjs* | 20b |
| intermission | антракт | *ant-ráhkt* | 29e |
| international | международный | *mizh-du-na-ród-nyj* | 18b |
| Internet | Интернет | *in-tyr-nyét* | 20d |
| Internet auction | Интернет-аукцион | *in-tyr-nyét-a-uk-tsy-ón* | 20d |
| Internet browser | Интернет-броузер | *in-tyr-nyét-bráh-u-zir* | 20d |
| Internet service provider (ISP) | Интернет-провайдер | *in-tyr-nyét-pra-váhj-dyr* | 20d |
| Internet user | пользователь | *pól-za-va-til'* | 20d |
| | интернета | *in-tyr-nyé-ta* | |
| interrogative | вопросительный | *vap-ra-sí-til'-nyj* | 8a |
| interrupt | прерывать | *pri-ry-váht'* | 17a |
| interruption | помеха | *pa-myé-kha* | 17a |

| | | | |
|---|---|---|---|
| intersection | перекрёсток | *pi-rik-ryós-tak* | 34c, 34d, 37b |
| interview | интервью | *in-tyr-v'yú* | 20a, 20b |
| intestines | кишечник, кишки *(pl)* | *ki-shéhch-nik, kish-kí* | 12a |
| intonation | интонация | *in-ta-náh-tsy-ya* | 8a |
| introduce someone | представить | *prit-stáh-vit'* | 16b |
| invertebrate | беспозвоночное | *bis-paz-va-nóch-na-ye* | 15a |
| invest | вложить | *vla-zhýt'* | 26 |
| investigator | следователь | *sli-da-va-tyél'* | 42 |
| investment | вложение, | *vla-zhéh-ni-ye,* | 26 |
| | капиталовложение | *ka-pi-ta-la-vla-zheh-ni-ye* | |
| invite | пригласить | *prig-la-sít'* | 17a |
| iPod | айпод | *áhj-pad* | 25j |
| Iran | Иран | *i-ráhn* | 31b |
| Ireland | Ирландия | *ir-láhn-di-ya* | 31b |
| Irish | ирландец (-дка) | *ir-láhn-dits (-tka)* | 31d |
| iron (appliance) | утюг | *u-tyúk* | 25g |
| iron (metal) | железо | *zhy-lyé-za* | 13c |
| iron, to | гладить | *gláh-dit'* | 25g |
| ironic | ироничный | *i-ra-ních-nyj* | 11e |
| irony | ирония | *i-ró-ni-ya* | 11e |
| irregular | неравномерный | *ni-rav-na-myér-nyj* | 4e |
| irresponsible | безответственный | *bi-zat-vyét-stvi-nyj* | 11e |
| irrigation | ирригация | *i-ri-gáh-tsy-ya* | 14a |
| irritable | раздражительный | *raz-dra-zhý-til'-nyj* | 11e |
| Islam | ислам | *is-láhm* | 11d |
| Islamic | исламский | *is-láhm-skij* | 11d |
| island | остров | *óst-raf* | 13b |
| Israel | Израиль *(m)* | *iz-rhá-il'* | 31b |
| Israeli | израильтянин (-нка) | *iz-ra-il'-tyáh-nin (-nka)* | 31d |
| it | оно | *a-nó* | 8c |
| It can't be! | Не может этого быть! | *ni mó-zhyt éh-ta-va byt'* | 21c |
| It seems to me | Мне кажется, что | *mnye káh-zyh-tsa shto* | 17b |
| It's midnight | Полночь | *pól-nach* | 4b |
| | Сейчас полночь | *si-cháhs pól-nach* | |
| It's obvious that | Очевидно, что | *a-chi-víd-na shto* | 17b |
| Italian (person) | итальянец (-нка) | *i-tal'-yáh-nits (-nka)* | 31d |
| Italian | итальянский | *i-tal'-yáhn-skij* | 31d |
| italics | курсив, | *kur-síf,* | 19d, 20b |
| | курсивный шрифт | *kur-sív-nyj shrift* | |
| Italy | Италия | *i-táh-li-ya* | 31b |
| itch | чесаться | *chi-sáh-tsa* | 41a |

| | | | |
|---|---|---|---|
| **J** | | | |
| jacket | куртка/жакет | *kóort-ka/zha-kyét* | 25k |
| Jacuzzi | джакузи | *dzha-kóo-zi* | 23d |
| jail, prison | тюрьма | *tyur'-máh* | 42 |
| jam | варенье | *va-ryé-n'ye* | 24j |
| janitor | уборщик *(m)* | *u-bór-shchik* | 38d, 39a |
| | (-щица) *(f)* | *(u-bór-shchi-tsa)* | |
| January | январь *(m)* | *yn-váhr'* | 31b |

| Japan | Япония | *i-pó-ni-ya* | 31b |
| Japanese | японский | *i-pón-skij* | 31d |
| Japanese | японец (-ка) | *i-pó-nits (-nka)* | 31d |
| jaw | челюсть *(f)* | *chyé-lyust'* | 12a, 41b |
| jazz | джаз | *dzhahs* | 25j, 29c |
| jealous | ревнивый | *riv-ní-vyj* | 11e |
| jest, joke | шутка | *shóot-ka* | 17a |
| Jew | еврей *(m)* | *yev-ryéj* | 11d |
| jewel | драгоценный камень | *dra-ga-tséh-nyj káh-min'* | 25i |
| | *(m)* | | |
| jeweler | ювелир | *yu-vi-lír* | 25i |
| jewelry | драгоценности *(pl)* | *dra-ga-tséh-nas-ti* | 25i |
| Jewish | еврейский | *yev-ryéj-skij* | 11d |
| job, work | работа | *ra-bó-ta* | 11f, 29d, |
| | | | 39a, 39d |
| jog | бегать | *byé-gat'* | 28a |
| joint | сустав | *sus-táhv* | 12a |
| joke | шутить | *shu-tít'* | 17a |
| joker | шутник | *shut-ník* | 11e |
| journalist | журналист (-ка) | *zhur-na-líst (-ka)* | 20a, 39a |
| joy | радость *(f)* | *ráh'dast'* | 21a |
| joyous | радостный | *ráh'das-nyj* | 21a |
| Judaism | иудейская религия | *iu-dyéj-ska-ya ri-lí-gi-ya* | 11d |
| judge | судья *(m&f)* | *sud'yáh* | 42 |
| judge, to | судить | *su-dít'* | 42 |
| judgment | решение, | *ri-shéh-ni-ye,* | 22a |
| | благоразумие | *bla-ga-ra-zóo-mi-ye* | |
| juice | сок | *sok* | 24k |
| juicer | соковыжималка | *só-ka-vy-zhy-máhl-ka* | 23d |
| July | июль *(m)* | *i-yúl'* | 5b |
| June | июнь *(m)* | *i-yún'* | 5b |
| justice | справедливость *(f)* | *spra-vid-lí-vast'* | 22a, 42 |

## K

| karaoke | караоке | *ka-ra-ó-ke* | 25j |
| Kazakhstan | Казахстан | *ka-zakh-stáhn* | 31b |
| Kenya | Кения | *kyé-ni-ya* | 31b |
| kettle | чайник | *cháhj-nik* | 23d |
| key | ключ | *klyuch* | 23d, 36b |
| key | клавиша | *kláh-vi-sha* | 20b, 26 |
| keyboard (keypad) | клавиатура | *kla-vi-a-tóo-ra* | 19e, 20b, |
| (on keyboard) | (клавиша) | *kláh-vi-sha* | 26, 39c |
| kick | удар (ногой) | *u-dáhr (na-gój)* | 28b |
| kidney | почка | *póch-ka* | 12a, 41a |
| Kiev | Киев | *kí-if* | 31c |
| kill | убить | *u-bít'* | 40b |
| kilogram | килограмм | *ki-la-gráhm* | 3a |
| kilometer | километр | *ki-la-myétr* | 3a |
| kind | добрый | *dób-ryj* | 11e |
| kindhearted | добросердечный | *dab-ra-sir-dyéch-nyj* | 11e |
| kindness | доброта | *dab-ra-táh* | 11e |

| king | король *(m)* | *ka-ról'* | 28a |
| kiosk | киоск | *ki-ósk* | 37b |
| kiss, to | целовать | *tsy-la-váht'* | 11c |
| kiss | поцелуй *(m)* | *pa-tsy-lóoj* | 11c, 21b |
| kissel | кисель *(m)* | *ki-syél'* | 24k |
| Kisses | Целую | *tsy-lóo-yu* | 19c |
| kitchen | кухня | *kóokh-nya* | 23b |
| kitchen furniture | кухонная мебель | *ku-khón-na-ya myé-bil'* | 23d |
| knapsack | рюкзак | *ryuk-záhk* | 28b, 32, 37c |
| knee | колено | *ka-lyé-na* | 12a |
| knife | нож | *nozh* | 23d, 24l, 40b |
| Knock it off! | Прекрати! | *prik-ra-tí* | 21c |
|  | Перестань! | *pi-ri-stáhn'* |  |
| know | знать | *znaht'* | 22b |
| knowledge | знание | *znáh-ni-ye* | 22a |
| knowledgeable | знающий | *znáh-yu-shchij* | 22a |
| kopeck | копейка | *ka-pyéj-ka* | 26 |
| Korea | Корея | *ka-ryé-ya* | 31b |
| Kyrgyzstan | Кыргызстан | *kyr-gys-stáhn* | 31b |

**L**

| labor/trade union | профсоюз | *praf-sa-yús* | 44 |
| laboratory | лаборатория | *la-ba-ra-tó-ri-ya* | 13c, 38c |
| ladder | лестница | *lyés-ni-tsa* | 40a |
| lady | дама | *dáh-ma* | 11a |
| lake | озеро *(sg)*, озёра *(pl)* | *ó-zi-ra, a-zyó-ra* | 13b, 37a, 37c |
| lamb | ягнёнок, баранина | *ig-nyó-nak, ba-ráh-ni-na* | 15a, 24c |
| lamp | лампа | *láhm-pa* | 23c, 36c |
| land, to | приземляться | *pri-zim-lyáh-tsa* | 33c |
| land | земля | *zim-lyáh* | 13b |
| landlord | хозяин дома | *kha-zyáh-in dó-ma* | 23g, |
|  | арендодатель | *a-rin-da-dáh-til'* | 27 |
| landscape | пейзаж | *pij-záhsh* | 13b, 29b |
| lane (traffic) | полоса | *pa-la-sáh* | 34c |
| language lab | лингафонный кабинет | *lin-ga-fón-yj ka-bi-nyét* | 38c |
| laptop | лаптоп | *léhp-tóp* | 20b |
| larch | лиственница | *líst-vi-ni-tsa* | 14c |
| laser | лазер | *láh-zyr* | 43 |
| laser (printer) | лазерный *(adj) (m)* | *láh-zir-nyj* | 20b |
| last | последний | *pas-lyéd-nij* | 4e |
| last, to | продолжаться | *pra-dal-zháh-tsa* | 4e |
| late | поздно *(adv)* | *póz-na* | 4e, 33b, 35 |
| Latin America | Латинская Америка | *la-tíns-ka-ya a-myé-ri-ka* | 31b |
| latitude | широта | *shy-ra-táh* | 13e |
| Latvia | Латвия | *láht-vi-ya* | 31b |
| laugh | смеяться | *smi-yáh-tsa* | 11e, 21a |

| laughter | смех | *smyekh* | 11e, 21a |
| laundromat | автоматическая прачечная | *av-to-ma-tí-chis-ka-ya práh-chish-na-ya* | 25g |
| laundry room | прачечная | *práh-chish-na-ya* | 25g |
| lava | лава | *láh-va* | 13b |
| lavatory | туалет, уборная | *tu-a-lyét, u-bór-na-ya* | 33c |
| law (single law) | закон | *za-kón* | 44 |
| | законодательство, по закону | *za-ka-na-dáh'til'-stva, pa za-kó-nu* | 42 |
| law (law in general) | законоведение | *za-ka-na-vyé-di-ni-ye* | 38e |
| lawn | лужайка/газон | *lu-zháhj-ka/ga-zón* | 23a |
| lawn mower | косилка/ газонокосилка | *ka-síl-ka/ga-zó-na-ka-síl-ka* | 23a |
| lawn mower (motor) | механическая газонокосилка | *mi-kha-ní-chis-ka-ya ga-zó-na-ka-síl-ka* | 23a |
| lawsuit | иск | *isk* | 42 |
| lawyer | адвокат *(m&f)* | *ad-va-káht* | 39a |
| lawyer (jurist) | юрист | *yu-ríst* | 42 |
| laziness | леность *(f)* | *lé-nast'* | 11e |
| lazy | ленивый | *li-ní-vyj* | 11e |
| lead (for pencils) | грифель *(m)* | *grí-fil'* | 38b |
| lead (metal) | свинец *(n)* | *svi-nyéts* | 13c |
| lead *(adj)* | свинцовый | *svin-tsó-vyj* | 13c |
| leader | лидер | *lí-dir* | 44 |
| leaf | лист *(sg)*, листья *(pl)* | *list, líst-ya* | 14a |
| learn | научиться, учить, изучать | *na-u-chí-tsa, u-chít', i-zu-cháht'* | 22b 38f |
| learn by heart/ memorize | выучить наизусть | *vý-u-chit' na-i-zóost* | 38f |
| lease (term) | срок аренды | *srok a-ryén-dy* | 27 |
| leather | кожа *(n)* | *kó-zha* | 13c, 25l |
| leather *(adj)* | кожаный *(adj)* | *kó-zha-nyj* | 13c, 25l |
| leave, depart | уйти, уехать | *uj-tí, u-yé-khat'* | 3e |
| lecture, to | читать лекцию | *chi-táht' lyék-tsy-yu* | 17a, 38f |
| lecture | лекция | *lyék-tsy-ya* | 17a, 38f |
| left *(adj)* | левый | *lyé-vyj* | 3d |
| legislation | законодательство | *za-ka-na-dáh-til'-st-va* | 44 |
| legislative *(adj)* | законодательный *(m)*, законодательное *(n)*, законодательная *(f)* | *za-ka-na-dáh-til'-nyj, za-ka-na-dáh-til'-na-ye, za-ka-na-dáh-til'-na-ya* | 44 |
| lemon | лимон | *li-món* | 14d, 24f |
| lemonade (carbonated) | лимонад | *li-ma-nát* | 24k |
| lender (creditor) | кредитор | *kri-dí-tor* | 27 |
| length | длина | *dli-náh* | 3a |
| lengthen | удлинять | *u-dli-nyáht'* | 25m |
| lens | линза | *lín-za* | 25d |
| leopard | леопард | *li-a-páhrt* | 15a |
| less | меньше | *myén-she* | 3c |
| lesson | урок | *u-rók* | 38f |
| letter (alphabet) | буква | *bóok-va* | 8a |
| letter (message) | письмо | *pis'-mó* | 19e |

| | | | |
|---|---|---|---|
| letter carrier, mailman | почтальон | *pach-tal'-yón* | 19f |
| lettuce | салат | *sa-láht* | 14e, 24e |
| liberal | либеральный | *li-bi-ráhl'-nyj* | 11e |
| librarian | библиотекарь (-рша) | *bib-li-a-tyé-kar' (-rsha)* | 38d |
| library | библиотека | *bib-li-a-tyé-ka* | 20a, 38c |
| license plate | номерной знак | *na-mir-nój znahk* | 34e |
| lie | ложь *(f)*, враньё *(coll)* | *losh, vran'-yó* | 17a |
| lie down | лечь | *lyech* | 3e |
| lie, to | лгать, соврать | *lgaht', sa-vráht'* | 17a |
| life | жизнь *(f)* | *zhyzn'* | 11c |
| life jacket | спасательный жилет | *spa-sáh-til'-nyj zhy-lyét* | 33c |
| lift | поднимать | *pad-ni-máht'* | 3e |
| light *(adj)* | лёгкий | *lyókh-kij* | 3b, 11a, 13d, 32 |
| | светлый | *svyét-lyj* | 7a |
| light | свет *(n)* | *svyet* | 6a, 13a, 23e, 36c |
| light a candle | зажечь свечу | *za-zhéhch svi-chóo* | 11d |
| light blue | голубой | *ga-lu-bój* | 7a |
| light bulb | лампочка | *láhm-pach-ka* | 25b |
| lighter | зажигалка | *za-zhy-gáhl-ka* | 25e |
| lightly | легко | *likh-kó* | 11a, 13d |
| lightning | молния | *mól-ni-ya* | 6a |
| lights (automobile) | фары *(pl)* | *fáh-ry* | 34e |
| like | нравиться | *nráh-vi-tsa* | 21b |
| lilac | сирень *(f)* | *si-ryén'* | 14b |
| limit (cash/withdrawal) | лимит | *li-mít* | 26 |
| line (mark) | линия/черта | *lí-ni-ya/chir-táh* | 2b, 19d |
| line (queue) | очередь *(f)* | *ó-chi-rit'* | 26 |
| link | веб-ссылка | *vyép-ssýl-ka* | 20d |
| lion | лев *(sg)*, львы *(pl)* | *lyef, l'vy* | 15a |
| lip | губа | *gu-báh* | 12a, 41h |
| liposuction | липоотсасывание | *lí-pa-at-sáh-sy-va-ni-ye* | 45b |
| lipstick | губная помада | *gub-náh-ya pa-máh-da* | 25f |
| liqueur | ликёр | *li-kyór* | 24k |
| liquid | жидкость *(f)* | *zhýt-kast'* | 13c |
| listen, to | слушать | *slóo-shat'* | 12c, 17a, 20b, 38f |
| liter | литр | *litr* | 3a |
| literal | буквальный | *buk-váhl'-nyj* | 17a |
| literally | буквально | *buk-váhl'-na* | 17a |
| literature | литература | *li-ti-ra-tóo-ra* | 29d, 38e |
| Lithuania | Литва | *lit-váh* | 31b |
| litigate | судиться | *su-dí-tsa* | 42 |
| little | мало *(adv)* | *máh-la* | 3c |
| live | жить | *zhyt'* | 11c |
| live in/on | жить в/на | *zhyt' v/na* | 11f, 23f |
| liver | печень *(f)*, печёнка | *pyé-chin', pi-chyón-ka* | 12a, 24c |
| living room | гостиная | *gas-tí-na-ya* | 23b |
| loan | заём | *za-yóm* | 26 |
| | ссуда | *ssóo-da* | 27 |

| lobby | вестибюль *(m)*, фойе | *vis-ti-byúl', faj-yé* | 29a, 29e, 36b |
|---|---|---|---|
| lobster | омар | *a-máhr* | 15d, 24d |
| local authorities | местные власти | *myés-ny-i vláhs-ti* | 44 |
| local call | местный телефонный разговор | *myés-nyj ti-li-fó-nyj raz-ga-vór* | 18b |
| local network | местная сеть, локальная | *myést-na-ya syet', la-káhl'-na-ya* | 20b |
| located | расположенный, размещённый | *ras-pa-ló-zhy-nyj, raz-mi-shchóy-nyj* | 13e |
| location | местонахождение, месторасположение, | *mye-sta-na-khazh-dyé-ni-ye, myes-ta-ras-pa-la-zhéh-ni-ye,* | 13e |
| | расположение | *ras-pa-la-zhéh-ni-ye* | 27 |
| London | Лондон | *lón-dan* | 31c |
| long | длинный | *dlí-nyj* | 3b, 38f |
| long ago | давно | *dav-nó* | 4a |
| long-distance call | междугородный телефонный разговор | *mizh-du-ga-ród-nyj ti-li-fó-nyj raz-ga-vór* | 18b |
| long-term (lease) | длительный срок | *dlí-til'-nyj srok* | 27 |
| longitude | долгота | *dal-ga-táh* | 13e |
| look | смотреть, глядеть | *smat-ryét', gli-dyét'* | 12c, 20b |
| look after | ухаживать | *u-kháh-zhy-vat'* | 41a |
| look for something | искать что-нибудь | *is-káht' shtó-ni-but'* | 25a |
| loose | свободный | *sva-bód-nyj* | 251 |
| loose change | мелочь *(f)* | *myé-lach* | 26 |
| lose | проиграть | *pra-ig-ráht'* | 28b |
| lose elections | проиграть *(p)*, проигрывать *(i)*, выборы | *pra-i-gráht', pra-í-gry-vat', vý-ba-ry* | 44 |
| lose weight | похудеть | *pa-khu-dyét'* | 11a |
| lost and found | бюро находок | *byu-ró na-khó-dak* | 33a |
| lot | земельный участок | *zi-myél'-nyj u-cháhs-tak* | 27 |
| loudspeaker | громкоговоритель *(m)* | *grom-ka-ga-va-rí-til'* | 20e |
| louse | вошь *(sg, f)*, вши *(pl)* | *vash, fshy* | 15d |
| love | любовь *(f)* | *lyu-bóf'* | 11c, 11e, 21b |
| love, to | любить | *lyu-bít'* | 11c, 11e, 21b |
| lover | любовник *(m)*, любовница *(f)* | *lyu-bóv-nik, lyu-bóv-ni-tsa* | 10b |
| lower class | низший класс | *nís-shyj klahs* | 45b |
| loyal | преданный, постоянный | *pryé-da-nyj, pa-sta-yáh-nyj* | 11e |
| luggage rack | багажная полка | *ba-gáhzh-na-ya pól-ka* | 36b |
| lunch | обед | *a-byét* | 24a |
| lung | лёгкое *(n)* | *lyókh-ka-ye* | 12a, 41a |
| lymphatic glands | лимфатические железы *(pl)* | *lim-fa-tí-chis-ki-i zhéh-li-zy* | 41a |

# M

| macaroni | макароны | *ma-ka-ró-ny* | 24g |
| machine gun | автомат | *af-ta-máht* | 40b |
| madness | сумасшествие | *su-ma-shéhst-vi-ye* | 11e |
| magazine | журнал | *zhur-náhl* | 20a, 25o, 38b |
| magistrate | мировой судья *(m&f)* | *mi-ra-vój sud'-yáh* | 42 |
| maid | горничная *(f)* | *gór-nich-na-ya* | 36b |
| mail | почта | *póch-ta* | 19f |
| mail a letter | послать письмо | *pas-láht' pis'-mó* | 19f |
| mailbox (inbox) | почтовый ящик | *pach-tó-vyj yáh-shchik* | 19a, 19f, 23a |
| mainframe | мейнфрейм | *myéjn-fryéjm* | 20b |
| majority | большинство | *bal'-shyn-stvó* | 44 |
| make a call | позвонить | *paz-va-nít'* | 18b |
| make friends | подружиться | *pa-dru-zhý-tsa* | 10b |
| make the bed | застлать постель, застелить | *za-stláht' pas-tyél', za-sti-lít'* | 23f |
| make-up | косметика | *kas-myé-ti-ka* | 25f |
| male | мужской | *mush-skój* | 11a |
| malicious | зловредный | *zla-vryéd-nyj* | 11e |
| mammal | млекопитающееся животное | *mli-ka-pi-táh-yu-shchij-sya zhy-vót-na-ye* | 15a |
| man | мужчина *(m)* | *muzh-chí-na* | 11a |
| manager | заведующий, заведующий (-ая), менеджер | *za-vyé-du-yu-shchij, za-vyé-du-yu-shchij (-a-ya), myé-nad-zhyr* | 36b, 39d, 26 |
| mandarin | мандарин | *man-da-rín* | 14d, 24f |
| many | много | *mnó-ga* | 3c |
| Many thanks! | Спасибо большое! | *spa-sí-ba bal'-shó-ye* | 16c |
| шар | карта | *káhr-ta* | 13e, 37b, 38b |
| maple | клён | *klyon* | 14c |
| March | март | *mahrt* | 5b |
| margin(s) | поле (-я) | *pó-lye (pa-lyáh)* | 19d |
| marital status | семейное положение | *si-myéj-na-ye pa-la-zhéh-ni-ye* | 11f, 39b |
| marker | фломастер | *fla-máhs-ter* | 19e, 25c |
| market | рынок | *rý-nak* | 24n, 39d |
| marketing | маркетинг | *máhr-ki-tink* | 26 |
| marriage, matrimony | женитьба | *zhy-nít'-ba* | 11c |
| married | женатый *(m)*, замужняя *(f)* | *zhy-náh-tyj, za-móozh-nya-ya* | 11c, 11f, 39b |
| masculine (manly) | мужественный | *móo-zhyst-vin-yj* | 11a |
| masculine (grammar) | мужской | *mush-skój* | 8a |
| massage | массаж | *ma-sáhsh* | 12d, 37a |
| masterpiece | шедевр | *shy-déhvr* | 29b |
| match | спичка | *spích-ka* | 25e |
| material | материал | *ma-ti-ri-áhl* | 13c |
| mathematician | математик *(m&f)* | *ma-ti-máh-tik* | 39a |
| mathematics | математика | *ma-ti-máh-ti-ka* | 38e |

| matter | вещество | *vi-shchist-vó* | 13c |
|---|---|---|---|
| mausoleum | мавзолей | *mav-za-lyéj* | 37b |
| maximum | максимум | *máhk-si-mum* | 3b |
| May | май | *mahj* | 5b |
| May I? | Можно? | *mózh-na* | 16c |
| mayonnaise | майонез | *ma-i-néhs* | 24j |
| mayor | мэр | *mehr* | 44 |
| mean, bad | противный | *pra-tív-nyj* | 11e |
| mean, to | значить | *znáh-chit'* | 17a |
| meaning | значение | *zna-chyé-ni-ye* | 17a |
| meat | мясо | *myáh-sa* | 24c |
| mechanic | механик | *mi-kháh-nik* | 34c, 39a |
| mechanical | механический | *mi-kha-ní-chis-kij* | 25b |
| medical instruments | медицинские инструменты | *mi-di-tsýn-ski-i in-stru-myén-ty* | 41a |
| medicine (drug) | лекарство, медикамент | *li-káhr-stva, mi-di-ka-myént* | 25h, 41a |
| medicine (field of study) | медицина | *mi-di-tsý-na* | 38e |
| meet, run into someone | встретить | *fstryé-tit'* | 16b |
| melon | дыня | *dý-nya* | 14d |
| membrane | мембрана | *mimb-ráh-na* | 14a |
| memory | запоминающее устройство | *za-pa-mi-náh-yu-shchi-ye ust-rójst-va* | 20b |
| memory | память | *pah-mit'* | 18a |
| memory card | карта памяти | *káhr-ta páh-mi-ti* | 18a, 25d |
| mend | починить | *pa-chi-nít'* | 25g |
| menstruation | менструация | *min-stru-áh-tsy-ya* | 41a |
| mention | упомянуть, заметить | *u-pa-mi-nóot', za-myé-tit'* | 17a |
| menu | меню | *mi-nyú* | 20b, 24g |
| Merge | Сливающееся движение | *sli-váh-yu-shchi-i-sya dvi-zhéh-ni-ye* | 34d |
| meridian | меридиан | *mi-ri-di-áhn* | 13e |
| message | сообщение, записка | *sa-ap-shchyé-ni-ye, za-pís-ka* | 18b, 36b |
| messenger | мессенджер | *myé-sin-dzhyr* | 20d |
| metal | металл | *mi-táhl* | 13c |
| metal *(adj)* | металлический | *mi-tah-lí-chis-kij* | 13c |
| meteor | метеор | *mi-ti-ór* | 13a |
| meter | метр | *myetr* | 3a |
| Mexico | Мексика | *myék-si-ka* | 31b |
| mezzanine | мансарда | *man-sáhr-da* | 27 |
| microbe | микроб | *mik-róp* | 15d, 45b |
| microcomputer | микрокомпьютер | *mik-ra-kamp'-yú-tar* | 20b |
| microphone | микрофон | *mik-ra-fón* | 20e |
| microscope | микроскоп | *mik-ras-kóp* | 13c |
| microwave | микроволна | *mik-ra-val-náh* | 43 |
| microwave oven | микроволновая печь, микроволновка | *mík-ra-val-nó-va-ya pyech, mík-ra-val-nóf-ka* | 23d |

| | | | |
|---|---|---|---|
| middle class | средний класс | *sryéd-nij klahs* | 45b |
| midnight | полночь *(f)* | *pól-nach* | 4a |
| Milan | Милан | *mi-láhn* | 31c |
| mild | лёгкий | *lyókh-kij* | 24p |
| mildly | легко | *likh-kó* | 24p |
| militia | милиция | *mi-lí-tsy-ya* | 34b |
| militiaman | милиционер *(m&f)* | *mi-li-tsy-a-nyér* | 34b |
| milk | молоко | *ma-la-kó* | 24h, 24k |
| millimeter | миллиметр | *mi-li-myétr* | 3a |
| mind | ум | *oom* | 22a |
| mineral | минерал | *mi-ni-ráhl* | 13c |
| mineral spring | минеральный источник | *mi-ni-ráhl'-nyj is-tóch-nik* | 37a |
| mineral water | минеральная вода | *mi-ni-ráhl'-na-ya va-dáh* | 24k |
| minimum | минимум | *mí-ni-mum* | 3b |
| minister | министр | *mi-nístr* | 44 |
| minivan | миниавтобус | *mi-ni-af-tó-bus* | 34a |
| minority | меньшинство | *min'-shyn-stvó* | 44 |
| Minsk | Минск | *minsk* | 31c |
| mint | мята | *myát-ta* | 14e, 24j |
| minus | минус | *mí-nus* | 1e, 6c |
| minute | минута | *mi-nóo-ta* | 4c |
| mirror | зеркало | *zyér-ka-la* | 23c, 36c |
| Miss, Ms., Mrs. | госпожа | *gas-pa-zháh* | 16b |
| missile | ракета | *ra-kyé-ta* | 43 |
| mitten | рукавица | *ru-ka-ví-tsa* | 25k |
| mixer | миксер | *mík-sir* | 23d |
| modem | модем | *mó-dym* | 20b |
| moderator | модератор | *ma-di-ráh-tar* | 20d |
| modest | скромный | *skróm-nyj* | 11e |
| modesty | скромность *(f)* | *skróm-nast'* | 11e |
| molar | коренной зуб | *ka-ri-nój zoop* | 41b |
| Moldova | Молдова | *mal-dó-va* | 31b |
| mole | крот | *krot* | 15a |
| molecule | молекула | *ma-lyé-ku-la* | 13c |
| mom | мама | *máh-ma* | 10a |
| moment | момент | *ma-myént* | 4c |
| monarchy | монархия | *mo-náhr-khi-ya* | 44 |
| monastery | монастырь *(m)* | *ma-nas-týr* | 11d |
| Monday | понедельник | *pa-ni-dyél'-nik* | 5a |
| money | деньги *(pl)* | *dyén'-gi* | 26 |
| monitor | монитор, экран | *ma-ni-tór, ik-rán* | 20b |
| monk | монах *(m)* | *ma-náhkh* | 11d |
| monkey | обезьяна | *a-biz'-yáh-na* | 15a |
| monorail | однорельсовая железная дорога | *ad-na-ryél'-sa-va-ya zhy-lyéz-na-ya da-ró-ga* | 43 |
| month | месяц | *myé-sits* | 4c |
| monthly payment | ежемесячная плата | *í-zhy-myé-sich-na-ya pláh-ta* | 27 |
| monument | монумент | *ma-nu-myént* | 29b |
| monument (tombstone) | памятник | *páh-mit-nik* | 37b |

| | | | |
|---|---|---|---|
| mood (inclination) | наклонение | *nak-la-nyé-ni-ye* | 8a |
| mood (feeling) | настроение | *na-stra-yé-ni-ye* | 11e, 21a |
| moon | луна | *lu-náh* | 5c, 6a, 13a |
| moonlight | лунный свет | *lóon-yj svyet* | 13a |
| morality | мораль *(f)* | *ma-ráhl'* | 45b |
| more | больше, ещё | *ból'-she, i-shchyó* | 3c |
| morning | утро | *óot-ra* | 4a |
| mortgage | ипотека, | *i-pa-tyé-ka,* | 27 |
| | ссуда на жильё | *ssoó-da na zhyl'-yó* | |
| Moscow | Москва | *mask-váh* | 31c |
| mosquito | комар | *ka-máhr* | 15d |
| motel | мотель *(m)* | *ma-tél'* | 36a |
| moth | моль *(f)* | *mol'* | 15d |
| mother | мать *(f)* | *maht'* | 10a |
| mother-in-law | свекровь *(f)* | *svi-króf'* | 10a |
| motion | движение | *dvi-zhéh-ni-ye* | 3e |
| motor | мотор | *ma-tór* | 11e |
| motto | девиз | *di-vís* | 26 |
| mountain | гора | *ga-ráh* | 13b |
| mountain ash | рябина | *ri-bí-na* | 14c |
| mountain bicycle | горный велосипед | *gór-nyj vi-la-si-pyét* | 37a |
| mountain climbing | скалолазание | *ska-la-láh-zyn'-ye* | 28b, 37c |
| mouse | мышь *(f)* | *mysh* | 15a, 20b, 39c |
| moustache | ус(ы) *(m)* | *óso(ý)* | 12a |
| mouth | рот | *rot* | 12a, 41b |
| move *(v)* (a file) | переместить *(p)*, | *pi-ri-mis-tít',* | 20b |
| | перемещать *(i)* | *pi-ri-mi-shchyáht'* | |
| move (something) | двинуть, переехать | *dví-nut', pi-ri-yé-khat'* | 3e, 23f |
| move (oneself) | переехать | *pi-ri-yé-khat'* | 11f |
| move out | уйти из дома | *uj-tí iz dó-ma* | 11c |
| movie, film | кинофильм | *ki-na-fil'm* | 29a |
| movie camera | киноаппарат | *ki-na-a-pa-ráht* | 25d |
| movie star | звезда экрана *(m&f)* | *zviz-dáh yk-ráh-na* | 29a |
| movie theater | кинотеатр | *ki-na-tyáhtr* | 29a |
| MP3 player | эмпи три/Мп3 плеер | *éhm-pi trí/éhm-pi-trí plyé-ir* | 25j |
| Mr. | господин | *gas-pa-dín* | 16b |
| muffler | глушитель *(m)* | *glu-shý-til'* | 34e |
| mugginess | сырость *(f)* | *sý-rast'* | 6a |
| mule | мул | *mool* | 15a |
| multicolored | многоцветный | *mna-ga-tsvyét-nyj* | 7b |
| multifunctional card (banking/ATM) | многофункциональная карточка | *mno-ga-funk-tsy-a-náhl'-na-ya káhr-tych-ka* | 26 |
| multimedia | мультимедия | *móol'-ti-mí-di-ya* | 20b |
| multimedia file | мультимедийные файл | *mul'-ti-mi-díj-nyj fahjl* | 20b |
| multiply | умножить | *um-nó-zhyt'* | 1e |
| multivitamins *(pl)* | мультивитамины *(pl)* | *móol'-ti-vi-ta-mí-ny* | 28b |

| mumble, murmur | бормотать | *bar-ma-táht'* | 17a |
| Munich | Мюнхен | *myún-khin* | 31c |
| murder | убийство | *u-bíjst-va* | 40b |
| murderer | убийца | *u-bíj-tsa* | 40b |
| muscle | мышца | *mýsh-tsa* | 12a, 41a |
| museum | музей | *mu-zyéj* | 29b, 37b |
| mushroom | гриб | *grip* | 14e, 24e |
| music | музыка | *móo-zy-ka* | 25j, 29c, |
| | | | 38e |
| musician, player | музыкант (-ша) | *mu-zy-káhnt (sha)* | 29c, 39a |
| Muslim | мусульманский | *mu-sul'-máhn-skij* | 11d |
| mussel | мидия | *mí-di-ya* | 24d |
| mute | немой | *ni-mój* | 12c |
| My God! | Боже мой! | *bó-zhy moj* | 21c |
| my | мой *(m)*, моё *(n)*, | *moj, ma-yó,* | 8c |
| | моя *(f)*, мои *(pl)* | *ma-yáh, ma-í* | |
| My name is... | Меня зовут... | *mi-nyáh za-vóot* | 11f, 16b |
| mystery novel | детективный роман | *dy-tyk-tív-nyj ra-máhn* | 20a, 25o |

**N**

| nag | пилить | *pi-lít'* | 17a |
| nail | гвоздь *(m)* | *gvost'* | 25b |
| nail polish | лак для ногтей | *lahk dlya nag-tyéj* | 12d, 25f |
| naive | наивный | *na-ív-nyj* | 11e |
| napkin | салфетка | *sal-fyét-ka* | 23d, 241 |
| narrow | узкий | *óos-kij* | 3b, 251 |
| nation | страна | *stra-náh* | 13e, 31a |
| nationality | национальность *(f)* | *na-tsy-a-náhl-nast'* | 11f, 39b |
| natural | естественный | *is-tyést-vi-nyj* | 13b |
| natural gas | природный газ | *pri-ròd-nyj gahs* | 13c |
| natural resources | полезные ископаемые | *pa-lyéz-ny-ye is-ka-páh-i-* | 45a |
| | | *my-ye* | |
| natural sciences | естественные науки *(pl)* | *is-tyést-vi-ny-i na-óo-ki* | 38e |
| nature | природа | *pri-ró-da* | 13b |
| near | при, около | *pri, ó-ka-la* | 8d, 37d |
| neat | аккуратный | *a-ku-ráht-nyj* | 11e |
| neck | шея | *shéh-ya* | 12a |
| necklace | ожерелье | *a-zhy-ryél'-i* | 25i |
| need | нужда, | *nuzh-dáh,* | |
| | необходимость *(f)* | *ni-ap-kha-dí-mast'* | 21a |
| need, to | нуждаться | *nuzh-dáh-tsa* | 21a |
| needle | игла | *ig-láh* | 41b |
| nephew | племянник | *pli-myáh-nik* | 10a |
| nerves | нервы *(pl)* | *nyér-vy* | 41a |
| nervous system | нервная система | *nyérv-na-ya sis-tyé-ma* | 41a |
| net | сеть *(f)* | *syet'* | 28b |
| network | сеть *(f)* | *syet'* | 20b, 20e |
| network connection | сетевое соединение | *si-ti-vó-ye sa-i-di-nyé-ni-ye* | 20b |
| neuter | средний | *sryéd-nij* | 8a |
| neutron | нейтрон | *nijt-rón* | 43 |
| never | никогда | *ni-kag-dáh* | 4e |

| New Year | Новый год | *nó-vyj god* | 5e |
| New Year's Eve | канун Нового года | *ka-nóon nó-va-va gó-da* | 5e, 30a |
| newlyweds | молодожёны *(pl)* | *ma-la-da-zhó-ny* | 11c |
| news | новость *(sg, f)* | *nó-vast'* | 20a |
| newscast | новости *(pl)* | *nò-vas-ti* | 20b |
| newspaper | газета | *ga-zyé-ta* | 20a, 25o |
| next | следующее *(adj) (n)* | *slyé-du-yu-shchi-ye* | 20b |
| nice, pleasant | приятный | *pri-yáht-nyj* | 11e, 21b, 24p |
| nice (person) | симпатичный | *sim-pa-tích-nyj* | 11a |
| niece | племянница | *pli-myáh-ni-tsa* | 10a |
| night | ночь *(f)* | *noch* | 4a |
| nightclub | ночной клуб | *nach-nój kloop* | 37a |
| night school | вечерняя школа | *vi-chyér-ni-ya shkó-la* | 38a |
| nightgown | ночная рубашка | *nach-náh-ya ru-báhsh-ka* | 25k |
| nightingale | соловей | *sa-la-vyéj* | 15b |
| nine | девять | *dyé-vit'* | 1a |
| nineteen | девятнадцать | *di-vit-náh-tsat'* | 1a |
| ninety | девяносто | *di-vi-nó-sta* | 1a |
| ninth | девятый | *di-vyáh-tyj* | 1b |
| nitrogen | азот | *a-zót* | 13c |
| no | нет | *nyet* | 16c |
| no one | никто | *nik-tó* | 3c |
| No Parking! | Нет стоянки! | *nyet sta-yáhn-ki* | 34d |
| No Passing! | Обгон воспрещён! | *ab-gón vas-pri-shchyón,* | |
| | Нет обгона! | *nyet ab-gó-na* | 34d |
| No Thoroughfare! | Нет проезда! | *nyet pra-yéz-da,* | |
| | Нет сквозного проезда! | *nyet skvaz-nó-va pra-yéz-da* | 34d |
| No U-Turn! | Нет разворота! | *nyet raz-va-ró-ta* | 34d |
| noise | шум | *shoom* | 12c |
| noisy | шумный | *shóom-nyj* | 12c |
| nominative | именительный | *i-mi-ní-til'-nyj* | 8a |
| non-fiction | документальная литература | *da-ku-min-táhl'-na-ya li-ti-ra-tóo-ra* | 20a |
| noodles | лапша *(coll)* | *lap-sháh* | 24g |
| noon | полдень *(m)* | *pól-din'* | 4a |
| north | север | *syé-vir* | 3d |
| North America | Северная Америка | *syé-vir-na-ya a-myé-ri-ka* | 31b |
| Norway | Норвегия | *nahr-vyé-gi-ya* | 31b |
| Norwegian (person) | норвежец (-жка) | *nar-vyé-zhyts (-shka)* | 31d |
| Norwegian | норвежский | *nar-vyésh-skij* | 31d |
| nose | нос | *nos* | 12a |
| nostril | ноздря | *nazd-ryáh* | 41a |
| not bad | неплохо | *ni-pló-kha* | 16a |
| note | заметка, нота, записка | *za-myét-ka, nó-ta, za-pís-ka* | 20a, 29c, 19f |
| notebook | тетрадь *(f)* | *tit-ráht'* | 38b |
| notebook | ноутбук, книжка-раскладушка | *nó-ut-buk, knísh-ka-ras-kla-doósh-ka* | 20b |
| notepad | блокнот | *blak-nót* | 25c |
| nothing | ничего | *ni-chi-vó* | 3c |

| noun | существительное | *su-shchis-tví-til'-na-ye* | 8a |
| novel | роман | *ra-máhn* | 20a, 25o, 29d |
| November | ноябрь *(m)* | *na-yáh-bar'* | 5b |
| Novosibirsk | Новосибирск | *na-va-si-bírsk* | 31c |
| now | сейчас/теперь | *si-cháhs/ti-pyér'* | 4e |
| nowhere | никуда | *ni-ku-dáh* | 3d |
| nuclear energy | ядерная энергия | *yáh-dir-na-ya y-néhr-gi-ya* | 13c, 43 |
| nuclear industry | ядерная промышленность | *yáh-dir-na-ya pra-mýsh-li- nast'* | 43 |
| nuclear weapon | ядерное оружие | *yáh-dir-na-ye a-róo-zhy-ye* | 45b |
| nucleus | ядро | *id-ró* | 14a |
| nudism | нудизм | *nóo-dizm* | 45b |
| number | число *(n)* | *chis-ló* | 1d, 8a |
| numeral | числительное | *chis-lí-til'-na-ye* | 8a |
| nun | монахиня *(f)* | *ma-náh-khi-nya* | 11d |
| nurse | медицинская сестра, медсестра | *mi-di-tsýn-ska-ya sist-ráh, mit-sist-ráh* | 39a, 41a |
| nut | орех | *a-ryékh* | 24f |
| nylon | нейлоновый | *nij-ló-na-vyj* | 25l |

| **O** | | | |
| oak | дуб | *doop* | 14c |
| oats | овёс | *a-vyós* | 24i |
| object | дополнение | *da-pal-nyé-ni-ye* | 8a |
| oboe | гобой | *ga-bój* | 29c |
| obstinate | неуклонный | *ni-uk-ló-nyj* | 11e |
| occasionally | иногда | *i-nag-dáh* | 4a, 4e |
| occupation | занятие | *za-nyáh-ti-ye* | 39a |
| ocean | океан | *a-ki-áhn* | 13b |
| October | октябрь *(m)* | *ak-tyáh-bar'* | 5b |
| octopus | осьминог | *as'-mi-nók* | 15d |
| odd, strange | странный | *stráh-nyj* | 11e |
| offend | обидеть | *a-bí-dit'* | 17a |
| office | контора, офис | *kan-tó-ra, ó-fis* | 39d, 26 |
| office hours | часы *(pl)* приёма | *chi-sý pri-yó-ma* | 41b |
| often | часто *(adv)* | *cháhs-ta* | 4e |
| oil | масло | *máhs-la* | 13c, 24j, 34e |
| OK, good | хорошо | *kha-ra-shó* | 16c |
| old | старый | *stáh-ryj* | 11b |
| old man | старик | *sta-rík* | 11a |
| older | старше | *stáhr-she* | 11b |
| omelet | омлет | *am-lyét* | 24g |
| on | на | *nah* | 8d |
| on sale | на распродаже | *na ras-pra-dáh-zhy* | 25a |
| On the whole | В общем | *v óp-shchim* | 21c |
| on time | вовремя | *vóvrye-mya* | 4e, 33b, 35 |
| once | однажды | *ad-náhzh-dy* | 4e |

| once more | ещё раз | i-shchyó rahs | 4e |
| one | один | a-dín | 1a |
| one hundred | сто/сотня | sto/sót-nya | 1a |
| one million | миллион | mi-li-ón | 1a |
| one thousand | тысяча | tý-si-cha | 1a |
| One Way | Одностороннее движение | ad-na-sta-ró-ni-ye dvi-zhéh-ni-ye | 34d |
| one-half | пол-/половина | pol-/pa-la-ví-na | 1c |
| onion | лук | look | 14e, 24e |
| online | он-лайн | an-láhjn | 20d |
| only | только | tól'-ka | 4e |
| opaque | непрозрачный | ni-praz-ráhch-nyj | 7b, 13d |
| open | открыт, | at-krýt', | 20b, |
| | открывать | at-kry-váht' | 25a |
| open a browser | открыть (p) браузер, | at-krýt' bráh-u-zir, | 20b |
| | открывать (i) | at-kry-váht' | |
| open a file | открыть (p) файл, | at-krýt' fahjl, | 20b |
| | открывать (i) | at-kry-váht' | |
| open a program | открыть (p) программу, | at-krýt' prag-ráh-mu, | 20b |
| | открывать (i), | at-kry-váht', | |
| | войти (p) в программу, | vaj-tí f prag-ráh-mu, | |
| | идти (i) | it-tí | |
| opening (n) | открытие | at-krý-ti-ye | 20b |
| opera | опера | ó-pi-ra | 29c |
| operating room | операционная | a-pi-ra-tsy-ó-na-ya | 41a |
| operating system | оперативная система | a-pi-ra-tív-na-ya sis-tyé-ma | 20b |
| operation | операция | a-pi-ráh-tsy-ya | 41a |
| operator | телефонист(ка) | ti-li-fa-níst(ka) | 18b |
| opinion | мнение | mnyé-ni-ye | 22a |
| opposition (political) | оппозиция | a-pa-zí-tsy-ya | 44 |
| optimism | оптимизм | ap-ti-mízm | 11e |
| optimist | оптимист | ap-ti-míst | 11e |
| optimistic | оптимистичный | ap-ti-mis-tích-nyj | 11e |
| option | опция | óp-tsy-ya | 20b |
| or | или | í-li | 8h |
| oral | устный | óos-nyj | 17a |
| orange (fruit) | апельсин | a-pil'-sín | 14d, 24f |
| orange (color) | оранжевый | a-ráhn-zhy-vyj | 7a |
| orbit | орбита | ar-bí-ta | 13a |
| orchestra | оркестр | ar-kyéstr | 29c |
| order | приказ | pri-káhs | 17a |
| order, to (command) | приказать | pri-ka-záht' | 17a |
| order | заказать | za-ka-záht' | 24o |
| order a call, to acquire | заказать разговор | za-ka-záht' raz-ga-vór | 18b |
| organ (instrument) | орган | ar-gáhn | 29c |
| organ (body part) | орган | ór-gan | 12a |
| organic | органический | ar-ga-ní-chis-kij | 13c |
| original | оригинальный | a-ri-gi-náhl'-nyj | 11e |
| ostrich | страус | stráh-us | 15b |

| | | | |
|---|---|---|---|
| **our** | наш *(m)*, наше *(n)*, | nahsh, náh-shy, | 8c |
| | наша *(f)*, наши *(pl)* | náh-sha, náh-shy | |
| **out** | из | is | 8d |
| **outlet** | розетка | ra-zyét-ka | 25b |
| **outlet (phone)** | (телефонная) розетка | (ti-li-fó-na-ya) ra-zyét-ka | 18a |
| **output** | аутпут | áh-ut-put | 20b |
| **outside** | снаружи, извне *(adv)* | sna-róo-zhy, iz-vnyé | 3d, 37d |
| **outskirts** | окраины *(pl)* | ak-ráh-i-ny | 31a |
| **oven** | духовка | du-khóf-ka | 23d |
| **owl** | сова | sa-váh | 15b |
| **owner** | владелец *(m)*, | vla-dyé-lits, | 26 |
| | владелица *(f)* | vla-dyé-li-tsa | |
| **ox** | вол | vol | 15a |
| **oxygen** | кислород | kis-la-rót | 13c |
| **oyster** | устрица | óost-ri-tsa | 15d, 24d |
| **P** | | | |
| **P. S.** | постскриптум | past-skríp-tum | 19d |
| **Pacific Ocean** | Тихий океан | tí-khij a-ki-áhn | 13b |
| **pack** | упаковать (-ся) | u-pa-ka-váht' (-tsa) | 32 |
| (one's bags/luggage) | | | |
| **package** | посылка | pa-sýl-ka | 19f |
| **pad** | блокнот | blak-nót | 19e |
| **pagan** | язычник | i-zých-nik | 11d |
| **page** | страница | stra-ní-tsa | 19e, 19f |
| **pail** | ведро | vid-ró | 23d |
| **pain** | боль *(f)* | bol' | 41a |
| **paint** | краска | kráhs-ka | 7c, 29b |
| **paint, to** | красить | kráh-sit' | 23f |
| **painter (artist)** | художник (-ница) | khu-dózh-nik (-ni-tsa) | 7c, 39a |
| **painter (walls)** | маляр | ma-lyáhr | 39a |
| **painter (workman)** | маляр | ma-lyáhr | 7c |
| **painting** | картина | kar-tí-na | 23c |
| **pair** | пара | páh-ra | 25n |
| **pajamas** | пижама | pi-zháh-ma | 25k |
| **palate** | нёбо | nyó-ba | 41b |
| **palm** | пальма | páhl'-ma | 14c |
| **pamphlet, brochure** | брошюра | bra-shóo-ra | 20a, 31a |
| **pan** | сковорода | ska-va-ra-dáh | 23d |
| **pants** | штаны | shta-ný | 25k |
| **panty** | трусики *(pl)* | tróo-si-ki | 25k |
| **pantyhose** | колготки *(pl)* | kal-gót-ki | 25k |
| **paper** | бумага | bu-máh-ga | 19e, 25c, 38b, 39c |
| **parade** | парад | pa-ráht | 30a |
| **paragraph** | абзац | ab-záhts | 19d |
| **parallel port** | параллельный порт | pa-ra-lyél'-nyj port | 20b |
| **parenthesis** | круглая скобка | króog-la-ya skóp-ka | 19d |
| **Paris** | Париж | pa-rísh | 31c |
| **park** | парк | pahrk | 37b |
| **park (a car)** | поставить машину | pa-stáh-vit' ma-shý-nu | 34c |

| parking | парковка, | par-kóf-ka, | 23a, |
| | стоянка | sta-yáhn-ka | 34c |
| parking (spot/place) | парковочное место, | par-kó-vach-na-ye myés-ta, | 27 |
| | парковка (slang) | par-kóf-ka | |
| parking zone | парковочная зона | par-kó-vach-na-ya zó-na | 34c |
| parliament | парламент | par-láh-mint | 44 |
| parliamentary | парламентские | par-láh-mints-ki-i | 44 |
| elections | выборы | vý-ba-ry | |
| parrot | попугай | pa-pu-gáhj | 15b |
| parsley | петрушка | pit-róosh-ka | 14e, 24j |
| part | часть (f) | chahst' | 3c |
| participle | причастие | pri-cháhs-ti-ye | 8a |
| (verbal adjective) | | | |
| particle | частица | chis-tí-tsa | 13c |
| party | вечеринка | vi-chi-rín-ka | 30b |
| party in power | партия власти | páhr-ti-ya vláhs-ti | 44 |
| pass | обогнать | a-bag-náht' | 34c |
| pass an exam | выдержать экзамен | vý-dír-zhat' yk-záh-min | 38f |
| pass by | пройти | praj-tí | 3e |
| pass | передача, пас | pi-ri-dáh-cha, pahs | 28b |
| passenger | пассажир (-ка) | pa-sa-zhýr (-ka) | 33c, 34b |
| passport | паспорт | páhs-part | 11f, 31a, |
| | | | 32, 36b |
| passport control | паспортный | páhs-part-nyj kant-ról' | 32 |
| | контроль (m) | | |
| password | пароль | pa-ról' | 19a |
| past | прошлое | prósh-la-ye | 4e |
| pastry | пирожное | pi-rózh-na-ye | 24g |
| patience | терпение | tir-pyé-ni-ye | 11e, 21a |
| patient | пациент | pa-tsy-éhnt | 41a |
| patient (adj) | терпеливый | tir-pi-lí-vyj | 11e, 21a |
| patronymic | отчество | ót-chist-va | 11f |
| paw | лапа | láh-pa | 15a |
| pay phone | телефон-автомат | ti-li-fón-af-ta-máht | 18a |
| pay | платить | pla-tít' | 25a, 26, |
| | | | 36b |
| pay (buy) by check | купить (p) чеком, | ku-pít' chyé-kam, | 25a |
| | покупать (i) | pa-ku-páht' | |
| payment | оплата, платёж | a-pláh-ta, pla-tyósh | 26 |
| pea | горох (coll), | ga-rókh, | 14e, |
| | горошина (sg) | ga-ró-shy-na | 24e |
| peace | мир | mir | 44 |
| peach | персик | pyér-sik | 14d, 24f |
| peanut | арахис (coll) | a-ráh-khis | 24f |
| pear | груша | gróo-sha | 14d |
| pear tree | грушевое дерево | gróo-shi-va-ye dyé-ri-va | 14c |
| pedal | педаль (f) | pi-dáhl' | 34a |
| pedestrian | пешеход | pi-shy-khót | 34b |
| pedestrian crossing | пешеходный переход | pi-shy-khód-nyj pi-ri-khót | 34c, 37b |
| peel | очистить | a-chís-tit' | 24o |
| pelican | пеликан | pi-li-káhn | 15b |

| | | | |
|---|---|---|---|
| pen | ручка | *róoch-ka* | 2b, 7c, 19e, 25c, 38b, 39c |
| penalty shot, kick | штрафной удар | *shtraf-nój u-dáhr* | 28b |
| pencil | карандаш | *ka-ran-dáhsh* | 2b, 19e, 25c, 38b, 39c |
| penguin | пингвин | *pin-gvín* | 15b |
| penicillin | пенициллин | *pi-ni-tsy-lín* | 25h |
| peninsula | полуостров | *pa-lu-óst-rof* | 13b |
| pepper | перец | *pyé-rits* | 24j |
| percent | процент | *pra-tséhnt* | 1f |
| percentage rate | процентная ставка | *pra-tséhnt-na-ya stáhf-ka* | 27 |
| perch | окунь | *ó-kun'* | 24d |
| perfection | совершенство | *sa-vír-shéh-stva* | 11e |
| perfective | совершенный | *sa-vir-shéh-nyj* | 8a |
| perfume | духи *(pl)* | *du-khí* | 12d, 25f |
| peripherals | периферические устройства | *pi-ri-fi-rí-chis-ki-ye ust-rójst-va* | 20b |
| permissions *(pl)* | права *(pl)* доступа | *pra-váh dós-tu-pa* | 20b |
| person | лицо | *li-tsó* | 8a |
| person-to-person | от лица к лицу | *at li-tsáh k li-tsóo* | 18b |
| personal computer | персональный компьютер | *pir-sa-náhl'-nyj kamp'-yú-tar* | 20b |
| perspire | потеть | *pa-tyét'* | 6b |
| persuade, convince | убедить | *u-bi-dít'* | 22b |
| pessimism | пессимизм | *pi-si-mízm* | 11e |
| pessimist | пессимист | *pi-si-míst* | 11e |
| pessimistic | пессимистичный | *pi-si-mis-tich-nyj* | 11e |
| pet | домашнее животное | *da-máhsh-ni-ye zhy-vót-na-ye* | 15a |
| petal | лепесток | *li-pis-tók* | 14a, 14b |
| petroleum | нефть *(f)* | *nyeft'* | 13c |
| pharmacist | фармацевт *(m&f)*, аптекарь *(m)* (-рша) | *far-ma-tséhft, ap-tyé-kar' ('-rsha)* | 25h, 39a |
| philosophy | философия | *fi-la-só-fi-ya* | 38e |
| phone book | телефонная книга | *ti-li-fó-na-ya kní-ga* | 18a |
| phone booth | телефонная будка | *ti-li-fó-na-ya bóot-ka* | 18a |
| phone camera | телефонная камера | *ti-li-fó-na-ya káh-mi-ra* | 18a |
| phone card | телефонная карточка | *ti-li-fó-na-ya káhr-tach-ka* | 18a |
| phonetics | звуковая система | *zvu-ka-váh-ya sis-tyé-ma* | 8a |
| photo | фотография | *fa-ta-gráh-fi-ya* | 20a, 25d |
| photocopier | копировальная машина | *ka-pi-ra-váhl'-na-ya ma-shý-na* | 39c |
| photosynthesis | фотосинтез | *fa-ta-sín-tis* | 14a |
| phrase | фраза/оборот | *fráh-za/a-ba-rót* | 19d |
| physical | физический | *fí-zí-chis-kij* | 13c |
| physicist | физик *(m&f)* | *fí-zik* | 39a |
| physics | физика | *fí-zi-ka* | 13c, 38e |
| piano | пианино | *pi-a-ní-na* | 29c |
| pick flowers | собрать цветы | *sab-ráht' tsvi-tý* | 14b |

| | | | |
|---|---|---|---|
| pick up the phone | взять трубку | vzyáht' tróop-ku | 18b |
| pickpocket | карманщик | kar-máhn-shchik | 40b |
| pie | пирог | pi-rók | 24g |
| piece | кусок | ku-sók | 24o |
| pig | свинья | svin'-yáh | 15a |
| pill | таблетка | tab-lyét-ka | 25h, 41a |
| pillow | подушка | pa-dóosh-ka | 23d, 36c |
| pillowcase | наволочка | náh-va-lach-ka | 23d |
| pilot | лётчик, пилот | lyót-chik, pi-lót | 39a |
| pimple | прыщ | prysh | 41a |
| PIN (personal | личный код/личный | lích-nyj kot/lích-nyj | 26 |
| identification number) | (идентификационный) | (i-din-ti-fi-ka-tsy-ón-nyj) | |
| | номер | nó-mir | |
| pine | сосна | sas-náh | 14c |
| pineapple | ананас | a-na-náhs | 14d, 24f |
| ping-pong | пинг-понг | pink-pónk | 28b |
| pink | розовый | ró-za-vyj | 7a |
| pipe | трубка | tróop-ka | 25e |
| pistol | пистолет | pis-ta-lyét | 40b |
| piston | поршень (m) | pór-shyn' | 34e |
| place | место | myés-ta | 3d, 33c |
| place of birth | место рождения | myés-ta razh-dyé-ni-ya | 11f, 39b |
| place of employment | место работы | myés-ta ra-bó-ty | 11f, 39b |
| place of residence | местожительство, | myes-ta-zhý-til'-stva, | 11f, |
| | место проживания | myés-ta pra-zhi-váh-ni-ya | 27 |
| plain | равнина | rav-ní-na | 13b |
| plain-looking, simple | простой | pra-stój | 11a, 22a |
| plainly, simply | просто | prós-ta | 11a, 22a |
| planet | планета | pla-nyé-ta | 13a |
| plant | растение (-ье) | ras-tyé-ni-ye | 14a |
| plant (factory) | завод | za-vót | 39d |
| plastic | пластик | pláhs-tík | 13c |
| plastic card (plastic) | пластиковая | pláhs-ti-ka-va-ya | 26 |
| | карточка | káhr-tych-ka | |
| plate | тарелка | ta-ryél-ka | 23d, 24l |
| platform | платформа | plat-fór-ma | 35 |
| platinum | платина | pláh-ti-na | 13c |
| platter, dish | блюдо | blyú-da | 24l |
| play | пьеса | p'yé-sa | 20a |
| play (a game) | играть в... | ig-ráht' v | 28a |
| play | поставить пластинку, | pas-táh-vit' plas-tín-ku, | 20b |
| (a record, tape, disc) | кассету, диск | ka-syé-tu, disk | |
| play (an instrument) | играть | ig-ráht' | 28a, 29c |
| | (на инструменте) | (na in-stru-myén-te) | |
| player | игрок (m&f) | ig-rók | 28b |
| playful | шутливый | shut-lí-vyj | 11e |
| playwright | драматург (m&f) | dra-ma-tóorg | 29e |
| plea | заявление | za-iv-lyé-ni-ye | 42 |
| pleasantly | приятно | pri-yáht-na | 24p |
| Please! | Пожалуйста! | pa-znáh-lus-ta! | 16c |
| pliers | плоскогубцы (pl) | pla-ska-góop-tsy | 25b |

| plot | сюжет | *syu-zhéht* | 20a, 29d, 29e |
| plough | пахать | *pa-khát'* | 14a |
| plug | штепсель *(m)*, вилка | *shtéhp-sil', víl-ka* | 18a, 25b |
| plum | слива | *slí-va* | 14d, 24f |
| plum tree | сливовое дерево | *sli-vó-va-ye dyé-ri-va* | 14c |
| plumber | слесарь *(m)* | *slyé-sar'* | 39a |
| plumbing | водопровод | *va-da-pra-vót* | 25b |
| plural | множественное число | *mnó-zhys-tvi-na-ye chis-ló* | 8a |
| plus | плюс | *plyus* | 1e, 6c |
| pneumonia | воспаление лёгких | *vas-pa-lyé-ni-ye lyókh-kikh* | 41a |
| pocket | карман | *kar-máhn* | 25g |
| poem (long) | поэма | *pa-éh-ma* | 20a |
| poem (short) | стихотворение | *sti-khat-va-ryé-ni-ye* | 20a |
| poet | поэт *(m)*, поэтесса *(f)* | *pa-éht, pa-y-téh-sa* | 29d |
| poetry | поэзия | *pa-éh-zi-ya* | 20a, 25o, 29d |
| point (geometry) | точка | *tóch-ka* | 2b |
| point (score) | очко *(sg)*, очки *(pl)* | *ach-kó, ach-kí* | 28b |
| Poland | Польша | *pól'-sha* | 31b |
| Pole | полюс | *pó-lyus* | 13e |
| Pole | поляк (полька) | *pa-lyáhk (pól'-ka)* | 31d |
| police | милиция | *mi-lí-tsy-ya* | 40b, 40c |
| police department (station) | отделение милиции | *at-di-lyé-ni-ye mi-lí-tsy-i* | 42 |
| police officer | милиционер | *mi-li-tsy-a-nyér* | 39a, 40b |
| policy | политика | *pa-lí-ti-ka* | 44 |
| Polish | польский | *pól'-skij* | 31d |
| politics | политика | *pa-lí-ti-ka* | 44 |
| pollen | пыльца | *pyl'-tsáh* | 14a |
| pollution | загрязнение | *zag-riz-nyé-ni-ye* | 13c |
| polyester | полиэфир | *pa-li-y-fír* | 251 |
| pond | пруд | *proot* | 37c |
| pool | бассейн | *ba-syéjn* | 36b |
| poor *(n & adj)* | бедняк *(n) (m)*, беднячка *(n) (f)*, бедный *(adj) (m)*, бедная *(adj) (f)* | *bid-nyáhk, bid-nyáhch-ka, byéd-nyj, byéd-na-ya* | 11e, 45b |
| Poor man! | Бедняга! | *bid-nyáh-ga* | 21c |
| Poor woman! | Бедняжка! | *bid-nyáhsh-ka* | 21c |
| poppy | мак | *mahk* | 14b |
| population | население | *na-si-lyé-ni-ye* | 27 |
| porch | крыльцо | *kryl'-tsó* | 23a |
| pork | свинина | *svi-ní-na* | 24c |
| porno movie | порнографический фильм | *par-na-gra-fí-chis-kij fil'm* | 29a |
| pornography | порнография | *par-na-gráh-fi-ya* | 45b |
| portable radio | транзисторный приёмник | *tran-zís-tar-nyj pri-yóm-nik* | 20b |
| portal | портал | *pór-tal* | 20d |
| porter | носильщик | *na-síl'-shchik* | 35, 36b |

| portly | полный | *pól-nyj* | 11a |
|---|---|---|---|
| portrait | портрет | *part-ryét* | 29b |
| **Portuguese (person)** | португалец (-лка) | *par-tu-gáh-lits (lka)* | 31d |
| **Portuguese** | португальский | *par-tu-gáh'l-kij* | 31d |
| post office | почта, почтовое | *póch-ta, pach-tó-va-ye* | 19f |
| | отделение | *at-di-lyé-ni-ye* | |
| postcard | открытка | *at-krýt-ka* | 19f |
| pot | кастрюля | *kast-ryúh-lya* | 23d |
| potato | картофель *(coll, m)*, | *kar-tó-fil',* | 14e, 24e |
| | картошка *(coll)*, | *kar-tósh-ka,* | |
| | картофелина *(sg)* | *kar-tó-fí-li-na* | |
| pound (U.K.) | фунт | *foont* | 26 |
| pour | налить | *na-lít'* | 24o |
| poverty | бедность | *byéd-nast'* | 45b |
| powder | порошок | *pa-ra-shók* | 25h |
| practical | практичный | *prak-tích-nyj* | 11e |
| practicality | практичность *(f)* | *prak-tích-nast'* | 11e |
| Prague | Прага | *práh-ga* | 31c |
| praise | хвалить | *khva-lít'* | 17a |
| pray | молиться | *ma-lít-tsa* | 11d, 17a |
| prayer | молитва | *ma-lít-va* | 11d, 17a |
| preach | проповедовать | *pra-pa-vyé-da-vat'* | 17a |
| precipitation | осадки *(pl)* | *a-sáhd-ki* | 6a |
| predicate | сказуемое | *ska-zóo-i-ma-ye* | 8a |
| preface | предисловие | *pri-dis-ló-vi-ye* | 29d |
| prefer | предпочесть | *prit-pa-chyést'* | 21b |
| preferable | предпочтительный | *prit-pach-tí-til'-nyj* | 21b |
| preference | предпочтение | *prit-pach-tyé-ni-ye* | 21b |
| pregnancy | беременность *(f)* | *bi-ryé-mi-nast'* | 11c |
| pregnant | беременная | *bi-ryé-mi-na-ya* | 41a |
| preposition | предлог | *prid-lók* | 8a |
| prepositional | предложный | *prid-lózh-nyj* | 8a |
| prescription | рецепт | *ri-tséhpt* | 25h, 41a |
| present | настоящее | *nas-ta-yáh-shchi-ye* | 4e |
| president | президент | *pri-zi-dyént* | 44 |
| previous | предыдущий | *pri-dy-dóo-shchij* | 4e |
| price | цена | *tsy-náh* | 24m, 25a, 36b |
| priest | священник | *svi-shchyé-nik* | 11d, 39a |
| principal's office | кабинет директора | *ka-bi-nyét di-ryék-ta-ra* | 38c |
| print | шрифт | *shrift* | 20a |
| print *(n)* | распечатка | *ras-pi-cháht-ka* | 20b |
| print *(v)* | напечатать *(p)*, | *na-pi-cháh-tat',* | 20b |
| | печатать *(i)*, | *pi-cháh-tat',* | |
| | вывести *(p)* на печать, | *vý-vis-ti na pi-cháht',* | |
| | выводить *(i)* | *vy-va-dít'* | |
| printed matter | бандероль *(f)* | *ban-dy-ról'* | 19f |
| printer | принтер | *prín-tyr* | 20b, |
| | печатник | *pi-cháht-nik* | 39c |
| printer cartridge | картридж | *káhrt-ridzh* | 20b |
| printing | печатание | *pi-cháh-ta-ni-ye* | 20a |
| printing *(n)* | вывод на печать | *vý-vat na pi-cháht'* | 20b |

| | | | |
|---|---|---|---|
| **private bank** | частные банк | *cháhs-nyj bahnk* | 26 |
| **private transportation** | личный транспорт | *lích-nyj tráhns-part* | 34c |
| **problem** | проблема, задача | *pràb-lyé-ma, za-dáh-cha* | 1f, 22a, 38f |
| **processor** | процессор | *pra-tséh-sar* | 20b |
| **products** *(pl)*, merchandise | товары *(pl)* | *ta-váh-ry* | 25a |
| **profession** | специальность *(f)*, профессия | *spi-tsáhl'-nast', pra-fyé-si-ya* | 11f, 33a, 39b |
| **professional** | профессиональный работник | *pra-fi-si-a-náhl'-nyj ra-bót-nik* | 11f |
| **professor** | профессор *(m&f)* | *pra-fyé-sar* | 16b, 38d, 39a |
| **program (software)** | программа, прога *(slang)* | *prag-ráh-ma, pró-ga* | 20b |
| **projector** | проектор | *pra-éhk-tar* | 20e |
| **promise** | обещание | *a-bi-shcháh-ni-ye* | 17a |
| **promise, to** | обещать | *a-bi-shcháht'* | 17a |
| **pronoun** | местоимение | *mis-ta-i-myé-ni-ye* | 8a |
| **pronounce** | произнести | *pra-iz-nis-tí* | 17a |
| **pronunciation** | произношение | *pra-iz-na-shéh-ni-ye* | 8a, 17a |
| **properties** *(pl)* | свойства *(pl)* | *svójst-va* | 20b, 20d |
| **propose** | предложить | *prid-la-zhýt'* | 17a |
| **prose** | проза | *pró-za* | 29d |
| **prostitute** | проститутка | *pras-ti-tóot-ka* | 39a |
| **prostitution** | проституция | *pras-ti-tóo-tsy-ya* | 45b |
| **protect** | защитить | *za-shchi-tít'* | 40a |
| **proton** | протон | *pra-tón* | 43 |
| **proud** | гордый | *gór-dyj* | 11e |
| **proverb** | пословица | *pas-ló-vi-tsa* | 8a |
| **provided that** | при условии, что | *pri us-ló-vi-i shto* | 8h |
| **province** | провинция | *pra-vín-tsy-ya* | 13e |
| **proximity** | близость | *blí-zast'* | 27 |
| **prune** | чернослив *(coll)* | *chir-na-slíf* | 14d, 24f |
| **psychiatrist** | психиатр | *psi-khi-áhtr* | 39a |
| **psychologist** | психолог *(m&f)* | *psi-khó-lak* | 39a |
| **psychology** | психология | *psi-kha-ló-gi-ya* | 38e |
| **public prosecutor** | народный обвинитель *(m&f)* | *na-ród-nyj ab-vi-ní-til'* | 42 |
| **public transportation** | общественный транспорт | *ab-shchyést-vi-nyj tráhns-part* | 34c |
| **publish** | публиковать | *pub-li-ka-váht'* | 20a |
| **publisher** | издатель *(m)* (-ница) | *iz-dáh-til' (ni-tsa)* | 20a |
| **pull** | потянуть | *pa-ti-nóot'* | 3e |
| **pulse** | пульс | *pool's* | 41a |
| **pumpkin** | тыква | *týk-va* | 14e |
| **punctuation** | знаки препинания | *znáh-ki pri-pi-náh-ni-ya* | 19d |
| **pupil** | ученик (-ница) | *u-chi-ník (-ni-tsa)* | 38d |
| **purchase** | покупка | *pa-kóop-ka* | 25a |
| **pure** | чистый | *chís-tyj* | 7b, 13d |
| **purple** | лиловый | *li-ló-vyj* | 7a |

| push | толкать *(i)* | *tal-káht'* | 3e |
| | толкнуть *(p)* | *talk-noot'* | |
| push (lawn) mower | ручная газонокосилка | *ruch-náh-ya ga-zó-na-ka-síl-ka* | 23a |
| put | ставить | *stáh-vit'* | 3e |
| put a room in order | убрать комнату | *u-bráht' kóm-na-tu* | 23f |
| put down | положить | *pa-la-zhýt'* | 3e |
| put on | одеть, надеть | *a-dyét', na-dyét'* | 25m |
| put on makeup | краситься | *kráh-si-tsa* | 12d |
| pyramid | пирамида | *pi-ra-mí-da* | 2a |

**Q**

| quantity | количество | *ka-lí-chist-va* | 3c |
| queen | королева | *ka-ra-lyé-va* | 28a |
| question | вопрос | *vap-rós* | 38f |
| question mark | вопросительный знак | *vap-ra-sí-til'-nyj znahk* | 19d |
| quickly | быстро *(adv)* | *býst-za* | 3e |
| quiet *(adj)* | тихий | *tí-khij* | 17a |
| quiet | тишина | *ti-shy-náh* | 17a |
| Quiet! | Тихо! | *tí-kha* | 21c |
| quietly | тихо | *tí-kha* | 17a |
| quotation marks | кавычки | *ka-vých-ki* | 19d |

**R**

| rabbi | раввин | *ra-vín* | 11d |
| rabbit | кролик | *kró-lik* | 15a |
| race | пробег, гонки *(pl)* | *pra-byék, gón-ki* | 28b |
| racism | расизм | *ra-sízm* | 45b |
| radiator | радиатор | *ra-di-áh-tar* | 34e |
| radio | радио | *ráh-di-a* | 20b, 23d, 36c |
| radioactive wastes | радиоактивные отходы | *ra-di-a-ak-tív-ny-ye at-khó-dy* | 13c |
| rafting | сплав на плотах | *splahf na pla-táhkh* | 28b |
| rag | тряпка | *tryáhp-ka* | 23d |
| railroad | железная дорога | *zhy-lyéz-na-ya da-ró-ga* | 35 |
| rain | дождь *(m)* | *dosht'* | 6a |
| raincoat | плащ, дождевик | *plahshch, dazh-di-vík* | 25k |
| rainy | дождливый | *dazhd-lí-vyj* | 6a |
| raise, to | вырастить | *vý-ras-tit'* | 14a |
| rap | рэп | *rehp* | 25j |
| rape | изнасилование | *iz-na-sí-la-va-ni-ye* | 40b |
| rape, to | изнасиловать | *iz-na-sí-la-vat'* | 40b |
| rare | редкий *(adj)* | *ryét-kij* | 4e |
| rarely | редко | *ryét-ka* | 4e |
| raspberry | малина *(coll)* | *ma-lí-na* | 14d, 24f |
| rat | крыса | *krý-sa* | 15a |
| ratio | отношение | *at-na-shéh-ni-ye* | 1e |
| razor | бритва | *brít-va* | 12d, 25f |
| read | прочитать | *pra-chi-táht'* | 20a, 38f |
| reader | читатель *(m)* (-ница) | *chi-táh-til' (-ni-tsa)* | 20a |

| reading | чтение | *chtyé-ni-ye* | 38f |
|---|---|---|---|
| real estate | жилая недвижимость | *zhy-láh-ya nid-vi-zhý-mast'* | 27 |
| real estate agency | агентство недвижимости | *a-gyént-stva nid-vi-zhý-mas-ti* | 27 |
| **Really?** | Действительно?, Правда?, На самом деле? | *dist-ví-til'-na, práhv-da, na sáh-mam dyé-li* | 21c |
| rearview mirror | зеркало заднего вида | *zyér-ka-la záhd-ni-va ví-da* | 34e |
| reason | причина, основание | *pri-chí-na, as-na-váh-ni-ye* | 22a, 22b |
| receipt | квитанция | *kvi-táhn-tsy-ya* | 26, 36b |
| receive | получить *(p)*, получать *(i)* | *pa-lu-chít', pa-lu-cháht'* | 19a, 19f |
| receiver, tuner | приёмник | *pri-yóm-nik* | 20b |
| receiver (microphone) | микрофон | *mik-ra-fón* | 18a |
| recent | недавний *(adj)* | *ni-dáhv-nij* | 4e |
| recently | недавно *(adv)* | *ni-dáhv-na* | 4a, 4e |
| recommend | рекомендовать | *ri-ka-min-da-váht'* | 17a |
| record, to | записывать (музыку) | *za-pí-sy-vat' (móo-zy-ku)* | 20b |
| record player | проигрыватель *(m)* | *pra-íg-ry-va-til'* | 20b, 38b |
| recording | запись | *záh-pis'* | 25j |
| rectum | прямая кишка | *pri-máh-ya kish-káh* | 41a |
| red | красный | *kráhs-nyj* | 7a |
| "red eye" | "красные глаза" *(pl)* | *kráhs-ny-i gláh-za* | 25d |
| red-haired | рыжий, рыжеволосый | *rý-zhyj, ry-zhy-va-ló-syj* | 11a |
| reduction (of payment) | снижение платы | *sni-zhéh-ni-ye pláh-ty* | 27 |
| referee | судья *(m&f)* | *sud'-yáh* | 28h |
| reference book | справочник | *spráh-vach-nik* | 20a, 25o |
| referendum | референдум | *ri-fi-ryén-dum* | 44 |
| refinancing | рефинансирование | *ri-fi-nan-sí-ra-va-ni-ye* | 27 |
| reflect | отразить | *at ra-zít'* | 22b |
| reform | реформа | *ri-fór-ma* | 44 |
| refrigerator | холодильник | *kha-la-díl'-nik* | 23d |
| region | район, область *(f)*, регион | *raj-ón, ób-last', ri-gi-ón* | 13e, 44 |
| registered letter | заказное письмо | *za-kaz-nó-ye pis'-mó* | 19f |
| registration | регистрация | *ri-gist-ráh-tsy-ya* | 38f |
| relate (connect) | связать | *svi-záht'* | 17a |
| relate (narrate) | рассказать | *ras-ka-záht'* | 17a |
| relative | родственник | *rót-stvín-ik* | 10a |
| relax *(v)* | расслабиться *(p)*, расслабляться *(i)* | *ras-sláh-bi-tsa, ras-sla-blyáh-tsa* | 37a |
| relief | облегчение | *ab-likh-chyé-ni-ye* | 21a |
| religion | религия | *ri-lí-gi-ya* | 11d |
| remain | остаться | *a-stáh-tsa* | 30b |
| remember | помнить | *póm-nit'* | 22b |
| remote control | дистанционное управление | *dis-tan-tsy-ó-na-ye up-rav-lyé-ni-ye* | 20b |
| rename | переименовать *(p)*, переименовывать *(i)* | *pi-ri-mi-na-váht', pi-ri-mi-nó-vy-vat'* | 20b |

| | | | |
|---|---|---|---|
| **rent** | плата за квартиру | *pláh-ta za kvar-tí-ru* | 23g |
| **rent, to** | снять | *snyaht'* | 23g |
| **rent** *(v)* | взять *(p)*/брать *(i)*/ | *vzyaht'/braht'/* | 37a |
| | взимать *(i)* на прокат | *vzi-máht' na pra-káht* | |
| **rent** *(v)* **(to someone)** | здать *(p)* комнату/дом, | *sdáht' kóm-na-tu/dom,* | 27 |
| | здавать *(i)* | *sda-váht'* | |
| **rent** *(v)* **(from someone)** | снять *(p)* комнату/дом, | *snyáht' kóm-na-tu/dom,* | 27 |
| | снимать *(i)*, | *sni-máht',* | |
| | заарендовать *(p)*, | *za-a-rin-da-váht',* | |
| | арендовать *(i)* | *a-rin-da-váht',* | |
| **rental** *(n, adj)* | аренда | *a-ryén-da* | 27 |
| **repairman** | монтёр (-ша) | *man-tyór (-sha)* | 39a |
| **repeat** | повторить | *paf-ta-rít'* | 17a, 38f |
| **repetition** | повторение | *paf-ta-ryé-ni-ye* | 17a |
| **reply** | ответ (-ное письмо) | *at-vyét (-na-ye pis'-mó)* | 19f |
| **reply, to** | ответить | *at-vyé-tít'* | 19f |
| **report** | доклад | *dak-láht* | 17a |
| **report, to** | доложить | *da-la-zhýt'* | 17a |
| **reporter** | корреспондент (-ка) | *ka-ris-pan-dyént (-ka)* | 20a |
| **reproach** | упрёк | *up-ryók* | 17a |
| **reproach, to** | упрекнуть | *up-rík-nóot'* | 17a |
| **reptile** | пресмыкающееся | *pris-my-káh-yu-shchi-i-sya* | 15c |
| **republic** | республика | *ris-póob-li-ka* | 44 |
| **request** | просьба | *prós'-ba* | 17a |
| **request, to** | просить | *pra-sít'* | 17a |
| **rescue** | спасать | *spas-sát'* | 40a |
| **reservation** | заказанный стол (-ик), | *za-káh-za-nyj stol(-ik),* | 24m |
| | броня | *bra-nyáh* | 36b |
| **reserve** | забронировать | *zab-ra-ní-ra-vat'* | 36b |
| **reserved** *(adj)* | сдержанный | *sdyér-zhy-nyj* | 11e |
| **reserved** | заказано | *za-káh-za-na* | 24m |
| **residence (place)** | жильё | *zhyl'-yó* | 27 |
| **resistant** | стойкий | *stój-kij* | 13d |
| **resolution** | разрешение | *raz-ri-shéh-ni-ye* | 25d |
| **resort** *(n)* | курорт | *ku-rórt* | 37a |
| **respiratory system** | дыхательные органы | *dy-kháh-til'-ny-ye ór-ga-ny* | 41a |
| **responsibility** | ответственность *(f)* | *at-vyét-stvi-nast'* | 11e |
| **responsible** | ответственный | *at-vyét-stvi-nyj* | 11e |
| **rest** | отдыхать | *ad-dy-khát'* | 12b |
| **restaurant** | ресторан | *ris-ta-ráhn* | 24m |
| **restless** | беспокойный | *bis-pa-kój-nyj* | 11e |
| **retire** | уйти на пенсию | *uj-tí na pyén-si-yu* | 39d |
| **retirement** | пенсия | *pyén-si-ya* | 39d |
| **return** | вернуть, вернуться | *vir-nóot', vir-nóo-tsa* | 3e, 30b |
| **review** | обозрение | *a-baz-ryé-ni-ye* | 20a |
| **revolution** | революция | *ri-va-lyú-tsy-ya* | 44 |
| **revolver** | револьвер | *ri-val'-vyér* | 40b |
| **rheumatism** | ревматизм | *riv-ma-tízm* | 41a |
| **rhinoceros** | носорог | *na-sa-rók* | 15a |
| **rhythm** | ритм | *ritm* | 29c |
| **rice** | рис | *ris* | 24g, 24i |

| | | | |
|---|---|---|---|
| **rich** *(n & adj)* | богач *(n) (m)*, | *ba-gáhch,* | 11e, 45b |
| | богачка *(n) (f)*, | *ba-gáhch-ka,* | |
| | богатый *(adj) (m)*, | *ba-gáh-tyj,* | |
| | богатая *(adj) (f)* | *ba-gáh-ta-ya* | |
| **riding lawn mower** | райдер | *ráhj-dir* | 23a |
| **rifle** | ружьё, винтовка | *ruzh-yo, vin-tóf-ka* | 40b |
| **right** | правый *(adj)*, | *práh-vyj,* | 3d, |
| | правильный | *práh-víl'-nyj* | 38f |
| **right, privilege** | право | *práh-va* | 42 |
| **right away** | сейчас, сейчас же | *si-cháhs, si-cháhs zhy* | 4e |
| **ring** | кольцо | *kal'-tsó* | 25i |
| **ring tone(s)** | рингтон, | *ríng-tón,* | 18a |
| | мелодии для | *mi-ló-di-ii dlya só-ta-* | |
| | сотового телефона | *va-va ti-li-fó-na* | |
| **ripe** | зрелый | *zryé-lyj* | 14a |
| **ripen** | созреть | *saz-ryét'* | 14a |
| **river** | река | *ri-káh* | 13b, 37c |
| **roaming** | роуминг, | *ró-u-mink,* | 18a |
| | гостевая сеть | *gas-ti-váh-ya syet'* | |
| **roast beef** | ростбиф | *rast-bíf* | 24g |
| **rob** | грабить | *gráh-bit'* | 40b |
| **robber** | грабитель *(m)* | *gra-bí-til'* | 40b |
| **robbery** | грабёж, ограбление | *gra-byósh, ag-rab-lyé-ni-ye* | 40b |
| **robot** | робот | *ró-bat* | 43 |
| **robust** | крепкий | *kryép-kij* | 13d |
| **rock, stone** | камень *(m, sg)*, | *káh-min',* | 13b |
| | камни *(pl)* | *káhm-ni* | |
| **rock (music)** | рок (-н-ролл) | *rok, rak-yn-ról* | 25j, 29c |
| **roll** | булка | *bóol-ka* | 24g |
| **roll of film** | катушка | *ka-tóosh-ka* | 25i |
| **romance** | роман | *ra-máhn* | 20a, 25o |
| **romantic** | романтичный | *ra-man-tích-nyj* | 11e |
| **Rome** | Рим | *rim* | 31c |
| **roof** | крыша | *krý-sha* | 23a, 34e |
| **room** | комната | *kóm-na-ta* | 23b, 36b |
| **rooster** | петух | *pi-tóokh* | 15b |
| **root** | корень *(m)* | *kó-rin'* | 1e, 14a, 41b |
| **rose** | роза | *ró-za* | 14b |
| **rotten** | гнилой | *gni-lój* | 14a |
| **roughly** | грубо | *gróo-ba* | 13d |
| **round** | круглый | *króog-lyj* | 11a |
| **(row) boat (to rent)** | лодку | *lót-ku* | 37a |
| **ruble** | рубль *(m)* | *roobl'* | 26 |
| **rude, rough** | грубый | *gróo-byj* | 11e, 13d |
| **ruler** | линейка | *li-nyéj-ka* | 2b, 19e, 38b, 39c |
| **rum** | ром | *rom* | 24k |
| **rumor** | слух | *slookh* | 17a |
| **run** | бег | *byek* | 28b |
| **run, to** | бегать | *byé-gat'* | 3e, 12b |

| Ru-net | рунет | roó-nyet | 20d |
| (Russian Internet) | | | |
| runway | лётная дорожка | lyót-na-ya da-rósh-ka | 33c |
| rush hour | час пик | chahs pik | 34c |
| Russia | Россия | ra-síj-ya | 31b |
| Russian | русский | róos-kij | 31d |
| Russian (person) | русский (-ая) | róos-kij (-a-ya) | 31d |
| Russian Federation | Российская | ra-síj-ska-ya fi-di-ráh- | 44 |
| | Федерация | tsy-ya | |
| rye | рожь (f) | rozh | 24i |

**S**

| sad | грустный, | gróos-nyj, | |
| | тоскливый, | task-lí-vyj, | 11e, |
| | печальный | pi-cháhl'-nyj | 21a |
| sadness | грусть (f), | groost', | |
| | тоска, | tas-káh, | 11e |
| | печаль (f) | pi-cháhl' | 21a |
| safari | сафари | sa-fáh-ri | 37a |
| safe | сейф | syejf | 26 |
| safe deposit box | сейфовый ящик | syéj-fa-vyj yáh-shchik | 26 |
| saint | святой | svi-tój | 11d |
| salad | салат | sa-láht | 24e, 24g |
| salary | зарплата | zar-pláh-ta | 26 |
| sale | распродажа | ras-pra-dáh-zha | 25a |
| salmon | сёмга | syóm-ga | 15c, 24d |
| salt | соль (f) | sol' | 13c, 24j |
| salty | солёный | sa-lyó-nyj | 24p |
| salutation | приветствие | pri-vyét-stvi-ye | 19d |
| sand | песок | pi-sók | 13b |
| sandwich | бутерброд | bu-ter-brót | 24g |
| sarcasm | сарказм | sar-káhzm | 11e |
| sarcastic | саркастичный | sar-kas-tích-nyj | 11e |
| sardine | сардина | sar-dí-na | 15c, 24d |
| satellite | спутник | spóot-nik | 13a, 43 |
| satisfaction | удовлетворение | u-dav-lit-va-ryé-ni-ye | 21a |
| satisfied | удовлетворён(-ный), | u-dav-lit-va-ryón(-yj), | |
| | довольный | da-vól'-nyj | 21a |
| Saturday | суббота | su-bó-ta | 5a |
| saucer | блюдце | blyú-tsy | 23d, 241 |
| sauna | сауна | sáh-u-na | 37a |
| sausage | колбаса | kal-ba-sáh | 24c, 24g |
| save | сберечь, отложить | sbi-ryéch, at-la-zhýt' | 26 |
| save | сохранить (p), | sakh-ra-nít', | 20b |
| | сохранять (i) | sakh-ra-nyáht' | |
| save as | сохранить (p) как, | sakh-ra-nít' kahk, | 20b |
| | сохранять (i) | sakh-ra-nyáht' | |
| saw | пила | pi-láh | 25b |
| saxophone | саксофон | sak-sa-fón | 29c |
| say, tell | сказать | ska-záht' | 17a |
| scallion | зелёный лук | zi-lyó-nyj look | 14e, 24e |

| | | | |
|---|---|---|---|
| **scanner** | сканнер | *skáh-nir* | 20b |
| **scarf** | шарф | *shahrf* | 25k |
| **scene** | картина | *kar-tí-na* | 29e |
| **scenery** | декорация | *di-ka-ráh-tsy-ya* | 29e |
| **school yard** | школьный двор | *shkól'-nyj dvor* | 38c |
| **school year** | школьный год | *shkól'-nyj got* | 38a |
| **science fiction** | научная фантастика | *na-óoch-na-ya fan-táhs-ti-ka* | 20a, 25o |
| **scientific research** | научное исследование | *na-óoch-na-ye is-lyé-da-va-ni-ye* | 43 |
| **scientist** | учёный *(m)* (-ная) | *u-chyó-nyj (-na-ya)* | 39a |
| **scissors** | ножницы *(pl)* | *nózh-ni-tsy* | 12d, 19e, 39c, 40c |
| **score** | счёт | *shchyot* | 28b |
| **scorpion** | скорпион | *skar-pi-ón* | 15d |
| **screen** | экран | *yk-ráhn* | 25d, 29a, 39c |
| **screen, monitor** | экран | *yk-ráhn* | 20b |
| **screw** | винт, болт | *vint, bolt* | 25b |
| **screwdriver** | отвёртка | *at-vyórt-ka* | 25b |
| **scroll down** | сместить *(p)* курсор вниз, смещать *(i)* | *smis-tít' koór-sar vnis, smi-shchyáht'* | 20b |
| **scroll up** | сместить *(p)* курсор вверх, смещать *(i)* | *smis-tít' koór-sar vvyerkh, smi-shchyáht'* | 20b |
| **sculptor** | скульптор *(m&f)* | *skóol'p-tar* | 29b |
| **sculpture** | скульптура | *skul'p-tóo-ra* | 29h |
| **sea** | море | *mó-rye* | 6a, 13b, 37c |
| **seagull** | чайка | *cháhj-ka* | 15b |
| **seal** | тюлень *(m)* | *tyu-lyén'* | 15c |
| **search *(n)*** | поиск | *pó-isk* | 20d |
| **search *(v)*** | поискать *(p)*, искать *(i)* | *pa-is-káht', is-káht'* | 20d |
| **season** | время года | *vryé-mya gó-da* | 5c |
| **seat** | место | *myés-ta* | 29a, 35 |
| **seat** | сидение | *si-dyé-ni-ye* | 33c, 34a, 34e, 35 |
| **seat belt** | привязной ремень *(m)* | *pri-viz-nój ri-myén'* | 33c, 34e |
| **second floor** | второй этаж | *fta-rój y-táhzh* | 27 |
| **second (order)** | второй | *fta-rój* | 1b |
| **second (time)** | секунда | *si-kóon-da* | 4c |
| **secretary** | секретарь *(m)* (-рша) *(f)* | *sik-ri-táhr'(-rsha)* | 38d, 39a |
| **sectional home** | секционный дом | *sik-tsy-ón-nyj dom* | 27 |
| **security** | безопасность | *bi-za-páhs-nast'* | 20d |
| **sedative** | успокоительное | *us-pa-ka-í-til'-na-ye* | 41a |
| **see** | видеть | *ví-dit'* | 12c, 31a |
| **See you!** | Пока! | *pa-káh* | 16a |

| See you soon! | До скорого (свидания)! | *da skó-ra-va (svi-dáh-ni-ya)* | 16a |
|---|---|---|---|
| seed | семя *(sg)*, семена *(pl)* | *syé-mya, si-mi-náh* | 14a |
| self-service | самообслуживание | *sá-ma-ab-slóo-zhy-va-n'ye* | 24m, 34c |
| self-timer | автотаймер | *áhf-ta-táhj-mir* | 25d |
| sell | продать | *pra-dáht'* | 25a |
| seller (of an apartment) | продавец квартиры | *pra-da-vyéts kvar-tí-ry* | 27 |
| semicolon | точка с запятой | *tóch-ka s za-pi-tój* | 19d |
| send | отправить | *at-práh-vit'* | 19f |
| send | послать | *pas-láht'* | 3e |
| sender | отправитель *(m&f)* | *at-pra-ví-til'* | 19a, 19f |
| sense | чувство | *chóo-stva* | 12c |
| sense, feel | чувствовать | *chóost-va-vat'* | 12c, 21a |
| sensitive | чувствительный | *chu-ství-til'-nyj* | 11e |
| sentence | приговор | *prí-ga-vór* | 42 |
| sentence | предложение | *prid-la-zhéh-ni-ye* | 8a, 19d |
| sentimental | сентиментальный | *sin-ti-min-táhl'-nyj* | 11e |
| separate | разойтись | *ra-zaj-tís'* | 11c |
| | отдельный *(m)*, | *at-dyél'-nyj,* | 27 |
| | отдельное *(n)*, | *at-dyél'-na-ye,* | |
| | отдельная *(f)* | *at-dyél'-na-ya* | |
| separation | расход | *ras-khód* | 11c |
| September | сентябрь *(m)* | *sin-tyáh-bar'* | 5b |
| series (TV) | многосерийная передача | *mna-ga-si-ríj-na-ya pi-ri-dáh-cha* | 20b |
| serious | серьёзный | *sir'-yóz-nyj* | 11e |
| sermon | проповедь *(f)* | *pró-pa-vit'* | 17a |
| serve | подать | *pa-dáht'* | 24o |
| server | сервер | *syér-vir* | 19a |
| service | обслуживание | *ap-slóo-zhy-va-n'ye* | 24m, 36b |
| service (prayer) | служба | *slóozh-ba* | 11d |
| service provider | провайдер | *pra-váhj-dir* | 19a |
| set the table | накрыть на стол | *na-krýt' na stol* | 23f, 24o |
| seven | семь | *syem'* | 1a |
| seventeen | семнадцать | *sim-náh-tsat'* | 1a |
| seventh | седьмой | *sid'-mój* | 1b |
| seventy | семьдесят | *syém-di-sit* | 1a |
| several | несколько | *nyés-kal'-ka* | 3c |
| sew | зашить | *za-shýt'* | 25g |
| sewing machine | швейная машина | *shvyéj-na-ya ma-shý-na* | 23d |
| sex | пол, секс | *pol, sehks* | 39b, 45b |
| sexual act | сексуальный/ половой акт | *sik-su-áhl'-nyj/pa-la-vój ahkt* | 45b |
| sexual orientation | сексуальная ориентация | *sik-su-áhl'-na-ya a-ri-in-táh-tsy-ya* | 45b |
| sexual relationship | сексуальное отношение, половые отношения *(pl)* | *sik-su-áhl'-na-ye at-na-shéh-ni-ye, pa-la-vý-ye at-na-shéh-ni-ya* | 45b |

| | | | |
|---|---|---|---|
| sexually-transmitted disease (venereal disease) | венерическое заболевание | *vi-ni-rí-chis-ka-ye za-ba-li-váh-ni-ye* | 45b |
| shadow, shade | тень *(f)* | *tyen'* | 6a |
| shaft | приводной вал | *pri-vad-nój vahl* | 34e |
| shake hands | пожать руку | *pa-zháht' róo-ku* | 16a |
| shame | стыд | *styt* | 21a |
| shampoo | шампунь *(m)* | *sham-póon'* | 12d, 25f, 36c |
| sharp | острый | *óst-ryj* | 24p |
| sharpen a pencil | отточить карандаш | *a-ta-chít' ka-ran-dáhsh* | 38b |
| sharpness | резкость | *ryés-kast'* | 25d |
| shave | побриться | *pa-brí-tsa* | 12d |
| she | она | *a-náh* | 8c |
| sheep | баран *(m)*, овца *(f)* | *ba-ráhn, af-tsáh* | 15a |
| sheet (bed) | простыня | *pras-ty-nyáh* | 23d, 36c |
| sheet of paper | лист бумаги | *list bu-máh-gi* | 25c, 39c |
| shelf | полка | *pól-ka* | 23a |
| shiny | светящийся | *svi-tyáh-shchij-sya* | 7b |
| shirt | рубашка | *ru-báhsh-ka* | 25k |
| shock | состояние шока | *sas-ta-yáh-ni-ye shó-ka* | 40c |
| shoe | туфель *(sg, m)*, туфли *(pl)*, ботинок *(sg)*, ботинки *(pl)* | *tôo-fil', tóof-li, ba-tí-nak, ba-tín-ki* | 25n |
| shoot | стрелять | *stri-lyát'* | 40b |
| shop, store | магазин | *ma-ga-zín* | 25a |
| shop | идти, ходить за покупками | *it-tí, kha-dít' za pa-kóʋp-ka-mi* | 25a |
| short | низкий рост | *nís-kij rost* | 11a |
| short (thing) | короткий | *ka-rót-kij* | 3b |
| short waves | короткие волны | *ka-rót-ki-ye vól-ny* | 20b |
| shorten | укоротить | *u-ka-ra-tít'* | 25m |
| shorts | трусы | *tru-sý* | 25k |
| shoulder | плечо | *pli-chó* | 12a |
| shout | крик | *krik* | 40a |
| shout, to | кричать | *kri-cháht'* | 17a, 40a |
| shout(ing) | крик | *krik* | 17a |
| shovel | лопата | *la-páh-ta* | 25b |
| show | выступление | *vys-tup-lyé-ni-ye* | 29c |
| show (movies) | сеанс | *si-áhns* | 20b |
| show (TV) | передача | *pi-ri-dáh-cha* | 20b |
| shower | душ | *doosh* | 12d, 23a, 36c |
| shrimp | креветка | *kri-vyét-ka* | 15d, 24d |
| shut up | заткнуться | *zatk-nóo-tsa* | 17a |
| Shut up! | Заткнись! | *zatk-nís'* | 21c |
| shuttle bus (route taxi) | маршрутное такси | *marsh-róot-na-ye tak-sí* | 34c |
| shy | застенчивый | *za-stén-chi-vyj* | 11e |
| shyness | застенчивость *(f)* | *za-stén-chi-vast'* | 11e |
| sick | больной | *bal'-nój* | 11a, 41a |

| sidewalk | тротуар | *tra-tu-áhr* | 34c, 37b |
|---|---|---|---|
| sight | зрение | *zryé-ni-ye* | 41a |
| sign | подписать | *pat-pi-sáht'* | 19d, 26 |
| sign a lease /sale | заключить *(p)* договор, | *za-klyu-chít' da-ga-vór,* | 27 |
| (agreement) | заключать *(i)* | *za-klyu-cháht'* | |
| signal | сигнал | *sig-náhl* | 34c |
| signature | подпись *(f)* | *pót-pis'* | 11f, 19a, 19d, 26, 39b |
| silence | молчание | *mal-cháh-ni-ye* | 17a |
| silent | молчаливый | *mal-cha-li-vyj* | 17a |
| silk | шёлк | *sholk* | 13c |
| silk *(adj)* | шёлковый | *shól-ka-vyj* | 251 |
| silkworm | шёлковичный червь *(m)* | *skol-ka-vích-nyj chyerf'* | 15d |
| silver | серебро | *si-rib-ró* | 13c, 25i |
| silver *(adj)* | серебряный | *si-ryéb-ri-nyj* | 7a |
| silver fir tree | пихта | *píkh-ta* | 14c |
| simple | простой | *pras-tój* | 11e |
| simply | просто | *prós-ta* | 11e |
| simultaneous | одновременный | *ad-na-vri-myé-nyj* | 4e |
| since | с, в течение | *s, f ti-chyé-ni-ye* | 4e |
| since (causal) | поскольку | *pas-kól-ku* | 8h |
| sincere | искренний | *ísk-ri-nij* | 11e |
| sincerely | искренно | *ísk-ri-na* | 11e |
| sincerity | искренность *(f)* | *ísk-ri-nast'* | 11e |
| sing | петь | *pyet'* | 29c |
| singer | певец *(m)*, певица *(f)* | *pi-vyéts, pi-ví-tsa* | 25j, 29c |
| single, unmarried | неженатый *(m)*, незамужняя *(f)* | *ni-zhy-náh-tyj, ni-za-móozh-nya-ya* | 11c, 11f, 39b |
| single room | комната на одного | *kóm-na-ta na ad-na-vó* | 36b |
| singular | единственное число | *i-díns-tvi-na-ye chis-ló* | 8a |
| sink | раковина | *ráh-ka-vi-na* | 23a, 36c |
| siren | сирена | *si-ryé-na* | 40a |
| sister | сестра | *sist-ráh* | 10a |
| sister-in-law | невестка | *ni-vyést-ka* | 10a |
| sit down | сидеть | *si-dét'* | 3e, 33c |
| six | шесть | *shehst'* | 1a |
| sixteen | шестнадцать | *shys-náh-tsat'* | 1a |
| sixth | шестой | *shys-tój* | 1b |
| sixty | шестьдесят | *shys-di-syáht* | 1s |
| size | размер | *raz-myér* | 3b, 25n, 25k, 27 |
| skate | конёк *(sg)*, коньки *(pl)* | *ka-nyók, kan'-ki* | 28b |
| skate, to | кататься на коньках | *ka-táh-tsa na kan'-káhkh* | 28b |
| ski trail | лыжня | *lyzh-nyáh* | 37c |
| skiing | катание на лыжах | *ka-táh-ni-ye na lý-zhakh* | 28b, 37c |
| skin | кожа | *kó-zha* | 12a |
| skinny | худой | *khu-dój* | 11a |
| skip a class | пропустить класс | *pra-pus-tít' klahs* | 38f |

| skip school (play hooky) | прогулять школу | *pra-gu-lyáht' shkó-lu* | 38f |
|---|---|---|---|
| skirt | юбка | *yúp-ka* | 25k |
| skis | лыжи | *lý-zhy* | 28b |
| sky | небо, небеса *(pl)* | *nyé-ba, ni-bi-sáh* | 6a, 13b |
| sleep | спать | *spaht'* | 12b |
| sleeping bag | спальный мешок | *spáhl'-ny mi-shók* | 37c |
| sleeve | рукав | *ru-káhf* | 25g |
| slide | диапозитив | *di-a-pa-zi-tíf* | 25d |
| sliding door | раздвижная дверь *(f)* | *raz-dvizh-náh-ya dvyer'* | 36c |
| slippers | тапки, тапочки *(pl)* | *táhp-ki, táh-pach-ki* | 25n |
| Slovakia | Словакия | *sla-váh-ki-ya* | 31b |
| slow | медленный *(adj)* | *myéd-li-nyj* | 3e, 4e |
| slow down | снизить скорость | *sní-zit' skó-rast'* | 34c |
| slowly | медленно *(adv)* | *myéd-li-na* | 3e, 4e |
| small, little | маленький, малый | *máh-lin'-kij, máh-lyj* | 3c, 11a, 251 |
| small letter | маленькая буква | *máh-liń-ka-ya bóok-va* | 19d |
| smart, clever | умный, сообразительный, смышлёный | *óom-nyj, sa-ab-ra-zí-til'-nyj, smysh-lyó-nyj* | 11e |
| smell | запах | *záh-pakh* | 12c |
| smell, to | нюхать | *nyú-khat'* | 12c |
| smile | улыбка | *u-lýp-ka* | 11e, 21a |
| smile, to | улыбаться | *u-ly-báh-tsa* | 11e, 21a |
| smoke | дым | *dym* | 13c, 40a |
| smooth | гладкий *(surface)*, плавный *(motion)* | *gláht-kij, pláv-nyj* | 13d |
| snack *(m)* | закуска | *za-kóos-ka* | 24a |
| snack, to | закусить, перекусить | *za-ku-sít', pi-ri-ku-sít'* | 24a |
| snack bar | закусочная | *za-kóo-sach-na-ya* | 24m |
| snake | змея | *zmi-yáh* | 15c |
| sneeze | чих | *chikh* | 41a |
| sneeze, to | чихнуть | *chíkh-nóot'* | 41a |
| snob | сноб | *snob* | 11e |
| snobbery | снобизм | *sna-bízm* | 11e |
| snow | снег | *snyek* | 6a |
| snowball tree | калина | *ka-lí-na* | 14c |
| so, therefore | так что | *takh shto* | 8h |
| so-so | так себе | *tahk si-byé* | 16a |
| So? | Ну и что? | *nu i shto* | 9 |
| soap | мыло | *mý-la* | 12d, 25f |
| soccer | футбол | *fud-ból* | 28b |
| socialism | социализм | *sa-tsy-a-lízm* | 44 |
| sociology | социология | *sa-tsy-a-ló-gi-ya* | 38e |
| sock | носок *(sg)*, носки *(pl)* | *na-sók, nas-kí* | 25n |
| sodium | натрий | *náht-rij* | 13c |
| sofa | диван/софа | *di-váhn/sa-fáh* | 23c |
| Sofia | София | *sa-fí-ya* | 31c |
| soft | мягкий | *myáhkh-kij* | 13d |
| softly | мягко | *myáhkh-ka* | 13d |

| software | математическое обеспечение | *ma-tí-ma-tí-chis-ka-ye a-bis-pi-chyé-ni-ye* | 20b |
|---|---|---|---|
| solar cell | солнечный элемент | *sól-nich-nyj y-li-myént* | 45a |
| solar energy | солнечная энергия | *sól-nich-na-ya y-néhr-gi-ya* | 13c, 45a |
| solar system | солнечная система | *sól-nich-na-ya sis-tyé-ma* | 13a |
| soldier | солдат (-ка) | *sal-dáht (-ka)* | 39a |
| solid | твёрдый | *tvyór-dyj* | 13c |
| soluble | растворимый | *rast-va-rí-myj* | 13d |
| solution | решение *(n)* | *ri-shéh-ni-ye* | 1f |
| some | некоторое | *nyé-ka-ta-ra-ye* | 3c |
| son | сын | *syn* | 10a |
| son-in-law | зять *(m)* | *zyaht'* | 10a |
| song | песня | *pyés-nya* | 25j, 29c |
| soon | скоро | *skó-ra* | 4e |
| sorrow | печаль *(f)*, скорбь *(f)* | *pi-cháhl', skorp'* | 21a |
| soul | душа | *du-sháh* | 11d |
| sound, to | звучать | *zvu-cháht'* | 12c |
| sound | звук | *zvook* | 12c |
| sound track | звуковая дорожка | *zvu-ka-váh-ya da-rósh-ka* | 20e |
| soup | суп | *soop* | 24g |
| sour | кислый | *kís-lyj* | 24p |
| sour cherry | черешня *(coll)* | *chi-ryésh-nya* | 14d, 24f |
| sour cream | сметана | *smi-táh-na* | 24h |
| south | юг | *yuk* | 3d |
| South America | Южная Америка | *yúzh-na-ya a-myé-ri-ka* | 31b |
| souvenir shop | сувенирный магазин | *su-vi-nír-nyj ma-ga-zín* | 25a |
| sovereign democracy | суверенная демократия | *su-vi-ryé-na-ya di-mak-ráh-ti-ya* | 44 |
| Soviet Union | Советский Союз | *sa-vyéts-kij sa-yús* | 31b |
| sow | сеять | *syé-it'* | 14a |
| spa | спа | *spah* | 37a |
| spa resort | курорт спа | *ku-rórt spah* | 37a |
| space | космос/пространство | *kós-mas/prast-ráhnst-va* | 13a |
| space flight | космический полёт | *kas-mí-chis-kij pa-lyót* | 43 |
| space shuttle | космический челнок | *kas-mí-chis-kij chil-nók* | 43 |
| Spain | Испания | *is-páh-ni-ya* | 31b |
| spam (e-mail) | почтовый спам | *pach-tó-vyj spahm* | 19a |
| Spaniard | испанец (-нка) | *is-páh-nits (-nka)* | 31d |
| Spanish | испанский | *is-páhn-skij* | 31d |
| spark plug | пробка | *próp-ka* | 34e |
| sparkling | сверкающий | *svir-káh-yu-shchij* | 7b |
| sparrow | воробей | *va-ra-byéj* | 15b |
| speak, talk | говорить | *ga-va-rít'* | 17a |
| speakers *(pl)* | колонки *(pl)*, спикеры *(pl)* | *ka-lón-ki, spí-ki-ry* | 20b |
| special delivery | срочная почта | *sróch-na-ya póch-ta* | 19f |
| specialist | специалист | *spi-tsy-a-líst* | 41a |
| species | вид | *vit* | 14a |
| speech, talk | речь *(f)* | *ryech* | 17a |
| speed | скорость *(f)* | *skó-rast'* | 3b, 34c |

| | | | |
|---|---|---|---|
| **speed limit** | ограничение скорости | *ag-ra-ni-shyé-ni-ye skó-ras-ti* | 34d |
| **speed up** | увеличить скорость *(f)* | *u-vi-lí-chit' skó-rast'* | 34c |
| **speedometer** | спидометр | *spi-dó-mitr* | 34e |
| **spelling** | орфография, правописание | *ar-fa-gráh-fi-ya, pra-va-pi-sáh-ni-ye* | 19d |
| **spend** | потратить | *pa-tráh-tit'* | 25a |
| **spend time** | провести время | *pra-vís-tí vryé-mya* | 4e |
| **sphere** | шар | *shahr* | 2a |
| **spicy** | пикантный | *pi-káhnt-nyj* | 24p |
| **spider** | паук | *pa-óok* | 15d |
| **spinach** | шпинат | *shpi-náht* | 14e, 24e |
| **spine, backbone** | позвоночник | *paz-va-nóch-nik* | 12a |
| **spirit** | дух | *dookh* | 11d |
| **spiritual** | духовный | *du-khóv-nyj* | 11d |
| **splint** | шина | *shý-na* | 40c |
| **spoon** | ложка | *lósh-ka* | 23d, 241 |
| **sporadic** | спорадический | *spo-rah-dí-chis-skij* | 4e |
| **sport** | спорт | *sport* | 28b |
| **sports center/club** | спортивный центр/клуб | *spar-tív-nyj tsehntr/kloop* | 28b |
| **sports facility** | спортивное учреждение | *spar-tív-na-ye uch-rizh-dyé-ni-ye* | 28b |
| **sports fan** | спортивный болельщик (-ица) | *spar-tív-nyj ba-lyél'-shchik (-i-tsa)* | 28b |
| **spot, stain** | пятно | *pit-nó* | 25g |
| **spouse** | супруг *(m)*, супруга *(f)* | *sup-róog, sup-róo-ga* | 11c |
| **spring** | весна | *vis-náh* | 5c |
| **square** *(adj, geometry)* | квадратный | *kvad-ráht-nyj* | 3a |
| **square** (urban place) | площадь *(f)* | *pló-shchat'* | 37b |
| **square meter** | квадратный метр (abbreviation: кв.м) | *kvad-ráht-nyj myetr* | 27 |
| **squash** | кабачок (-чки) *(pl)* | *ka-ba-chók* | 14e, 24e |
| **squirrel** | белка | *byél-ka* | 15a |
| **St. Petersburg** | (Санкт-) Петербург | *(sáhnkt-) pi-tir-bóork* | 31c |
| **stable** | устойчивый | *us-tój-chi-vyj* | 13d |
| **stadium** | стадион | *sta-di-ón* | 28b |
| **stage** | сцена | *stséh-na* | 29e |
| **stairs** | лестница | *lyéhs-ni-tsa* | 23a, 27, 36b |
| **stamp** | марка | *máhr-ka* | 19f, 28a |
| **stamp collecting** | филателия | *fi-la-téh-li-ya* | 28a |
| **stand in line** | стоять в очереди | *sta-yáht' v ó-chi-ri-di* | 26 |
| **staple** | скобка | *skóp-ka* | 19e, 25c, 40c |
| **stapler** | стейплер | *stéhjp-lir* | 19e, 25c, 39c |
| **star** | звезда *(sg)*, звезды *(pl)* | *zviz-dáh, zvyóz-dy* | 6a, 13a |
| **start (the car)** | завести машину | *za-vis-tí ma-shý-nu* | 34c |

| state | государство, штат | *ga-su-dáhr-stva, shtaht* | 11f, 13e, 44 |
|---|---|---|---|
| state, to | изложить, заявить | *iz-la-zhýt', za-i-vít'* | 17a |
| State Assembly | Государственная Дума | *ga-su-dáhr-stvi-na-ya dóo-ma* | 44 |
| state bank | государственные банк | *ga-su-dáhr-stvi-nyj bahnk* | 26 |
| statement | изложение, заявление | *iz-la-zhéh-ni-ye, za-iv-lyé-ni-ye* | 17a |
| station (radio) | радиостанция | *ra-di-a-stáhn-tsy-ya* | 20b |
| statistics | статистика | *sta-tís-ti-ka* | 1f, 38e |
| steak | бифштекс | *bif-shtéhks* | 24g |
| steal | украсть | *uk-ráhst'* | 40b |
| steamer | пароварка | *pa-ra-váhr-ka* | 23d |
| steel | сталь *(f)* | *stahl'* | 13c |
| steering wheel | руль *(m)* | *roól'* | 34e |
| stem | стебель *(m)* | *styé-bil'* | 14a |
| step | ступень *(f)* | *stu-pyén'* | 23a |
| stepbrother | сводный брат | *svód-nyi braht* | 10a |
| stepfather | отчим | *ót-chim* | 10a |
| stepmother | мачеха | *máh-chi-kha* | 10a |
| stepsister | сводная сестра | *svód-na-ya sist-ráh* | 10a |
| stereo | стерео | *styé-ri-a* | 20b |
| stethoscope | стетоскоп | *sty-tas-kóp* | 41a |
| stew/simmer | тушить | *tu-shýt'* | 24b |
| stewed fruit juice | компот | *kam-pót* | 24k |
| still | ещё пока | *i-shchyó pa-káh* | 4e |
| still life | натюрморт | *na-tyur-mórt* | 29b |
| stingy | жадный | *zháhd-nyj* | 11e |
| stock | сток, акция | *stok, áhk-tsy-ya* | 26 |
| stock market | биржа | *bír-zha* | 26 |
| stocking | чулок *(sg)*, чулки *(pl)* | *chu-lók, chul-kí* | 25n |
| stomach | желудок | *zhy-lóo-dak* | 12a, 41a |
| stool | табурет | *ta-bu-ryét* | 23c |
| stop | остановка | *as-ta-nóf-ka* | 35 |
| stop, to | остановиться | *as-ta-na-ví-tsa* | 3e |
| Stop! | Стоп! | *stop* | 34d |
| stork | аист | *áh-ist* | 15b |
| storm | буря | *bóo-rya* | 6a |
| storm cloud | туча | *tóo-cha* | 13b |
| story | рассказ | *ras-káhs* | 17a |
| stout, full-figured | толстый | *tól-styj* | 11a |
| stove | плита | *pli-táh* | 23d |
| straight, blunt | прямой | *pri-mój* | 11e |
| strawberry | клубника *(coll)* | *klub-ní-ka* | 14d, 24f |
| street | улица | *óo-li-tsa* | 11f, 37b, 39b |
| street drugs *(pl)* | уличные наркотики *(pl)* | *óo-lich-ny-ye nar-kó-ti-ki* | 45b |
| street sign | уличный знак | *óo-lich-nyj znahk* | 37b |
| strength | сила | *sí-la* | 11a |
| stress (accent) | ударение | *u-da-ryé-ni-ye* | 8a |

| | | | |
|---|---|---|---|
| strike | забастовка | *za-bas-tóf-ka* | 42 |
| string (musical instrument) | струна | *stru-náh* | 29c |
| string | верёвка, бечёвка | *vi-ryóf-ka, bi-chyóf-ka* | 19e, 25c |
| striped | полосатый | *pa-la-sáh-tyj* | 25l |
| strong | сильный, крепкий | *síl'-nyj, kryép-kij* | 11a, 11e, 13d |
| strongly | сильно, крепко | *síl-na, kryép-ka* | 11a, 11e, 13d |
| stubborn | упрямый | *u-pryáh-myj* | 11e |
| student | студент (-ка) | *stu-dyént (-ka)* | 37d |
| study | изучить *(p),* изучать *(i)* | *iz-u-chít', i-zu-cháht'* | 22b |
| study | учиться | *u-chí-tsa* | 38f |
| stupid | глупый | *glóo-pyj* | 11e |
| style | стиль *(m)* | *stil'* | 29d |
| subject (line) | предмет письма, тема | *prid-myét pis'-máh, tyé-ma* | 19a |
| subject (topic, theme) | предмет | *prid-myét* | 38e |
| subject (grammar) | подлежащее | *pad-li-zháh-shchi-ye* | 8a |
| subsidy | субсидия | *sup-sí-di-ya* | 27 |
| substance | вещество | *vi-shchist-vó* | 13c |
| subtract | вычесть | *vý-chist'* | 1e |
| subway (metro) | метро *(indecl)* | *mit-ró* | 35 |
| sue | подать в суд на ... | *pa-dáht' f soot na ...* | 42 |
| suffer | страдать | *stra-dáht'* | 41a |
| suffix | суффикс | *sóo-fiks* | 8a |
| sugar | сахар | *sáh-khar* | 24j |
| suggest | предложить | *prid-la-zhýt'* | 17a |
| suit | костюм | *kas-tyúm* | 25k |
| suitcase | чемодан | *chi-ma-dáhn* | 32 |
| sulfur | сера | *syé-ra* | 13c |
| sum | сумма | *sóom-a* | 1f |
| summarize | суммировать, резюмировать | *su-mí-ra-vat', ri-zyu-mí-ra-vat'* | 17a |
| summary | сводка, резюме | *svót-ka, ri-zyu-méh* | 17a |
| summer | лето | *lyé-ta* | 5c |
| summons | вызов | *vý-zov* | 42 |
| sun | солнце | *són-tse* | 5c, 6a, 13a |
| sunburn | солнечный ожог | *sól-nich-nyj a-zhók* | 37d |
| Sunday | воскресенье (-ние) | *vas-kri-syé-n'ye* | 5a |
| sunlight | солнечный свет | *sól-nich-nyj svyet* | 13a |
| sunny | солнечный | *sól-nich-nyj* | 6a |
| sunset | закат | *za-káht* | 4a |
| suntan | загар | *za-gáhr* | 37c |
| suntan, to | загореть | *za-ga-ryét'* | 37c |
| supermarket | супермаркет, супер | *su-pir-máhr-kit, sóo-pir* | 24n |
| superstitious | суеверный | *su-ye-vér-nyj* | 11e |
| surgeon | хирург *(m&f)* | *khi-róork* | 39a, 41a |

| surprise | удивление | *u-div-lyé-ni-ye* | 21a |
| surprise, to | удивиться | *u-di-ví-tsa* | 21a |
| swallow | ласточка | *láhs-tach-ka* | 15b |
| swear (in court) | клясться | *klyáhs-tsa* | 17a |
| swear (profanity) | ругнуться | *rug-nóo-tsa* | 17a |
| sweater | свитер | *serí-tyr* | 25k |
| Swede | швед (-ка) | *shvyet (-ka)* | 31d |
| Sweden | Швеция | *shvyé-tsy-ya* | 31b |
| Swedish | шведский | *skvyét-skij* | 31d |
| sweet (taste) | сладкий | *sláht-kij* | 24p |
| sweet (dear) | милый | *mí-lyj* | 11e |
| sweets | сладкое | *sláht-ka-ye* | 24g |
| swim | плыть | *plyt'* | 28b |
| swimming | плавание | *pláh-va-ni-ye* | 28b |
| swimming pool | бассейн, | *ba-syén,* | 23a |
| | плавательный | *pláh-va-til'-nyj* | |
| | бассейн | *ba-syén* | |
| switch | выключатель *(m)*, | *vy-klyu-cháh-til',* | 23a, |
| | переключатель *(m)* | *pi-ri-klyu-cháh-til'* | 36c |
| switch off | потушить, | *pa-tu-shýt',* | 36c |
| | выключить | *výk-lu-chit'* | |
| switch on | включить | *fklyu-chít'* | 36c |
| Switzerland | Швейцария | *shvij-tsáh-ri-ya* | 31b |
| swollen | распух(-ший) | *ras-póokh (-shyj)* | 41a |
| syllable | слог | *slok* | 8a |
| symbol | символ | *sím-val* | 17a |
| symbol (geometry) | знак | *znahk* | 1f |
| sympathetic | сочувственный | *sa-chóost-vi-nyj* | 21a |
| sympathy | сочувствие | *sa-chóost-vi-ye* | 21a |
| symphony | симфония | *sim-fó-ni-ya* | 30c |
| synagogue | синагога | *si-na-gó-ga* | 11d, 37b |
| synthetic | синтетический | *syn-ty-tí-chis-kij* | 13d |
| syringe | шприц | *shprits* | 41a |
| syrup | сироп | *si-róp* | 25h |

**T**

| T-shirt | майка | *máhj-ka* | 25k |
| table | стол | *stol* | 23c, 241, |
| | | | 36c |
| tablecloth | скатерть *(f)* | *skáh-tirt'* | 23d, 241 |
| tablet | таблетка | *tab-lyét-ka* | 25h, 41a |
| tableware | столовый прибор | *stah-ló-vyj pri-bór* | 23d |
| tail | хвост | *khvost* | 15a |
| tailor | портной *(m)* | *part-nój* | 39a |
| Tajikistan | Таджикистан | *tad-zhy-ki-stáhn* | 31b |
| take | взять | *vzyaht'* | 25a |
| take a course | прослушать курс | *pras-lóo-shat' koors* | 38f |
| take a picture | сфотографировать | *sphah-ta-gra-fí-ra-vat'* | 25d |
| take a shower | принять душ | *pri-nyáht' doosh* | 12d |
| take a trip | совершить | *sa-vir-shýt' pu-ti-shéhst-* | 37a |
| | путешествие | *vi-ye* | |

| take an exam | сдавать экзамен | *sda-váht' yk-záh-min* | 38f |
| take back | вернуть | *vir-nóot'* | 25a |
| take in tow | брать на буксир | *braht' na buk-sír* | 34a |
| take off, to (flight) | взлететь | *vzli-tyét'* | 33c |
| take off, to (remove) | снять | *snyaht'* | 25m |
| take place | иметь место | *i-myét' myés-ta* | 4e |
| takeoff | взлёт, вылет | *vzlyot, vý-lit* | 33c |
| talk | разговор | *raz-ga-vór* | 11e |
| talkative | разговорчивый, болтливый | *raz-ga-vór-chi-vyj, balt-lí-vyj* | 11e |
| tall | высокий | *vy-só-kij* | 3b, 11a |
| tampon | тампон | *tam-pón* | 25f |
| tanker truck | цистерна | *tsys-téhr-na* | 34a |
| tape | плёнка | *plyón-ka* | 25j |
| tape recorder | магнитофон | *mag-ni-ta-fón* | 38b |
| tariff | тариф | *ta-ríf* | 32 |
| taste | вкус | *fkoos* | 12c |
| tasty | вкусный | *fkóos-nyj* | 24p |
| tax | налог | *na-lók* | 27 |
| taxi | такси | *tak-sí* | 34a |
| tea | чай | *chahj* | 24k |
| teach | преподавать, учить / обучать | *pri-pa-da-váht', u-chít'/a-bu-cháht'* | 38f |
| teacher | учитель *(m)*, учительница *(f)* | *u-chí-til', u-chí-til'-ni-tsa* | 38d, 39a |
| team | команда | *ka-máhn-da* | 28b |
| teapot | заварочный чайник | *za-va-rách-nyj cháhj-nik* | 23d |
| technical school | техникум | *tyéch-ni-kum* | 38a |
| technician | техник *(m&f)* | *tyéch-nik* | 38d, 39a |
| telecommunication | телесвязь *(f)* | *ti-li-zvyáhs* | 18a, 43 |
| telephone (set) | телефон | *ti-li-fón* | 18a, 18b, 23e, 36c, 39c |
| telephone number | номер телефона, телефонный номер | *nó-myer ti-li-fó-na, ti-li-fó-nyj nó-mir* | 11f, 39b 18b |
| television | телевидение | *ti-li-ví-di-ni-ye* | 20b, 23e |
| television set | телевизор | *ti-li-ví-zar* | 20b, 23e, 36c |
| telex machine | телекс | *tyé-líks* | 18a |
| tell a story | рассказать, рассказ | *ras-ka-záht', ras-káhs* | 17a |
| temperature | температура | *tim-pi-ra-tóo-ra* | 6c, 41a |
| temple | храм | *khrahm* | 11d, 37b |
| temporary | временный | *vryé-min-nyj* | 4a, 4e |
| ten | десять | *dyé-sit'* | 1a |
| tenant | арендатор, квартирант | *a-rin-dáh-tar, kvar-ti-ráhnt* | 27 23g |
| tennis | теннис | *téh-nis* | 28b |
| tennis court | теннисный корт | *téh-nis-nyj kórt* | 23a |
| tennis shoes | кроссовки | *kra-sóf-ki* | 25n |
| tense | время | *vryé-mya* | 8a |
| tent | палатка | *pa-láht-ka* | 37c |

| | | | |
|---|---|---|---|
| tenth | десятый | *di-syáh-tyj* | 1b |
| terminal | терминал | *tir-mi-náhl* | 20b |
| terrace | терраса | *ti-ráh-sa* | 23a |
| terrain course | терренкур | *ti-rin-kóor* | 28b |
| territory | территория | *ti-ri-tó-ri-ya* | 13e |
| text | текст | *tyekst* | 19d |
| text messaging | обмен сообщениями | *ab-myén sa-ab-shchyé-ni-ya-mi* | 18a |
| textbook | учебник | *u-chyéb-nik* | 25o, 38b |
| textile | текстиль *(m)* | *tiks-stíl'* | 13c |
| thank | поблагодарить | *pa-bla-ga-da-rít'* | 17a, 21a |
| Thank God! | Слава Богу! | *sláh-va bó-gu* | 21c |
| Thank you! | Спасибо! | *spa-sí-ba* | 16c |
| thankful | благодарный | *bla-ga-dáhr-nyj* | 21a |
| thankfulness | благодарность *(f)* | *bla-ga-dáhr-nast'* | 21a |
| that, which | что | *shto* | 8f |
| that | тот *(m)*, то *(n)*, та *(f)* | *tot, to, tah* | 8b |
| That's none of your business! | Не твоё дело! | *ni tva-yó dyé-la* | 21c |
| The line is busy! | Линия занята! | *lí-ni-ya záh-ni-ta* | 18b |
| theater | театр | *tyahtr* | 29e |
| their | их | *ikh* | 8c |
| theme | тема | *tyé-ma* | 29d |
| then | тогда | *tag-dáh* | 4e |
| there | там, туда | *tahm, tu-dáh* | 3d, 37d |
| thermal energy | тепловая энергия | *tip-la-váh-ya y-néhr-gi-ya* | 45a |
| thermometer | термометр | *tir-mó-mitr* | 6c, 25h, 41a |
| thermostat | термостат | *tir-ma-stáht* | 6c, 36c |
| thesis (diploma project) | дипломный проект | *dip-lóm-nyj pra-éhkt* | 38f |
| they | они | *a-ní* | 8c |
| thick | толстый | *tóls-tyj* | 3b |
| thief | вор | *vor* | 40b |
| thin | тонкий | *tón-kíj* | 3b, 11a |
| think | подумать | *pa-dóo-mat'* | 22b |
| thinly | тонко | *tón-ka* | 11a |
| third | третий | *tryé-tij* | 1b |
| third floor | третий этаж | *tryé-tij y-táhzh* | 27 |
| third world | третий мир | *tryé-tij mir* | 44 |
| thirst | жажда | *zháhzh-da* | 12b |
| thirteen | тринадцать | *tri-náh-tsat'* | 1a |
| thirty | тридцать | *trí-tsat'* | 1a |
| this | этот *(m)*, это *(n)*, эта *(f)* | *éh-tat, éh-ta, éh-ta* | 8b |
| This is terrible/awful! | Это ужасно!, Это кошмар! | *éh-ta u-zháhs-na, éh-ta kash-máhr* | 21c |
| This is wonderful! | Это замечательно! | *éh-ta za-mi-cháh-tíl'-na* | 21c |
| This is... | Говорит... | *ga-va-rít* | 18b |
| thorn | шип | *shyp* | 14b |
| those | те *(pl)* | *tye* | 8b |
| thought | мысль *(f)*, мышление | *mysl', mysh-lyé-ni-ye* | 22a |

| threat | угроза | *ug-ró-za* | 17a |
| threaten | пригрозить | *prig-ra-zít'* | 17a |
| three | три | *tri* | 1a |
| throat | горло | *gór-la* | 41a |
| through | через | *chyé-ris* | 3d, 8d, 37d |
| throw up, vomit | вырвать | *výr-vat'* | 41a |
| thumb | большой палец | *bal'-shój páh-lits* | 12a |
| thunder | гром | *grom* | 6a |
| Thursday | четверг | *chit-vyérk* | 5a |
| tick | клещ | *klyeshch* | 15d |
| ticket | билет | *bi-lyét* | 28b, 31a, 35 |
| tide | прилив | *pri-líf* | 13b |
| tidy up | убрать | *ub-ráht'* | 23f |
| tie | галстук | *gáhls-tuk* | 25k |
| tiger | тигр | *tigr* | 15a |
| tight | тесный | *tyés-nyj* | 251 |
| time (as in every time) | раз | *rahs* | 4a |
| time (in general) | время | *vryé-mya* | 4a |
| timer | таймер | *táhj-mir* | 25d |
| timetable, schedule | расписание | *ras-pi-sáh-ni-ye* | 4e, 35 |
| timpani | тимпан | *tim-páhn* | 29c |
| tincture of iodine | настойка йода | *nas-tój-ka jóh-da* | 40c |
| tint | оттенок | *at-tyé-nak* | 7c |
| tip | чаевые *(pl)* | *chi-i-vý-i* | 24m |
| tip, to | дать на чай *(p)*, давать на чай *(i)* | *daht' na cháhj da-váht na cháhj* | 24m |
| tire | шина | *shý-na* | 34a, 34e |
| tired | усталый | *u-stáh-lyj* | 12b |
| title (appellation) | форма обращения | *fór-ma ab-ra-shchyé-ní-ya* | 16b |
| title (inscription) | заглавие, заголовок | *zag-láh-vi-ye, za-ga-ló-vak* | 20a |
| title (right of ownership) | титул (право собственности) | *tí-tul (práh-va sóp-s-vi-nas-ti)* | 27 |
| to | к | *k* | 3d, 8d |
| to the east | на восток | *na vas-tók* | 37d |
| to the left | налево | *na-lyé-va* | 3d, 37d |
| to the north | на север | *na syé-vir* | 37d |
| to the right | направо | *nap-ráh-va* | 3d, 37d |
| to the south | на юг | *na yúk* | 37d |
| to the west | на запад | *na záh-pat* | 37d |
| toad | жаба | *zhá-ba* | 15c |
| toast | тост | *tost* | 17a, 24o |
| toaster | тостер | *tós-ter* | 23d |
| tobacco | табак | *ta-báhk* | 25e |
| today | сегодня | *si-vód-nya* | 4a |
| toe | палец ноги | *páh-lits na-gí* | 12a |
| toilet (fixture) | унитаз | *u-ni-táhz* | 23a, 36c |
| toilet (room) | туалет, уборная | *tu-a-lyét, u-bór-na-ya* | 23b, 36c |
| toilet paper | туалетная бумага | *tu-a-lyét-na-ya bu-máh-ga* | 36c |

| token | жетон | *zhy-tón* | 18a |
|---|---|---|---|
| tolerance | терпимость *(f)* | *tir-pí-mast'* | 21a |
| tolerate | терпеть, допустить | *tir-pyét', da-pus-tít'* | 21a |
| tomato | помидор | *pa-mi-dór* | 14e, 24e |
| tomorrow | завтра | *záhft-ra* | 4a |
| tongue | язык | *i-zýk* | 12a, 41b |
| tonight | вечером | *vyé-chi-ram* | 4a |
| tonsils | аденоиды | *a-dy-nó-i-dy* | 41a |
| Too bad! | Жаль!, (Как) жалко! | *zhahl', (kahk) zháhl-ka* | 21c |
| tools | инструменты | *in-stru-myén-ty* | 23d, 25b, 33c |
| tooth | зуб | *zóop* | 12a, 41b |
| toothache | зубная боль | *zub-náh-ya bol'* | 41b |
| toothbrush | зубная щётка | *zub-náh-ya shchyót-ka* | 12d, 25h, 41b |
| toothpaste | зубная паста | *zub-náh-ya páhs-ta* | 12d, 25h, 41b |
| toothpick | зубочистка | *zu-ba-chíst-ka* | 24l |
| tornado | смерч | *smyérch* | 6a |
| touch | прикосновение | *pri-kas-na-vyé-ni-ye* | 12c |
| touch, to | коснуться | *kas-nóo-tsa* | 12c |
| tour | тур | *toor* | 37a |
| tourism | туризм | *tu-rízm* | 37a |
| tourist | турист | *tu-ríst* | 31a |
| toward | к | *k* | 3d, 37d |
| towel | полотенце | *pa-la-tyén-tsy* | 12d, 36c |
| tower | башня | *báhsh-nya* | 27, 37b |
| townhouse | таунхаус | *táh-un-háh-us* | 27 |
| track | рельс | *ryel's* | 35 |
| track and field | лёгкая атлетика | *lyókh-ka-ya at-lyé-ti-ka* | 28b |
| trade (buying-selling) | купля-продажа | *kóop-lya-pra-dáh-zha* | 26 |
| traffic | дорожное движение | *da-rózh-na-ye dvi-zhéh-ni-ye* | 34c |
| traffic light | светофор | *svi-ta-fór* | 34c, 37b |
| tragedy | трагедия | *tra-gyé-di-ya* | 20a, 29e |
| trailer | прицеп | *pri-tséhp* | 34a |
| train | поезд | *pó-ist* | 35 |
| transfer (n) (money) | перевод *(n)* (денег) | *pi-ri-vót (dyé-nik)* | 26 |
| transformer | трансформатор | *trans-far-máh-tar* | 25b |
| translate | перевести | *pi-ri-vis-tí* | 17a |
| translation | перевод | *pi-ri-vót* | 17a |
| transmission | передача | *pi-ri-dáh-cha* | 20b |
| transmission box | коробка передач | *ka-róp-ka pi-ri-dáhch* | 34e |
| transparent | прозрачный | *praz-ráhch-nyj* | 7b, 13d |
| transplant | пересадить | *pi-ri-sa-dit'* | 14a |
| travel | путешествие | *pu-ti-shéhst-vi-ye* | 31a |
| travel agency | туристическое агентство | *tu-ris-tí-chis-ka-ye a-gyént-stva* | 31a, 37a |
| traveler's check | дорожный чек | *da-rózh-nyj chyek* | 26, 36b |
| tray | поднос | *pad-nós* | 23d, 24l, 33c |

| | | | |
|---|---|---|---|
| treatment | курс лечения | *koors li-chyé-ni-ya* | 41a |
| tree | дерево *(sg)*, | *dyé-ri-va,* | 14c |
| | деревья *(pl)* | *di-ryév-ya* | |
| trial | судебный процесс | *su-dyéb-nyj pra-tséhs* | 42 |
| triangle | треугольник | *tri-u-gól'-nik* | 2a |
| trigonometry | тригонометрия | *tri-ga-na-myét-ri-ya* | 2b, 38e |
| trip, journey | поездка | *pa-yést-ka* | 31a, 37c |
| trombone | тромбон | *tram-bón* | 29c |
| tropic | тропик | *tró-pik* | 13e |
| trousers | брюки | *bryú-ki* | 25k |
| trout | форель *(f)* | *fa-ryél'* | 24d |
| truck | грузовик | *gru-za-vík* | 34a |
| trumpet | труба | *tru-báh* | 29c |
| trunk (of car) | багажник | *ba-gáhzh-nik* | 34e |
| trunk (of tree) | ствол | *stvohl* | 14a |
| trust | доверить | *da-vyé-rit'* | 21a |
| try on | примерить, | *pri-myé-rit',* | 25m |
| | померить | *pa-myé-rit'* | |
| tuba | туба | *tóo-ba* | 29c |
| Tuesday | вторник | *ftór-nik* | 5a |
| tulip | тюльпан | *tyul'-páhn* | 14b |
| tunnel | туннель *(m)* | *tu-néhl'* | 34c |
| turbulence | болтанка | *bal-táhn-ka* | 33c |
| turkey | индейка/индюшка | *in-dyéj-ka/in-dyúsh-ka* | 15b, 24c |
| Turkey | Турция | *tóor-tsy-ya* | 31b |
| Turkmenistan | Туркменистан | *turk-mi-ni-stáhn* | 31b |
| turn | поворот | *pa-va-rót* | 34c |
| turn off (a computer) | выключить *(p)* | *vý-klyu-chit'* | 20b, 20e |
| | (компьютер) | *(kamp'-yú-tar)* | |
| | выключать *(i)* | *vy-klyu-cháht'* | |
| turn on (a computer) | включить *(p)* | *fklyu-chít'* | 20b, 20e |
| | (компьютер) | *(kamp'-yu-tar)* | |
| | включать *(i)* | *fklyu-cháht'* | |
| turn, to | повернуть, | *pa-vir-nóot',* | 3e, 37d, |
| | повернуться | *pa-vir-nóo-tsa* | 3e |
| turn pages | переворачивать | *pi-ri-va-ráh-chi-vat'* | 20a |
| | страницы | *stra-ní-tsy* | |
| turn signal | поворотный сигнал | *pa-va-rót-nyj sig-náhl* | 34e |
| turnip | репа | *ryé-pa* | 14e |
| turtle | черепаха | *chi-ri-páh-ka* | 15c |
| TV station | телестанция | *ti-li-stáhn-tsy-ya* | 23a |
| twelve | двенадцать | *dvi-náh-tsat'* | 1a |
| twenty | двадцать | *dváh-tsat'* | 1a |
| twin | близнец | *bliz-nyéts* | 10a |
| two | два | *dvah* | 1a |
| type | напечатать | *na-pi-cháh-tat'* | 38f |
| typewriter | пишущая машинка | *pí-shu-shchi-ya* | 19e, 39c |
| | | *ma-shýn-ka* | |
| typist | машинистка | *ma-sky-níst-ka* | 38f, 39a |

## U

| | | | |
|---|---|---|---|
| **ugliness** | уродство | *u-rót-stva* | 11a |
| **ugly** | уродливый, | *u-ród-li-vyj,* | 11a, |
| | некрасивый | *ni-kra-sí-vyj* | 251 |
| **Ukraine** | Украина | *uk-ra-í-na* | 31b |
| **unacceptable** | неприемлемый | *ni-pri-yém-li-myj* | 21b |
| **uncle** | дядя/дядька *(m)* | *dyáh-dya/dyáht'-ka* | 10a |
| **under** | под | *pat* | 3d, 8d |
| **underage/minor** *(n)* | несовершеннолетний | *ni-sa-vir-shy-na-lyét-nij,* | 45b |
| | *(m)*, | | |
| | несовершеннолетняя | *ni-sa-vir-shy-na-lyét-* | |
| | *(f)* | *nya-ya* | |
| **underclass** | андеркласс | *áhn-dar-kláhs* | 45b |
| **underclothes** | бельё | *bil'-yó* | 25g |
| **underground parking** | подземная | *pat-zyém-na-ya ahv-ta-* | 27 |
| | автостоянка | *sta-yáhn-ka* | |
| **underline** | подчеркнуть | *pat-chirk-nóot'* | 19d |
| **understand** | понять | *pa-nyáht'* | 22b, 38f |
| **underwear** | бельё *(coll)* | *bil'-yó* | 25k |
| **undress (take off)** | снять, раздеться | *snyaht', raz-dyét'-tsa* | 25m |
| **uneducated** | необразованный | *ni-ab-ra-zó-van-yj* | 11e, 38f |
| **unemployment** | безработица | *biz-ra-bó-ti-tsa* | 39d, 45b |
| **unhappy** | несчастливый | *ni-shchis-lí-vyj* | 11e |
| **United States** | Соединённые Штаты | *sa-i-di-nyó-ny-ye shtáh-ty* | 31b |
| **universe** | вселенная | *fsi-lyé-na-ya* | 13a |
| **university** | университет | *u-ni-vir-si-tyét* | 38a |
| **unlawful, illegal** | незаконный *(adj)* | *ni-za-kó-nyj* | 42 |
| **unpleasant** | неприятный | *ni-pri-yáht-nyj* | 11e, 21b |
| **unreserved** | несдержанный | *ni-sdyér-zhy-nyj* | 11e |
| **until, till** | до, пока | *do, pa-káh* | 8h |
| **until** | до тех пор | *da tyekh por* | 4e |
| **up** | вверх | *vvyérkh* | 3d |
| **upload** | поместить *(p)* на сервер, | *pa-mis-tít' na syér-vir,* | 20d |
| | помещать *(i)*, | *pa-mi-shcháht',* | |
| | загрузить *(p)* файл, | *zag-ru-zít' fahjl,* | |
| | загружать *(i)* | *zag-ru-zháht'* | |
| **upper class** | верхний класс | *vyérkh-nij klahs* | 45b |
| **upper-middle class** | верхний средний | *vyérkh-nij sryéd-nij* | 45b |
| | класс | *klahs* | |
| **urinary system** | мочеводные | *ma-chi-vód-ny-ye* | 41a |
| | органы | *ór-ga-ny* | |
| **urinate** | мочиться | *ma-chí-tsa* | 41a |
| **URL** | урл (also уэрэл, урла) | *oórl (also u-e-réhl,* | 20d |
| | (spelled *url*) | *oór-la)* | |
| **use, help** | польза | *pól'-za* | 11e |
| **useful** | полезный | *pa-lyéz-nyj* | 11e |
| **useless** | бесполезный | *bis-pa-lyéz-nyj* | 11e |
| **usually** | обычно | *a-bých-na* | 4e |
| **Uzbekistan** | Узбекистан | *uz-bi-ki-stáhn* | 31b |

# V

| | | | |
|---|---|---|---|
| **vacation** | отпуск | *ót-pusk* | 30a, 37c, 38a |
| **vacuum cleaner** | пылесос | *py-li-sós* | 23d |
| **valley** | долина | *da-lí-na* | 13b |
| **van** | автобус | *af-tó-bus* | 34a |
| **vapor** | пар | *pahr* | 13c |
| **vase** | ваза | *váh-za* | 23d |
| **VCR** | видеомагнитофон | *vi-di-a-mag-ni-ta-fón* | 20e |
| **veal** | телятина | *ti-lyáh-ti-na* | 24c |
| **vegetable** | овощ *(m)* | *ó-vashch* | 14e, 24e |
| **vegetable garden** | огород | *a-ga-rót* | 14e, 23a |
| **vegetarian** *(adj)* | вегетарианский *(m)*, | *vi-gi-ta-ri-áhn-skij,* | 24p |
| | вегетарианское *(n)*, | *vi-gi-ta-ri-áhn-ska-ye,* | |
| | вегетарианская *(f)* | *vi-gi-ta-ri-áhn-ska-ya* | |
| **vegetation** | растительность *(f)* | *ras-ti-tíl'-nast'* | 13b |
| **vehicle** | машина | *ma-shý-na* | 34a |
| **vein** | вена | *vyé-na* | 41a |
| **verb** | глагол | *gla-gól* | 8a |
| **verbal adverb** | деепричастие | *di-i-pri-cháhs-ti-ye* | 8a |
| **verdict** | решение суда | *ri-shéh-ni-ye su-dáh* | 42 |
| **vertebrate** | позвоночное | *paz-va-nóch-na-ye* | 15a |
| **vest** | жилет | *zhy-lyét* | 25k |
| **Victory Day, May 9** | День Победы, | *dyen' pa-byé-dy,* | 30a |
| | Девятое Мая | *dye-vyáh-ta-ye máh-ya* | |
| **videocassette** | видеокассета | *vi-di-a-ka-syé-ta* | 20e |
| **videogame** | видио-игра | *ví-di-a-ig-ráh* | 20b |
| **videotape** | видеоплёнка | *vi-di-a-plyón-ka* | 20e |
| **view** | вид (из окна) | *vit (iz ák-náh)* | 27, 36b |
| **village** | деревня, *(large)* село | *di-ryév-nya, si-ló* | 13e |
| **village (subdivision)** | посёлок | *pa-syó-lak* | 27 |
| **vinegar** | уксус | *óok-sus* | 24j |
| **violet** | фиалка | *fi-áhl-ka* | 14b |
| **violin** | скрипка | *skríp-ka* | 29c |
| **virtual reality** | виртуальная | *vir-tu-áhl'-na-ya* | 20d |
| | реальность | *ri-áhl'-nast'* | |
| **virtual space** | виртуальное | *vir-tu-áhl'-na-ye* | 20d |
| | пространство | *prast-ráhn-stva* | |
| **virtual tour** | виртуальный тур | *vir-tu-áhl'-nyj toor* | 27 |
| **virus** | вирус | *ví-rus* | 20b, 45k |
| **visa** | виза | *ví-za* | 32 |
| **vision** | видение | *vi-dé-ni-ye* | 12c |
| **visit** | посетить | *pa-si-tít'* | 30b |
| **visit** *(v)* **(go to)** | посетить *(p)* веб-сайт, | *pa-si-tít' vyép-sáhjt,* | 20d |
| **(a website)** | посещать *(i)* | *pa-si-shchyáht'* | |
| **vitamin** | витамин | *vi-ta-mín* | 25h, 28b |
| **vocabulary** | словарный запас | *sla-váhr-nyj za-páhs* | 17a |
| **vocational school** | школа трудового | *shkó-la tru-da-vó-va* | 38a |
| | обучения | *a-bu-chyé-ni-ya* | |
| **vodka** | водка | *vót-ka* | 24k |
| **voice** | залог | *za-lók* | 8a |

| voice mail | голосовая почта | *ga-la-sa-váh-ya póch-ta* | 18a |
| voice message | голосовое сообщение | *ga-la-sa-vó-ye sa-ab-shchyé-ni-ye* | 18a |
| volcano | вулкан | *vul-káhn* | 13b |
| volleyball | волейбол | *va-li-ból* | 28b |
| volume | объём | *ab'-yóm* | 3a |
| vote | голос | *gó-las* | 44 |
| vowel | гласная | *gláhs-na-ya* | 8a |
| voyage | рейс | *ryejs* | 37a |

**W**

| wage, salary | заработок, зарплата | *záh-ra-ba-tak, zarp-láh-ta* | 39d |
| waist | талия | *táh-li-ya* | 12a |
| wait | подождать | *pa-dazh-dáht'* | 4e |
| Wait a minute! | Одну минуту! | *ad-nóo mi-nóo-tu* | 21c |
| wait for, expect | ждать, ожидать | *zhdaht', a-zhy-dáht'* | 19f |
| waiter | официант | *a-fi-tsi-áhnt* | 24m |
| waitress | официантка | *a-fi-tsi-áhnt-ka* | 24m |
| wake up somebody, to | разбудить | *raz-bu-dít'* | 36b |
| wake up, to | проснуться | *pra-snóot-tsa* | 12b |
| walk | прогулка | *pra-góol-ka* | 3e |
| walk, to | идти, ходить | *it-tí, kha-dít'* | 3e, 12b |
| walking tour | пешеходная прогулка | *pi-shy-khód-na-ya pra-góol-ka* | 37a |
| wall | стена | *sti-náh* | 23a |
| walnut | грецкий орех | *gryéts-kij a-ryékh* | 14d, 24f |
| want, to | хотеть | *kha-tyét'* | 21a |
| war | война | *vaj-náh* | 44 |
| warm | тёплый *(adj)* | *tyóp-lyj* | 11e |
| warm up | согреться | *sag-ryé-tsa* | 6b |
| warn | предупредить | *pri-dup-ri-dít'* | 17a |
| warning | предупреждение | *pri-dup-rizh-dyé-ni-ye* | 17a, 20b |
| wash | стирка *(coll)* | *stír-ka* | 25g |
| wash, to | помыть | *pa-mýt'* | 12d, 23f |
| wash clothes | постирать | *pa-sti-ráht'* | 23f |
| wash dishes | помыть посуду | *pa-mýt' pa-sóo-du* | 23f |
| wash one's hair | вымыть/помыть голову | *vý-myt'/pa-mýt' gó-la-vu* | 12d |
| wash oneself | помыться | *pa-mýt-tsa* | 12d |
| washing machine | стиральная машина | *sti-ráhl'-na-ya ma-shý-na* | 23d |
| wasp | оса | *a-sáh* | 15d |
| wastepaper basket | корзина (-нка) для бумаг | *kar-zí-na (-nka) dlya bu-máhk* | 39c |
| watch | часы *(pl)* | *chi-sý* | 4d, 25i |
| water | вода | *va-dáh* | 13b, 13c, 14a, 23e, 24k |
| water, to | полить | *pa-lit'* | 14a |
| water park (water attractions) | водные аттракционы *(pl)* | *vód-ny-ye at-rak-tsy-ó-ny* | 37a |
| water pollution | загрязнение воды | *zag-riz-nyé-ni-ye va-dý* | 45a |

| water supply | водоснабжение | va-do-snab-zhéh-ni-ye | 27 |
| water skiing | катание на водных лыжах | ka-táh-ni-ye na vód-nykh lý-zhakh | 28b |
| watercolor | акварель *(f)* | ak-va-ryél' | 29b |
| watermelon | арбуз | ar-bóos | 14d, 24f |
| wave | волна | val-náh | 13b |
| we | мы | my | 8c |
| weak | слабый *(adj)* | sláh-byj | 11a, 11e, 13d |
| weakly | слабо *(adv)* | sláh-ba | 11a, 13d |
| weakness | слабость *(f)* | sláh-bast' | 11a |
| weapon | оружие | a-róo-zhy-ye | 40b |
| wear | носить | na-sít' | 25m |
| weather | погода | pa-gó-da | 6a |
| weather forecast | прогноз/сводка погоды | prag-nós/svót-ka pa-gó-dy | 6c |
| web designer | веб-дизайнер | vyép-di-záhj-nir | 20d |
| web forum | веб-форум | vyép-fó-rum | 20d |
| web link | веб-ссылка | vyép-ssýl-ka | 20d |
| wedding | свадьба | sváhd'-ba | 11c, 30a |
| Wednesday | среда | sri-dáh | 5a |
| week | неделя | ni-dyé-lya | 4c |
| weekend | конец недели | ka-nyéts ni-dyé-li | 5a |
| weigh | весить | vyé-sit' | 24o |
| weigh oneself | взвеситься | vzvyé-si-tsa | 11a |
| weight | вес | vyes | 3a, 11a, 32 |
| weight lifting | поднятие тяжести | pad-nyáh-ti-ye tyáh-zhys-ti | 28b |
| well | хорошо | kha-ra-shó | 11e, 24p |
| west | запад | záh-pat | 3d |
| whale | кит | kit | 15c |
| what | что | shto | 8g, 9 |
| What bad luck! | Вот, не повезло! | vot ni pa-viz-ló | 21c |
| What luck! | Вот, повезло! | vot pa-viz-ló | 21c |
| What time is it? | Который сейчас час?, Сколько сейчас времени? | ka-tó-ryj si-cháhs chahs, skól'-ka si-cháhs vryé-mi-ni | 4b 4b |
| What's got into you? | Что с тобой? | shto s ta-bój | 21c |
| What's new? | Что нового? | shto nó-va-va | 16b |
| What's today's date? | Какое сегодня число? | ka-kó-ye si-vód-nya chis-ló | 5d |
| What's your name? | Как вас зовут? *(pol)*, Как тебя зовут? *(fam)* | kahk vahs za-vóot, kahk ti-byáh za-vóot | 11f, 16b |
| wheat | пшеница | pshy-ní-tsa | 24i |
| wheel | колесо | ka-li-só | 34e |
| when | когда | kag-dáh | 8g, 8h, 9 |
| where | где | gdye | 3d, 8g, 9 |
| Where to? | Куда | ku-dáh | 9 |
| whether | ли | li | 8h |
| which | который | ka-tó-ryj | 8g |
| while | пока | pa-káh | 4e, 8h |
| whiskey | виски | vís-ki | 24k |

| | | | |
|---|---|---|---|
| whisper | шепнуть | *shyp-nóot'* | 17a |
| white | белый | *byé-lyj* | 7a |
| white-haired | беловолосый | *bí-la-va-ló-syj* | 11b |
| (whitewater) rafting | рафтинг/сплав на плоту | *ráhf-tink/splahf na pla-tóo* | 37a |
| who | кто | *kto* | 8f, 8g, 9 |
| whose, of which | чей *(m)*, чья *(f)*, чьё *(n)* | *chyej, ch'yah, ch'yo* | 8f, 8g |
| why | почему | *pa-chi-móo* | 8g, 9 |
| wide | широкий | *shy-ró-kij* | 3b |
| wide angle | широкий угол | *shy-ró-kij oó-gal* | 25d |
| widow | вдова *(f)* | *vda-váh* | 11c |
| widower | вдовец *(m)* | *vda-vyéts* | 11c |
| width | ширина | *shy-ri-náh* | 3b |
| wife | жена | *zhy-náh* | 10a, 11c |
| wikipedia, (wiki) | википедия, (вики) | *vi-ki-pí-di-ya, ví-ki* | 20d |
| willing | готовый | *ga-tó-vyj* | 11e |
| willow | ива | *í-va* | 14c |
| win | выиграть | *vý-ig-rat'* | 28b |
| win elections | выиграть *(p)*, выигрывать *(i)*, выборы | *vý-ig-rat', vy-íg-ry-vat', vy-ba-ry* | 44 |
| wind energy | энергия ветра | *y-néhr-gi-ya vyét-ra* | 45a |
| window | окно | *ak-nó* | 20b, 23a, 27, 33c, |
| | окно машины | *ak-nó ma-shy'-ny* | 34e |
| window (store) | касса | *káh-sa* | 35 |
| | витрина | *vit-rí-na* | 25a |
| window sill | подоконник | *pa-da-kón-ik* | 23a |
| windshield | ветровое стекло | *vit-ra-vó-ye stik-ló* | 34e |
| windshield wiper | дворник | *dvór-nik* | 34e |
| wine | вино | *vi-nó* | 24k |
| wine glass | рюмка | *ryúm-ka* | 24l |
| wing | крыло | *kry-ló* | 15b, 33c |
| winter | зима | *zi-máh* | 5c |
| wire | проволока, провод | *pró-va-la-ka, pró-vat* | 25b |
| wisdom | мудрость *(f)* | *móod-rast'* | 11e, 22a |
| wisdom tooth | зуб мудрости | *zoop móod-ras-ti* | 41b |
| wise | мудрый *(adj)* | *móod-ryj* | 11e |
| with | с, со | *s, so* | 8d |
| With best wishes! | С наилучшими пожеланиями! | *s na-i-lóot-shy-mi pa-zhy-láh-ni-yah-mi* | 19c |
| With love! | С любовью! | *s lyu-bóv'-yu* | 19c |
| withdraw | снять со счёта | *snyаt' sa shchyó-ta* | 26 |
| within | в течение | *f ti-chyé-ni-ye* | 4e |
| witness | свидетель *(m)* (-ница) *(f)* | *svi-dyé-til' (-ni-tsa)* | 42 |
| witty | остроумный | *ast-ra-óom-nyj* | 11e |
| wolf | волк *(m)*, волчица *(f)* | *volk, val-chí-tsa* | 15a |
| woman | женщина | *zhéhn-shchi-na* | 11a |

| Women's Day | Женский день *(m)* | *zhéhn-skij dyen'* | 5e, 30a |
| wonderful (ly) | прекрасно | *prik-ráhs-na* | 16a |
| wool | шерсть *(f)* | *shehrst'* | 13c |
| woolen | шерстяной | *shyr-sti-nój* | 251 |
| word | слово | *sló-va* | 8a, 17a, 19d |
| word processing | обработка текста | *ab-ra-bót-ka tyéks-ta* | 20b |
| word processor | текстовой редактор | *tiks-ta-vój ri-dáhk-tar* | 19e, 20b, 39c |
| work | работать | *ra-bó-tat'* | 39d |
| workday | рабочий день *(m)* | *ra-bó-chij dyen'* | 5a |
| working class | рабочий класс | *ra-bó-chij klahs* | 45b |
| world | мир | *mir* | 13a |
| world-wide web | всемирная паутина | *vsi-mír-na-ya pa-u-tí-na* | 20d |
| worm | червь *(m)*, червяк | *chyerf', chir-vyáhk* | 15d |
| wrench | гаечный ключ | *gáh'ich-nyj klyuch* | 25b |
| wrestling | борьба | *bar'-báh* | 28b |
| wrist | кисть *(f)* | *kíst'* | 12a |
| wristwatch | ручные часы *(pl)* | *ruch-ný-ye chi-sý* | 4d |
| write | написать | *na-pi-sáht'* | 19f, 38f |
| writer | писатель *(m)*, писательница *(f)* | *pi-sáh-til', pi-sáh-til'-ni-tsa* | 29d, 39a |
| writing desk | письменный стол | *pís'-mi-nyj stol* | 23c, 39c |
| wrong | неправильный | *ni-prah-víl'-nyj* | 38f |
| Wrong number! | (Вы набрали) неправильный номер! | *(vy nab-ráh-li) ni-práh-vil'-nyj nó-mir* | 18b |
| www(. -dot) | вэ-вэ-вэ /три вэ (-точка), три дабл ю | *véh-véh-véh/tri véh (-tóch-ka), trí dáhbl yu* | 20d |

**X**

| X rays | рентген | *rin-gyén* | 40c, 41b |

**Y**

| yawn | зевнуть | *ziv-nóot'* | 17a |
| yawn | зевок | *zi-vók* | 17a |
| year | год (годы *pl*) | *got (gó-dy)* | 4c |
| yell | орать | *a-ráht'* | 17a |
| yellow | жёлтый | *zhól-tyj* | 7a |
| yes | да | *dah* | 16c |
| yesterday | вчера | *fchi-ráh* | 4a |
| yet | ещё | *i-shchyó* | 4e |
| Yield | уступать дорогу | *us-tu-páht' da-ró-gu* | 34d |
| yoga | йога | *jó-ga* | 28b |
| you *(fam/pol)* | ты, вы | *ty, vy* | 8c |
| You're welcome! | Пожалуйста! | *pa-zháh-lus-ta* | 16c |
| young | молодой | *ma-la-dój* | 11b |
| young man | молодой человек, юноша, парень *(m)* | *ma-la-dój chi-la-vyék, yú-na-sha, páh-rin'* | 11a |
| young woman | девушка, молодая женщина | *dyé-vush-ka, ma-la-dáh-ya zhéhn-shchi-na* | 11a |

| younger | моложе, младше | *ma-ló-zhe, mláht-she* | 11b |
| your (fam) | твой *(m)*, твоё *(n)*, | *tvoj, tva-yó,* | 8c |
| | твоя *(f)*, твои *(pl)* | *tva-yáh, tva-í* | |
| your (pl/pol) | ваш *(m)*, ваше *(n)*, | *vahsh, váh-shy,* | 8c |
| | ваша *(f)*, ваши *(pl)* | *váh-sha, váh-shy* | |
| Yours | Твой (-я) *(fam)*, | *tvoj, tva-yáh,* | 19c |
| | Ваш (-а) *(pol)* | *vahsh, váh-sha* | |
| Yours sincerely! | Искренне твой! *(fam)* | *ísk-rí-nye tvoj* | 19b |
| | (Ваш) *(pol)* | *(vahsh)* | |
| youth | юность *(f)*, молодость | *yú-nast', mó-la-dast'* | 11b |

## Z

| zebra | зебра | *zyéb-ra* | 15a |
| zero | ноль *(m)* | *nol'* | 1a, 6c |
| zip code | почтовый индекс | *pach-tó-vyj ín-dyks* | 19f, 39b |
| zipper | молния | *mól-ni-ya* | 25g |
| zoo | зоопарк | *za-a-páhrk* | 15a |
| zoology | зоология | *za-a-ló-gi-ya* | 38e |
| zoom | зум | *zoom* | 25d |
| zoom lens | зум линза | *zoom lín-za* | 25d |

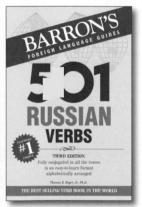